T0327084

DEMOCRACY IN OUR AMERICA

PAUL W. KAHN

Democracy in Our America

CAN WE STILL GOVERN OURSELVES?

Yale

UNIVERSITY PRESS

NEW HAVEN & LONDON

Published with assistance from the Mary Cady Tew Memorial Fund.

Yale University Press books may be purchased in quantity for educational,
business, or promotional use. For information, please e-mail sales.press@yale.
edu (U.S. office) or sales@yaleup.co.uk (U.K. office).

Set in Times Roman type by Integrated Publishing Solutions,
Grand Rapids, Michigan.
Printed in the United States of America.

Library of Congress Control Number: 2022934849
ISBN 978-0-300-25742-7 (hardcover : alk. paper)

A catalogue record for this book is available from the British Library.

This paper meets the requirements of ANSI/NISO Z39.48-1992
(Permanence of Paper).

10 9 8 7 6 5 4 3 2 1

To the volunteers of Killingworth

CONTENTS

Preface: Political Theory and Political Practice Today   ix

Acknowledgments   xv

PART ONE. TWO COMMUNITIES, ONE PROBLEM

1 A Constitutional Coup   3

2 Killingworth Copes   31

PART TWO. DEMOCRATIC PARTICIPATION AND CIVIL SOCIETY

3 Self-Government as Volunteering   59

4 Civil Society: Democracy and Authority   100

PART THREE. PUBLIC OPINION NATIONALIZES AND DIVIDES

5 Talking to Each Other   139

6 Killingworth Disrupted   167

7 What Can Be Done?   203

Notes   223

Index   279

PREFACE: POLITICAL THEORY AND
POLITICAL PRACTICE TODAY

THE 2016 PRESIDENTIAL ELECTION WAS a shock to many people, including political theorists. We had spent several decades elaborating theories of the basic
structure of a liberal, constitutional order in which equality and dignity were
first principles. Suddenly, we confronted the possibility that voters were far less
committed to these principles than we assumed. Few academics had been thinking about the foundations of a populism fueled by white nationalism. Our failure to see the political upheaval coming to the United States raised memories of
a similar failure at the time of the collapse of the Soviet Union. In both cases,
scholars had failed to keep up with a rapidly changing reality.

For decades, most political theorists have placed themselves in one of two
camps. The first explores questions of political legitimacy, asking what justifies
the exercise of authority. Is it consent or justice, the vote or deliberation? Does
legitimacy arise from the source of political power, from the design of political
institutions, or from the policies pursued by government? These are questions
of political philosophy. Students coming into this field begin by reading classic
works, from Aristotle to John Rawls. The second camp thinks that these philosophical questions have no objective answers. The study of politics, in their
view, should be a social science—a fact-based inquiry using quantifiable data
to measure the consequences of political choices. Students coming into this
field learn techniques of quantification and analysis.

Scholars in both camps, however, generally agreed on the relevant questions. The fundamental issue for both camps has been, as famously expressed by
Robert Dahl, "Who governs?"[1] For the political philosophers, that means, "Who

should govern?" For the empiricists, it means, "Who wins the competition for resources and power?" Before 2016, the two camps shared a broad research agenda. Both investigated the design of institutions, including the role of expert agencies, courts, and lobbyists. Both pursued inquiries into political parties, political speech, and voter turnout. They looked at how markets and politics interact and worried about the ways in which power created by the former can dominate the latter. Both camps were concerned with the position of minorities and questioned which minorities deserve what kinds of legal protection. Both explored the relationship between domestic political order and transnational institutions. Populism, to the extent that either camp thought about it at all, was mainly a problem of constitutional backsliding in the fragile democracies of eastern Europe and Latin America.

The 2016 election revealed that American political institutions are not as strong as we thought. Some wondered if we are in a sort of Weimar moment. Germany in the 1920s also had liberal theorists and political economists who argued about the grounds of political legitimacy and the design of political institutions. But the politics they theorized was not the politics in which they found themselves by the early 1930s.[2] Our political situation, too, might not match our theories. The shift from one political world to another could be a matter of eighty thousand votes scattered across three states. It could be as rapid as the replacement of one Supreme Court nominee by another.[3] Four years later, the presidential election turned on even fewer votes scattered across four states. More shocking still, on the day Congress counted the electoral votes, a white nationalist mob invaded the Capitol. Was this our version of the 1923 Munich Putsch?

Everyone sees that American politics has become more polarized over the past two decades. It has become more intolerant and more threatening, even as it has become less serious and more entertaining. The consequences were all too evident in the failed response to the pandemic in the spring of 2020. Public health became a victim of our polarized politics. Donald Trump called himself a "wartime president" in the early days of the pandemic. The war, however, was of his own making, and it had begun well before the virus arrived. By 2016, our culture war had become a civil cold war. With the arrival of the pandemic, the casualties of this war included the dead and injured.

To explain voter anger, many commentators have focused on the ever-increasing inequality in income and wealth: the 1 percent versus everyone else.

The redistributive measures required to reduce this inequality have never featured prominently in constitutional law or human rights.[4] A rising group of scholars argues that the structural weakness of the American political order has been its inclination to protect private property over social welfare, even as other scholars show us just how deep and pervasive inequality has become.[5] This focus on inequality aligns scholarship with a growing progressive political movement. Scholars and activists agree that inequality reached a tipping point with the Great Recession, producing an explosion of populist politics on the right and the left.

This material inequality is real and troubling, but it would be a mistake to focus on it as the fundamental explanation for the state of American politics. Facts do not generate political responses. It is the other way around: political responses identify which facts matter and how they matter. Inequality and economic insecurity gain their political salience against the background of changing beliefs and practices. Voters make judgments based on their expectations and their values. These, in turn, are a function of how they imagine themselves and their communities. Right-wing and left-wing populism look at the same inequalities but see the facts differently. To explain political responses, we must pay attention to forms of communication, the cultivation of resentment, the collapse of traditional civil society institutions and authorities, and the character of family life and religious practices. We have to expand our inquiry to look at how people live and work today, how they experience their communities of home, religion, work, and politics. If we seek to explain national politics by looking primarily to the collapsed economies of the Rust Belt and Appalachia, we will miss the broader picture of what is happening to democracy in America.

Politics is always embedded in forms of life—that is, in what we do and what we find meaningful. Our unhappy politics reflects our unhappy lives. We need, accordingly, to have a better sense of the sources and character of that unhappiness. Why so much tension, anxiety, and anger—well before the pandemic arrived? Survey data will take us only so far, because politics is an expressive and interpretive activity. Competing political positions offer different narratives to explain the sources of our problems and what might be done about them. Narratives of progress compete with narratives of collapse. Broadening the picture allows us to better understand, not just our political pathologies, but also our political possibilities.

In the face of so much cynicism about politics today, scholars have a special responsibility to explain the value of political engagement. Voters need to be reminded that the great American project has been a political project. The measure of success of a work in political theory lies less in the creativity of its proposals than in its calling to mind practices and beliefs that have slipped from view. The task is not to invent something new but to recover what we may be losing. Judith Shklar expressed this idea well: "The most obvious task of political theory has always been the elucidation of common experience, the expression of what is inarticulately known to groups of people at any time. It is the reexamination of inherited ideas, their adaptation and even their utter rejection. It is not a work of discovery, but one of illumination through discussion. . . . We share a variety of common encounters and reactions, and to give these a coherent form, a clear voice, is the task of political theory."[6]

The lesson of 2016 to scholars was "get real." I take that lesson to heart by staying close to the political practices and beliefs of the local community that I know best. My objective is to speak of and to the common sense of the community. As a work of common sense, this book is both an interpretation of politics and a political intervention. It is a work of local political theory, meaning that it takes the perspective of a participant-theorist. In Shklar's terms, I aim to give coherent form to our common encounters. I discuss politics in a way that is itself meant to be a part of politics. The arguments I make are not those I would make in a campaign, but they are the sorts of things I would say over a long dinner conversation with neighbors.

Turning to the local does not mean turning from the national. Just the opposite: I begin with the national and then turn to the local to better understand the state of the nation. Today, even a small town participates in national media, national commerce, national culture, and national politics. For generations, we approached national issues from the perspective of local experience. Today, the direction has reversed: we come to the local already deeply embedded in the national. Local political practices offer, therefore, a lens through which we can examine the impact of changes in our social, cultural, and economic lives on our capacity for self-government. This approach is hardly new, but it remains timely.[7]

The small New England town at the center of this inquiry is my own: Killingworth, Connecticut, population 6,400. Elections in Killingworth are often close; outcomes are unpredictable. About half the voters register as "unaffiliated." The others divide about evenly between Democrats and Republicans.

Voters elected Democrats to fill most local positions in 2015. Just one year later, the town voted for Trump. A year after that, the campaign for local offices was marked by signs proclaiming, "Drain the Killingworth Swamp." Political combat became so intense that a federal lawsuit was filed alleging a conspiracy to keep the Conservative Party candidate off the ballot. By 2019, big money had arrived. Traditionally, campaigns had cost on the order of $5,000 to $7,000. That year, the Republican Party and its candidate for first selectman reported spending around $40,000. In 2020, the town voted for Joe Biden, but there is no evidence that Trump voters had changed their minds: Trump received more votes than he had in 2016. But as in much of the nation, Biden voters turned out in even greater numbers.

In 2017, Fred Dudek was the Republican candidate for first selectman. He was a community leader who grew up in town, led the volunteer fire department, and served in town government for many years. He had started as a Democrat but switched to the Republicans decades ago. In 2019, the candidate spending all that money, Francesco Lulaj, had lived in town ten years and had no history of participation in local governance. No one I knew could remember seeing him at a town meeting. He unabashedly put his membership in the Catholic church at the center of his campaign; he drove to campaign events in a Ferrari. One had to wonder what battle was really being fought in the election. I was particularly puzzled because three years earlier, Francesco had been the first person from whom I had heard the charge, "Hillary Clinton is a murderer." I had more than a scholar's interest in this question because his opponent, the incumbent Catherine Iino, is my wife.

When we arrived in Killingworth in 1996, it was not a deeply partisan place. Its first selectman, David LeVasseur, was a local lawyer with a keen interest in the history of the town. He was a Republican but had been cross-endorsed by the Democrats. When he was appointed to a state office in 2001, he was replaced by David Denvir, another local lawyer already serving as a selectman. Both were members of the now vanishing breed of New England Republicans—small business owners dedicated to the success of local commerce, prudent financial management, good schools, participation in civic organizations, and local autonomy.[8] Killingworth politics began to grow deeply contentious with the rise of a conservative splinter group within the Republicans. The constant pressure on the right resulted in primary after primary. Reporting on the Republican primaries for local office in 2013, the *New Haven Register* described Killingworth as "[the] small town that has become the election primary capital of Middlesex Country, if not all of Connecticut."[9]

By 2016, many voters in town were anxious; some were angry. Why? The unemployment rate was low and the median income high. The schools won national awards, the public facilities were working well, and the woods remained pristine. The sources of unease lie in the way we live today. Family, employment, community, and faith no longer work together to support a common political project. This is a problem everywhere, not just in Killingworth and not just in small towns. Everywhere, unease leads to distrust, and that leads to conflict. Killingworth is worth studying, not because it is different in these respects, but because its small size and long history offer a microcosm in which we can see more clearly the gap between our aspirations for collective self-government and how we live our lives.

Our national political polarization may overwhelm Killingworth's capacity for self-government. If not, it will be because Killingworth can still call upon a long tradition of volunteerism. Self-government in Killingworth means volunteering, whether in a conference room at town hall, the fire station next door, the ambulance service up the street, or the library down the street. I do not imagine that these practices of volunteering can be replicated throughout America. An urban area cannot rely upon a volunteer fire department. Volunteering in Killingworth, however, is not just about providing services. Residents take responsibility for creating and maintaining a public ethos of care. Citizen participation will take different shape in different settings—community groups, political movements, charities, unions, church organizations, environmental groups, and youth movements—but the end is the same: to build an ethos of care.

I am hardly the first person to see the vital connection between volunteering and the quality of democratic life. Alexis de Tocqueville was the first, and there have been many since. He, too, turned to the New England town to learn about the state of American politics. Killingworth poses the political question we all face: Are we to be a nation of aggrieved voters, or are we to be citizen volunteers seeking to create and maintain a self-governing community?

ACKNOWLEDGMENTS

FOR FIFTEEN YEARS, I HAVE BEEN learning about Killingworth politics and civil society from my spouse, Catherine Iino. Without our nightly discussions of the news of the day, this book would not have been possible. While she has been indispensable to the project, the views expressed are my own. The virtues of political disagreement—a theme of the book—begin in the household.

In writing the book, I formally interviewed about twenty-five members of the community. I want to thank each of them for taking the time to engage with me, even when they knew that our politics did not align. Many of these interviews took place under the difficult circumstances of the Covid-19 pandemic. I am especially grateful for the extra effort many took to connect and to engage frankly with me. I owe a special note of thanks, as well, to Tom Lentz, our town historian, and to the clerk's office in town hall.

My long-time editor at Yale University, William Frucht, deserves a special note of thanks. Twice, Bill read the entire manuscript with great care. His detailed comments on an early draft contributed greatly to the final shape of the project.

Several colleagues and friends read and commented on the entire manuscript. I want to thank in particular Samuel Moyn, Bruce Ackerman, Aziz Rana, and Benjamin Berger. I also had the support of "Team Killingworth," an extraordinary group of Yale Law students who helped with the many detailed research projects that this work spawned: Emma McDermott, Susan Wang,

Gavin Jackson, Sierra Stubbs, and Josh Lefkow. I also want to thank Noah Kazis, a rising leader in the field of local government and land use (and my son-in-law), who on numerous occasions corrected my errors and pointed me in the right direction. Last, I am grateful as ever for the help of my assistant, Barbara Mianzo.

PART ONE

TWO COMMUNITIES,

ONE PROBLEM

I regularly move between two settings that offer radically different perspectives on the American political scene. One is Yale Law School, where everyone focuses on national politics. We all read the *New York Times* every morning. Students imagine the school as a launching pad for entry into institutions of national power. Some want to be public officials; some want to be leaders in the private sector. All aspire to influence national policy. In this, they are following their teachers. Many faculty members have served in national office; most worked for federal judges early in their careers; and some are federal judges. When their attention shifts from national institutions and policies, it moves to the international, not the local.

Most members of this community know little or nothing about their local representatives and institutions. I regularly ask my students to name their state representatives—not their representatives in Congress but those elected to their statehouses. Rarely can anyone do this. Neither can the faculty. My colleagues know substantially more about Congress than about the New Haven Board of Alders.

The second setting is some twenty-five miles east of the Yale campus: the small town of Killingworth, one of the oldest in Connecticut. The first settlers arrived in the early 1660s, only some forty years after the Pilgrims settled at Plymouth. Catherine and I live in a two-hundred-year-old farmhouse on thirty acres of land bordered by state forest. Like the town, the house mixes the old and the new; generations of occupants have added on and updated. What was once the outhouse became a doghouse; the hayloft is now a study; the milking shed is a workshop. Former pastures have become forests; the pigsty is now a vegetable garden. I think of us as caretakers of this land and these buildings.

We have lived in Killingworth for twenty-five years. For the past twelve years, Catherine has served as first selectman—an old New England term for mayor. In our house, political discussion easily moves from American policy in the Middle East to traffic flow at the town dump. Health care discussions move between reforming the Affordable Care Act and getting flu vaccines to seniors living in the retirement community down the road. One evening we will be talking with European friends about the appropriate response to Brexit; the next, we are talking with neighbors about how the town should respond to the state legislature's failure to pass a budget.

Often, I try to bring what I have learned in Killingworth to bear on discussions in the law school. My colleagues have gotten used to hearing questions from me that begin, "In Killingworth . . . ." Of course, scale matters: Killingworth is not a model for national politics. Nevertheless, the town has been the site of significant changes in civil society and in the formation of public opinion over the past few decades. Similar changes have occurred around the nation. The town's small size lets us see better what these changes have meant for ordinary citizens as well as for our collective efforts at democratic self-government.

There is no direct path from the local to the national, but there may be an indirect one. That possibility begins with putting my two communities in contact. Chapter 1 offers a view from the Yale Law School of the state of the nation's politics in the era of Donald Trump. I describe his presidential administration as an attempted "constitutional coup." The election of Joe Biden put an end to that attempt for now. Six months into the new administration, however, the threat of right-wing, authoritarian populism continues to shape much of our national political life. Chapter 2 moves from the national to the local. It offers a view from Killingworth, where changes in practices and beliefs also pose an existential threat to self-government. Democratic self-government in Killingworth relies upon volunteers, but the same forces that threatened constitutional order in Washington threaten volunteerism in town. These are the national and local faces of politics today.

A Constitutional Coup

To instruct democracy, if possible to reanimate its beliefs, to purify its mores, to regulate its movements, to substitute . . . knowledge of its true interests for its blind instincts; to adapt its government to time and place; to modify it according to circumstances and men: such is the first duty imposed on those who direct society in our day.
—Alexis de Tocqueville, Democracy in America

WE ARE A NATION COMING APART. We had a riot in the Capitol and a national pandemic that overwhelmed our hospitals. As I write, the United States has passed seventy-three million Covid-19 cases with over 870,000 deaths. These numbers—which will only be higher when you read this—are incredible for a country that just a few years ago was the world's economic, technological, and political leader. Until vaccines became widely available in the first half of 2021, we were unable to contain the pandemic. We certainly had the ability to do so; we lacked the political will. Our initial response looked more like that of Brazil, Mexico, and Russia than that of Germany, Taiwan, Australia, or New Zealand. We had the material resources of the latter nations but the politics of the former. Like them, we were led by an authoritarian populist.

Ironically, this disastrous response pointed to the success of the Trump administration. When the pandemic arrived, President Trump had already spent three years dismantling and undermining national institutions. Experienced professionals had been dismissed as agencies were hollowed out. Science was rejected as a basis for policy; the regulatory agenda was abandoned; internal checks were undermined. In place of good-faith administration, we got cronyism. It seemed never to have occurred to the administration's leaders that they might actually have to govern—that is, lead the nation through a crisis. Three years into the Trump administration, not enough competent professionalism remained at the top levels of government to respond effectively, even had Trump been so inclined. The Centers for Disease Control's initial efforts to create a test for the virus failed from incompetence, the stockpiles of emergency supplies had been allowed to deteriorate, the Food and Drug Administration followed Trump's promotion of untested "miracle" drugs, and the Transportation Security Administration could not manage to screen passengers returning from abroad. Trump responded to the crisis with denial; it would, he said, go away by itself, and anyway it was not his problem. How did the nation so easily discard its practices and traditions at the urgings of a corrupt real estate developer supported by right-wing provocateurs?

A Pathological Turn

Trump's 2016 Electoral College victory depended on a small fraction of the total votes, distributed across three states.[1] To explain that margin, commentators often point to a series of extraordinary interferences with the ordinary course of the election: most prominently, Federal Bureau of Investigation director James Comey's letter to the U.S. Congress, a week before the election, stating that he had reopened an investigation into the private email server Hillary Clinton had used while serving as secretary of state; the WikiLeaks release of thousands of stolen emails from the account of Clinton campaign chair John Podesta; and Russian manipulation of social media to inflame social divisions and depress Democratic (especially Black) voter turnout.[2] Yet the election had to be close enough for these interventions to make a difference. Even had Trump lost, scholars would still have the substantial task of explaining how so many voters could support him. Those voters backed him again in 2020. They will be here long after Trump is gone.

Voters were well aware of Trump's character. They saw his performance in nationally televised debates and heard his *Access Hollywood* tape.[3] Reporters investigated his questionable business practices, multiple bankruptcies, lies, ignorance, abuse of the courts, personal vendettas, misogyny, racism, and xenophobia. Voters were told all of this, and they voted for him anyway. The reports continued during his four years in office, yet still more voters supported him in 2020. Connecticut went for Hillary Clinton in 2016, but 41 percent of its voters chose Trump. In 2020, Trump still received close to 40 percent of the state's vote, and more actual votes than four years earlier. A state where 40 percent of the voters are prepared to support a populist authoritarian is already a fragile democracy.

Democracy is not just any choice by the people. It requires more than showing up at the polling booth. It requires citizens who take their political responsibilities seriously and act for the right reasons. Those reasons include respect for individual dignity, for the rule of law, and for representative institutions. Citizens can choose to reevaluate laws and reconstruct institutions. They can do this within or without the ordinary institutions of change, including the process of constitutional amendment. But if these choices are made casually or thoughtlessly, or if they are based on hatred directed at other members of the polity, then democracy has taken a pathological turn. Our democracy took a pathological turn in 2016.

The fragility of our democracy lies in an absence of citizen commitment to the necessary institutions of our political life. This is more than taking the time to vote, although it is noteworthy that in 2016 about 40 percent of eligible voters failed to participate and in 2020 a third did not vote.[4] Commitment begins with paying attention and learning about government practices and citizen responsibilities. Americans frequently do not know about their own political institutions or how the system works to produce laws and policies.[5] Many voters are enthralled by right-wing propaganda sites that deliberately misrepresent facts.[6] The quality of political debate has declined as discussion has given way to tweets, conspiracy theories, and bots. By 2016, many voters approached politics as a form of entertainment: a competition between red and blue teams with no clear rules except winner takes all. Trump ran for president as the entertainer-in-chief.

Of those who voted for Trump, few had any idea what policies he would pursue. That Trump's support remained stable over his entire administration suggests that voters were not moved by expectations respecting particular policies. He promised better health insurance, more manufacturing, a rebound of the coal industry, and infrastructure investment. He promised that Mexico would pay for a border wall and that he would restore law and order. None of this happened, but that made no difference to his base. More surprising, even his failure to respond in a timely fashion to the pandemic and the recession that accompanied it made little difference to his supporters. Team loyalty mattered most.

A Constitutional Coup

Having not expected Trump's victory, the academic community was unprepared for the administration that followed. Scholars predicted that Trump would move toward the center once in office. He would, they thought, be checked by the courts, the press, the independent agencies, the political exigencies of Congress and the state houses, and by allies and international institutions. By 2020, most of those domestic institutions had been undermined, and America was in retreat around the world. By July of that year, the federal government was deploying a secret army on the streets of an American city, Portland, Oregon. As the pandemic raged, Trump attacked the leaders of America's major cities, calling them radicals, socialists, and anarchists.

The Obama administration had been committed to the ideal of a progressive, modern welfare state. It privileged expertise in the form of policy planning. It pursued multilateralism on issues of trade, climate change, and security. At the end of his term, Barack Obama's approval rating was close to 60 percent.[7] Employment was back to what it had been before the 2009 recession.[8] The American troop presence in Iraq and Afghanistan had declined from about 140,000 to about 15,000.[9] There was growing unhappiness with income inequality, but there was no social crisis drawing masses of people into the streets to demand regime change. The Occupy movement had disappeared. The Black Lives Matter movement was drawing attention to a serious problem but was hardly disrupting national political institutions. There was unhappiness with Washington gridlock, but apart from the Senate's refusal to consider Obama's judicial nominees, there was no major unsettling of institutions. Yet an election that yielded no popular mandate enabled a serious effort to displace our liberal constitutional system.

The Trump administration was unable or unwilling to consolidate political support among a majority of the voters.[10] It never achieved that level of approval for its trademark policies of cutting taxes, eliminating Obamacare, building a border wall, or abandoning environmental regulation.[11] Nevertheless, it governed as if it had a mandate for radical change. It passed little legislation, even with a Republican Congress for its first two years. The changes it pursued took the form of deconstructing national institutions, practices, and norms. No one quite knew what political vision drove the administration, beyond Trump's personal self-aggrandizement.[12] This confusion of personal power with political institutions is characteristic of populist autocratic regimes.[13]

Trump ran the government as if it were a personal fiefdom. He refused to cooperate with congressional oversight, including impeachment proceedings. He attacked the independence of federal agencies. He did not tolerate any point of independence within the government, purging the ranks of the inspectors general in federal agencies.[14] Senior positions were no longer subject to confirmation by the Senate but were filled by "acting" appointments.[15] He pulled back from multilateral institutions while attacking traditional allies. He aligned himself with undemocratic regimes, even with those accused of major violations of human rights. He expressed support for populist political movements that undermined the rule of law in Hungary, Poland, and Brazil. He challenged the assessments of his own intelligence agencies, particularly when they touched on Russian actions. He favored the dismantling of the European Union.[16]

Many of Trump's accomplishments were achieved through "not doing."[17] This made public assessment difficult, since a failure to act often lacks visibility. Agency after agency stopped enforcing regulations.[18] In many departments and agencies, the administration simply declined to fill leadership positions.[19] When appointments were made, the appointees did not last long.[20] Substantively, agencies aligned themselves with the regulated; they withdrew rules rather than pursued enforcement.[21] This was the pattern across broad swathes of federal responsibility—for example, the environment, immigration, financial markets, and occupational safety. One did not know whether it was policy, incompetence, or corruption.

In foreign policy, too, Trump's disruption was largely a matter of not doing. We no longer did nation building, but neither did we do free trade, the Iran Nuclear Deal, or the Paris Climate Agreement. We withdrew from the World Health Organization and threatened withdrawal from NATO, the World Trade Organization, and the United Nations.[22] America's leadership of the Western alliance collapsed. Trump's effort to align with Russia puzzled both liberals and conservatives. Foreign observers were not the only ones struggling to understand what had happened. Even the American military no longer knew which side we would take in potential conflicts.

America had been a liberal democracy committed to the rule of law. Was it still? The Trump administration declined to accept adverse judicial rulings. When it failed in its effort to end the Deferred Action for Childhood Arrivals program, for example, it simply refused to process new applications.[23] It acted to subvert the administration of criminal justice.[24] When presidential cronies were convicted of federal offenses, Trump issued pardons and commutations.[25] Enforcement of federal civil rights substantially ended, except on behalf of Christian religious groups. The administration not did not just reject the International Criminal Court; it threatened judges and prosecutors with personal sanctions.[26]

Courts are intimately connected to our understanding of democracy, because they not only protect the innocent but police the integrity of government. At no point in Trump's administration, however, was there any acknowledgment of the idea of law as a limit on power. During his 2016 campaign, Trump questioned the motives of individual judges.[27] In office, the attack on the courts continued, with the president denigrating "Obama judges" and threatening the Ninth Circuit Court of Appeals.[28] Judicial appointments—including to the Supreme Court—were deeply politicized.[29]

The president forced out one attorney general, Jeff Sessions, for failing to protect him from a process of legal accountability. He tried to use the Justice Department to bring criminal charges against his political opponents.[30] His next attorney general, William Barr, undermined the department's own investigative processes. The administration's motto might have been "politics before law." The effort to politicize the courts created a circuslike atmosphere after the 2020 election. Dozens of frivolous lawsuits were filed, apparently in the belief that judges appointed by Trump would support his effort to overturn the election.

Just as the institutions of legality were attacked, so was the exercise of free speech. The American constitutional regime has tightly bound democracy to the rule of law, on the one hand, and to free speech, on the other. These twin pillars of law and freely formed public opinion give a distinct shape to our constitutional democracy. Courts protect individual and minority rights, while the press leads the formation of public opinion by reporting on and critiquing policies, politicians, and government officials. A constitutional democracy checks democratic populism by placing legal limits on power and protecting the critical function of public opinion formation.

The Trump administration tried to subordinate the press to its own political aims. Threats against an independent press included terminating press briefings, limiting reporter access, denying press credentials, privileging right-wing media, threatening lawsuits, and endlessly lying.[31] The president not only lied but constantly demanded misrepresentations from others.[32] This began on the first day of his administration, with an obvious lie about the size of the crowd at the inauguration ceremony. There was often no reason to believe what the administration said—a point driven home when the president told the nation that Covid-19 would not be a problem.[33] The lying was linked to the president's repeated allegations of "fake news" directed against true reports by reputable institutions, and his efforts at rallies and on Twitter to prompt attacks on reporters. The press, he repeatedly claimed, was "the enemy of the people."[34]

Disregard for law and the attacks on the press are the tools of authoritarian regimes everywhere. Such regimes fear they cannot survive in the full light of truth, which is the object of both the judicial process and responsible reporting. The independence of the universities came under administration attack for the same reason. These attacks included persistent efforts to delegitimize academic science and to characterize campus speech as wholly corrupted by ideologically driven political correctness.[35]

The Trump regime may fairly be said to have attempted a "constitutional coup."[36] An ordinary coup is an extralegal seizure of power, in which the perpetrators aim to occupy government positions. A constitutional coup uses the ordinary institutions of governance to alter the basic form of government. An ordinary coup discards the mechanisms of election; a constitutional coup discards the mechanisms of constitutional amendment.

We misread contemporary events if we bring to them a twentieth-century idea of what a coup looks like: tanks in the streets, political leaders exiled or jailed, violence between factions, elections suspended, declarations of martial law, and the closing down of a free press. To insist on that model of a coup is like insisting that contemporary warfare must consist of tank and artillery battles fought between mass-conscript armies on the plains of Europe. Today's wars can occur in a zone of indistinction in which we cannot separate combatants from civilians, the public from the private, the domestic from the foreign, or news from propaganda.[37] This indistinction has now appeared in domestic politics: agency has become uncertain, and it is difficult to separate the private from the public, the domestic from the foreign, and news from propaganda. We do not really know whether 2016 was an ordinary election or an attack by a foreign power. Perhaps it was both.[38]

A regime of hostility to law, minorities, immigrants, political opponents, a free press, independent agencies, civil society institutions, science, transnational institutions, and the Western alliance is simply not the liberal constitutional order that was in place up until 2016. America under Trump was becoming an authoritarian democracy similar to those in Hungary, Poland, Turkey, and Russia. In each of these countries, electoral means have been used to consolidate political institutions around an authoritarian, populist leader who pursues a domestic politics of friends and enemies.[39] Trump tried the same. Thus, when the Black Lives Matter movement protested police killings in the middle of the pandemic, Trump threatened and then deployed a hastily assembled national police force to intervene violently against protestors, whom he described as terrorists and anarchists.[40] He intervened over the opposition of local leaders. As in other authoritarian regimes, this violence went forward without public transparency. It was carried out by unidentified actors who did not bear clear marks of authority or hold themselves out to public scrutiny.[41]

Constitutional Coup or Informal Amendment?

An authoritarian regime aligning itself with like-minded regimes abroad while abandoning the rule of law at home represents a change of constitutional magnitude. This is not, however, the first time in American history that there has been an effort at regime change outside of the formal process of constitutional amendment. Most famously, Franklin Roosevelt successfully overcame the Supreme Court's defense of a nineteenth-century regime of laissez-faire. Without formal amendment, he introduced a new constitutional regime that embraced the social welfare state with its heavy regulatory agenda.

Few people today think of the New Deal transformation as a constitutional coup. We speak instead of "informal amendment."[42] No doubt, those who resisted the changes considered them to be something akin to a coup—certainly unconstitutional.[43] These resisters have mostly dropped from our collective memory. Is talk of a constitutional coup today merely the grumbling expression of an angry political opposition?

Was Trump a new Roosevelt? Roosevelt was responding to a genuine crisis, while Trump, when confronted with the real crises of his times—the pandemic and climate change—failed to respond. Trump focused on imagined threats from immigrants, minorities, and trade partners; Roosevelt fought the Second

World War. Yet in a democracy, the people are entitled to decide for themselves when radical change is required. If they think there is a crisis justifying change, is that not enough? After all, at the time of the American Revolution, the loyalists asserted that there was no crisis, for the colonies enjoyed substantial personal liberty and rising wealth.[44]

If we are to understand the difference between an informal amendment and a constitutional coup as more than the different perspectives of winners and losers, we need some criteria. We can find them in the formal amendment procedures set forth in article 5 of the Constitution. An amendment requires more process and more popular support than does ordinary electoral or legislative success.[45] As my colleague Bruce Ackerman has argued, we are right to ask of informal regime change that it meets the same standards of supermajority support and sustained deliberation required of article 5 amendments.[46]

Before we discard a constitutional regime, we should collectively give the proposed change considerable thought, examining both costs and benefits. We need to ask how contemporary circumstances make the existing regime inadequate to our political aspirations. We need to listen to those who defend the status quo, even as we explore the possibility of change. Those who support change need to offer a concrete proposal that can be studied and debated. We need collectively to reach a decision after this critical deliberation, and that decision should be supported by a supermajority. Roosevelt was elected four times, including a landslide in 1936, after he had introduced the policies of the New Deal.[47] The supermajority requirement may seem unfair to an existing majority, but a regime change will have most of its effects on future generations. The supermajority requirement is a sort of representational stand-in for those future generations who will bear the costs of our errors.

We should be particularly wary of efforts at regime change by a faction that has suddenly achieved electoral success without having set forth and defended, over some significant time, a proposal for change. The decision for change should represent a new national commitment, not opportunism by a faction that happened to succeed in one electoral cycle. We need to guard against decisions that arise from temporary passions, for the regime will remain long after the passions dissipate.

Trump was no Roosevelt. During his time in office, there was never a serious public debate over his proposed changes—not in Congress and not among the states. There was no vetting in public opinion or even any real deliberation.

There was no clearly formulated proposal or articulated plan around which a debate could have been organized. Was there, for example, a decision not to staff administrative agencies in order to limit their roles? Or was the administration simply unable to manage the appointment process? If the people do not know what is happening and why, there can be no consensus for change.

Trump's efforts to undermine rights, institutions, and relationships were not the consequence of a sustained supermajority that chose to pursue an informal procedure of regime change. He lost the popular vote; he did not have majority approval for even one day while in office. The election of 2018 was a further repudiation of his transformative efforts. Even in the Senate, in which Republicans gained three seats, Democratic candidates outpolled Republicans by some twelve million votes.[48] Trump, himself, was voted out of office in 2020. However, were Trump to be reelected by a majority in 2024—along with Republicans gaining control of the House and Senate—claims for informal amendment would look entirely different. Trump could indeed assert that he was the new Roosevelt. We are not yet done with this debate over our national regime.

Accounts of Democratic Failure

Accounts of political polarization and the rise of Trump tend to focus on one of two large themes: economic inequality or cultural disregard. The former matches the ideological inclinations of the left—workers are falling behind—and the latter matches those of the right—traditional values are not respected.

Study after study has tracked the growth of sharp inequalities of class: the rich have been getting much richer while everyone else has fallen behind. Thomas Piketty's *Capital in the Twenty-First Century,* the best known of these studies, tells us that we are suffering from a structural problem of capitalism itself: finance will take an increasing share of the return on investment, leaving workers (and everyone else) further and further behind. Other studies focus on the decline of unions, leaving workers unable to bargain effectively with employers. Still others focus on globalization, identifying competition with low-wage workers abroad as the source of the problem. No doubt, all of these factors contribute to growing inequality.[49]

Progressive activists often act as if the facts of inequality—like the facts of environmental degradation or climate change—will generate their own politics. They think of their own politics as "fact based" and believe that the extension of knowledge will lead to greater political alignment with the agenda of the left. That there has lately been a shift of college-educated voters toward the Democratic Party gives some support to this view.[50] Nevertheless, politics remains overwhelmingly a domain of opinion, not facts.[51] Growing inequality does not explain why, for example, a program to extend affordable health care became an object of populist wrath. Facts operate in an already charged political field. Consider the pandemic of 2020. The same virus had different political meanings in New York and Texas, producing different responses.

Catherine frequently reminds me that people—rich and poor—vote their values, not their interests.[52] Or rather, they understand their interests only from within their values. I answer that we have no reason to trust their values if they are not paying attention or are paying attention only to propaganda. She responds that the problem, then, is to get them to pay attention to better sources of information. Tocqueville made the same point by speaking of "self-interest well understood."[53] The political issue, of course, is how to persuade people to understand their self-interests "well."

Those who explain the state of national politics by pointing to cultural rather than economic inequality take a values approach. Right-wing populism, they argue, responds to the failure of coastal elites to respect the values and lifestyles of traditional communities. These commentators see the culture wars through a lens of community disrespect rather than of class inequality.[54] The problem is not simply disagreement over values—over, for example, abortion, gun ownership, religion, and gender identity. The problem is distain for those who hold so-called traditional values or who do not achieve success as measured by advanced degrees.

Many of those who put religion, family, and nation at the center of their moral universe believe that their opponents think of them as morally corrupt, uneducated, lazy, and racist. They have been called "deplorables," a word that reeks of disdain.[55] Evangelicals, in particular, feel that their political opponents would deny them a public space in which to express the values with which they were raised. The new populism makes a claim for public recognition by groups that believe they have been ignored by the traditional leadership of both political parties.

With these charges, the populist right effectively turns the moral tables: those who would label them deplorable are the ones who are closed-minded and incapable of respecting difference. Coastal elites are charged with writing off the vast middle of the country, believing it to be full of gun-wielding, homophobic racists rather than hard-working families raising their children with traditional moral values. This story of abandonment and condemnation is made vivid in popular accounts, such as J. D. Vance's *Hillbilly Elegy* and Arlie Hochschild's *Strangers in Their Own Land*.[56] Vance speaks as an insider, Hochschild as an outside observer. Both accept the idea that these communities have fallen from public view and that the polarization of national politics represents a backlash against the values of the governing elite.

Vance describes Scots-Irish communities in Appalachia and Ohio caught up in substance abuse, economic dysfunction, and failed families. He has a mixed attitude toward these communities, which he considers home. On the one hand, he moralizes, arguing that individuals are responsible for their own failures and should—like him—discipline themselves and their children to seize available opportunities. On the other hand, he believes that the elite society he entered through Yale Law School ignores these communities.

Hochschild tells a similar story about a Louisiana community with Cajun roots. It is a community of strong families organized around evangelical faith. It is also a community collapsing from environmental degradation. She finds that these families are more distrustful of the federal government than of the corporations that are literally killing them. Like Vance, she argues for recognition and engagement across a cultural divide.

Vance, Hochschild, and others trying to grasp what is going on in the American heartland accurately describe views held by many people.[57] Certainly, no one should reject a plea for recognition or ignore the economic, environmental, and social suffering of these communities. Perception across a cultural and geographic divide, however, is likely to be inaccurate in both directions. Propagandists on the right want to convince voters from these communities that a cosmopolitan elite views them as morally offensive. They are matched by propagandists on the left trying to convince voters that government elites are controlled by global capitalists and financiers intent on denying a living wage to the working class. The two views are not wholly incompatible, which is why there is always hope for a convergence of left and right at the extremes.

But both of these accounts direct attention away from the fact that the beneficiaries of the modern social welfare state have largely been the white working class. There is a good deal of irony in the image of lower-middle-class citizens asserting that government has ignored them while they enjoy the benefits of

Medicare and Social Security—the largest domestic welfare programs.[58] These programs substantially eliminated abject poverty among the elderly by addressing the structural subordination of the working class—particularly the white working class.[59]

The story is much the same across the federal government's regulatory agenda. Cleaning the nation's air and water, for example, is not a project only for elites but a direct, life-enhancing benefit to the poor and lower middle class. As Hochschild shows, their communities have been the sites of dumping of hazardous, carcinogenic waste. Their children have suffered asthma from air pollution, their elderly from chronic respiratory problems.[60]

Environmental regulation is only one example among many. The beneficiaries of consumer protection measures, of financial regulation, and of labor and employment laws have been the working class. Everyone benefits from support for public education, but it has been of particular importance to members of the lower middle class. Personal success stories in these communities are almost always stories of taking advantage of educational opportunities. Vance's own success begins with public education. Claims of cultural disregard and economic inequality also ignore the millions upon millions of lower-middle-class and poor families who have been the beneficiaries of the Obama administration's extension of health insurance. If we measure concern by action, the powerful center of modern American domestic politics has been the welfare of the working class.[61] This hardly means that enough has been done. It is only to say that much of our modern politics has focused on amelioration of the conditions of the working class.

Of course, one can recognize the material benefits of national programs but still believe that they express an elite paternalism joined with cultural distain. For this reason, arguments about the facts may have little effect on political beliefs. Passing legislation that extended health insurance to millions of lower-income Americans did not persuade Trump's constituents that government was acting on their behalf. Rather, it created a new ground of attack that helped Trump get elected. How exactly would repealing that law express regard for the millions who would then be left without health care or with more expensive health insurance?

Charges of cultural disregard often speak the language of religion. Trump spoke of "a war on Christmas." His support is strongest among evangelicals. Again, we need to separate propaganda from policy. The Religious Freedom

Restoration Act of 1993 was introduced by Chuck Schumer in the House and Ted Kennedy in the Senate. It passed unanimously in the House and lost only three votes in the Senate; it was signed by President Bill Clinton.[62] Many of the religious victories in the Supreme Court in recent years have been based on this act, including the recognition of religious exceptions to Obamacare's requirement that employers support health insurance coverage of employees' access to reproductive-health services.[63]

To observe these facts is not to deny that there is widespread belief in the claim of cultural disregard, just as there is growing economic inequality. Government interventions do not act on an empty field. People's attitudes emerge from the meanings already at work in their lives. These meanings are not abstract norms. They are created and sustained in common practices—in the way we speak and listen to each other, lend our support, or express our disapproval. To observe Killingworth is to consider the close and intimate relationship between civil society and public governance, between the worlds we create for ourselves in family, work, and church, on the one hand, and the ways in which we tend to the public space and practices, on the other.

In Killingworth, wealth inequality and feelings of cultural disregard are certainly present. Those with few economic resources are angry that their taxes never go down. They feel they are being priced out of the town. Some longtime residents are angry about the "elites," who occupy the wealthier developments built in the 1990s. Yet these factors don't go very far in explaining changing beliefs and practices. There are few poor residents, and most townspeople benefit from the schools and parks that came with the new residents. Nevertheless, the community of volunteers is under deep stress, and the town did vote for Trump in 2016. There is much disquiet to be explained.

Public Opinion: Division and Entertainment

My law school colleagues consider it so important to follow national events that they think they are engaged politically when they are just keeping up with the news. They are not wrong. In a democracy, contributing to public opinion formation is itself an important political activity. That contribution begins with participation in a common world of information, observation, and discussion. James Madison observed in the Federalist No. 49 that "all governments rest on opinion." Not the facts, but how we account for them, drives our political practices.

A deeply polarized politics is one in which the two sides' narratives are far apart. For the political right, government is the enemy, working with intellectual and cultural elites against the interests of the people. Many believe that scientists conspire against God and free enterprise, minorities and women unfairly displace white men through affirmative action, immigrants invade the nation, unborn babies are killed, and free markets promote well-being. For the political left, everything is the opposite: government is a progressive force, the elites who are working against the people are the corporations and banks, science is the only rational basis for policy, structural racism is a deep and abiding reality, women have a right to control their own bodies, and unregulated markets favor the wealthy.

Those who listen to or read the same sources of information and commentary come to share a way of imagining politics. These communities of opinion are much thicker today than are communities defined by geography.[64] Members of the former know how to engage each other, even when they are otherwise strangers. Members of the latter—including my Killingworth neighbors—may not know how to speak to each other. They cannot be sure whether they are speaking to someone who reads the *New York Times* or watches Fox News.

In the postwar decades, national opinion formation depended on the medium of television. Americans everywhere looked to figures like Walter Cronkite and David Brinkley to learn about daily events and to respond to extraordinary crises. There was not a lot of difference among the three national networks. Together, they assured that acceptable opinion operated within a limited range and with a shared set of facts. The two political parties operated within a common world maintained by public opinion.[65] It was two parties, one system. The parties remain, but the system does not.

There is no longer a shared public opinion. While there had long been an alternative world of far-right, conservative opinion—from the John Birchers, at one end, to the readers of the *National Review,* at the other—the collapse of a single system of public opinion really took off with the arrival of Rush Limbaugh's nationally syndicated radio program in 1988. This was followed by the launch of Fox News in 1996.[66] By the time of the 2016 election, there was an entire ecosystem of right-wing media quite distinct from the traditional sources of information and opinion.

This ecosystem was not in the business of covering the news under the standards of professional journalism but instead melded ideology, propaganda, and entertainment. The news it offered often struck the mainstream as conspiratorial fantasy bordering on delusion. Stories of criminality and sexual abuse—including pedophilia—were manufactured, circulated, and reinforced as part of the political campaign against Hillary Clinton. After describing allegations linking the Clintons to the Jeffrey Epstein child sex abuse scandals, the authors of *Network Propaganda* summarize: "In the grip of the propaganda feedback loop, the right-wing media ecosystem had no mechanisms for self-correction, and instead exhibited dynamics of self-reinforcement, confirmation, and repetition so that readers, viewers, and listeners encountered multiple versions of the same story, over months, to the point that both recall and credibility were enhanced."[67]

Bitter division in public opinion is not new in America history. Today, however, these divisions extend well beyond opinions. We do not agree on facts or even on who can reliably determine facts, for the assault from the right includes attacks on science and expertise. These divisions are exacerbated by the changing forms of media. The laptop and the smartphone are replacing the television as opinion-shaping portals.[68]

Shifts in technology have consequences beyond their information content. This was no less true in the time of Martin Luther than it is in the time of Mark Zuckerberg.[69] The printing press greatly expanded access to biblical texts translated into the vernacular. Reading the Bible became a family activity, changing the character of parental roles.[70] With the invention of printing, libraries displaced the monasteries as the place of the book. Libraries meant universities. The secularization of printing brought a reimagining of the relations among writing, reading, and the political community. Modern politics emerged with an investment in new, organizing texts. In 1803, the Supreme Court declared "a written constitution" to be "the greatest improvement on political institutions."[71] The Court might have said the same of newspapers, for they also characterized politics in an age of printing.[72]

A similar story can be told about the emergence of the political lecture in the nineteenth century. Here, too, expectations had been formed by religious practice—in this instance, the sermon. In the eighteenth century, Killingworth residents spent their Sundays listening to the Congregational pastor speak for many hours. By the nineteenth century, public speaking was a critical part of the democratic political project.[73] Politicians spoke to crowds whose attention spans had been formed in church. Citizens were prepared to listen to public addresses lasting hours. The best of these were filled with the cadences and images of the King James Bible.[74] The revival meetings that marked the first and second Great Awakenings had effectively modeled a new form of political engagement. Something of this tradition continues in the evangelical meeting quality of the Trump rally. Not only did Trump appear with evangelical preachers, but he appeared in place of them.[75]

Today's media are far different from the religiously inflected print and speaking cultures of the eighteenth and nineteenth centuries. Family ritual for most Americans no longer includes Bible reading. That was replaced first by radio and then, in the second half of the twentieth century, by television. Families would gather in the evening to watch their shows. They lived with the new rhythms of entertainment: *TV Guide* replaced the calendar of saints. Temporal experience was divided in new ways. Each show alternated segments of content and advertising.[76] Viewers became accustomed to a twelve-minute window of content followed by a string of thirty-second advertisements.[77]

Today, with the proliferation of small screens, there is no family gathering at all. Electronic media moved us indoors, then splintered us within the home and fractured our shared time. Contemporary forms of media have moved even further in the direction of shortened attention spans and rapid messaging. Almost everything on the small screen is measured by its entertainment value, meaning its ability to hold the viewer's attention. Not surprisingly, the most important form of political communication today—especially for Trump—is Twitter.[78] This is politics for those whose attention span has been reduced to seconds. Politics appears within an endless stream of messaging that randomly juxtaposes life-and-death matters with celebrity revelations, photos of friends, and chatter about families and travel.

One hundred fifty years ago, it was hard to know where religion ended and politics began. Today, we do not know where entertainment ends and politics begins.[79] Pressure on this line is not new. Network news has struggled to maintain separation between politics and entertainment for decades.[80] Was the news to be measured by profit or public service?[81] Careers were made and lost over this question. The networks, however, were not allowed to make this decision wholly on their own. There was, until 1987, a federal "fairness doctrine," requiring broadcasters to recognize their public responsibility to provide "balanced" coverage of contending political positions.[82] Rush Limbaugh's radio show began one year after the fairness doctrine was abolished. Conservative talk radio exploited the new deregulation of the airways, just as Fox News exploited the new digital access of cable. The new social media have no memory of the fairness doctrine. For them, public service journalism was not even a question until the backlash to their facilitation of extravagant misrepresentations in the 2016 election. In 2020, Facebook and Twitter came under enormous pressure to monitor the misinformation on their platforms.[83] In January 2021, they found it necessary to act against President Trump.

Today's social media do not generate content. Instead, the users—who do generate content—are the product that is sold to customers, the advertisers. To increase the supply of product, users must be kept in a state of addictive suspense, enthralled as to what might come next.[84] What comes next is no longer determined by the network lineup. It is, instead, produced by an algorithm: the pace of change has gone from thirty minutes to less than thirty seconds. This, too, is not entirely new. Conservative talk radio also had to enthrall an audience for hours on end. Both forms of communication—the talk show host going on for hours and the endless social media account—are designed to allow viewers and listeners to easily come in and out. Content must be transitory yet support a single, broad narrative that is immediately accessible whenever a listener arrives. Outrage at elites serves these ends. So, however, does outrage at Trump.

When politics is an element of the entertainment business, we do not know what is serious and what is not. At a Trump rally, were those chants of "Lock her up!" politics or entertainment? They were politics become entertainment—a mob whipped into a destructive passion.[85] Lynchings, too, were once entertainment.[86] There is something of the lynching in the careless disregard for truth, law, dignity, and rights on display in much of our politics today.

Out of this maelstrom of entertaining self-display and profit-seeking manipulation came Donald Trump—the star of a reality TV show. Before he became president, he was as likely to be talking sex with Howard Stern as to be leading the birther movement on Fox News. Stern has made close to a billion dollars melding sex and outrage on the radio; Rupert Murdoch made billions from a media empire that turned news into entertainment. Trump himself was not just talking; he was advertising. Even his run for president was about pushing his brand.[87] Not surprisingly, speculation on the right as to who might follow Trump often focuses on Tucker Carlson, another TV personality whose role is to meld politics with entertainment.

The arrival of the internet might have contributed to a politics built on respect for science and investigative journalism. On the internet, everyone can be a fact checker. Never has so much information been available so widely. That the information is available, however, does not mean that people will use it. Information does not announce its own weight or relevance. What we seek out depends on what we expect when we go online. We expect to be entertained, not educated.

Often the entertainment sought on the internet is pornographic and violent.[88] Violent video games are played everywhere, and not just by adolescent boys. Close to 70 percent of Americans play video games, and more than 90 percent of those rated for ten-year-olds and older contain violent imagery.[89] Sex and violence dominate the web, just as they have long dominated popular entertainment. All of this produced candidate Trump: an entertainer threatening violence and reveling in pornographic behavior. Trump's *Access Hollywood* sex tape, for example, had little effect on his public standing because, for an electorate whose political expectations were shaped by entertainment, it presented nothing new.

By the beginning of the new millennium, both the old and the new media were treating politics as a form of entertainment. Traditional media approached politics as if it were more like a sports competition than a debate. The networks emphasized who was ahead, who had a good week or a bad week, who was gaining or losing. This horse-race model is coupled to a focus on personal interest stories, again as if the media were covering athletes. For the traditional media, the Olympics and presidential races share much more than a four-year cycle.

The sports competition model tended to normalize a candidate who was far from normal. To be treated equally was to appear as if equal. Trump was, moreover, the first among equals, because he was first in viewer interest. He was so good for ratings that he did not need to buy advertising to dominate the media. He was enormously profitable for traditional media, whose political operations had not been robust profit centers for some time.[90]

While traditional media were trying to create interest in politics as a competitive sport, their competitors were covering politics as if it were pornography. Pornography trades on fantasy and scandal, not truth. In 2016, Trump was the candidate of sexual transgression. News in the mode of pornography is not simply covering a campaign; it is participating in it. Is Fox News or Newsmax a news source, an entertainment venue, or an arm of the Trump political apparatus? What is Breitbart? Or is Trump himself better understood as an element of an entertainment empire? In a politics of entertainment, the traditional distinction between public and private disappears just as surely as that between fact and fiction. What is WikiLeaks: news, entertainment, instrument of a political party, or tool of a foreign power?

Distinctions between truth and falsehood, and between fact and opinion, simply do not count in a world of entertainment. We do not ask if entertainment is true; we ask whether it holds our attention. Democracies have no way of insisting that voters be serious or that they pay attention to the credibility of their information sources. It is not possible to insist that voters leave their conspiracy theories and their prejudices outside the voting booth. A mob can succeed as an entertainment venture even as it fails as politics.

When politics becomes entertainment, political research becomes market research. The same firms using the same techniques have both political and corporate clients.[91] They do research and provide data to support more effective client advertising to attract customers/voters. For the modern political campaign, data analysis is far more important than endorsement by opinion leaders. Indeed, the whole idea of endorsement seems antiquated.[92] Instead of endorsements by opinion leaders, good polling numbers by themselves add to a candidate's attractiveness. To follow politics today is to read polls, not editorials.

As an entertainment market, politics is dominated less by competitive pricing than by monopoly pricing: those who will not or cannot pay the monopoly price are not worth pursuing. Politicians thus write off entire segments of voters—for example, Hillary Clinton's "deplorables" or Mitt Romney's "47 percent."[93] There is no longer an effort to form a consensus and thus no need to aim for policies at the center. Trump made clear that he simply did not care about the citizens who did not vote for him. In 2020, the Democrats were divided over a strategy of trying to attract the moderate right or to increase voter participation on the left. That battle is likely to continue; it, too, will be driven by polling numbers.

Preparing for Trump: Politics and Myth

Trump voters are more puzzling than Trump himself. He is a recognizable type: narcissism, racism, xenophobia, misogyny, and corruption are familiar characteristics of the autocrat. We don't normally elect such people president. How did Trump fit within the constellation of beliefs and practices that was the Republican Party?[94] That party already relied on voters who listened to Rush

Limbaugh and Sean Hannity, kept their televisions on Fox News, believed the conspiracy-laden messages of Alex Jones, and had faith in the fundamentalists' promise of the coming rapture.[95]

Trump's support of the birther movement, which carried him to political prominence, enabled him to overcome his reputation as an unethical real-estate developer. The success of that movement tells us a great deal about his voters. The birthers made a claim of fact, suggesting hidden knowledge, and linked it to a claim of conspiracy perpetrated by threatening forces—Muslims, socialists, and the deep state. They invented an anticolonialist socialist out of Barack Obama's father; foreign birth out of dark skin; and Muslim faith out of time abroad. The birthers did not say that they disagreed with President Obama's policies; they attacked his legitimacy by insisting he was born outside the country. We see a similar pattern with opposition to environmental regulation. Those opposed to the Paris Climate Accords do not say that they disagree with the government's policy choices; they deny that global climate change is occurring.[96] Again, they allege conspiracies by hidden elites.

These terms—hidden facts, conspiracies, and secret forces—work on the mythical imagination. Why did the Republican Party become the home of mythical politics? Both parties confronted the same media technologies and the same social and economic conditions. But history matters: a left-wing populism of class never recovered from its defeats early in the twentieth century and from the failure of the union movement in the postwar decades.[97] More fundamentally, the dynamics of the two political parties were substantially different in the last decades of the twentieth century.

The Democrats, since the 1960s, have become a coalition of identity-driven groups, loosely aligned behind progressive policies. Their disputes are over how far left to move. The Republicans, during this same period, became an awkward union of a business elite and a white working-class base. The GOP's defining problem was to hold these two wings together when their interests lay in quite different directions.[98] At the heart of the party was a truth that could not be spoken: neither wing cared for or had any interest in the other's success. Because no one was able to speak this truth, the two factions could not usefully inform and educate each other. This division created the opening for a mythical politics carried by the new media and operating as a form of entertainment.

Two trends, accelerating in the 1970s, were especially important to the development of the modern Republican Party. First, there was a movement toward a global regulatory order. Global markets require global regulation. In earlier eras, that order was produced by hegemonic colonial powers. After the Second World War, hegemony took the form of American-driven transnational institutions in which states would participate on a formally equal basis.[99] Second, and more or less simultaneously, the Republican base was shifting in reaction to the progressive movements of the 1960s. It became increasingly white, male, and fundamentalist.

Because business leaders so often complain of regulatory burdens, we tend not to see the deep complementarity of trade and regulation. Expansion of trade is always accompanied by an expansion of regulation, first by national governments and then by transnational institutions. Early capitalism required an aggressive state to open and maintain markets—foreign and domestic—and to create an orderly property and contract regime.[100] Late capitalism requires an aggressive state to maintain a transnational legal order and to regulate global competition. The European Union, the largest open market in the world, is dense with regulation.

Of course, just like every other effort to create public goods, a global trade framework also creates possibilities for free riding and opportunism. Whatever problems and opportunities might arise for individual corporate interests—all of which want to shift burdens away from themselves—the promise is that in a common global order, governments will reliably secure public goods that no single firm can achieve on its own. Corporate interests, accordingly, are not against regulation per se. Even human rights can be a necessary condition of expanding markets. Bluntly put, genocide and torture are bad for business.

The new globalism required professional administrators: an international class of policy analysts, lawyers, financiers, and managers. This was the promise of the American era of global hegemony. It was also the promise of the European Union and, more recently, the promise of a newly emergent China, which needs the WTO no less than its competitors do. Schools of public policy, business, law, and management flourished. This elite easily moved back and forth between the private sector and public administration, as well as across borders. Their common backgrounds and interests led them to see problems and solutions in the same way. They shared a belief in neoliberalism and generally paid little attention to social and economic divisions within nations.[101]

As the neoliberal trade regime was expanding, the Republican Party was reacting to the cultural and political upheavals of the 1960s. By the 1970s, the antiwar movement, the civil rights movement, and the feminist movement had converged to create an impression of popular consensus around a progressive social agenda. Young people were bringing the culture of the university into the mainstream of American politics. Women and minorities were entering political life and changing the national center of gravity.[102]

Each of these movements triggered its own opposition, and these merged to form the base of the modern Republican Party. The antiwar movement brought forth an opposition organized around claims of respect for the military and a more militarized foreign policy. The civil rights movement brought forth an opposition in defense of the structure of white privilege, more popularly framed as defense of suburban life.[103] The feminist movement triggered a defense of traditional family values organized largely through Christian fundamentalist groups focused on opposition to abortion.[104] The Christian right became a substantial and reliable voting bloc, constituting more than 20 percent of the electorate.[105]

Groups opposing the progressive movements of the 1960s and 1970s shared loosely overlapping memberships, all of whom found a home in the Republican Party. The new party had to meld a right-wing populism—nationalist, racist, antifeminist, and evangelical—to the very different conservativism of the business elite. "Values conservatism," supported largely by non-college-educated whites living outside urban areas, entered a forced marriage with "market conservativism," whose adherents were largely university-educated, wealthy, and living in cities and suburbs.

Republican voters were increasingly culturally driven nationalists, while Republican funders were corporate interests. The former were antielitist; the latter were the elite. The former were suspicious of anything beyond the nation's borders, of university-based expertise, and of claims for diversity. The latter affirmed all of these. This uneasy union of opposites was entirely visible in the Republican ticket of 2008, which paired the center-right internationalist John McCain with the populist Sarah Palin. Who represented modern Republicans? The jolt of enthusiasm that Palin's nomination injected into McCain's moribund campaign gave a clear sign of which wing was ascendant.

The two wings found common ground in their fear of the left. Even here, however, there were differences. The corporate elite feared that the left would pursue redistributive policies both domestically and internationally. The populists had no reason to oppose redistribution—they were the beneficiaries of the largest of these programs, Social Security and Medicare—but they feared a social and cultural agenda of racial, gender, and ethnic equality. The corporate elite had no reason to oppose the progressives' cultural and social ambitions. In the places where they lived and worked, no one wanted to think of themselves as racist, sexist, or nationalist. They attended the same universities, lived in the same neighborhoods, and often exchanged the same offices—as administrations changed—with the elite of the Democratic Party.

Managing this tension between the base and the elite became the modern Republican Party's central problem. In large part, it meant suppressing the politics of class by emphasizing a politics of white racial identity and Christian belief. You could not find a lot of birthers on Wall Street, but neither could you find corporate leaders speaking out against the movement. A party unable or unwilling to deliver programs that advanced its base's economic well-being had no choice but to raise its attacks on opponents to an ever-higher pitch. Democratic leadership was cast as the enemy; minorities were depicted as un-American. Government programs became "giveaways" to undeserving minorities; regulatory interventions became abuses of federal power that cost jobs. These views had long inhabited the far-right side of Republican politics. Now they became the main message.

To advance this essentially reactive and defensive politics, the party hit upon a coordinated, two-step approach: first, find "experts" to challenge the epistemic consensus; second, rely on propagandists to fill the disrupted space.[106] This approach is familiar from creation science, which emerged as a serious movement in the 1960s and 1970s.[107] Believers in the revealed truth of creation—mythical thinking—needed to be reassured that their position could be defended against modern science. Creation scientists were not speaking to the biologists, geologists, and physicists of the modern university. They were not "debating" experts in their fields. Rather, they were creating a space within which the believer could feel secure against scientific challenge. Their role was to reassure the modern believer that "we have our own science," which effectively means that they can give free rein to their faith.

This pattern of alternative experts creating a space for the mythical imagination came to characterize right-wing populist politics in diverse fields. Exxon, for example, funded research designed to question climate change well after its own scientists concluded that climate change was indeed a fact.[108] The tobacco industry funded research to deny the health consequences of smoking. The attack on the science easily morphed into an attack on the scientists as conspiring elites.[109] No reasonably well educated person, including those running the corporations, believed these claims, but educated people were not the audience. Well-financed conservative think tanks churned out dissensus views on finance, schools, housing, drug pricing, banking, risk regulation, and climate change. The corporate leaders did not really expect large swings of policy based on this "research." Policy would yield to the facts in the long term. Climate change was a problem; smoking did cause cancer. The corporate interest was in slowing the rate of change. Today, it is telling that a majority of Republicans believe that colleges and universities have had a negative effect on society.[110]

Absent the preparatory work of challenging the epistemic consensus, the agitator would have little credibility. Limbaugh, for example, had little more than a high school education; Hannity has two years of college.[111] They do not speak the language of experts. They rely on others to open a space for their conspiracy-laden harangues. The movement is always from scientific disruption to mythical belief. Consider climate change. Only if that change is not a fact to be acknowledged is it possible to allege that those who support ameliorative action are conspiring to destroy the nation's economy.

The Republican base was cultivated by an unrelenting attack on progressive policies, focusing on undeserving others ("makers versus takers," in the Romney campaign's well-crafted phrasing) and liberty-denying regulatory regimes.[112] Cultural issues—particularly gun rights and opposition to abortion—were added to cement the fundamentalist and rural votes. In office, however, Republicans cut taxes and pursued moderate deregulation. On foreign policy and national security, they were hardly different from the Democrats.[113] On the Supreme Court, it could be hard to tell the Democrats and the Republicans apart: *Roe v. Wade* survived.

In the end, Republican politics proved more powerful than Republican governance.[114] Establishment Republicans believed, at first, that Trump would fall into line, governing according to their neoliberal agenda. He did support the tax breaks and deregulation they would have wanted from any Republican candidate. But Trump never stopped campaigning while in office. He rode those mythical forces from neoliberalism to right-wing authoritarianism. The Republican Party did not remake him in its image; he remade the party.

Practicing politics as entertainment, Trump gave voice to emotions and beliefs that are not ordinarily expressed in public debate. In 2016, he accused Hillary Clinton of being a criminal, a sexual predator, and a national security threat. This is the standard practice of propaganda: to invert the truth. It was, after all, Trump who allegedly committed fraud, practiced sexual predation, and posed a national security threat. He regularly threw back at his accuser whatever allegations were made against him, at one point even claiming that Clinton was responsible for the birther campaign against Obama and for Trump's own failure to pay federal taxes.[115] Both are mind-boggling claims, which was just their point: to disorient anyone who tried to take his speech seriously while exciting his supporters by pushing the borders of the outrageous. Trump's claims of massive election fraud in 2020 had the same character. As he tried to persuade Republican officials to discard the actual votes in their states, he made more and more extreme claims of fraud—claims that no court would accept but that his followers believed.

Constitutional Coup or Civil War?

Democratic politics holds up a mirror to ourselves, for politicians appeal to what they imagine to be our values and interests. Looking into that mirror today, many citizens do not like what they see. For those citizens who did not see themselves represented in the values and policies of the Trump administration, the problem is more than a loss in one electoral cycle. That sort of loss is part of politics. Trump's 2016 victory, however, was different. It felt to them like a military defeat—as if their country had been occupied by an enemy. In 2020, Trump supporters experienced that same sense—not loss but defeat.

How did Trump voters imagine their responsibilities as citizens? Indeed, what were we thinking? I say "we" because, in a democracy, we are collectively responsible for our community's political choices. Those of us who opposed Trump failed to persuade our fellow citizens. They won; we all, collectively, chose Trump. If this idea of collective responsibility sounds strained or out of place, if we think instead that "they did this to us," then we are no longer a single, self-governing community. We are, in Lincoln's famous words, a house divided, which cannot stand.

Can we? I have described the Trump administration as attempting a constitutional coup, but our situation may better be described as a civil war. A civil war occurs when conflict is beyond the power of ordinary political institutions to resolve. Today, neither elections nor court judgments can resolve our differences. Similarly, representative institutions, including Congress, are incapable of resolving differences. They, too, have become sites of polarized conflict.

Just as contemporary coups look different from those of earlier eras, so do civil wars. We are no longer fighting over a line of territorial division. There are red and blue states, but the war goes on deep within each state. The sides in this new war are just as divided, polarized, and intolerant as those in earlier civil wars. If this war is less violent—though it is hardly nonviolent—than the earlier wars, it is not because we have more regard for each other. Rather, it is because we have less regard for politics. Citizens are no longer willing to sacrifice themselves for their political beliefs. They would rather just turn the channel. After Vietnam, Iraq, and mutual assured destruction, the age of sacrificial politics may be at an end.[116]

In America today, we are past the point at which the red and the blue constitute a single national community. Each side has pulled away from the other; neither has sympathy for the other. This is why Trump's support remained stable even as a pandemic swept the country. Neither the nation of the red nor that of the blue can imagine moving to the other side. That would be defeat at best and treason at worst. In this conflict, issues are symbols—markers of the divide—not problems to be solved. This extends from guns to abortion, from Christian fundamentalism to pandemic relief. No institution, whether the Centers for Disease Control or the Supreme Court, has managed to escape the conflict. No act is too trivial or too commonsensical to escape the war: for example, wearing face masks. Always the question is, "Which side are you on?"

As in most wars, the sources of these deep passions are not entirely clear. Political partisanship has become tribal. Fellow members are "patriots," while the opposition is the "enemy of the people." The strength of these beliefs became stunningly clear when the pandemic arrived. The Trump administration saw the arrival of the virus on the two coasts—blue nation strongholds—as if it were a plague descended upon an enemy state. They were not about to offer help to the enemy.[117] By the time they realized that red states were not immune to the virus, it was too late. The pattern had been set; the forms of response had been politicized. The cost was hundreds of thousands of lives.

All of the changes in national political life that I have described in this chapter have appeared in Killingworth. Some have gathered strength; some have been resisted. They arrive not as generalizations or in returns to survey questions—

the view from Yale Law School—but in the beliefs and practices of my neighbors. These changes bear on the forms of civil participation, the content of our
local dialogues, and the way in which we participate (or fail to participate) in local
governance. As at the national level, our long-standing political institutions—
beginning with the town meeting—are no longer serving our democratic ideals.

Although Killingworth is special and unique to many of its residents, from a
national perspective there is nothing special about the town. Local changes over
the past several decades echo changes occurring everywhere. Killingworth no
longer has the extended families, churches, farms, and close associations that
once characterized community life. The nature of work and the workplace have
changed; the communications revolution has arrived. Patterns of civility are
strained; practices of volunteering are no longer so common. Those who have
lived here for many decades ask, "What is happening to us?" They wonder
whether their town can survive what the nation has become.

2

Killingworth Copes

I confess that in America I saw more than America; I sought there an
image of democracy itself, of its penchants, its character, its prejudices,
its passions; I wanted to become acquainted with it if only to know at
least what we ought to hope or fear from it.
—*Alexis de Tocqueville,* Democracy in America

TOCQUEVILLE CAME TO AMERICA IN 1831 to learn of the possible future of democracy in his own country, France. He observed that the desire for equality
had become the dominant force in world history. So powerful and pervasive
was this force, he thought it part of a divine plan: "The gradual development of
equality of conditions is therefore a providential fact."[1] By equality, he meant a
social condition, not a legal right. An equal society was one without hierarches
of religion, class, guild, family, or tradition. Everywhere, people wanted a leveling of social distinctions.

While Tocqueville thought the general movement toward social equality was
inevitable, no single political form followed from that movement. He saw two
paths into the egalitarian future: that of the mob and that of civil society.[2] The
mob leads to a populist authoritarian regime: all citizens are equal because one
leader has all the power. Civil society pursues equality through citizen participation in countless associations that form and reform in the pursuit of projects
and interests. Equality, on this view, is realized not in the relationship of the
individual to the whole of the people but in the individual's participation alongside others in multiple associations and organizations.

This tension—populist authoritarianism or liberal democracy?—is especially pressing in our own era. The choice is measured not in numbers at the polls but in how we live our lives. The authoritarian and the liberal democrat do not just favor different policies; they are different people. They operate with different norms, interests, and beliefs—that is, with different narratives of self, society, and polity. Thus, the election of Trump posed the question: "Who are we?"

Tocqueville worried that France was headed down the authoritarian path. He came to America in 1831 to explore the alternative path, which he thought was most clearly at work in the self-governing New England townships. If Tocqueville could have revisited America in the past few years, he would have found the constitutional coup I described in the last chapter threatening to take the nation down the path of authoritarian populism. But what would he have seen if he returned to New England?

In Killingworth, he would have found much the same institutional structure that he saw in 1831—direct democracy in the town meeting, a board of selectmen, and many unpaid elected officials. Had he attended a town meeting, however, he would have found something unrecognizable: an almost empty room. Had he gone looking for the civil society organizations that were central to his view of American democracy, he would have found only remnants. He would have found a persistent faction of mostly older joiners, along with a larger culture of families trying to live without the support of relatives, neighbors, government, and civil society—not on farms but in suburban homes. He might have concluded that the strained condition of democratic self-government in Killingworth has some relation to the constitutional coup in Washington. That Killingworth voted for Trump in 2016 might not have surprised him. He might have seen a connection between the local contraction of civil attachments and the rise of a national politics of division and anger: "Sentiments and ideas renew themselves, the heart is enlarged, and the human mind is developed only by the reciprocal action of men upon one another."[3]

A Difficult Year

The coronavirus arrived in New York City sometime in early 2020. By March, the New York metropolitan area, including western Connecticut, was in its worst public health crisis since the influenza pandemic of 1918. Thousands died; many tens of thousands were ill. The national government was absent, even as the disease spread across state lines and the economy collapsed. Like other threatened communities, Killingworth was on its own.

Catherine, recently elected to her sixth term as first selectman, was at first reluctant to shut town hall. Residents expect to be able to enter the building to obtain permits, do title searches, register their dogs, and pay their taxes. They expect to be able to walk into her office and complain or just chat. The building is the place for evening meetings of the committees and boards that carry on the work of the town. More than that, it is a symbol of the community as an ongoing enterprise. Go to the town website, and you are greeted with a photograph of the building from 1896, when it was a farmhouse up the road from the Congregational Church.

Catherine's hopes to remain open did not last long, for she was responsible for the safety of town employees. An old farmhouse does not permit much social distancing. Online, the town reinvented itself, putting public safety responsibilities first. The public health official gained a new prominence. The ambulance association took on a new role: transporting patients with Covid-19 symptoms to the hospital. All meetings, formal and informal, moved to cyberspace. The town faced a particular problem in providing residents the ability to join the public meetings of its committees and boards. Residents had to learn new cyber skills; they also had to learn patience.

Some things, however, required urgent action. Like so many other communities, the town found itself without adequate personal protective equipment. Town volunteers started sewing masks and eventually produced thousands of them. Annette Cook, who previously ran a business making handbags, volunteered her equipment and her labor. On her own, she produced 5,500 masks. The masks were distributed free to emergency responders, essential workers, and anyone else who needed one, which at times seemed like the entire town. Reflecting on her astounding production at the end of the year, Annette wrote, "If there is one highlight from 2020 it is the Killingworth community proving we can help each other." She told me, "In a situation totally out of your control, and you're helpless, what you can do is help somebody else. And that's empowering."

As the pandemic continued to wreck the economy, Killingworth found that it had increasing numbers of families in need. Unemployment in town doubled, then tripled. The Lions Club stepped forward with a food drive. Members stood at the entrance to the town dump with nets into which residents could throw cans or boxes while maintaining social distance. Several times, a local restaurateur, Francesco Lulaj, delivered three hundred meals to seniors living at Beachwood, a moderate-income retirement community. Helping Hands, a volunteer food bank, expanded its operations. Before the pandemic, it had provided holiday meals to about thirty families; now, it was doing so for some sixty families. Annette, who would take nothing for the masks she produced, donated contributions she received to Helping Hands. The churches—Congregational, Catholic, and Evangelical—paid special attention to the needs of their senior members. The Lions took responsibility for seniors without a faith community.

Other residents volunteered to shop for elderly or immune-deficient neighbors. Catherine and I—both over sixty-five—did not go to a grocery store for many months. A neighbor brought us groceries until delivery services became available. Volunteers came forward to take trash to the dump for community members who found the social distancing rules arduous. The town library started a curbside pickup service.

Every night, Catherine produced a town bulletin, "Killingworth Copes," informing residents of public health measures, infection and morbidity statistics, volunteer opportunities, and available services. For the first couple of months, this bulletin was bleak as the virus spread through the state and region. To our west, there were major hot spots, including New Haven. Hartford, to the north, was having severe problems. To the east, the incidence of the virus dropped off rapidly. Killingworth was just on the border between areas of high and low incidence. Thanks to the volunteers, the town managed to get through the summer with only about twenty cases and three deaths. Three is not a small number for a town of our size. Most residents had only one or two degrees of separation from a disease victim. One of those who died lived just down the street from us; one ran a popular garage. By the end of the year, Killingworth had seen around two hundred cases and five deaths.

"Killingworth copes" is a good description of how the town managed. Residents pitched in; no one who asked for help went unanswered. Yet some residents complained about the nightly bulletin, particularly when the news was bad. Catherine's daily reports were often about disease, death, social distancing, and prohibited activities. She did not reflect the optimism residents were hearing from the president, who said that the virus posed no significant threat and would just disappear "like a miracle."[4] Some residents wondered why she had to report bad news at all.

Allegations of fake news soon arrived via social media. Conventional public health advice was challenged. Residents were sternly lectured by critics to "do their own research," followed by links to right-wing sources. When the governor started to reimpose restrictions as the second wave arrived in the fall, some residents openly rebelled, announcing that no one was going to tell them when they could go out or where they could go. These were local skirmishes in America's civil war. Even when promising news on vaccine research emerged, a conspiracy theory circulated charging that the vaccine was only another tool for government surveillance.

Other points of suspicion emerged. The town budget for the coming year is adopted each spring. Because the economic impact of the pandemic was uncertain, residents were naturally nervous about taking on new financial commitments. The board of finance and the selectmen pared the budget down by delaying capital expenditures and maintenance projects. They were, however, contractually committed to small salary increases for the half a dozen unionized town employees. Following the usual practice, they extended the same increases to the few nonunionized coworkers in town hall—a small price to pay for worker harmony—but froze salaries for management. Nevertheless, a charge circulated that that town officials "were giving themselves raises." Because the state had suspended the ordinary requirement of budget approval by Town Meeting or referendum, some residents were convinced that town officials would take advantage of the situation to enrich themselves.[5]

General suspicions quickly led to specific acts of resistance, particularly over social distancing and mask-wearing. The town dump—actually a transfer station—is a center of civic life. It sits next to the little league field and the site of the seasonal farmers' market. Even with town hall shuttered, the dump remained in operation as an essential service. It could not, however, continue as a place at which residents gather on Saturday mornings to chat and catch up on local gossip. Once the town required that no one linger and everyone wear a mask—necessary steps as the second wave hit the town that fall—the dump became a site of contention.

Resistance began with the employees. One refused to cooperate and left. On my frequent trips to the dump, I noticed that another employee could never seem to wear a mask properly, leaving it hanging around his chin. He nevertheless chatted with the regulars, some of whom lowered their own masks when speaking with him. Some residents defended him; others complained about his behavior, asking why they should suffer a health risk at the dump. In the end, a sort of compromise was reached. He would mostly stand inside the little shed by the dumpster. His friends would stand outside and chat through an open door. The problem was managed; Killingworth coped.

In 2020, Killingworth had to deal with not only the pandemic but also the Black Lives Matter movement. Killingworth is 96 percent white, but as the movement gained traction in the spring and early summer of 2020, many residents joined public actions in the surroundings towns and cities. Some erected Black Lives Matter signs on their property. Others responded by trashing the signs at night. This led to a lively debate on an online discussion board. One of the more controversial entries in that debate came from Cheryl Fine, the only member of the board of finance to have voted against the town budget that spring. When a neighbor complained that her BLM sign had been repeatedly trashed by trespassers in the middle of the night, Cheryl posted this message:

> BLM is funded by violent Marxists whose goal is to destroy the western nuclear family and our Judeo-Christian based values. This past weekend they attacked many churches—burned a 250-year-old church in Calif., defaced Catholic statues. They are also rabidly anti-Semitic. They are co-opting the genuine protests seeking equal treatment to fit their agenda to destroy the USA. . . . Their head fundraiser was convicted of bombings—only served 16 of 58 yr sentence. Pardoned by Bill Clinton. All three head women claim to be well trained Marxists—their words. Don't just believe the superficial information. Always dig deep and know the facts for yourself.

Her statement captures a familiar set of ideas, associating conspiracies, Marxism, destruction of church and family, attacks on the nation, Bill Clinton, violence, and a claim to serious research ("dig deep"). There is simultaneously an affirmation of American values—"genuine protests seeking equal treatment"—alongside suspicion of those claiming these values. When I asked Cheryl about this posting, at first she said she could not remember it. When I read it to her, she acknowledged it and told me that she got her information directly from the BLM website. She also told me that she gets most of her news from apps on her phone, saying that she "spends way too much time" with them. These allegations did circulate on some conservative news apps; perhaps Cheryl confused some of her sources.[6]

I do not believe that Cheryl thought of herself as representing a political position—just the opposite. She complained about how people make "assumptions" about a person just by virtue of their party affiliation. She was, she said, reporting the results of her research in that post. But what is she looking to when she "digs deep"? One answer appeared immediately in the exchange: someone posted a link to a Fox News story entitled, "Catholic Churches Burned, Vandalized over Weekend as Police Investigate: 'Where's the Outrage?'" The story provided no evidence whatsoever of a connection to BLM; it simply strung together reports of fires at a few churches across the country, some of which may have been accidental; one was caused by a schizophrenic off his meds.[7]

Cheryl's posting drew both objections and support. Some supporters of her views told BLM advocates either to keep their views to themselves or to move to a city, away from this "white area." This invoked countercharges that the BLM critics should keep their opinions to themselves. Cheryl told me that she did not follow the discussion.

This is Killingworth today. A place of volunteers helping each other manage the town and deliver services, on the one hand, and of ideologically driven suspicions and attacks, on the other. Cheryl shows us that people do not fall simply on one side or the other of this divide. She has long been an active volunteer in the Congregational Church, serves on town boards, and serves on the Republican town committee. At the same time, some of her social media posts can sound as if they came from a right-wing agitator. She, along with many others in town, expresses a desire for dialogue across political divisions, but there is little prospect for such a discussion actually to occur. The two sides do not share enough of a common world to support an exchange of views. Are we really going to have a dialogue on the Marxist threat to the American family and Christian faith?

A tendency toward incivility is not limited to political discourse. A posting on Facebook asking whether neighbors can do anything to tend to an abandoned house with an overgrown lawn quickly became confrontational when someone responded that people should "mind their own business" and "not trespass." An inquiry about a town noise ordinance became a shouting match over who was a good neighbor: the guy with the noisy leaf blower or the neighbor wondering if he has to tolerate this at seven o'clock on a Saturday morning?

Political discourse is swept up into this broader incivility. For better and for worse, our politics reflects who we are, how we act toward each other, and what we think we owe each other. Residents of Killingworth often want to avoid open discussion of politics, but there is no line distinguishing the political from the social. Self-governance does not begin in town hall but starts with volunteers producing masks for the guys at the dump, just as political discourse begins with the sign along the road and the online exchange.

Killingworth managed to deal with the pandemic because it could draw on the willingness of community members to volunteer. Whether it can continue to manage depends on its ability to sustain that ethos of volunteerism. Tellingly, the woman who initially posted about the vandalism of her BLM sign announced, after several rounds of "dialogue," that she was withdrawing from further participation. She had reached her limit; she was no longer willing to tolerate the threats and abuse.[8] When engaged citizens are attacked as Marxists and anti-Semitic destroyers of families and faith, they will hesitate to get involved. They will hesitate even more when vandals appear at night. Some will turn away completely. Polarization then becomes an existential threat to the life of the town. This is how the national crisis reaches into the life of a small town.

A Countrypolitan Town

Killingworth is not a typical American town. It is smaller, whiter, wealthier, older, and less urban than the average.[9] Its population of 6,400 is made up of 2,700 households, of which African Americans and Hispanics are each about 0.5 percent.[10] The median household income in 2019 was $110,543. The median value of a house was $365,300, and 93 percent of the houses are owner-occupied. The town has little commercial development. Once a rural farm town, it has a lot of open space and an extensive system of roads. One selectman likes to remind us that our eighty miles of roads are our largest infrastructure investment. There is also a lot of water in town. Reservoirs provide water to much of south-central Connecticut, and water companies own a good deal of undeveloped land. There is a state park, a state forest, and several town parks—all limiting development. More land is kept from development by two large hunting and fishing clubs.

Residents joke that Killingworth's only local products are water and rocks. In the nineteenth century, the water powered numerous mills. The dams still dot the town. Farming here was always a tough business. Killingworth seems to have been favored as a rock depository of the Last Glacial Maximum, about twenty thousand years ago, which is why it is difficult to dig a hole to plant a tree. The underlying bedrock has the form of a large upward dome, fittingly called "the Killingworth dome." This geology accounts for the reservoirs and the height of the town. Just seven miles north of Long Island Sound, parts of the town are well over five hundred feet above sea level. In winter, I often drive home from rain in New Haven to snow in Killingworth. Alongside the rocks and water, Killingworth has an abundance of history. It has been practicing self-government for over 350 years. At the time of the Revolution, the town had a population of about 2,000, of whom about 200 went to war and 17 died. By the time Tocqueville toured New England, Killingworth was already close to 200 years old.

If any place in America can govern itself well, it should be Killingworth.[11] The town does not have deep divides of race and class. There are few very wealthy residents, but also very few poor residents.[12] It is solidly middle class. There is a community of modest homes for seniors—the homes to which Francesco delivered free meals during the pandemic. For the most part, however, it is expensive to live in Killingworth, with its two-acre residential zoning, lack of public transport, and absence of public services. We supply water to the state, but with the exception of the seniors' community, every house in town has its own well. Similarly, there are no public sewers; everyone must maintain their own septic system. As Tom Haggerty, a member of the planning and zoning commission, puts it, "It takes money to live here." Many residents, he adds, want to keep it that way. Other residents can barely make ends meet.

Killingworth copes, but it would not take much—a couple of dozen volunteers choosing to stay home—for it to fail in much the same way as the national government failed in its pandemic response. Services would go neglected; families and individuals would be on their own. The wealthy would still do well; everyone else would struggle materially and psychologically. The town cannot afford to pay for the public services it receives from volunteers. Without them, who would plan its budgets or maintain its parks? Who would drive the ambulances and put out the fires? Who would produce the masks and make sure they got to those who need them?

The Art of Governance

The Covid-19 crisis reminds us that the problems for local government are not different in kind—though vastly different in scale—from those facing the nation.[13] In Killingworth, there are, first, the problems of passing a budget and raising taxes. Residents are generally no happier about paying local taxes than they are about paying federal taxes. The town has to educate the young and take care of the elderly. Balancing development—commercial and residential—against environmental preservation is no less pressing locally than nationally. The town must maintain its facilities and infrastructure. Killingworth is small enough that it has no local police force, relying on a "resident" state trooper—a state officer posted to the town. Yet the town confronts the same problems of drug abuse and domestic violence as the rest of the nation. Not so long ago, we were surprised by a bank robbery at the town's lone bank branch. While Killingworth does not have to deal with foreign states, it does have to deal with intergovernmental relations. The state capital, Hartford, often looks to residents like a foreign place. Dealing with state officials requires building alliances with other small towns. It also requires recognizing potential adversaries—often the state's large cities, with their different agendas.

The routine provision of public services and record-keeping, alongside maintenance of roads and facilities, take most of the time of town employees and leaders. As with national and state government, however, crisis is the test of leadership. For elected leaders, the art of governance is that of responding to the unpredictable: storms, fire, injury, disputes between neighbors, accidents, and most recently, the pandemic. The first selectman's role is to bring neighbors together to reach a practical solution to the problem at hand. The town staff can do little on its own. This was the story of pandemic response. The town needed face masks: volunteers started sewing; a distribution table was set up at the dump; personal delivery was arranged for those who could not get there. None of this was legally required; no one had a right to these services. None of it was written down in a manual or set of regulations. No one was assigned these responsibilities in advance.

Covid-19 was not unusual in this respect. When a storm sweeps in, knocking trees into the streets, it is not the time to debate the merits of privatization. We do not consult a regulatory manual or wait for the specialists. The chainsaws come out, the generators go on, the middle school becomes an emergency shelter, and the first selectman gets on the phone to harass, demand, and threaten the utility company to get the power back up.

While the problems are similar across levels of government, the art of governance is not. Catherine likes to point out that Killingworth is the same size as Wasilla, Alaska, where Sarah Palin served as mayor before becoming governor.[14]

Running a small town, Catherine explains, is not a qualification for national office because governance of a small town is direct, unmediated, and personal. National office, on the other hand, requires rules, bureaucratic order, representation of multiple interest groups, and hierarchical authority. Personally delivering masks is a virtue for small town leadership; it relates not at all to managing production and importation of hundreds of millions of masks by the national government.

Mayors of small towns do not advance their careers by becoming mayors of ever larger towns and cities. First selectman is not an entry-level position for a career in public sector management. Some towns near Killingworth are turning to professional management in place of public governance. They hire a town manager and replace the board of selectmen structure with a town council. Town managers do have a career path of advancing to ever larger jurisdictions. This sort of professionalization is also expensive. Killingworth lacks the tax base and the willingness to expend the resources on a town manager. It prefers to cope, as it has done for over three hundred years.

Democracy and Distrust

Many of the problems tearing at our national political fabric became apparent in Killingworth some time ago. Their effect has been to undermine what Tocqueville saw as the virtue of local governance: its character as a school of liberty. He did not mean a school in managerial techniques but a school in character formation: "Without the institutions of a township a nation can give itself a free government, but it does not have the spirit of freedom. . . . Despotism suppressed in the interior of the social body reappears sooner or later on the surface."[15]

Over the past twenty years, the town's political discourse has grown less civil. Recent political campaigns have been marked by subtle threats of violence, a turn toward secrecy, the propagation of conspiracy theories, a willingness to misrepresent, and a personalizing of political differences. "Fake news" showed up in Killingworth before it became a national issue; so did "Lock her up." The connection between political speech and speaking truthfully was deliberately broken by a small group of residents. Traditions of civility are easily disturbed and hard to recover. When political exchange becomes volatile, people are more likely to withdraw—to stay home—than to confront the disrupters.

More residents come to suspect their neighbors' motives. They are quick to denounce town decisions and quick to see conspiracies.

An extreme form of distrust is suspicion of criminal intent. Efforts to introduce criminal charges into ordinary politics characterized Trump's presidential campaigns. Once in office, he pressed the Justice Department to bring charges against his political opponents.[16] Here, too, Killingworth led the way. Catherine has twice been the target of efforts to have state officials investigate her actions. The first involved rental of a town-owned building to the local historical society; the second concerned a decision to allow a citizen group to use a conference room in town hall to make phone calls in support of a budget referendum. Legally, nothing came of these efforts, but the same was true of Trump's charges. The point is not the criminal process itself but the accusation. These allegations increase distrust among residents, who are unlikely to know the truth of the matter.

Recently, one of the selectmen proposed expanding our local food pantry's hours of operation, arguing that it was not right for Killingworth families placed in need by the pandemic to have to travel to a regional food bank. She thought the town should take care of its own. Others argued that the regional center could do a better job and that some residents might prefer not to reveal their financial difficulties to their neighbors. Mercedes Ricciuti, then the director of Helping Hands, told me that she would sometimes recommend to residents that they go to the regional center because it offered a wider range of items, including fresh produce and meat, than was available here. Allegations were soon being made that Helping Hands was turning families away.

Disagreement over how to manage the relationship between the local and the regional food bank seems like the sort of thing that should be resolved through discussion. But this discussion led only to bad feelings. Partisan suspicions arose and rippled outward as others got drawn into the debate. Catherine was confronted with personal accusations: a wedge issue, forcing a partisan stand, was being created regardless of whatever good intentions might have been there at the beginning. Amid the controversy, Mercedes resigned. She perceived a personal attack with no regard for her thirteen years of volunteer service managing Helping Hands. Instead of receiving recognition, she felt "insulted."

Today, even a food pantry can become a site of partisan suspicion. Programs like the food bank require volunteers, but when they become sites of partisan controversy, volunteers are inclined to withdraw. There are not a lot of people ready and willing to take their place. The food bank was adopted by the Killing-worth Women's Organization—a move Mercedes had herself recommended three years earlier. Maybe that will save it, but already there is controversy over how it will be run.

The expression of distrust comes most often from the right—for example, with the controversy over the BLM signs. But not always. To combat dangerous weed growth over barriers along some of the roads that traverse wetlands, Cath-erine approved limited use of an herbicide. She did so after research on its en-vironmental effects and consideration of alternatives. Some local environmen-talists were outraged and accused her of betrayal. Catherine invited them to volunteer to study the problem and propose alternatives. None has been sug-gested, but this year there was no spraying by the town. Is that the success of local government responding to constituent pressure, or is it a failure to pursue the public interest because of a few residents' shrill response? We will answer that question one way if the overgrown vegetation leads to traffic accidents and another way if nothing happens. As a resident, I can see one thing happening already: an explosion of stilt grass, an invasive weed that is taking over lawns in town. When I complain about that, am I pursuing a special interest or the public interest?

Road maintenance is an important part of town government, and weeds are hardly the only problem. The most controversial issue is chip sealing—a pro-cess of spreading loose gravel over the road, which passing cars then press into the surface over the course of a few days. Catherine describes this as "the most dangerous" decision a local politician faces. Residents are outraged by the peb-bles hitting their cars and inconveniencing children on bicycles. They demand that it cease immediately. They do not believe explanations that this is the best way to maintain the roads. They threaten to park their cars in such a way as to block the process. This passion cannot be a response to only a few days of in-convenience. It expresses a deeper anxiety, a suspicion that whatever they suf-fer is the consequence of a malevolent intention. Complaining about herbicides or pebbles—not to speak of the salaries of town officials—residents do not believe officials are acting in good faith. They lack trust.

Without trust, democracy loses more than participant volunteers; it loses its very point. Politics becomes nothing more than a competition to take control to help friends and hurt enemies. These views can be self-fulfilling, if attacks grounded on suspicion drive away residents who might otherwise volunteer. In Washington, moderate Republicans responded to the changing atmosphere within their party by simultaneously denouncing the party's direction and announcing their retirements. Killingworth residents just stay home. There is a visible graying of those serving on town committees and in civil society organizations. Everyone to whom I speak raises the same concern: Where are the younger adults to replace the aging volunteers?

Jim Lally, a longtime member of the ambulance association board, worries about maintaining volunteer emergency medical services in town: "What I don't want is to have a professional ambulance have to come to us . . . where we have to pay them . . . because we don't have enough responders. That would be catastrophic. But that's where we are now. We need to get more interest. . . . I just hope people see the need more than there is now."[17]

Jim's view is seconded by Rob Clark, who says, "Recruitment at KAA [Killingworth Ambulance Association] has been a concern ever since I joined in 2000." Dan O'Sullivan, the current president of the association, reports that recruitment is adequate for now because younger people are joining as part of their training to become health care professionals. The fire department, too, has become a training program for young people who want to become professional firefighters. Of course, that would be in some other town with a professional department. These forms of recruitment tend to be transient: they give volunteers the tools they need to professionalize and move on.

We might think of the food bank as the local face of welfare, chip sealing as the local face of infrastructure, and weed eradication as the local face of environmental policies. Same problems, but different scale and different tools of governance. Still, it is difficult to be one sort of citizen locally and another nationally.[18] The same residents, in the same voting booths, pull the levers for national and local candidates.

The sources of our political challenges, locally and nationally, are not hard to identify: increased economic insecurity; collapse of traditional authority structures in civil society; disappearance of local media and rise of the new media, including social media; decline of traditional churches and growth of religious fundamentalism; changes in the family and the nature of family life; and the rise of globalism and a cultural cosmopolitanism.[19] I heard references to many of these factors when Ed Ricciuti, Mercedes's husband, explained to me why he voted for Trump in 2016, after having voted twice for Obama.

Ed and Mercedes moved to Killingworth in 1972, looking for a rural community in which they could afford some land. They purchased a house on a lot of more than seven acres. He set into farming, hunting, and fishing while pursuing a profession as a freelance writer. In his first decade in town, he was an active volunteer, but eventually work had him traveling too much to take on local responsibilities. Mercedes's volunteer service started later. In the early 2000s, some of her friends were looking for someone to take over the operation of Helping Hands. Mercedes hesitated, but changed her mind when the local priest delivered a homily on how one should offer a "helping hand" to neighbors. As if directed at her, the priest repeated the phrase "helping hand." Mercedes got the message and took up the position.

Ed came to town as a Democrat, but he switched his registration to "unaffiliated" when he started thinking of himself as a small businessman. In the past ten years, he has become a Republican. Mercedes has remained a lifelong Democrat. About their political disagreement, she says, "it's so hard," but "I'm not getting divorced over this." About the virtues and pleasures of life in Killingworth, Ed, Mercedes and I all agree. National politics is another matter.

Ed says that more than half of his support for Trump was based on his view of gun rights. He is an avid hunter, but that is not the whole of it. He thinks that we may need literally to defend ourselves against big government. He worries that the Democrats are becoming socialists, by which he means they support "big government." He thinks that Obama "apologized" too much to foreign countries, that he was weak on "law and order," and that race relations became worse during his time in office. Ed describes the Black Lives Matter movement as a "terrorist" group. He fears the cities and the politics they support. He describes an economic situation in which, over his career, it became harder and harder to earn a living as a writer, to the point where it is virtually impossible now. He has seen Saint Lawrence, the local Catholic Church, grow and then shrink. His own children have scattered across the country.

In his eighties, Ed teaches martial arts in a building next to, and owned by, the Congregational Church. One has a sense that he is practicing self-defense physically and spiritually. He remembers the decades after their arrival as a period when he was very close to his neighbors, most of whom have now died. He has always opposed development in town and is both pleased and surprised that the town has managed to maintain its rural character—despite a threefold increase in population since he arrived.

Ed wants to stand up for himself, and he wants the country to stand up for itself. Guns are linked to independence, and for him Killingworth reflects the value of independence. When I asked him where he gets his national news, he said that while he used to watch all the network news shows, today he watches only Fox. Mercedes says, "He loves Fox." She watches the morning and evening news shows but avoids Fox. Ed says he seeks more news diversity "on the computer," but his list of sources does not intersect with mine, beginning with the absence of the *New York Times* and the *Washington Post*. As for local news, they both say there are no longer any sources. Neither has much use for local social media. Mercedes describes the largest local site, Killingworth Stompin' Ground, a group forum on Facebook, as having become a "bitching session," while Ed proudly notes that the site has banned him—Ed tends to speak his mind.

Ed recalls an era of neighborliness, civic engagement, and local bipartisanship, with fluid movement between parties. I often hear of this earlier era from older residents. Most did not make the shift to Trump as Ed did; many have maintained an ethos of volunteerism. Among them is Mercedes, who not only volunteered to run Helping Hands but is also the municipal agent for the elderly. She is the closest thing Killingworth has to a town social worker. She is sometimes fondly called the "protector" of the elderly. At Helping Hands, she worked to make sure everyone had enough to eat; as agent, she works to make sure seniors get the advantages of rental and fuel assistance through state programs.

As Ed explains his views, he points to many of the changes that I investigate in this study: development, financial strain, religious decline, children leaving, nationally driven cultural markers, Fox News, and an absence of local news. These changes are neither national nor local; they are simply everywhere, roiling the background conditions against which individuals form expectations and make choices. They are undermining the town's capacity to govern itself because they are undermining the development of the character traits required for self-governance to succeed. This is less an issue for someone like Ed, who at eighty-three is who he is. For younger residents, however, the changes that Ed reflects upon are not changes at all. Rather, they are simply characteristics of life in the town.

A town that relies on volunteers relies on its residents' virtue. Because Killingworth self-government puts volunteering first, the town's changing character is a sort of natural experiment testing the relationships among character, civil society, opinion formation, and democratic governance. Our virtues are on display in volunteering to produce and distribute masks. Our vices are on display when partisan attacks, fraudulent accusations, and conspiracy theories drive volunteers back into their homes.

Beginning with Tocqueville

To deal with the modern problems of governance, Killingworth relies on institutional structures that have changed little since Tocqueville's time. Structure probably did not matter much when the town was a rural community of extended families.[20] The institutions were only prompts for residents to step forward to help each other. As volunteerism becomes more strained, however, institutions come to matter a great deal more. When Catherine first ran for first selectman, I suggested as her campaign slogan, "Proudly bringing Killingworth into the twentieth century." That was in 2009.

Tocqueville worried that in France the passion for equality had destroyed the old order without creating new institutions capable of restraining the destructive tendencies of democratic leveling. "Democracy has therefore been abandoned to its savage instincts; it has grown up like those children who, deprived of paternal care, rear themselves in the streets of our towns and know only society's vices and miseries."[21] He continues with some strikingly modern observations. Rich and poor, he says, have been brought closer together, but the result is increased suspicion of each other.[22] Local power centers have been destroyed, but the result has been to increase the power of central authority: "We have destroyed the individual entities that were able to struggle separately against tyranny; but . . . government alone . . . inherits all the prerogatives extracted from families, from corporations, or from men."[23] Religious institutions, too, he says, are so fearful of losing their position that they have become conservative opponents of the democratic impulse.[24] Today we, too, risk becoming those children following savage instincts. We are increasingly suspicious and increasingly centralized, and even our churches have entered the field of polarized politics.

France, Tocqueville thought, was taking a destructive path toward equality in institutions and markets, without marshaling creative alternatives. Americans had discovered those alternatives. Immigrants to America had left behind Old World hierarchies of class and religion. America, he thought, offered a naturally egalitarian society.[25] To make this argument, he had to distinguish the slave economy of the South from life in the North, as well as ignore hierarchies that seem obvious to us, such as gender and ethnicity. He asserted a privileged place for New England: "In the . . . New England states, the two or three principal ideas that today form the basis of the social theory of the United States were combined."[26] These were ideas of social equality, political participation, and citizen education. In the New England town, he believed, mores and institutions had created democratic self-government by a community of equals.

America had such natural advantages for the emergence of new forms of democracy that Tocqueville makes what to an American reader is a puzzling claim: "The Americans have a democratic social state and constitution, but they did not have a democratic revolution. They arrived on the soil they occupy nearly as we see them."[27] By revolution, he means not a change in political arrangements but a change in society: a "social revolution." American independence, he believes, led only to the redesign of some of its government institutions; it was already a deeply egalitarian society. There was no need to eliminate an aristocratic class or dismantle the church because these elements of class distinction never made the transatlantic crossing.

Tocqueville's key insight is to see that democracy is a condition of society before it is a practice of governance. It is a set of beliefs informing voluntary collaboration. Government alone cannot make society democratic. Conversely, an egalitarian society alone will not sustain democratic government. Successful democratic government requires mediating institutions of civil society that stand between government authority and equal citizens. Tocqueville worries that democracies, when they lose stable internal articulation, empower mobs, and mobs elect tyrants.[28] He believes that Americans, partly by chance, had found a set of midlevel institutions to break the tendency toward political centralization and thus toward authoritarianism. If today we are electing authoritarians, Tocqueville would advise us to look to the state of civil society, where our practices and beliefs are formed, sustained, and challenged.

Tocqueville approaches the New World as a sort of experimental testing ground for reform and reconstruction of the Old World.[29] This is not only what Tocqueville thought; it is what most Americans thought of themselves. Tocqueville speaks of their "irritable patriotism," meaning Americans will defend "all that is done in this country."[30] America was the model—the "shining city on a hill"—that all the world would follow, as nations became free and equal societies.

This American belief still exists, but often as a lost hope or a longing to "make America great again."[31]

Tocqueville does not look at laws and institutions as the products of an abstract science of politics—the view of many of the Founders.[32] He does not think America's Founders were better at political science than European politicians were. Rather, he studies the way in which legal and political institutions have a kind of symbiotic relationship with beliefs and practices concerning religion, family, gender, community, and commerce. He is interested in forms of spontaneous association, the ways in which people organize to express themselves and get things done. He studies democracy as a set of beliefs and social practices that sustain the ordinary affairs of life within self-governing communities. Before there are laws, there are mores. He is the first social theorist to focus on the importance of civil society to the character of political institutions.

At the center of his inquiry is the New England town: the earliest site for the realization of the democratic beliefs the colonists brought with them. These towns gave political expression to a modern culture of social equality. "In the heart of the township one sees a real, active, altogether democratic and republican political life reigning."[33] Tocqueville treats the Town Meeting as if it contains the DNA that went on to determine the course of American political life at successive levels of governmental organization. The towns remain, for him, the animating source of democratic mores: "It is . . . in the township that the force of free people resides. The institutions of a township are to freedom what primary schools are to science; they put it within the reach of the people; they make them taste its peaceful employ and habituate them to making use of it."[34] He sees a sort of virtuous circle between citizen and town. Citizens realize the value of freedom in the self-governing township, and the town trains its members to believe in the liberty on which it depends.

Tocqueville's enthusiasm for the Town Meeting was reflected at the time by American writers. Thoreau called the Town Meeting "the true Congress . . . in the United States," while Emerson said that the Town Meeting demonstrates "the great secret of political science" of "how to give every individual his fair weight in government."[35] He went on, "In these assemblies, the public weal, the call of . . . duty [and] religions were heard."[36] The idea of the Town Meeting as "the school of democracy" was often repeated; it remains an American myth.[37]

Although Tocqueville never came to Killingworth, it was much like the New

England towns that so impressed him. Its organizing features were those he described: the Town Meeting, yearly elections for multiple offices, rejection of representative government in favor of direct democracy, a board of selectmen with no authority to make law, commitment to ideals of private property and individual autonomy, a central role for the Congregational Church, and substantial independence from the state and national governments. In its first century, there was a requirement that all—that is, all adult males—participate at Town Meeting: "Ordered and Voted by the Town that if any man shall wholly absent himself [from] any Town Meeting shall pay twelve pence & if any man comes in late shall pay six pence."[38] The Congregational Church was disestablished as the state religion only in 1818. It was still effectively the town religion when Tocqueville visited New England.

By the 1830s, Killingworth was starting to decline. In the 1820 census, it recorded a population of 2,342.[39] Over the following decades, much of its population moved to better farmland in Ohio and northern New York. By 1930, its population had fallen below 500. Killingworth did not recover its 1830 population until the late 1960s, when the population once again climbed toward 2,500. Truly rapid growth occurred over the next three decades as the town reached its present population of about 6,400. By then, it had become a town of commuters rather than farmers.

Despite the demographic changes, town governance remains much as Tocqueville described it. Most important, Killingworth remains a direct democracy, with the Town Meeting as the town's legislative body. The town still has many—arguably too many—elected positions. Apart from extending voting rights to women, the biggest change since Tocqueville's time has been the receding place of the Congregational Church, which is no longer the center of town life. It is no longer even the largest church in town.

Although the structure of town governance has remained relatively unchanged since Tocqueville's time, civil society has changed dramatically. What to Tocqueville seemed a balance between social equality and political participation has now become a substantial imbalance. The modern Town Meeting is no longer an ideal expression of direct democracy; it is often quite the opposite. While decisions at Town Meetings are formally democratic, they are actually among the least democratic moments in the life of the town. Usually, few residents are in the room. A Town Meeting that no one attends cannot function as the school of democracy. Killingworth is well past the point at which all residents could fit into a room to argue the merits of an issue and then make a collective decision. This is not just a matter of size, for the town is also well past the point at which most residents want to attend such a meeting. The latter is a far more important change than the former. Direct democracy assumes that residents care about governing.

The result is that town authority is exercised by the few people who show up at a meeting. For the most part, they are there because they have a particular interest in the matters to be decided. Recently, for example, there was an issue of whether the chief of the volunteer fire department would be provided a vehicle at the town's expense. The board of finance, along with the board of selectmen, had decided that it was not necessary. The fire department had managed for decades without one. The committee members had not, however, thought of the dynamics of a town meeting at which the volunteer firefighters would show up to make known their views. The fire chief got his vehicle. This may have been the right decision, for the town can ill afford to alienate its volunteer firefighters. But was it democracy? It can be difficult to tell the difference between pluralist pursuit of self-interest and the public commitments of civil-society organizations. Even participants, if they are honest with themselves, may not know.

The founders of the American political project understood that a democracy cannot be better than its citizens. Government institutions might be designed to be "a machine that would go of itself," but absent character, that machine will run itself into the ground.[40] When Benjamin Franklin spoke of a "republic, if you can keep it," he was gesturing toward citizen character. George Washington's Farewell Address, too, spoke of the need for character, if the nation was to survive its infancy.[41] Character was at the heart of Tocqueville's inquiry. He looked for the ground of character in practices of religion, education, commerce, family, and informal associations. He thought all of these factors worked together to support local, self-government. From there, they could inform national political practices.

Let us not romanticize the past. Tocqueville's vision of America's passion for equality ignored women, minorities, and the poor. Even as he saw the society's virtues, he believed that America was likely heading toward a brutal race war: "the most horrible of all civil wars, and perhaps to the ruin of one of the two races."[42] A more inclusive vision, however, will not make democratic government run of itself. Participation without character can veer into authoritarian populism. This may not have been evident in the immediate aftermath of the

Cold War, when neoliberals proposed market-based solutions to most problems of governance. By 2020, it was the "democracy problem" everywhere.[43]

Tocqueville's faith in America was grounded in his belief that here voluntary civil society associations spontaneously arose to replace those traditional social institutions undermined by the spread of equality. He thought that the habits of sociability and self-governance taught in New England's small towns explained much about America's democratic ethos. For him, the line of cultural and political transmission went from the local to the national: beliefs and practices learned locally were carried to national institutions. "The dogma of the sovereignty of the people came out from the township and took hold of this government. . . . It became the law of laws."[44] There was a direct line, he thought, from the Town Meeting to Jacksonian democracy as a national project.

We are today at the far end of the growth of an ideology of equality. We are also at the far end of a decline in the kind of civil society Tocqueville observed. The rapid lapse in civil society has been well documented in Robert Putnam's *Bowling Alone*.[45] Absent that civil society, the line of transmission of values reverses. Instead of local virtues informing national politics, the character of national politics dominates local practices and beliefs. Older residents remember when personal character mattered more than party identity. Walt Adametz, who is now in his sixties and spent his entire life in Killingworth, describes contemporary town politics as "more hardcore." In the past twenty years, he says politics has "changed a lot in our small town." Where once "lively discussion" was bounded by a sense of neighborliness, now there is "more animosity" and it "festers all year round." He is describing the nationalization of local politics. In Killingworth today, we are increasingly red or blue.

In 2016, the largest campaign sign in town read, "God loves Trump and so does Killingworth." The sign may have violated local signage regulations. More important, it violated traditional religious mores. The God of New England did not so crassly and publicly intervene in local politics. The sign was intended to offend those local sensibilities. The sign went up after local Republicans had angrily denounced Democrats for displaying lawn signs saying, "Killingworth for Hillary." Their complaint was that the signs were misleading, since not all of Killingworth supported her. Apparently, they had no such qualms about which side God supported. This controversy was not about a failure to respect difference; it was about power. The violation of norms was an assertion of power: "We can do this" was the message. Power was now measured in an alignment with national politics.

In 2020, the sign went back up, but this time, it did not project power so much as its failure. God, one might reasonably think in the middle of a raging pandemic, has more to tend to than the Republicans in Killingworth. Whatever power the sign conveyed was now found in nostalgia for the shock of the earlier moment. By 2020, the shock was that Trump supporters had nothing new to say. They could not even come up with a new sign.[46]

Despite the reversal of transmission between the local and the national, Tocqueville's basic methodological insight remains compelling: the local provides a window into the beliefs and values that inform our political practices generally.[47] Studying the local, therefore, can help us to understand the changing character of American politics. What looks like a constitutional coup in Washington looks, in Killingworth, like a change in attitudes toward neighbors and organizations.[48]

We are not going to go back to a simpler time when Killingworth was a farm community, a full day's travel from the metropolitan areas of New Haven and Hartford. That we are not going back, however, is not an excuse to stay where we are. Political institutions designed in an earlier era are likely to malfunction when the background conditions shift. Public responsibility surely includes the responsibility to support the conditions of democracy's own survival.[49] It will not survive if we no longer believe in it or if we do not understand what it demands of each of us.[50] Equality, Tocqueville warned, is what we make it. He ends his seven-hundred-page study with lines that apply equally to our situation: "Nations of our day cannot have it that conditions within them are not equal; but it depends on them whether equality leads them to servitude or freedom, to enlightenment or barbarism, to prosperity or misery."[51]

PART TWO

DEMOCRATIC PARTICIPATION

AND CIVIL SOCIETY

By the end of the millennium, Killingworth had a population of 6,400—up from just 1,098 residents in 1960. Measured by income, wealth, property values, and school quality, it was a success. The town was thriving at the intersection of two distinctly American narratives: one expressing optimism about the possibility of individual accomplishment, the other, nostalgia for a traditional community. These stories embody different ideas of liberty: the former emphasizes a lack of dependence on others; the latter emphasizes membership in a self-governing community. On the first view, liberty lies in the individual alone; on the second, it is the ability to work with others in a community of equals. Autonomy and community are my themes in the next two chapters.

Autonomy is expressed in the classic narrative of the American dream: a story of individual opportunity, hard work, and economic advance.[1] "Advance" often suggests movement—first immigration across the ocean and then onward to a frontier that, by the end of the nineteenth century, was increasingly metaphorical.[2] Each generation moves on; each is more successful than its parents were. For many people who came to Killingworth during the postwar boom, arrival marked the endpoint of a path of upward mobility. By the end of the century, newcomers were heading for the new developments that, by design, are poorly integrated into the historic parts of Killingworth.[3] Traveling the traditional routes through the town, one might not even be aware of these new neighborhoods. They often occupy a clearing in the woods through which a developer inserted an access road. Until the early twentieth century, many of these areas had been farmland. When the farms failed, they became woodlands. One of the oddities about New England is that it is far more wooded today than it was two hundred years ago.[4]

These new developments stand in contrast to the houses built for the first wave of urban exodus in the 1950s and 1960s. Those earlier entrants occupied split-level houses built right alongside the antique colonials, creating aesthetic confusion on the main roads. These houses attracted residents who wanted the space Killingworth offered but did not want to be by themselves. Their ideal of suburban life did not yet include the dream of purchasing private services and activities. Three decades later, developers were building homes that represent the privatization of success not as necessity but as luxury.[5]

Some people, however, embraced the second view of liberty: they moved to Killingworth not for a bigger house but for the life of a small town—a place away from the intense competition, endless professional demands, and affective anonymity of urban living. For this group, Killingworth represents a romantic recovery of small-town life. Some of these people first discovered the town as a vacation site: what were once second homes became primary. If the McMansions represent the values of the first group, the antique colonials sitting close to the old roads represent those of the second. To occupy these houses was to place oneself in public view and commit to keeping up a small part of the town's history. Today, those houses no longer speak to the condition of most young families. When Catherine and I moved here, all of the antique houses around us were occupied by families with children. Today, none are.

When the economic crisis hit in 2008, those who had come to Killingworth in pursuit of the first version of liberty had little sense of community to fall back on. As property values in town declined and some of the larger employers—Pfizer in Groton, Bristol-Myers Squibb in Wallingford—relocated out of state, residents began to sense their constrained possibilities.[6] This was hardly the expected endpoint of their American dream; it gave rise to an anger that simmered just below the surface. There was urgency without direction, a sense that everything had gotten both too complicated and too expensive. It became common to hear people speak of moving to low-tax states in the South. Some of the more vocal residents actually did.

In the competition between the supporters of autonomy and those of community, the latter are losing.[7] Tocqueville worried about the stability of liberty without community in a mass democracy. Too much liberty could shift to too much equality: "Democratic peoples love equality at all times, but in certain periods, they press the passion they feel for it to delirium. This happens at the moment when the old social hierarchy, long threatened, is finally destroyed after a last internecine struggle, and the barriers that separated citizens are finally overturned. Then men rush at equality as at a conquest, and they become attached to it as to a precious good someone wants to rob them of."[8] When the ideal of autonomy fails, resentment is often not far behind. That can produce Tocqueville's "delirium": a passionate demand for equality in the form of leveling. Nationally, that phenomenon looks like Trumpism. Locally, it can look like implacable distrust of authority and suspicion of the motives of anyone who suggests a reform or a new project. Privatization in the local community opens the way for nationalization of public opinion, and vice-versa.

The most important issue facing Killingworth today is not which party will win the next election. The deep, existential issue is whether residents will volunteer to take on the multiple tasks of self-governance. Volunteerism was already strained at the end of the millennium as residents increasingly felt the attraction of an autochthonous lifestyle. The polarization of public opinion that defines the age of Trump has further strained the town's ethos of volunteerism, without which it cannot survive as a self-governing community.

3

Self-Government as Volunteering

Take it to the people.
—*Richard Cabral, Killingworth first selectman, 2007–9*

WE OFTEN IDENTIFY DEMOCRACY WITH the voting booth. Democracy is performing better, we think, when more people vote. But voter turnout actually tells us little about the health of a democracy. A democracy flourishes when people vote for the right reasons and engage the political process in the right way. A mob at the polls is still a mob. Electoral success does not legitimate the violation of rights or the failure to respect the rule of law. It does not save citizens from suffering from mismanagement of domestic policy or dangerous foreign interventions.

In the face of poor voter turnout, political scientists ask whether and how participation rates effect outcomes, as if the point of an election were only to aggregate preferences.[1] Some conclude that in small communities, low voting rates do not matter much when the interests of those who vote align with those who do not.[2] In Killingworth, where Catherine won her first election by seventeen votes, that conclusion does not ring true—unless, of course, one believes that it does not matter who wins. Yet the scholars are right to ask how important voting is to democratic governance.[3]

In Killingworth, the voting booth is not the fundamental site of political engagement. The town is a direct, not a representative, democracy. The citizens gathered at the Town Meeting constitute the legislative branch of town government. The formal status of the Town Meeting, however, can lead scholars to make the opposite mistake of focusing on attendance at the meeting as the proper measure of local democracy.[4] The democratic life of Killingworth lies elsewhere: in the committees, boards, and civic organizations that carry out the town's affairs and perform the work of public administration and public service.

To participate in self-government in Killingworth is not to vote but to volunteer. It is to act with others, not to make a choice about who might act in one's place. It is one thing to spend a few minutes in a polling booth on Election Day; it is quite another to serve on one of the many boards and committees that meet on workday evenings throughout the year, and still another to serve in the fire department or on the ambulance crew. In town hall, on any weekday evening, there might be meetings of the board of selectmen, the board of finance, the zoning board of appeals, the inlands wetland commission, the planning and zoning commission, the public health committee, or an ad hoc committee planning an event like the town's recent 350th anniversary. Elsewhere in town, the library board or the school board might be meeting, while the firemen are training. There might also be meetings of the Killingworth Women's Organization (KWO), the Lions, or the parent-teacher organization (PTO). This is self-government as a practice of taking care.

Politics in Killingworth does not mean campaigns; it means participation. The most important function of campaigns is to encourage further volunteerism. To run for office is to volunteer. For most of the elected offices—there were twenty-three on the last ballot—candidates do little personal campaigning, even though these are partisan elections. Scholars who study local elections might describe them as "managerial" elections—that is, elections in which the issue is whether office holders have performed adequately.[5] Some of them are. In the 2019 cycle the candidate for town treasurer was cross-endorsed; in 2017, the town clerk was similarly cross-endorsed. These are paid positions that have been effectively professionalized. Most offices are not like this. The managerial perspective misses the way in which elections serve primarily as recruitment efforts for volunteers.

Elections are a means by which neighbors take turns volunteering to help the town. Residents are "drafted" by the Democratic or Republican town committees to run. For most positions, running means little more than having one's name posted in the party's roster of ballot positions. Only those running for first selectman do much campaigning—and even that is a recent phenomenon. By

2019, that office had become the site of intense partisan competition; it was functioning as a proxy for our national political confrontation.

The town is entirely dependent on citizen volunteers, including for essential services of fire protection and emergency medical intervention. There is no one else to do the work.[6] That work is both indoors and outdoors: service on committees and boards, in the parks and recreation facilities, and on the emergency response teams. Because volunteering is demanding, shifts in the way residents understand the meaning of citizenship are likely to appear here earlier and more visibly than in the voting booth. A low voter turnout may make little difference to the outcome of an election. A low turnout of volunteers for the ambulance service may mean that someone we know dies.

In August 2020, a tropical storm rolled through town, knocking out power, cell phone service, and cable connections. Roads were blocked by fallen trees. Because the trees were tangled in electric wires, neighbors could not use their chainsaws to clear the roads. When the power goes down, the well pumps stop; residents are without water. Ordinarily, the town opens an emergency operations center, and the middle school becomes a shelter for those in need. The presence of the coronavirus complicated this effort, but it did not change the familiar pattern of response. Volunteers mobilized to help neighbors.

In the middle of the crisis, the new emergency management director—a volunteer in his late twenties—quit. When the demands of the emergency mounted, he seemed unable to cope. He failed to communicate to residents; he was reluctant to provide services or take time out from work. He lashed out at the prior director, who had held the position for decades. He alienated other volunteers. Unable to mobilize the town's response, he quit, commenting that he was not getting paid. I asked Catherine why the town had turned to him in the first place. She explained, "He is the one who volunteered."

An older generation of residents, who grew up with an ethos of volunteering, is disappearing. The younger generation is less interested.[7] As soon as one asks, "Why me?" the ethos of volunteering has been lost.

Moving to Killingworth: A Politics of Common Sense

Catherine and I moved to Killingworth from New Haven in the summer of 1996. We were looking for a town with good public schools for our two daughters, ages ten and eight. Killingworth schools had a reputation for rapid improvement under an innovative superintendent. No one told us—and we did not think to ask—that just the year before, the school budget had failed in ten consecutive referenda. Nor did anyone tell us that the innovative superintendent was being forced out and would shortly resign. We did not look hard, because we had already fallen in love with the house: an old farm with gardens, fields, a pond, and woods, bordering a state forest. Another thing no one told us was how much work it takes to maintain this property.

Nor did they tell us how much work self-government would be. Moving from New Haven, I knew that urban areas pose special problems for self-government—problems of racial division and conflicts among different interest groups.[8] I hoped that democracy in a community without the divisions of modern urban America, and where political communication does not depend on money, would be more of an exercise in self-government than what I was used to.[9] I had read Tocqueville, who describes a close and intimate connection between civil society and local government. Local political life, he argued, is rooted in civil practices and beliefs—"mores." Americans, he observed, spontaneously join associations; they are naturally volunteers.[10] We were about to test his views.

I thought political accountability in a small town would be direct and effective because there would be little administrative bureaucracy or formal legality. I imagined local self-government to be continuous with the forms of civic organization. The same people would be active in both. There would, for example, be a direct line between the PTO and the local school board, or service organizations like the Lions and the first selectman's office. When the town confronted issues of land management, where else would it turn but to the land conservation trust? Similarly, issues relating to development would draw upon the resources of the chamber of commerce. Residents would contribute not just their time but also their expertise to the town.

I imagined town life as a conversation carried out in diverse forums but involving more or less the same people with the same general concerns. If a resident had a problem, he or she knew where to find the first selectman or which committee to approach. If a problem was not addressed, residents knew whom to hold accountable. Town officials could not hide from their constituents. No offices filled with bureaucrats occupied the space between residents and officials. Most state and national officials have a certain anonymity in their daily lives, since few people recognize them out of doors. Local officials cannot escape from their constituents, who freely approach them in the parks, in stores, and at the dump.[11]

Looking back, I see that I imagined town governance as a sort of enlarged faculty meeting. Self-government in the law school means faculty meetings, where we discuss endlessly but only occasionally take a vote. Mostly, we work things out through mutual and reciprocal efforts to persuade. We enjoy the debate as much as the resolution. We not only feel pride in running the school but experience ourselves as a community of mutual and reciprocal recognition. We are fundamentally a dialogic community, which may be why the analogy of faculty meeting to local government comes so naturally to a political theorist.[12] But as I learned during my first few years in town, municipal governance is not a faculty meeting. Residents have little patience for, or interest in, long discussions. They are uncomfortable debating their neighbors or defending their views in public.[13] A few residents have a reputation for always speaking at town meetings. It is not a good reputation to have.

Most residents prefer to limit their public expression of partisan disagreement to elections and, even then, only to the top offices. Within the ordinary operation of town institutions, there is a limited capacity to absorb outright political disagreement. The party division on the board of selectman, for example, rarely surfaces. Catherine has been on the board for more than twelve years. In that time, the board has acted unanimously in almost every case. In the mid-2000s, just before her election, the two Democratic members of the board developed an intense personal conflict. Their feud created substantial tension in the meeting room. Neither remained long in office.

These long habits of limited partisanship have begun to change, producing substantial discomfort among older residents. Year-round politics has become embedded in social media and is drifting off line into the institutions of governance. In 2019, Eileen Blewett, a Republican, was elected to the board of selectmen. Since her arrival, the board has started to have party-line votes, including on the membership of a charter revision commission.

For most of Catherine's first ten years on the board, Fred Dudek, a Republican, served with her. They voted together all the time. Despite their general agreement, Fred ran against Catherine for first selectman in 2017. He comes from the volunteer culture of the town and is generally uneasy with public disagreement of any sort. When the League of Women Voters arranged a debate among the candidates, Fred failed to appear. I heard that decision defended on the ground that participation would lend credibility to John Samperi, the Conservative Party candidate, who was publicly attacking the other candidates. To me, Fred's decision reflected a more general attitude. He had spent most of his life in town and had served in many positions, including seventeen years as fire chief. For him, politics was about taking care of common concerns, not about publicly expressing disagreement. Running for first selectman, he was volunteering to lead the town; he was not campaigning for elected office. As he explained, "I will continue to volunteer, win, lose, or draw. . . . I care about the community, and I care about the people in the community."[14]

Some of what I imagined back in the summer of 1996 turned out to be true. Residents can bring problems to the attention of their neighbors and town officials. It does not take any special expertise to ask how the schools are doing. Residents want to know where our high school graduates are going and how our schools compare to those of surrounding towns. When drugs appear in the schools, no formal studies are needed to identify the problem. If the roads are not maintained, our vehicles hit the potholes. If the sports fields are flooded, our children cannot play their scheduled games. If the dump is not functioning well, we wait in line in our pickup trucks. Local developers deal with the building inspector. When the inspector is not serving them well, they complain to the selectmen. The same is true of the zoning officer, the public health inspector, and the animal control officer. Particular problems may affect only a few residents, but everyone in town has an interest in maintaining a sense of well-being. No town official would ever think to ignore a problem because it affects only a few residents or voters of the other party. That hardly means that the problem will be remedied, only that the reasons for failure do not lie in partisan politics.

Most of the problems the town faces are visible to residents. Local politics is, accordingly, a matter of common sense in both meanings of the term: there is a common awareness of the problems, and responses do not require special expertise. When neither of these senses of "common" applies—when the problems are not visible and the response requires expertise—responsibilities lie elsewhere. We do not rely on town government to regulate the economy or to address long-term climate change. Because of this concern with the common, local government does not easily separate from civil society or even individual action. The Lions Club or KWO will step up to address a common problem—for example, families in need of assistance—but so will the neighbor who takes out a chainsaw to clear fallen trees.

We do rely on town government to maintain the local roads. In Killingworth, these include Lovers Lane, which provides a shortcut connecting the main north-south road to the old east-west road running from the Connecticut River to Hartford. Lovers Lane follows an old path, bordering an early burial ground that includes Native American graves. The road, unfortunately, sinks into the boggy ground on which it sits. It tends to flood, and in the winter the water freezes. As the weather changes, town officials must decide when to close the road. Doing so adds a few minutes of travel time to residents in the northwest quadrant of the town—including us. Close the road too early, and residents complain that the extra few minutes can mean life or death if a call for an ambulance goes out. Close it too late, and cars may slide off the road into the marsh.

A first selectman in the mid-2000s, Marty Klein, tired of the annual repairs for Lovers Lane. He decided to close the road permanently. He also thought he would get to the heart of the problem of flooding on local roads: beaver dams. He hired someone to kill the beavers. His political career soon ended. It turned out that many residents felt strongly about Lovers Lane and many were fond of the beavers. No one ran a cost-benefit analysis on road repair or beaver preservation. Rather, Marty had come in conflict with local public opinion, what amounted to our common sense. Marty erred not just in his judgment but also in his failure to follow an open process of wide consultation. Had he done so, he might have been persuaded to look for alternatives. That he was a retired chicken farmer may have inclined him toward the radical solution of just getting rid of the pests. His farmer's sense was no longer common sense.

The beavers presented a typical problem. A successful solution required building a consensus, not a managerial intervention. Another example of local common sense presented itself more recently when a family sought permission from the zoning board of appeals to build an apartment in their barn for a disabled adult child. At its initial hearing, the board denied the application, explaining that it lacks the authority to grant a variance based on financial or personal hardship. That much of the construction work had already been done was unfortunate but not sufficient. Soon, however, workarounds were suggested. Maybe the apartment could qualify as an office; perhaps the Americans with Disabilities Act (ADA) could ground an exception. After much consultation among Catherine, the family, the town lawyer, and the board, the ADA route was chosen. To disallow a plan to take care of the family member would have shown a lack of common sense. Why would neighbors do that to each other?

This idea of common sense as caring for the well-being of the community can, at times, take a distinctly less virtuous form: gossip. Neighbors tend to keep an eye on each other. Sometimes this means coming to their aid, as when my elderly neighbor was struggling with her heating bills. Sometimes it means spying and gossiping. I got these two forms of caring—caring for and caring about—mixed up shortly after we came to town.

A resident came to talk to me because she had heard I was a lawyer. She complained that a neighbor across the street from her was hounding and stalking her. She also alleged that the neighbor was spreading rumors about an older male friend who visited her while her children were in school and her husband was away. She told a complicated tale of innocence on her part and maliciousness on the part of the neighbor. I wanted to be helpful and started doing research on her legal options; I referred her to a lawyer. I was being drawn into a longer and broader feud. Years later, after I came to know her neighbor, I realized that I had no idea who was in the right in this dispute.

Killingworth does not have many fences, but residents recognize the truth of Robert Frost's line, "Good fences make good neighbors."[15] We all know where our property lines lie; many follow the remains of ancient stone walls. Those walls allow us to see over, but they also separate. That is pretty much how we feel about our neighbors. They are in our sight, but we do not want to be too close. A community is not a family, but neither is it a market. It requires maintaining a middle distance between the two. This is the space of common sense. Ed Ricciuti, after fifty years in town, captured this sense of neighborliness:

> Classic New England neighbors are a bit different than others. You do not have to be buddy-buddy just because you live near someone. On the other hand, you can still be a buddy when it counts. Case in point: When we moved here in Feb. 72, Walter Clarkson, then a major figure in town, lived near us on the corner of Stevens and Roast Meat. I said hello to him in passing a few times but that was all. Then, in zero-degree weather, we had a storm and power was out. Knock on back door. There was Walter with a pipe wrench, ready to help me turn off the water and drain the pipes in case I did not know how.[16]

Shortly after we moved in, I looked out the kitchen window and saw several horses race up our driveway, run past the barn, then gallop in circles around our back field before returning down the driveway. I was pretty sure these were the neighbor's horses. When I asked her about them, she denied they had any horses, even though I could see their paddock on the other side of a stone wall separating our properties. Town regulations require owners to maintain "adequate fencing . . . so as to confine all animals within the premises of the owner."[17] Perhaps she did not appreciate a new neighbor making inquiries. I was looking too closely across the stone wall.

A commitment to the common does not require residents to share their private lives or even to be close friends. It does require that we not be enemies, especially when we disagree, and that we be able to work together for the common good. In Killingworth today, there is less common sense because the idea of a common good makes less and less sense. Jennifer Patton, after living in Killingworth for about two years, explained:

> For me, there is not a sense of community; I love where we live, love where the kids go to school, but that's all we got from moving to Killingworth. . . . I always say there is no CVS; nothing in town. For a working mom, you want to stop somewhere quick for a gallon of milk, don't want to travel twenty minutes out of your way. If you want a dinner, [there is] only one place nice. . . . Put in a CVS or a Walmart, something where a mom could stop and grab pajamas and macaroni. North Haven, all these other towns, are more developed.

Jennifer commutes to work in New Haven; her husband commutes to Hartford. Her idea of community is less about recognizing a common good that already exists than it is about responding to her needs and concerns as a working mother.

Volunteerism: A Synergy of the Public and Private

On arrival in Killingworth, we did not know that the town depends entirely on resident volunteers. Nor did we have any idea of what it would take to maintain an old farmhouse with acres of fields and forests. It would be many years before I understood the connection between the two: the common character of the town and the old houses. For both town and home, one has a sense of struggling just to hold on.

The two are often threatened by the same event. When a storm comes through, the town must pick itself up, but so must our old farm. Trees are down on the roads, as well as in the gardens and across the paths. Lovers Lane floods, but so does our basement. Centuries ago, the same people who built Lovers Lane in a bog built our house at the foot of a hill. Emerald ash borers are destroying

our trees and those of the town; mosquitoes are spreading eastern equine en-
cephalitis on both public and private land.

By necessity, Catherine and I quickly found ourselves splitting responsibilities
as we moved from city to town life. She started participating in evening meetings; I started maintaining our property. A dozen years later, she was leading the
town. I was still struggling to keep the forests from swallowing up our fields,
the wildlife from destroying the gardens, and the buildings from falling down.
This division of labor is better thought of as outside versus inside work, not as
private versus public. Killingworth land—apart from the new developments—
flows seamlessly between private property, land trust ownership, water company
land, town land, and state forest and park. The deer, bears, coyotes, and occasional bobcat make no distinctions. The town's history is carried as much in the
private homes as in the public spaces. About 150 houses date from the late eighteenth and early nineteenth centuries. I have traced ours back to 1830 in town
records, but a number of architectural details suggest a late eighteenth-century
origin.

This intersection of the public and private is carried by the land itself. Walk-
ing south out my backdoor, I stay squarely in our fields and forest for about a
quarter of a mile, then run briefly along the edge of a neighbor's land before
hitting the land trust property. Crossing it, I enter the state forest. Heading west
for about a mile, I cross into the state park, where I turn north. I walk another
mile and exit onto a dirt road that passes alongside a hunting and fishing club,
crosses through water company land, and then joins a paved state road a couple
of hundred yards from our driveway. Ownership is diverse, but we all face the
same challenge of taking care of an essential part of Killingworth: its forests,
streams, paths, and wildlife. I realized this when a local developer bought a
neighboring plot of some twenty acres and clear-cut part of the woods to construct an artificial pond. Not only was he violating the land use regulations; he
was breaking my heart. For those of us who care about each tree on our property, this felt like a wound inflicted on the town. His sin was that he did not care.
A few years later, having done the damage, he moved away.

I quickly discovered that I could not take care of our property without a
pickup truck. There is the weekly hauling out of trash along with endless loads
of brush and debris. Construction materials for one project or another, along with
loads of manure and mulch, have to be brought in. I was learning how much of

rural life is necessarily do-it-yourself. Soon, I owned not just a pickup but also two chainsaws, a generator, pumps, a lawn tractor, a log splitter, and an endless array of power tools. While I was adjusting to a life driven by seasonal change, Catherine was adjusting to the weekly schedule of meetings as she volunteered for one committee after another. We learned from each other what was going in the part of town that the other did not see.

With the exception of the schools, which are part of a regional district consisting of Killingworth and the neighboring town of Haddam, the town has few employees.[18] There are three full-time elected officials: the first selectman, the clerk, and the tax collector. The treasurer, building inspector, zoning enforcement officer, animal control officer, assessor, and public health officer work part time. Apart from a finance director and a supervisor of the road crew, independent contractors provide other professional services as the need arises: the town engineer, the town attorney, the town accountant. The largest group of employees is the road crew, and there are only three or four of them.

The entire staff of town hall—part time and full time—is about ten people. They must tend to tax collections, financial accounting, assessments, elections, record keeping, maintenance of public facilities, licensing, permitting, and intergovernmental affairs. They must respond to residents in trouble and to natural disasters: hurricanes, floods, freezing, and now the pandemic. They cannot possibly do all of this and engage in planning and development of facilities and budgets. The town is run by volunteers. That is the fundamental difference between small town governance and every other form of governmental organization, whether urban, state, national, or transnational.

Some public services that are routine in urban areas are simply absent in Killingworth. The town has no police force. Were any strangers to start prowling around, they would be noticed. Local social media regularly has posts of the sort: "Stranger spotted late at night on Roast Meat Hill Road." If things were to get serious, there is the resident state trooper. "Serious" includes a string of nighttime robberies of returnable bottles from the bin at the dump. Those deposits help support the local scout troops.

The town's trash removal operation is three guys who work at the town dump for several hours a few days each week. Even there, it is do-it-yourself when you bring in your trash. The garden club provides public landscaping. Open space is maintained by the land conservation trust. Town land supports a community garden and numerous hiking trails—all maintained by volunteers. When a tree falls across a road, it is likely to be cut up and removed by neighbors before the maintenance crew arrives. The town has literally one traffic light.

Volunteering takes multiple forms. It begins with the volunteer fire department and volunteer ambulance service and extends to the library, the food pantry, and the land trust. Volunteers cut the hiking trails, plant the flowers along the roads, staff the emergency operations center, and organize and coach the sports teams. At times they even construct public facilities. When the town needed a new playing field, volunteers showed up with earth-moving equipment. Someone with building experience volunteers to supervise construction and landscaping. Jim Lally, Killingworth's citizen of the year in 2012, often contributes his construction crew to town projects, including a new emergency operations center, the maple sugar shack at the town-owned Parmalee Farm, and work on virtually every park and playing field in town. Fittingly, he has also served as chair of Killingworth's parks and recreation commission. Another local builder, Mike Milano, contributed expertise and equipment to several major projects at Parmalee, including creating an open pavilion out of an old pole barn, bringing in electric lines, and building public restrooms.

Volunteers are not just outside but in the offices. Weekday evenings, town hall fills with the many committees, boards, and panels that conduct the town's business. All are run by people like Tom and Lucinda Hogarty, who have lived in town about seven years, after moving here from a neighboring town where they found it hard to get involved. She is a retired public health official; he is a retired state trooper now working as a zoning enforcement officer in a neighboring town. She is chair of the library board, chaired the town's 350th anniversary committee, sits on the historic preservation review committee, and works with the KWO and the Killingworth refugee resettlement coalition. He is on the school building committee, the planning and zoning commission, the town barn renovation committee, and the alternative housing committee.

When the town relies on volunteers for so much, it is hard to say that voting and paying taxes exhaust one's civic responsibilities. Tax receipts could not begin to pay for the services the community requires. Without volunteers, the town would grind to a halt and burn to the ground. Volunteering in Killingworth is less doing something for others than doing something with others. It is not about charity but about community. One does not have to be selfless to volunteer; one has only to have a sense that one should do one's part. Of course, some volunteer work is charitable: for example, the food pantry and a weekend back-pack program for children who need nutritional assistance. These services, how-ever, are not what distinguishes the small town. Rather, the distinguishing fea-ture is the way self-governance operates through volunteerism.

In the past ten years, the largest public works project by far has been the development of Parmalee Farm—a 132-acre site of fields, trails, and facilities. The town bought the site in 2000 with a vague idea using it as a sports venue. That plan was poorly conceived and ultimately failed twice in referenda. The land was unused for a number of years, until a resident, Peg Scofield, asked the town if she could start a community garden there. A local contractor, Pete Venuti, volunteered to clear a space for the garden. That was the beginning of what has become an ongoing community project offering space for events, con-certs, and farmers' markets.

The development of Parmalee is a story of volunteerism. Tim Gannon, who has lived in town more than forty years, has been at the center of that story. He was in the first group of gardeners and gradually came to spend more and more of his time at Parmalee. Soon enough, he was the chair of the town's Parmalee Farm committee. A few years ago, he had the idea of building a sugar shack—sugar maples on the land were already being tapped. He started raising money, and pretty soon a handsome building was going up. Construction was done by volunteers, including a local roofer, Mike Young, who donated a metal roof. The yearly sugaring operation is now a part of town life, with sale of the syrup helping to support the farm.

As a Lion and member of the chamber of commerce, Tim helped to connect the farm to these networks of volunteers. The Lions, for example, took on a proj-ect to convert an old turkey shed into a pavilion for weddings and concerts. My eldest daughter was married there in 2015. Meanwhile, Bruce Dotson, the long-time leader of the land trust, developed the network of trails on the farm. Volun-teers have brought in power, cleared acres of land, rebuilt stone walls, and built public toilet facilities. The town could not begin to pay for these services, even with the occasional state grant.

Tim insists that he is not a political person, even though he was involved in the campaigns of the last two Republican candidates for first selectman. Still, he describes his recruitment technique in language strikingly similar to what Catherine uses to describe her efforts to find town volunteers. They both recruit by doing. They set an example and ask people to work alongside them, not to work in their place. Tim says he never asks anybody to do something that he would not be willing to do and likely be already doing. He found volunteers to mow the fields by simply going out and mowing. People would naturally ask if they could help, to which his answer is always, "Yes." Tim notes the same aging of the volunteers at the farm that I see everywhere in town. Of the group of regular volunteers upon whom he relies, none is younger than sixty-five.

A striking fact about Killingworth residents is that many would much rather give their time to the town than their money. No doubt for some this is because they are living at the edge financially. But the sentiment is broader and deeper. Many residents are instinctively against taxes but in favor of public service. They see taxes as something done to them. They are skeptical of requirements imposed by law and even think of law itself as a failure of community. To rely on law is to be governed rather than to govern oneself. An extreme form of this sentiment is evident in much of red America today in the controversy over face masks. Governors who resist issuing legal mandates requiring use of masks nevertheless go on to say that everyone should wear a mask. They speak of individual responsibility in place of legal requirements.[19]

Taxed as individuals, some residents respond as consumers, wanting more for less. Residents regularly come to Catherine's office to complain that their taxes are too high because, for example, they are not using the town's schools. They think of taxes as a fee for services and believe they should get a discount.[20] An older resident told me that she feels seniors should, at some point, no longer have to pay taxes in support of the schools. Recently, a resident from one of the more expensive new developments asked that the town make a special effort to repair her curb since her tax bill was particularly high. Her logic was, "If I pay more, I should get more." The request came with photos showing some stone curbing with small dents—damage unlikely to make it onto the town's repair list.

It is common around the country today to think of taxes as fees for services. What is less common is the attitude of those Killingworth residents who object to taxes but are quite prepared to volunteer their time and effort without putting a price on these activities. They do not ask whether they are getting their money's worth when they volunteer; they do not generally ask for a discount on their tax bill because they have contributed in-kind services. Neighbors who volunteer do not generally compare themselves to others; there are few complaints of free riding. The young emergency management director, who did not last through his first emergency, was the first person I heard of who thought of his services in monetary terms. He is not quite alone.

Just a few months later, I heard a somewhat similar story from a long-serving volunteer with the fire department. Speaking of recruiting difficulties, he mentioned the importance of a $2,000 rebate members receive on their property taxes. He sounded nostalgic for an earlier era of service, when the rebate would not have mattered. To the new recruits, it matters. I heard the same sort of thing about the ambulance association. Some of the most active volunteers in the past few years have been residents who needed the modest payment they received each time they respond to a call. I do not mean to suggest that there is anything wrong with taking these small financial benefits into consideration. They are there for a reason, and no one begrudges the volunteers these modest rewards. But there has been a change within the organizations in how members understand themselves. These might be the first steps toward professionalizing both services. Something similar is happening at Parmalee Farm. Bruce Dotson recently retired from the committee. He had developed and maintained the trails. So far, no one has volunteered to take up this task. Tim reports that the committee is seriously considering hiring someone to provide the service.

Of course, attitudes toward volunteering are not monolithic. On Facebook, someone posts that the old barn by the town hall needs a new coat of point. Immediately, some residents respond that they are ready with paintbrushes. Others reply that with modern lead abatement requirements, this is a job for professionals. Others assert that we already pay taxes for maintenance of town buildings and ask why the maintenance has not been kept up. Still others like the run-down, country look and fear that doing anything will raise taxes.

For many who did not grow up in a small town, volunteering does not come naturally. I would count myself among them, but Catherine is quite the opposite—and she grew up in New York City. Younger people often never get into the habit. Some people want simply to be left alone. But regardless of one's views of participation, to live in Killingworth is to rely on volunteers. There is not some other fire department or ambulance service you can hire. There is not some other civil service to manage the town. For most of what happens in town, there is no option of paying instead of volunteering.

Volunteering means participating in the work of the town regardless of whether a project falls within the formal authority of town government. The town is not experienced as a political entity separate from its civic organizations, just as town land is not distinguished from land trust land. The most visible blurring of the lines is with the fire department and the ambulance service, the two most prominent sites of volunteering. Each has its own buildings, uniforms, and equipment; each has a yearly public awards dinner. There is some overlap in membership, but different families tend to think of one or the other as their responsibility. The fire department, in particular, is a multigenerational affair, with at least three father-child relationships among those on active duty. Members of the ambulance service, too, report that they are following in their parents' footsteps: "My parents were actually founding members of the KAA [Killingworth Ambulance Association] in the early 1970s. Both were techs and served on the board for many years—my Mom longer than my Dad. . . . I learned volunteer service from my parents, so it really wasn't a question of 'if' I would become an EMT with the KAA but 'when.'"[21] Another reports, "Volunteering, firemen and EMS run in my family. So, that kind of got me into it."[22] This family tradition, however, is fading. Rob Clark, a twenty-year veteran of the association, reports: "My son followed me but only stayed a year or so before joining the Air Force. My daughter became an EMT but never served before joining the Peace Corps." A family tradition is hard to maintain when the children no longer expect to stay in town.

These organizations provide essential services for town residents, but residents have no idea whether they are formally part of the town. Indeed, it can be difficult to answer. The town purchases and owns much of the fire department's equipment; it owns the buildings, which are rented to the organizations for a token fee.[23] Members of the fire department and the ambulance association get modest tax breaks, insurance, and small pensions. But the selectmen have no direct authority over their operations. There are two elected fire commissioners, whose role is not to run the volunteer fire department but to act as liaison with town officials. The fire chief is neither elected by residents nor employed by the town but chosen by the members of the fire company. The ambulance service has no formal contact with the voters at all. The library receives about two-thirds of its annual funding from the town and operates out of a building the town owns. The town places two members on the fifteen-member library board. Volunteerism thus blurs the distinction between private and public.[24]

The history of the library is a similar story of volunteerism operating in a public-private space. The library was begun in 1964 by a group of about twenty town "mothers." The public school gave them some space in the back of the school library and a $25 loan to get started. At that time, Killingworth had only one school, which ran from kindergarten through eighth grade. Volunteers did all the work; everything—from books to shelving—was donated. Within a year, the school wanted its space back. The town had recently purchased its first town hall—an old farmhouse—and the selectmen agreed to let the library use two second-floor bedrooms. A call went out for donations of furniture, shelving, and a typewriter. Although it was now in the town hall, the library did not receive any money from the town until 1969, a year after its formal incorporation.

After eight years in town hall, the library moved down the road to a building on the traffic circle that the volunteer fire company had vacated in 1971, when a proper fire station opened. The vacated building had originally been a one-room schoolhouse. The fire company, which had itself incorporated in 1947, occupied it after the town elementary school opened in 1948. Here is how the library's own history describes the move from town hall to the old schoolhouse:

> Once again volunteers to the front! In order to move the thousands of books from upstairs in the Town Office Building, the town's pay-loader nestled up to the windows and the books, in carefully numbered boxes, were loaded on trucks, and various groups including the Lions and the town crew helped tote them into the new quarters.
>
> Following Killingworth tradition various organizations helped. The Lions gave the new desk and chair. Various homemakers' groups made the drapes, gave the children's table and individuals gave clocks, flags, pictures, screens for all the windows, electric fan, tiny refrigerator etc. And the Library was opened with a festive Silver Tea.[25]

This do-it-yourself ethos does not distinguish between public and private, between town and civil society.

After close to ten years of wholly volunteer operation, the library hired its first part-time, paid secretary. In 1995, it moved into a modern building with a separate children's wing, reading room, meeting room, and wi-fi service. Today, the library is a substantial operation, with a professional staff of two full-time and two part-time positions and a budget of around $300,000. Yet it is still very dependent upon volunteers. Working in teams of two, about twenty-five volunteers—mostly retired professional women—run the circulation desk. Lucinda, the chair of the board, describes the struggle the library faces in dealing with the

Killingworth ethos: "The library is doing very well on volunteers but poorly in fund raising."

The town's growth is symbolized by the changing use of that old building on the traffic circle: schoolhouse, firehouse, library. Each function left the building for a modern facility. After the new library was constructed, the building became the office of the resident state trooper and the town emergency operations facility. Both of these functions moved to a new dedicated facility in 2016. Today, the old building houses two food assistance programs, each run by volunteers with a financial subsidy from the town. There is a logic, or perhaps a sociology, in this pattern of movement; it traces the changing nature of public concern in a town that has become increasingly suburban over the past seventy years.

The Differences That Count

A town that depends so heavily on volunteers must pursue a politics of persuasion. No one will volunteer for an organization or activity that fails to respect his or her views. Political disagreement in Killingworth, therefore, forces us to ask whether we are still capable of governing ourselves through a politics of persuasion. If we cannot talk to each other, we will not volunteer to work with each other. But if we cannot speak to each other, who in this country can?

Killingworth lacks the social differences that have long been associated with polarization and marginalization. Very few residents are members of minority groups: a handful of Black families, a few Asians. About 0.6 percent of its families identify as Hispanic. I have never heard Spanish spoken in town. The town is 97.2 percent non-Hispanic white.[26] Killingworth does have a few very wealthy residents, but they are not generally involved in local politics or civil society. No one could identify them on the street or on a trail. Nor are there pockets of extreme poverty, although there is a retirement community of some 300 homes—out of a total of about 2,700—designed for seniors of modest means. A few families have children in the schools' free lunch program.[27] The town has four churches of different Christian denominations—no temple or mosque—but these no longer represent politically salient distinctions.

The absence of diversity led a student of mine, who visited shortly after we had left New Haven, to propose that we name our new home "White Flight Farm." He had a point. The absence of social differences is not, for Catherine and me, an attractive feature. There are many reasons—cultural, social, political, and economic—to prefer a more diverse population. Life in Killingworth would be more interesting, the schools might do a better job preparing young people for careers and national citizenship, and economic growth might be stronger were the town more diverse.

I regularly see postings on local social media that react to the self-centered satisfaction with the town—our "boosterism" ethos—characteristic of these sites: "When we moved to KW, this beautiful picturesque town you are all describing, my daughter was told a boy wasn't allowed to play with her because she's Brown. That's what happens in the 'blessed' town of which you speak. I recognize not ALL KW community members share this view, however, those who do not visibly share it don't speak up enough against it." Another consequence of the lack of diversity is a stunning ignorance about urban areas like New Haven or Hartford. Although both are just thirty minutes away, I often meet residents who have not been to either city for many years. Some have a fear of urban America. Ed Ricciuti, who lived in New York when he was young, tells me that when he has to go to New Haven, he "packs iron." Residents do not generally consider conditions in the cities to be their problem. Like the resident who did not want to see a BLM sign when she returned home from work, they become resentful when forced to confront urban problems.[28]

Despite its unattractive features, the town's homogeneity makes it easier to examine the strengths and weaknesses of its political institutions and social practices. The problems of race and class in America are deep and seemingly intractable, but they are not problems that Killingworth confronts in its ordinary practices of self-government. To put it bluntly, if middle-class white people are having trouble governing themselves well in Killingworth, we have reason to worry about our capacity for self-government on any scale.[29]

This experiment has been going on for centuries. The town began, in 1663, as a part of the Plantation of Homonoscitt.[30] In the first 150 years, homogeneity was measured by religious faith: Congregationalism was the established religion until statewide disestablishment in 1818. Until 1784, when Connecticut passed an "Act for Securing the Rights of Conscience," everyone had to pay a tax imposed by the ecclesiastical society, whether they belonged to the church or not. The new act secured religious freedom for those "professing the Christian religion," of whatever denomination, and released them from the obligation to support the Congregational Church.[31] By 1800, there were enough Episcopalians in the area to build a church, which still stands several miles from the town center. In the early decades of the twentieth century, diversity meant the arrival of poor southern and eastern Europeans—mostly Catholics—who found in Killingworth abandoned farmland on which they could pursue subsistence agriculture. The families that endured those decades of poverty are now the town's "old families." The ones that dominated the first two hundred years of town life have all but disappeared. I know only one person who traces her roots in town as far back as the early 1800s.

Suburban development did not hit Killingworth until the late 1950s. Before that, it was a rural community of farmers and local artisans. Older residents remember attending one-room schoolhouses, several of which are still standing. Electricity did not arrive until 1938, and it took ten years to be fully installed. Substantial development came only with the completion of the Connecticut Turnpike in 1958, making it possible to commute to work in the surrounding cities and plunging the town into an extended identity crisis: Is it a rural or a suburban community?

For some older families, this was not an easy transition. Joan Gay, who moved here in 1968, told me that in the first house they occupied, they were greeted by gunshots from the neighbors who were not happy to see new families move in. "After we met the neighbors, they finally confessed that they had done it to scare us, because they didn't want more people coming into town." Ed Ricciuti tells me a similar story, but with roles reversed: he greeted new neighbors with a gunshot—not directed at them but just to let them know that he was there and to indicate the sort of neighborhood into which they were moving. Ed was not from an old family, but he was definitely against development.

Despite Ed's efforts to slow development, the town was filling with young families. Joan speaks of a vibrant "community within a community" formed by the families with school-age children. This group, she says, were not part of the "patronage that existed in the town" but instead translated their vibrancy into new civil society organizations. This is when the Lions, the chamber of commerce, the ambulance association, and the library began. Joan herself was soon serving on the board of finance and leading the town Democrats.

Ed, who arrived just four years after Joan, describes a similar vibrancy. On arrival, he had three young children and a lot of energy. Quickly he found himself driving for the ambulance association, while serving on the boards of the land trust and the library. With children in the public schools, he did his part to take care of the land and his neighbors. Both Ed and Joan drifted away from volunteerism as their careers took them out of town.

The distinction between new and old residents that matters today is fixed by school attendance: you are a local if you went to school in town. Catherine and I frequently have to remind ourselves that some of our neighbors have been arguing with each other since grade school. They sized each other up long ago and are not going to change their opinions. For more than a decade, Catherine had to fend off such a feud between Walt and Fred—the road crew foreman and a selectman. When I asked Walt what was the source of the feud, he told me he did not know. Perhaps, after all these years, he has simply forgotten.

There is no way to undo the animosity between Walt and Fred. Indeed, there is little hope fully to understand the ways in which public roles and family life intersect. As road crew foreman, Walt supervised his son, Jeremy, who was the town mechanic. Jeremy and Fred became allies. When Jeremy purchased a local auto repair shop, Fred, who had recently left the board of selectmen to run for first selectman, went to work there part time. Had Fred won the race in 2017, one of his first acts would likely have been to try to fire Jeremy's father, Walt. Meanwhile, Walt's wife—Jeremy's mother—became a leader of the Conservative Party, which targeted the Republican leadership, including Fred. Fred started his political career as a Democrat and is married to Linda, whose family has deep roots in the town. Linda remained a Democrat, serving for years as town clerk, but is now retired. In the end, Fred lost the election, the Conservative Party survived, Walt stayed on the job, and we get our car serviced by Jeremy.

Apart from old feuds, the deepest disagreements in the town trace to different attitudes toward development. This difference cuts across the line between new and old residents. Some old residents are dedicated to preservation; others see their land as their most important source of wealth. Among the new residents, some came because of the town's rural character, others because houses were less expensive than in other suburbs. My neighbor Joseph Hutchins, who lives in an eighteenth-century house that was once a gristmill, is an example of the former. He works as a restorer at the Metropolitan Museum of Art in New York. He speaks of the thrill he finds in maintaining the old waterworks and preserving the remnants of the mill on his property: "The value of this place [his property] is in its continuity with the past, which I try not to break. . . . I want to leave the pieces [of the mill] in place so they will still be here when I am gone.

I get to work every day with things that the people [who occupied this house] worked with in 1780 with their own hands."

I am with Joseph in the preservationist camp. Francesco Lulaj, the Republican candidate for first selectman in 2019, is very much the opposite. About five years ago, he opened a restaurant in town, modeled on one that he had run in New Haven. One of his campaign promises was that he would call the chamber of commerce every day for news of any businesses that might be interested in coming to Killingworth. That position might be attractive to Jennifer, the young mother who wants more services in town. She told me she would like the town to look more like the close-in suburbs: "Knock everything down and develop." But her husband, she says, wants "to leave it exactly as it is." Steve and Carolyn Anderson are also divided. They moved here twenty-five years ago, attracted by the town's rural character. He is opposed to development in every form. She likes the rural character but would like to see some new restaurants in town.

This division of opinion does not track the Republican–Democrat divide. Carolyn and Steve have both occupied leadership roles in the Democratic Party. Arjumund, who lives in one of the more expensive new developments, agrees with Jennifer on development. He, too, would like to see a supermarket and other shops in town. Both register as Independents, but he leans Democratic while she leans Republican. Ed, who voted for Trump, opposes development. He represents an older generation of town Republicans who have been very active in land conservation. Of the new, younger leaders of the town Republican Party, including Francesco, Ed says he "does not recognize them."

Consider the Venuti family property, a central point of contention for the past two decades. This family, which has been in town for several generations, operated an excavation and construction business. That business occupied a small part of the largest undeveloped tract of privately owned land in town—some 350 acres. The Venutis would like to sell the land, but they would also like to preserve its undeveloped character. They would like, in other words, for the town to purchase the property and then maintain it as it is. This proposal has generated sustained controversy that I discuss in some detail in chapter 5. Here, the point is that an old family wants to profit from its ownership yet does not want development.

The town was recently embroiled in controversy over the development of a solar farm on a twenty-five-acre tract, along the main east-west road. Once farmland, it had returned to forest over the past fifty years. While local regulations zone the site as residential, solar facilities are chartered by the state, independently of local zoning ordinances. The immediate neighbors took the classic NIMBY attitude; they were for solar power, just not here. Supporters of the solar farm argued that it would not disrupt the town's rural character and would contribute to its tax base. Opponents responded with concerns about water runoff from the facility and its effect on local wildlife. We learned about the birds and insects that occupy the land.

These divisions over the pace and kind of development represent the sort of disagreements that local political institutions are designed to address. No one makes a claim of fundamental right; no single point of view is so dominant that those who do not share it are fated to lose. We think we have convincing reasons to hold to our own views; we are naturally inclined to think that what persuades us should persuade others. These issues do not fall along predictable party lines. They represent a difference of opinion, not polarization.

Much of the discussion of the solar farm proposal showed local politics at its best. Proponents of each side hoped to persuade their neighbors by pointing to common interests. Both sides assumed their neighbors would listen and respond. The first public meeting, however, had quite a different atmosphere. Residents met the proposal with angry accusations of bad faith and allegations that town officials were secretly conspiring with out-of-town interests. They feared that someone was trying to take advantage of them. Some outside investor, they were sure, would make money at the site and then abandon it, leaving them to bear the costs.

Catherine was the object of some of these charges, even though the decision was the responsibility of a state commission. She was targeted for a letter she had submitted to the commission, supporting the project if it could meet all relevant environmental standards. In her view, solar power was a good business for a town that neither wants nor is likely to develop any manufacturing or large-scale commerce. One can disagree, but expressions of outrage are intended to intimidate, not to persuade.

The solar farm debate fell into a common pattern. Those who respond first to a proposal are those most inclined toward suspicion. They are already angry and are looking for occasions to confirm their anger. In subsequent meetings, cooler heads enter the conversation. With respect to the solar farm, they overcame the hostile environment of the first meeting, collaborating on a common presentation to the state siting commission. They persuaded the commission not to allow the project to go forward by marshaling evidence of an environmental threat. Members of the commission observed that they rarely saw a community so well prepared in its presentation.

The difference between the first and the subsequent meetings is typical. The loudest voices in the room are full of suspicion and anger. The controversy over the sign supporting the BLM movement, discussed in the last chapter, also followed this pattern. The controversy began with a violent act of destruction. The initial post by the victim provoked anger and resentment among some residents. One post asked, "Why put up something [the BLM sign] that might be inflammatory?" It reflected an exhaustion with national debate: "When your neighbors come home from a long day at work, they don't want to be bombarded with a subject that can be an added stressor to your day." Perhaps trying to be humorous, the writer goes on to "suggest you post the sign facing your property where you can enjoy it." Whatever the intent, the post blames the victim for the violence and trespass that she suffered. Portraying the neighborhood as a retreat from a stressful world, the poster mocks a traditional form of political communication. Speaking of stress after a long day of work, the writer expresses the precariousness some residents feel. They tend to think of themselves as "victims."

Just as the subsequent meetings on the solar farm drew in residents who had a stake but do not ordinarily get involved, so did the exchange on the BLM sign. New responses criticized the expression of intolerance. It is as if a first hurdle must be overcome to motivate residents—apart from the "regulars"—to get involved. This is the also the pattern on school budget referenda: defeat on the first vote, a few cosmetic changes by the board, and passage on the subsequent vote.

Sometimes, however, there is no second meeting, and a good idea dies. Failure to adhere to a politics of respect, truthfulness, and common deliberation will debilitate democratic governance. It will leave residents frustrated and angry with the direction of town government, as well as with many of their neighbors. If residents are angry, they will not volunteer. If they don't volunteer, public facilities will degrade, services will disappear, infrastructure will decay, and development will be haphazard. Common commitments will be undermined, and whatever the town does, it will tend to do poorly.

Volunteerism in Town Hall

The original site of public participation was the Town Meeting. Here, residents are to speak for themselves and to speak their minds directly. So democratic are

Town Meetings that their first order of business is always self-organization. There are no permanent positions at the Town Meeting; no claim of authority can preempt the right of residents to govern themselves. Elected officials have no special authority; everyone has the same right to speak and to vote. The gathered citizens must first elect a moderator and choose a voting procedure.[32] They decide whether to use secret ballots or a show of hands. There are no absentee ballots, for the right is one of participation, not representation. Ideally, residents come to the meeting as equals and act together as the body politic. This ideal of generating a public out of the collective deliberation of private individuals can only work, however, if residents actually participate. Today, if a hundred residents show up, that is considered hugely successful. Attendance is often half of that.[33]

At every Town Meeting I have attended, the assembly has voted against secret ballots. Residents hold themselves accountable to each other by acting publicly. But in 2017, John Samperi, the Conservative Party candidate for first selectman, made an issue of this. He argued that the town charter should be amended to require secret ballots. Public voting, he felt, put too much pressure on those who do not agree with the general sentiment in the room. If the participants come to pursue their private interests, he has a point. Today, most of those who come to a meeting do so because they have a particular interest at stake: they come knowing exactly how they will vote.[34] Absent open deliberation among residents, the argument in favor of a public show of hands disappears, but then so do the reasons for a Town Meeting. If it is just a matter of voting, better to increase participation through a referendum.

The Town Meeting is hardly the only public meeting that Killingworth residents are asked to attend. Every committee and board conducts its business in public with a right of participation by residents. The number of such meetings seems endless. The board of selectmen meets every two weeks. The school board and the board of finance are just as important. Tom Hogarty, a member of the planning and zoning commission, believes that to be the most important committee in town. Peg Scofield, who reported on town meetings for the dozen years she put out *Killingworth Today,* adds the inland wetlands commission to the list of "major players." Together, these two committees control the pace of development. Then there are meetings of the public health committee, the board of zoning appeals, and the board of assessment appeals. There are meetings of ad hoc committees asked to look into projects such as the renovation of the town hall, the purchase of land, the construction of an emergency operations center, or the planning of special events, including the celebration of the town's 350th anniversary. Add to these the meetings of the political parties' town committees, the library board, and all of the civil society groups: an engaged citizen could easily spend three or four nights a week tending to town business in one forum or another. In fact, few residents come to these meetings—apart from those with an immediate interest.

These endless meetings are the lifeblood of the town. Every one of these committees is staffed by volunteers. That some are elected and others are appointed makes no difference in how they operate. Few residents could tell you which was which, and even those who are elected are not paid for their time. Standing for election to a position on these boards and committees is simply another form of volunteering. Because the town operates under state-mandated minority representation requirements for most of its formal committees, often there is no electoral opposition at all.[35] A party will put up just one candidate for a position on a board or committee that is required to have at least one member from that party.

Even when a position is contested, electoral loss is usually not the end of the matter. Just about anyone who is interested can find a position on one board or another. Stephanie, for example, lost her election to be a member of the planning and zoning commission. She was instead appointed to be the town's representative on the regional zoning committee.

The role of board members—elected or appointed—is not to impose their opinions but to set an agenda or propose a plan. Most boards and committees hope to avoid controversy, not just because it is unpleasant, but because the ideal is to reach consensus. Even with the minority representation requirement, decisions tend toward unanimity. The town's most difficult political moments are when it confronts an issue on which there will be winners and losers—for example, those neighbors objecting to a proposed solar field or parents objecting to the school board's decision to close an elementary school. Even the zoning board of appeals, which regularly denies applications for variances, is acting in a way that reduces animosity among neighbors. Few could tolerate living under a zoning regime in which some residents were allowed exemptions from generally applicable rules.[36]

The desire for inclusion and consensus does not promote efficiency, nor does it always promote equitable outcomes. It does promote a continued willingness to volunteer. Procedures that end with winners and losers would undermine the sense of a common project that is both the ground and the result of volunteer-ism. The most visible site of winning and losing is the biannual election for first selectman, which is also where the town experiences maximum polarization and maximum influence of national politics. The intensity of party competition is wholly disproportionate to the unanimity that reigns over the ordinary oper-ations of the board of selectmen.

If a disgruntled resident threatens a lawsuit, the town is likely to settle. In-deed, in the twenty-five years we have been here, very few lawsuits have gone to trial.[37] The town is extremely reluctant to spend money on an intratown dis-pute. This is not just a matter of cost; it is about sustaining an ethos of coop-eration. This attitude is formally set forth in the town plan for 2018: "For most [zoning] violations, a conversation between the Zoning Enforcement Officer and the offending party is sufficient to resolve the problem. When it is not, [a long legal procedure is available]. This procedure, although usually ultimately suc-cessful, is lengthy[,] sometimes taking months or years to be heard by the court, during which time the violation continues. There are also significant expenses to the Town in attorney and court fees."[38] What is true of zoning violations is true of other areas of regulation: conversation is always preferred to litigation.

In our first years in Killingworth, there was an issue about where to build a middle school. At a public meeting, various attractive locations were excluded from consideration because they were not for sale. I asked the first selectman why the town would not consider using its power of eminent domain to obtain what-ever property was most appropriate for the project. He looked at me as if I were a stranger, which I was. He told me in a very serious tone that the town "would never do that." If someone does not want to sell their property, the town will not force them into a sale. Neighbors do not act that way toward each other.

The meeting on the middle school built consensus. Twenty years later, a meet-ing of the school board on closing one of the two elementary schools in Haddam, the other town in the district, reached no consensus. It ended with an angry confrontation of parents shouting and hissing at each other, and a divided vote on the board. Closing a school was a situation of winners and losers. Local officials in Haddam, and even their state representative, were forced to take a position on the school closing. Some were voted out of office.

At the time of the middle school decision, I thought the first selectman's re-sponse a poor way to run the town. I could not fathom why the town would not use all of the legal resources available to build the school in the very best location in light of projections of the likely course of town development over the life of the school. Now, I think he was right.

Law does not get much done in town; volunteers do. Governance must tend to the ethos that supports volunteering. Absent that, the town cannot flourish; indeed, it cannot even survive. The decision to close the elementary school was an ugly moment of conflict, causing at least one school board member to consider whether to continue in her position. She had not volunteered for this sort of abuse.

This attitude of cooperation over regulation can cause problems when there are rules that actually should be enforced. The town has a problem with residents abusing their privilege of free use of the dump. That free use does not include refuse created by businesses—such as local contractors. To allow that use would effectively ask taxpayers to subsidize these businesses. Still, you need only spend a short while watching the pickup trucks coming into the dump to realize that this rule is regularly violated. But who is going to enforce it against neighbors whose contracting businesses may be under strain? The "dump guys" are there to help, not to enforce. Even Catherine hesitates to call out a violation at the dump. Formally, she is the police chief—that is, chief of a nonexistent department. Nevertheless, she was elected not to enforce rules but to keep the town going as an organization of volunteers.

This is a common pattern. The zoning enforcement officer or the animal control officer is there to help work things out. When neighbors have problems with each other, they are likely to call Catherine and ask for her help rather than hire a lawyer. For this reason, Catherine is often drawn into private disputes that are not formally within the town's jurisdiction. When residents complain about actions by the town—for example, when a snowplow destroys an improperly placed mailbox—the inclination is to respond sympathetically rather than to enforce a rule. A person willing to complain can get away with a lot.

Volunteers are generally amateurs. They can find it hard not to defer to experts, despite the rising antielitism of populist movements. The town has often been poorly served by professionals: for example, lawyers, accountants, public health officials, building inspectors, and union negotiators. Volunteers, for the most part, have no knowledge by which to judge professionals. They would have to hire another lawyer to evaluate the lawyer, another accountant to evaluate the accountant. The consequence is that these professional positions can become sinecures for which the town pays too much and gets too little. Catherine's first years in office involved reviewing and then declining to extend the contracts of many of these experts.

Order without Law Enforcement

Twenty-five years ago, Robert Ellickson published *Order without Law,* about a rural community—Shasta County, California—in which ranching was the dominant economic activity.[39] Ellickson was interested in how the community generated informal norms to allocate responsibility at points of interaction among neighbors. Who, for example, pays for fencing to control the movement of cattle across property lines? Who pays when cattle damage property or cause accidents? He discovered that residents in close-knit communities do not appeal to law enforcement, nor do they informally implement legal rules.[40] Rather, they create order without law by adopting rules that promote a common economic surplus.[41] The rules are accompanied by informal enforcement mechanisms that can include even the destruction of property.

Ellickson argued that the order that emerges naturally in a close-knit community promotes efficiency, as if the common project were to advance economic well-being. The system discourages shirking or freeriding. Maybe this is so in cattle country; it is not in Killingworth. From its earliest moments, Killingworth was a religious legal settlement, organized around ideas of community that began in the Congregational meetinghouse, not the market. The Congregational meeting centralized authority in a communal body that blurred the distinction between private and public. Law existed at this point of indistinction between a religious and a governmental assembly. Town officers selected at Town Meetings in 1740 included "Towns Men, Town Clerk, Constables, Grand Jurors, Town Treasurer, Collector of Town Rates, Collector of County Rates, Tithing Men, Surveyors of Highways, Fence Viewers, Leather Sealer, Haywards, Auditors, Keeper of the Pound Key, Packer of Beef, Pork, Etc., Sealer of Weights and Measures, Brander and Recorder of Horses."[42] This was a well-regulated community that did not hesitate to judge its members.

Today, Killingworth residents are like residents of Shasta County in their reluctance to turn to formal institutions, whether police or courts, to enforce rights against neighbors. Reviewing the records of the zoning board of appeals, it is striking how rarely a neighbor objects to an applicant's request for a variance. When the neighbors do appear, it is usually to say that they are working matters out with the applicant—for example, planting trees around a noncon-forming shed. Unlike residents of Shasta County, however, those of Killing-worth do not rely on informal norms of coordination. Conflicts, when they appear, are often personal, arising out of a perceived lack of respect. This perception is often framed as a claim of legal right—usually property—even if the mecha-nisms of resolution are informal. The two types of offenses—to dignity and to property—often merge.

A resident, Chip, thinks his neighbor, Mike, who is a builder, increased the flow of rain runoff onto his property. The dispute is framed as one involving wetlands protection, water rights, and development rights. Chip and Mike are unable to resolve the dispute. Chip is a long-standing volunteer with the fire de-partment, members of which took up his cause. His roots in the town are deep. His father served as a selectman, a leader of the Republican Party, president of the Lions, and a member of the local Masonic lodge. Mike is the largest devel-oper in town, deeply connected to the business community. His wife is the edi-tor of the publication of the local chamber of commerce; his mother-in-law has long been active on the Democratic town committee. He donated substantial construction work to help develop the Parmalee Farm buildings. The dispute between the two men refracts through webs of interconnection built up over decades. I hear about Chip's problems from my neighbor Joseph, who employs Chip to do yardwork.

Catherine is pressed to help settle the matter. She brings in the town engineer, who is assisted by Walt, the town foreman. Private contractors are brought in at the town's expense to deal with drainage issues. Disputes arise with them, but these are now for the town to manage. There are more complaints about perfor-mance—of who did what according to what standard. Determination of legal rights will not solve the dispute. The town lends its goodwill to help to find a solution that will allow each side to think it has won something. That is difficult, but part of what each side wins is the ability to blame the town for the problem.

Killingworth requires the same kinds of trust and common purpose that El-lickson saw in California. Shasta Country required voluntary participation in a common economic order; Killingworth requires voluntary participation in a common order of governance. Killingworth is actually in a weaker position than Shasta County. It has no way, not even an informal way, to enforce a re-gime of volunteerism. There is no public shaming mechanism beyond the expe-

rience of awkwardness when declining a request for help from the first selectman. That may no longer be enough.

Of Killingworth, Ellickson would say that most residents freeride and shirk
by relying upon their neighbors' volunteer services. Yet most are not even
aware of this. They simply do not think about how the town provides the services upon which they rely. This failure to appreciate one's own dependence on
others is a common phenomenon. It became vivid in the Covid-19 pandemic:
service providers, once invisible to the well-off, are now "essential workers."
What had been taken for granted has become very visible.

Participatory Pathologies

Today, with a population of about 6,400 residents, the town's actual number
of volunteers—excluding the fire and ambulance services, which together have
around fifty active participants—comes to no more than a couple hundred people.
That includes those who show up for an occasional project or event. The number
of volunteers running the town's formal institutions—all the boards and committees—is also around fifty. Maybe twenty serve on the committees that carry
out most of the administrative work of the town. Meetings of the local PTO usually draw about a dozen members. About twenty-five volunteers take turns running the library's circulation desk. The Killingworth Women's Organization has
about forty-five members, some of whom run the food pantry. The land trust has
many contributing members but only a few who volunteer to work. A few members
of the Congregational Church help with senior lunches. The Lions Club, the largest
service organization, has about fifty members, of whom around thirty are active.

There is, as one might expect, considerable overlap among these groups.
Charlie Smith, who has lived here fifty years, volunteers with the Lions, the
Congregational Church, the chamber of commerce, and the ambulance association. Cheryl Fine, who has lived here thirty years, has served on the board of
finance, the public health agency, and the long-term Covid-19 recovery committee. She is also the head deacon in the Congregational Church. Some years
back, she was on the board of the land trust. Tim Gannon, who now directs operations at Parmalee, has held the leadership positions in both the Lions and the
chamber of commerce. He says, "Volunteering is in my blood." To be a part of
a community is "what it's all about."

Often, the people who show up for formal committee work in town hall are the same ones who work in the civil society organizations. Dan and Jan O'Sullivan have lived in town more than thirty years. They came to Killingworth shortly after they got married, already committed to getting involved with church and community service. They were drawn first into work supporting the schools at the time of the multiple referenda, just before we arrived. Jan was soon president of the PTO of our elementary school. Dan was elected to the school board and became its president. Schools were only the beginning. Dan is the president of the Killingworth Ambulance Association and treasurer of the Lions. At the local Catholic church, he is a eucharistic minister, as well as chair of the finance committee. At town hall, he is a member of the energy task force. Jan is on the board of the historical society and of the Killingworth library. She is a lector at the church. She volunteers in a neighboring town for Birthright. She provides accounting services to the library at no cost—a contribution that the board chair describes as half-time work. For many years, she helped run Helping Hands, the town food bank. She also volunteers to help seniors with their tax returns.

When Catherine speaks to groups of residents, particularly to young people, she tries to make vivid Killingworth's tradition of democratic volunteerism. She tells them that governing is not something done to them but something "we do together." When John Samperi, the Conservative Party candidate in 2017, described local property taxes as the town reaching into his pocket to take his money, she responded that the town is all of us together, not an alien force acting on him. She asks residents to take up the responsibilities of citizenship, and she promises that rewards will come, in no small part, from the pleasures and satisfactions of working with neighbors to advance the good of the community.

Many of those to whom she speaks agree with these ideals. They respond the way they do to a good Sunday sermon. They respect the messenger, even though the message does not track much in their daily lives. Every once in a while, she comes home announcing a new convert: someone has agreed to get involved in a town project or perhaps even to allow their name to be placed on the ballot for a position on one of the boards and commissions. Conversion occurs one resident at a time. So does loss, as volunteers discover they have neither the time nor the energy to continue. In recent years, losses often outnumbered conversions. The volunteers are becoming older; the young are busy elsewhere.

Killingworth faces an existential question in finding ways to maintain sufficient volunteers to run the town. Well before the ambulances stop running, however, Killingworth self-government confronts pathologies that arise from a mismatch between its formal institutions and its residents' willingness to participate. Institutions of self-government designed in the eighteenth and nineteenth centuries are faltering.

Killingworth's problems of self-government arise not in spite of, but because of, its extremely democratic nature. The town has not fallen victim to a political machine.[43] It is not run by an entrenched minority of developers who managed to undermine democratic procedures. Nor has it been commandeered by an entrenched majority of homeowners. There is no deep division in the town between homeowners and renters, because there are hardly any renters.[44] Killingworth governance requires volunteers, but its actual practices can discourage volunteers. This is occurring at a time when residents' time for, and interest in, volunteering is already strained by the demands of career and family.

Killingworth was suffering from a range of democratic pathologies well before Donald Trump came to dominate the national scene. As early as twenty-five years ago, those committed to the idea of local politics as a common project of volunteering began to see something deeply disturbing. Institutions designed to be maximally participatory were beginning to operate in an undemocratic fashion. It was not just that people were failing to volunteer for service or come to town meetings. Equally important was the character of those who did come.

Capture: Self-Government Becomes Government by Faction

Killingworth residents vote. The participation rate in presidential elections is over 80 percent.[45] In years when only local offices are at stake, voter participation is around half that—again, not bad for local elections.[46] For educated and mobile residents, voting appears as a civic duty. It is also not much of a burden. It usually takes me less than five minutes to vote at the local elementary school. Participation at Town Meeting, on the other hand, is a mere fraction of voting rates—as low as 1 or 2 percent. The one local issue that regularly provokes attention is the annual referendum on the budget for the regional school district. Killingworth's contribution to the school district amounts to about 80 percent of the town's total expenses. Even here, voter participation rates are usually well under 25 percent.[47]

Catherine's predecessor as first selectman, Richard Cabral, had a standard response to every problem: "Let the people decide." He thought this was an easy matter—bring the issue up at a Town Meeting or go to a referendum. But with low participation, actually achieving democracy is not so easy. A Town Meeting may be deciding issues with fewer than fifty people in the room. Because of the small numbers, the board of selectmen follows a practice of referring major financial commitments—such as land purchases or bonding—to referenda. Voters can also petition to move an item from Town Meeting to a referendum. In recent years, the town budget—separate from the school budget—has occasionally been the subject of such petitions. Even on these referenda, turnout is usually little more than 10 percent. When decisions are made by mere fractions of the voters, the procedures of direct democracy no longer produce democratic outcomes.

For many residents, the political life of the town simply does not enter their horizon; they do not think of local politics as for them. Most residents are unaware of town problems, possibilities, or projects unless something involves them directly. Common sense can develop only if there is a fund of common knowledge, which means common experience. Absent local media or informal networks of communication, that knowledge is not likely to develop.

Eric Auer Jr.—single, thirty, and the owner of a small construction business—has lived in town most of his life. He never attends town meetings and knows no one of his age cohort who does. He told me that only once did he go to any sort of a political meeting: a Republican town committee meeting. He walked out after just a few minutes. He has neither the patience for nor an interest in local governance. His father, on the other hand, was someone with whom I spent many hours discussing local as well as national politics. Eric Sr. was an active volunteer, serving on the zoning board of appeals and the inland wetlands commission, and also helping with outdoor construction projects, such as the playing field that is now named for him. He was inducted into the Killingworth Hall of Fame in 2013 and was named 2014 Citizen of the Year by the Lions Club. He knew who was doing what in town and who could be trusted. I asked Eric Jr.'s work crew if they could name the first selectman. None could. This is typical of young adults in town.

Whatever the reasons for this failure to participate, the consequences are the same: the lower the level of participation, the more vulnerable the process is to capture by faction.[48] Town Meetings have no rule about the size of a quorum. Neither do referenda, with the exception of proposed charter revisions.[49] The democratic process can be no better than the values, beliefs, and practices of the participants. When residents do not show up at town meetings, it is as if our representatives and senators failed to show up on the floor of Congress to debate and to vote. For good or bad, those who are there make the decisions.

When the issue is new athletic fields, the soccer moms are there. When the issue involves land use, the local developers are there. When the issue is the town budget, the Conservative Party shows up in force. Because there are so few participants, it does not take many votes to win. The dynamic of the meeting is rarely that of a deliberative forum debating different ideas of the public interest. There is no expectation that minds will change. The soccer moms are not there to debate the merits of investing in a tennis court rather than a soccer field. They are there to get their field. The firefighters are there to get their chief's vehicle. When an issue involves an investment that does not align with any easily identifiable interest group, the decision is particularly vulnerable to the antitax group. For example, after many years of study by a dedicated group of volunteers, a proposal was put forth to rebuild the collapsing rear half of town hall. The proposal was voted down. The same happened with a proposal to convert a barn next to town hall into a public meeting space. These meetings did not rely upon or generate a common sense of the community. Rather, the community failed to show up.

If few people show up at the Town Meeting, even fewer show up at meetings of the school board, the board of selectmen, the finance committee, the planning and zoning commission, or the inland waters commission. People show up when they have an issue; they show up to make their case. Instead of sites of self-governance, the boards are treated as if they are administrative agencies. They may come to think of themselves that way as well.[50] Some board members serve a very long time and develop substantial expertise. Tom Lentz, the head of the planning and zoning commission, has been a member for over forty years. He may be the person most responsible for the shape of development in the town—a shape that includes two-acre building lots and could be described as "exclusionary zoning." It may well be that the homeowners in town would choose this policy. Tom has been repeatedly reelected, but he does not campaign. I cannot remember any occasion when the town has collectively engaged the issue apart from the meetings of the planning and zoning commission, which very few attend.[51]

Harassment: The Psychological Burden of Volunteering

Alongside the pathology of capture is the pathology of harassment. My introduction to this came at a meeting of the school board to discuss the proposed budget, shortly after we arrived in Killingworth. I was not then aware of the multiple referenda on a prior school budget or the allegations of embezzlement by the superintendent that had preoccupied the town in the years before we arrived. Comments from the floor were not questions but attacks from a few residents, who seemed deeply suspicious of the board members' motives. The attackers were trolling before the internet phenomenon arose. There was no coherence to their litany of accusations. Every response elicited a new and unrelated accusation. I wondered if they were schizophrenic. That impression may have been more accurate than I realized. Several years later, one of those who personally approached me to speak of his suspicions of the school board died by suicide.

What most impressed me about that meeting, however, was the effect these critics had on others in the room. Few of the other attendees were willing to enter a conversation characterized by incoherence and accusation. The effect on school board members was equally dramatic. I had a sense that they wanted to get out of the room as quickly as possible. There was no possibility of pursuing common deliberation, no way to take control of the discussion. They looked distressed and harassed.

Such public harassment has predictable long-term political effects. Residents do not want to come to meetings at which the discussion can take such an aggressive turn. There was a feeling that things could get out of control. I found myself checking to see if any police officers were in the room. Today, that sense of threat can be so great at some meetings that the resident state trooper may be asked to attend.

Harassment happens occasionally at public meetings but is constant online. There, too, it undermines the possibility of a useful exchange. It also undermines the possibility of public participation and volunteer service. Who wants to run for public office if it entails personal attacks? Tim Gannon described his reaction to the increased "nastiness" of public discourse in town: "The thing is, there are . . . people like me who would normally maybe get involved with politics but don't want to deal with the hassle [of being] attacked." Harassment, moreover, furthers capture: as fewer residents participate, it becomes easier for a small group to capture the institutions of governance.

Catherine is regularly attacked—trolled—for things she never said or did but about which some residents are outraged. In a recent election cycle, for example, a photo of her at the high school graduation circulated on social media. The photo purported to show her staging a protest by refusing to look at the American flag during the opening ceremonies. In fact, she was watching a student give a stunning performance of the national anthem. Some people who saw the photo were prepared to believe that she was part of a national conspiracy to undermine flag and country.

Just short of the conspiracy theorists and trolls are a much larger group of residents who are skeptical of all government activities. They equate public enthusiasm with a threat to raise taxes. The selectmen in the region have an acronym for this group: CAVE people, standing for "citizens against virtually everything." There is no possible budget they will support. They want no one to be a beneficiary of any town service of which they are not equal beneficiaries. I have seen them argue against town projects even when there is state and federal funding available. At one point, for example, the town hall renovation project would have been funded by a state grant. That made no difference to their opposition, and in the end, the town walked away from the grant. In part, they are standing on principle; in part, they simply do not believe such assurances. They fear that ultimately the town will have to pay, which means that their taxes will go up. They are the Killingworth equivalent of the voters who opposed the extension of Medicaid into their states, even when the federal government promised to pay 90 percent of the cost.[52]

The CAVE people attacked the school board's investment in computer technology on the grounds that they did not have computers when they went to school. No one, apparently, should have more than they had. They stopped the town hall renovations, arguing that it would be better for the building to fall down since "one only goes there to pay one's taxes." Recently, I heard a proposal no longer to pay for clearing the snow from our roads. Instead, local homeowners should take care of the roads in front of their own homes. This is autochthony not as a privilege of the wealthy but as a rebellion of the angry.

It would not be right to describe these opponents of town investments as narrowly self-interested. They suspect all authority, but they support each other. They join the Conservative Party; they rally for Trump. Some volunteer to serve on boards and committees. Resentment may be a better characterization of their attitude toward town governance. They worry that it is advancing the interests of others while imposing costs upon them.[53]

Two recent postings on Facebook capture this resentment. Matt Young, who was the Republican candidate for first selectman in 2013 and subsequently a member of the board of finance, has now moved to a lower-tax jurisdiction. He posted from Colorado: "The deck is stacked against the taxpayer in Connecticut.

The system has reached a point that a large voting group are also a recipient of some kind of state job or program. It's a shame." Cheryl Fine expressed a similar view: "I believe we should shift our budget to focus more on the services that serve those of all ages—the fire company, the library, police protection." She believes the town directs a disproportionate amount of its resources to the schools and children, often ignoring the needs of low-income seniors. She describes this group as a "forgotten class"—invisible to the "elites" who dominate town governance. In her view, the schools benefit a faction, not the town as a whole. The library, fire department, and police, on the other hand, serve everyone. Indeed, she would increase funding for these "general" services.

One can appreciate the sentiment of equality but wonder whether it is misplaced when children are viewed as a special interest. For those who struggle "to pay the mortgage and taxes"—Cheryl's words—care can easily be displaced by resentment toward those who benefit from town spending. Cheryl complains that too often the town acts as if "the taxpayer pocketbook is endless." Of this attitude, she says, "It offended me greatly." She seems to imagine the town budget as a zero-sum game: spending on one group—children—means not spending on another—seniors. She feels the conflict deeply and thinks it her responsibility to act on it when given the opportunity. Her message, she says, has not been well received by the "elites." She reports that some years back, while she served on the board of health, somebody told her that those who cannot afford to pay for services "should just move."

In this atmosphere of division, those who volunteer know that very few residents will stand up to defend them when the attacks begin. Few will thank them for their service. They will be trolled and accused of self-dealing. Facing this, individuals are often reluctant to run for office. They ask themselves, "Who needs this?" It can be a hard question to answer. Among the Democrats, it is increasingly difficult to find residents willing to run for office or serve on committees. Cheryl, who is a member of the town Republican committee, described a similar problem for the Republicans, when I asked her how she ended up in office: "When you're sitting in the [Republican] town committee and the party is looking for candidates, you open your mouth and say yes. I think I have learned my lesson."

Institutions of local self-government are not self-correcting; they do not naturally balance factions to produce a common good. Killingworth has no rules by which to stop harassment or prevent capture. It has no way to require residents to participate when they choose to stay home. It has no way even to communicate effectively with those who are busy elsewhere. Institutional design alone cannot substitute for common norms, common commitments, and common sense.[54]

Political Dysfunction

The problems of capture and harassment are so pervasive that they support a rule: the closer a political process is to the voters, the less democratic it becomes. The Town Meeting attended by a few dozen voters is now among the least democratic moments in town governance. This reverses one of the key assumptions behind American self-government. Distance is now inversely related to democracy. Tocqueville would easily recognize Killingworth's political institutions, but he would be astounded by the way they now undermine self-government. When most residents turn away, institutions designed for maximum openness become opaque structures opportunistically seized by factional interests.[55] Instead of settings for common discussion, joint activity, and reciprocal recognition, we get ideological division, resentment, and the pursuit of self-interest.

This transformation of local politics was on display in the election for first selectman in 2017. Access to the ballot ended up in federal court, after the Conservative Party candidate for first selectman, John Samperi, found himself stymied at town hall. When he went to file the paperwork certifying that he was the candidate chosen by the Conservative Party caucus, the town clerk told him that earlier that same day someone else had filed a certificate claiming that the party caucus had endorsed the Republican candidate, Fred Dudek, for the office. Had the party actually held two separate caucuses on the same day? That was unlikely. When two conflicting filings are made by representatives of the same party, the clerk is required by state law to reject both, leaving the party line empty on the ballot.

Eliminating the Conservative Party candidate, who many believed had previously drained votes from the Republicans, seemed the likely point of the earlier filing. In response to the clerk's action, John sued the town, the clerk, the Republican Party, and Fred.[56] He hired a prominent trial attorney from New Haven. None of this was inexpensive. After two hearings in federal court, Fred agreed to withdraw his name from the Conservative Party nomination, allowing John onto the ballot.

How, one wonders, could Killingworth politics spawn ballot access contro-versies that end up in federal court? I do not know who was behind this use of a little-known state law to try to keep the Conservative candidate off the ballot. I do wonder, however, who thinks it appropriate to approach local politics in this way. The controversy, moreover, did not end with the court settlement. John campaigned on the issue of corruption. He put up signs charging his opponents with criminal behavior. Some residents were shocked that such allegations would be made publicly in their town, where elections had traditionally been low-key and not particularly partisan. Those residents, however, had not been paying attention to what was happening to local politics. They could not imag-ine that such dirty tricks might already be a part of local politics.

Democracy, Volunteerism, and Self-Correction

Alienation from politics is a national problem. In Killingworth, alienation looks like this: potential volunteers stay home; an ethos of common sense is undermined by resentment and personal harassment; and campaigns become games in which people seek partisan advantage through dirty tricks. All of this debilitates the legitimating function of democratic institutions and undermines the possibility of volunteerism. This is a familiar story around the nation today.

We can argue that if residents choose not to participate in governance, if they pay no attention or allow themselves to be driven out of town meetings, then it is their own fault when decisions go against their understanding of the public interest. Presumably, if things get bad enough, they will choose to get involved. Something like this happened after Donald Trump was elected in 2016. Voter turnout in 2020 was the highest in a hundred years. But our political problems—national and local—are not easily fixed by an increase in turnout. The invasion of Congress by a mob of Trump supporters hoping to reverse the 2020 election results makes this entirely clear. Locally, some unhappy residents will move away; others may pay for private services to replace a public benefit. Residents may simply come to expect less from government or do without. There is no reason to think that a failure to leave represents a preference for the goods and services offered by this town as opposed to others.[57]

Of course, no one should care too much about Killingworth's problems—it is a well-off town that can fend for itself. But if those problems are grounded in social, cultural, and economic changes common to much of the nation, then Killingworth's problems are everyone's problems. Its practices and history also bring to the surface an idea of self-government that is richer and deeper than counting votes. We are not going back to small-town America, but we can search for and create diverse forms of participation in local associations that take responsibility for neighbors and neighborhoods. Killingworth raises a fundamental question: Is there a democratic cure for the problems of our democracy?

4

Civil Society:
Democracy and Authority

We the members of the Congregational Church in Killingworth, Conn,
and all others who shall hereafter become members, do hereby
constitute ourselves a body politic, and corporation.
—Motion approved on March 22, 1889

KILLINGWORTH'S POLITICAL PROBLEMS represent a third stage of democratic pathology. The first stage is formal exclusion from the institutions of self-government. Killingworth started with property, gender, and religious qualifications for participation. The second stage is granting the formal right to participate but failing to provide opportunities for its effective exercise. A legal right to vote can be undermined through public or private action—for example, inconvenient polling hours, gerrymandering, or harassment at the polls. For parents of young children or those who work late and out of town, the right to participate in town meetings may be more formal than real. The third stage arises not from exclusion or lack of opportunity but from changes in the underlying social order such that political institutions no longer map on to civil society.[1]

In this third stage, political institutions are available, but few residents pay any attention. Those who do pay attention may be quite unrepresentative of the town's population. When self-government becomes government by a few, we have to ask about the qualifications of those who choose to remain involved. Are experts or conspiracy theorists stepping forward? Are they concerned for the general welfare, or are they pursuing private interests?[2] As participation declines, we begin to worry about how the multiple tasks of governance will get done at all.

Because third-stage problems arise at the intersection of civil society and political order, there is no quick legal remedy. A court cannot order us to be better citizens, to pay attention, or to volunteer. No one can require us to stop listening to conspiracy mongers or put down the smartphone. Civil society is not re-formed on command. This was Tocqueville's point: democracy in America is a matter of values and beliefs—mores—that support practices and institutions.[3] Those conditions, he thought, arose "naturally" from the combined effects of geography, immigration, economics, religion, family, and interests. Today there is nothing natural about successful democratic practices.

Tocqueville wrote of the dependence of democratic politics on civil society: "In our time, freedom of association has become a necessary guarantee against the tyranny of the majority. . . . There are no countries where associations are more necessary to prevent the despotism of parties or the arbitrariness of the prince than those in which the social state is democratic."[4] In Killingworth, however, there is a gap between the institutions the town inherited and the society it has become. Is the town still socially suited for the volunteerism upon which its governance depends? Most Killingworth residents no longer have the time, and few have the interest, to volunteer. The natural interplay between civil society—family, work, religion, and civic associations—and political order no longer exists. Absent that interplay, governance through volunteering can produce the pathologies of harassment and capture that I described in chapter 3.

In Killingworth, political frustrations arise from the institutions of direct democracy; in Washington, from the institutions of representative democracy. Everywhere, reasonable people wonder why politics is so difficult today. Tocqueville's insight still applies: democracy without a supporting civil society may be more than we can handle. Civil society did more than bring people together in various associations. It created relationships of authority and deference: for example, minister-parishioner, teacher-student, parent-child, and professional-client. Traditional authority was as much about responsibility as about privilege. We should do away with privilege, but we cannot do away with responsibility. New England society was once surfeited with authority, but Killingworth has become a society without authority.

Democracy and Deference

Well before the normalization of the disruptive fringe in American politics, Hannah Arendt worried about the recession of political authority in modern life.[5] By authority, Arendt meant a practice of regarding the past, and particularly the founding act, as a source of legitimacy. The Romans invented this idea: they understood present politics as "augmenting" the city's founding. Politics was a structure of authority because its motivating force was to preserve and to augment, to grow from its origin. The problem of authority, accordingly, was that of establishing and maintaining a foundation.[6]

Arendt's idea of authority traces to Rome but resonates with some characteristically American beliefs. The authority of the Constitution derives not from its abstract excellence, however that might be measured, but from its origin in a founding act.[7] While the Declaration of Independence was the performative text bringing the nation into existence, the Constitution created the nation's legal and institutional order. This idea of authority finds direct contemporary expression in originalism as a method of constitutional interpretation and in the rhetoric of our most famous presidential addresses, including Lincoln's invocation of "our fathers" at Gettysburg.

Arendt's idea of authority nevertheless poses a puzzle in a democratic polity because it privileges the past over the present. It is a republican idea, not a democratic one. Its very point is to counter the political claims of a contemporary majority. This is why Arendt saw the Supreme Court as the site of political authority and also why the Court's power is often described as "counter-majoritarian."[8] Its role is to hold the nation to its constitutional commitments.[9] In Arendt's terms, the Court's primary responsibility is to explain how acts of government, including laws, can be seen as augmentations of the foundation.[10] When no such explanation is available, the act is unconstitutional.

At stake in Arendtian authority is how we imagine ourselves as part of a political community. Nationally, we link ourselves to the founding through a belief in the popular sovereign, imagined as the agent of national history: the "We the People" of the Constitution's first words.[11] Belief in the popular sovereign simultaneously founds individual responsibility and collective authority. These are reciprocal expressions of political belonging. This double character was long expressed in the blurring of any distinction between the military conscript and the volunteer. One enlisted out of deference to authority, the other from a sense of responsibility. This was not a difference that registered in political identity. No one asked a wounded veteran whether he was a volunteer or a conscript.

Locally, this reciprocity of responsibility and authority makes volunteerism something more than acting on personal values or interests. Taking up the work of town governance is neither charity nor hobby. It is an act of citizenship, not of personal generosity. Volunteerism rests on a sense of responsibility for a community that is more than an arbitrary collection of residents. The community has a life as a political entity with a distinct past that members see as their responsibility to carry into the future. Those who feel no such responsibility may live in the neighborhood, but they are not members of the political community. Older residents give voice to this view when they describe the occupants in the upscale developments as "New Yorkers."

When we perceive the town's past as significant to our own identity, we recognize its authority over us.[12] This town, not some other, claims us. Local authority draws residents to volunteer, and in doing so, it makes residents into citizens. Together, volunteers augment the town. Self-government, in short, is not just whoever shows up at the Town Meeting to pursue a personal interest. It is a taking care of the public project by residents who have come to view it as their own responsibility. The most active volunteers—people with widely diverse political views—share a concern that younger residents have little interest in this project. Absent that interest, they worry, the town will die: it will become just another suburb with no particular identity of its own.

Forms of association that once supported a relationship between authority and responsibility are in decline: church, family, and town. Absent these forms of living together—or their equivalent—we are increasingly on our own.[13] This is evident in the decline of attendance at church services and the rise of a self-help industry.[14] The ideology behind this industry is that the self is a project to be managed: we are each to make something of ourselves. The roles once served by ministers and community leaders are now filled by life coaches.[15] The past appears no longer as a source of authority to be augmented but as a source of injustice—personal and structural—to be eliminated. Not surprisingly, the most important book on justice in the last decades of the twentieth century began with an image of complete anonymity: there is no history, no place, and no association behind the "veil of ignorance."[16]

Contemporary politics, like much of contemporary political theory, often takes self-regard as a first principle.[17] Those residents coming to Catherine's office looking for a tax reduction because they do not use the schools are asking of the town: "What's in it for me?"[18] A neighbor complained of having to pay taxes to support the public library. If he does not use it, why does its support fall to him? The resignation of the emergency operations director, the difficulty of recruiting electoral candidates, and the worries about staffing the ambulance service all come down to the same question. So does the sparse attendance at town meetings. When people come to town meetings only to advance a personal interest, they are taking the same attitude toward their own legislative role: "What's in it for me?"

The decline of political authority is just one expression of a broader rise of individualism. We defer to authority, but who today thinks they should defer to anyone? I am constantly surprised to learn of residents in town who do not register their dogs or vaccinate their children. Their attitude seems to be, "Make me." The same attitude leads to constant speeding on narrow residential streets. In one neighborhood, a group of young teenagers on bicycles were harassing motorists and residents. Catherine received complaints and asked the resident state trooper to visit the family of the "gang leader." When the trooper arrived, the parents did not deny the allegations or defend their son's integrity. Instead, they verbally abused the trooper. Again, the attitude was, "Make me." Most residents at the dump wear a mask, following the directions of the large sign at the entrance. But whenever I am there, at least one person drives in and very ostentatiously refuses to wear one. He flaunts his power to refuse, knowing that the dump guys are not about to make him.

When no one believes in deference to anyone else, only numbers count. Think of Amazon ratings, in which every opinion counts equally. These ratings are precisely not the expert evaluations of Consumer Reports. We have become more Amazon than Consumer Reports. When everyone's opinion counts equally, the scientist speaking on climate change becomes just another person whose opinion we are free to reject.[19] Calls for deference immediately raise suspicions. We ask whose interests would be advanced. President Trump modeled this behavior when he rejected public health officials' advice for limiting the spread of Covid-19, suggesting that they were motivated by "politics."[20]

If everyone's opinion counts equally, common sense becomes the sense of the mob; it becomes non-sense. Individuals may think they are deciding for themselves when in fact they are simply repeating what "everyone is saying."[21] Thinking for oneself requires more than repeating what one heard on the radio, just as free choice requires more than wanting what everyone else wants. In the stock market, such thinking produces bubbles of irrational exuberance. In democratic politics, it produces populism.

Tocqueville saw evidence of this phenomenon in Jacksonian America: a democratic aversion to authority can produce exactly the opposite of reflection and choice. "The more conditions become equal, and the less men are individually strong, the more they easily let themselves go with the current of the crowd and have trouble holding alone an opinion that it has abandoned."[22] Democracy, he thought, succeeds only through an active and engaged civil society, for the reciprocal relationship of authority and responsibility is learned through practice. Civil society gives democracy a structure that resists the individualism of self-regard while keeping the mob at bay. Absent that structure, practicing self-government is like trying to run the schools without teachers: students cannot educate themselves.

Tocqueville was right to note that civil society organizations, alongside participatory mechanisms of governance, give shape to an otherwise formless equality. Organizations that build civic capacity bring together democracy and deference, or responsibility and authority. Formless equality has a way of turning into authoritarianism. The democratic egalitarianism that Tocqueville feared truly emerged only at the end of the twentieth century. When it did, it indeed produced the problems he worried about. This is the Killingworth dilemma: Can self-government work in a democratic society? That sounds paradoxical, but Tocqueville's work was devoted to explaining the paradox of a democracy destroyed by too much equality. The trolling on many social media sites offers a vivid example of "too much" equality, for on those sites there is neither authority nor responsibility.[23]

For hundreds of years, Killingworth had an abundance of authority. This was evident in the extraordinary stability of its political and civil-society institutions. These included family, church, professions, and commerce.[24] Of course, traditional practices should not become objects of nostalgia. Even as they formed the background condition of political institutions, they produced the first two forms of democratic pathology: exclusion and discrimination. When those practices fail, however, we can have the third form: mismatch. Too little authority can be just as problematic as too much. What will take the place of these traditional sources of direction and care?

Religion and Town

Religious Foundations

Killingworth's original practices of self-government were not just rooted in the Congregational Church but inseparable from it. How much did governance as volunteerism depend upon Congregationalist practices and beliefs? Do citizens act differently when they are accountable to each other not just at the Town Meeting but also at Sunday Meeting? Into the nineteenth century, Killingworth engaged in formal, public shaming of moral offenders before the congregation.[25]

The Congregational origin remains evident today. The modern Town Meeting has the same formal character as the church meeting. Both begin with the collective choice of a moderator, followed by public participation in a moderated debate, and decision by a show of hands rather than by secret ballot. In both church and town, the moderator is in charge of the meeting—not the first selectman and not the minister. The parishioners at meeting are the legislative assembly of the Congregational Church, just as the Town Meeting is the legislative assembly of the town. The parish, like the town, staffs numerous positions and committees with volunteers, from the deacons to the flower committee. Tom Lentz, the town historian, describes volunteerism in the contemporary church in words that could be directly applied to the town: "Besides those who serve as officers and on boards and committees and are voted on at annual meetings, there are, and have been from the beginning, a large number of volunteers without whom the church could not function. These volunteers are known as 'Silent Servers.'"[26]

The Silent Servers' contributions include teaching, leading youth groups, helping the sick, preparing meals for those in need, putting out the church newsletter, hosting coffee hours as well as lunches and dinners, running the church fair, and taking care of the church building and grounds. In short, volunteers do everything except occupy the role of minister. This is a pretty good description of town governance.

Arendt might see these practices as evidence of a unique political authority running back to the foundation of church and town. In truth, residents are no longer aware of this history, and if they were, most would be unlikely to care. Some residents—the "history buffs"—are curious about the origin of such practices, but they make no connection between that history and contemporary governance. Authority as augmentation of the founding is not a causal connection to be discovered but a collective belief in identity and responsibility. It is a matter, not of fact, but of the imagination. In Killingworth, political institutions maintain their traditional form less out of respect for the past than out of inertia. Town Meetings continue even though only a handful of residents participate. At the origin, participation in Sunday Meeting was mandatory.[27] The form remains, but the practice has drifted wide of that mark.

In 1667, the General Assembly of the Connecticut Colony "officially named the town and gave permission for establishing a church."[28] Membership in the community referred simultaneously to a religious and a political order. The former had normative priority: residents were Congregationalists first. The point of political organization was to secure and advance the community as a congregation.[29] In 1730, the farmers in the north part of town asked the town to allow them to form a new Ecclesiastical Society. They wrote: "If Faith comes by hearing the word Preached . . . then we hope no good man will Deny our Prayer & if we cannot be a Society we cannot hear the word Preached but seldom & so not have the means in order to Faith which makes our Case Lamentable."[30] They were not successful, but in 1734 they petitioned the General Assembly to be allowed to form a new society. That request was granted in 1735, when the General Assembly divided the town into two Ecclesiastical Societies. The Ecclesiastical Society was responsible for organizing the church; it was also responsible for the schools and graveyards. This gives a fair impression of the important areas of public life—church meetings, schools, and graveyards.

The two Ecclesiastical Societies formally separated into two towns in 1838. Today's Killingworth, in other words, started as a parish. A self-governing congregation became a self-governing town.[31] Early town buildings, including the "meeting hall," served both public and religious purposes—a distinction that would hardly have been recognized at the time. Despite statewide disestablishment in 1818, the Congregational Church remained central to town life deep into the twentieth century. The Old Town Hall, used until 1966, still sits in the backyard of the Congregational Church. Today, it is rented out as a martial arts studio—an apt symbol of the decline of religious authority.

An effective pastor was the town leader. While town and church offices were typically one-year appointments, pastors tended to serve for many years.[32] The first pastor for the northern Ecclesiastical Society, William Seward, served for forty-four years. His successor, Henry Ely, served nearly nineteen years. Tom Lentz explained the ministerial role to me: "The early pastors were by far the most important people in town. They were the only ones with an education, had a house built for them, and received the largest salary. They were often students of natural history, physicians, and scholars as exemplified by Jared Eliot, the pastor who followed Abraham Pierson." Abraham Pierson served as pastor from 1694 to 1701. During that time, he was also appointed the first rector of the Collegiate School, which later became Yale. He conducted the first classes in his home. Jared Eliot, pastor for fifty-six years, was a prominent physician, scientist, and agriculturist. He created an ironworks forge in Killingworth and invented a method for making iron from black sand. He was a friend of Benjamin Franklin, who visited him in Killingworth, and was elected a member of the Royal Society of London.[33]

The accounts of these early pastors prominently record the number of baptisms and marriages they performed: events no less central to the town's survival than to the congregation's. Residents would devote an entire day each week to church, listening to sermons that could last for hours and socializing with their neighbors over Sunday lunch. In an era when travel between homes was not easy and the work of farming tended to isolate families from one another, the church maintained the town's public space and time. Participation in that public life was part religious obligation, part civic responsibility, part socializing, part informational exchange, and part entertainment.

The line between public and private, secular and religious, remained unclear as long as congregation and town coincided. There is still a remnant of this convergence in the annual Memorial Day celebration, with a parade that ends at the Congregational Church. Veterans are honored and the first selectman addresses the residents from in front of the church building. If it starts to rain, however, the celebration moves into the church itself. At that point, with the residents in pews and the town leadership standing with the local religious authorities in the front, we reenact Killingworth's earliest practices—a convergence of sacred and public, of church and town. The difference is that in 1815, of the 233 families in town, 170 were Congregationalists. Today, of the 6,400 residents, around 225 are Congregationalists.

At the Memorial Day celebrations, the proceedings begin with a prayer from one of the religious leaders. The first selectman then speaks. She acknowledges the town's veterans, alive and dead, and tries to draw a lesson for residents from those past sacrifices. Sacrifice is exactly the concept that links the religious and the secular, the town to its foundation. If residents attend to that message, they are experiencing authority as augmentation. It may well be, however, that I am one of a very few listening closely for these connections, and I do so because it is Catherine speaking.

The church's significance for town residents in the nineteenth century is evident in their decision to impose an extraordinary tax upon themselves, about ten times the ordinary mill rate, in order to construct the church building that still dominates the town. The tax was imposed just before state disestablishment in 1818, but it continued to be collected by the Ecclesiastical Society after that date and was even legally enforced against those who resisted.[34] This model of public financing of a "private" entity continues today with important services— for example, the fire department and the library. These are secular organizations, but they occupy the same blurry border between private and public that was long the space of the Congregational Church.

As the town's population declined in the nineteenth and early twentieth centuries, the Congregational Church's finances grew increasingly precarious. By 1896, the congregation required a subsidy from a regional religious organization.[35] With the postwar population boom, the church grew and became more stable financially. By the turn of the millennium, however, it was again struggling to survive.[36] It even considered selling its parsonage.

Today, the church's finances have stabilized, but not because its membership is increasing. The slow, steady decline continues. Cheryl Fine, the head deacon, observes an absence of "people making a place for a spiritual life. . . . It just doesn't seem important to a lot of young families." As fewer families with children occupy the town, the shrinking membership skews more and more toward the elderly. The church's current financial stability is largely a consequence of the departure of its full-time minister, Martha Bays. After several years of temporary ministers, a permanent but part-time minister has been hired. In addition to reducing costs, the church has received state aid for the renovation of its historic building. The town may at some point have to decide whether to contribute to the building's preservation as a part of a common historical legacy, or maybe as part of a plan to attract tourism. The church building, too, may become part of the business of entertainment.

Looking back at the history of congregation and town, I am less sure that traditional practices of self-government should be described as "volunteerism." This ambiguity is well expressed in one of the earliest legal provisions of Massachusetts, which was also adopted by the Connecticut Colony.[37] To provide support for ministers, the law stated: "Eve[r]ie man voluntarily set downe what he is willing to alowe to that end & vse; and if any man refuse to pay a meet p[ro]portion, that he be rated by authority in some iust & equall way; and if after this any man withhould or delay due paym[ent] the civill power to be exercised as in other iust debts."[38] The voluntary seamlessly becomes a legal obligation: responsibility and authority have the same foundation. As long as citizens were committed members of the congregation, they no more asked, "Why volunteer?" than they asked, "Why go to Sunday Meeting?" Today, they ask both questions.

Religious Diversity and the Forms of Authority

Across the street from the Congregational Church is Saint Lawrence Catholic Church, built in the 1960s. Catholicism arrived in town with the European immigrants who took up subsistence farming at the start of the twentieth century. They found cheap land, for many of the farms had been abandoned during the nineteenth century. Today, Catholics constitute about a third of the town's population.[39] Saint Lawrence is now the largest church in town, with a membership of 678 families. Before the pandemic, 250–300 people would attend Mass on a typical weekend. Like the Congregationalists, however, the Catholics face an uncertain future as participation declines and financial resources become more tenuous. The Saint Lawrence population, too, is aging. Many Catholic families want to have their children participate through confirmation, but that is often the endpoint of their involvement.

Down the road from the Congregational and Catholic churches is the third of the town's three major churches: the Living Rock Church. It was built by an evangelical group that came to town in 1992.[40] Its membership is about 120 families or 250 individuals, making it slightly larger than the Congregational Church. These members are mostly not from Killingworth. The fourth and final church is a small Episcopal church, located in a beautiful antique building, dating from 1817. Its location, in the woods about three miles from the town center, speaks to the marginal place of non-Congregationalists at the time.[41] It claims some fame as the church that figures in the 1940 best-seller *Forty Years a Country Preacher*.[42] For some decades, however, it has been too small to have a regular minister.

The three central churches offer three different forms of community, each with its own idea of authority. The Congregationalists choose their minister; the evangelical minister creates his congregation. The Catholic priest is assigned by a central administration. These different authority structures reflect different forms of religiosity. More important, they intersect in different ways with the volunteerism necessary to town life.

The evangelical community is organized around the individual experience of transcendence: Jesus appears to the believer as his or her "personal savior."[43] The evangelicals make the written text of the Bible fundamental. Because the text is understood as the revealed word, every believer stands in the same position of receiving the text from God. Individual reception depends on neither theological doctrine nor relationships among members of the congregation. It is, rather, a singular experience that opens a space for charismatic leadership. The minister models the congregant's personal relationship to Christ. He has no ritual to proffer; his role is not to mediate for the parishioner between the sacred and the secular but to demonstrate what can be only personal and direct.

A religion that emphasizes the direct presence of the sacred cannot claim institutional authority for its ministry. There is no formal qualification for this ministry, no reporting to higher authority, no supervision within a larger bureaucracy. The Living Rock Church came into being when its pastor, the Reverend Ryan Young, gathered a following and split off from an existing church in a neighboring town.[44] His authority extends only as far and as long as he can persuade others to join or remain in his church.

Charismatic authority can be deep when the parishioners trust their pastor. The Living Rock Church displays features of such personal trust. It has been in town for close to thirty years under its founding pastor, whose sermons weave his personal experience into his exhortations to the congregation. He asks them to bring God's word and the Kingdom of God to the world. It is a mission-driven church, with an active mission in Ukraine, support for a ministry in Bridgeport, and links to Jews for Jesus. The church has a location in Killingworth, but it does not have a "mission" in Killingworth.

This church is not a local institution, either in its self-conception or in the town's view. It was started by families from elsewhere who happened to purchase land in Killingworth. When asked about the size of their membership, the church office manager was quick to point out their geographical diversity: "Unlike most of the churches in town, our members come from many towns, from Branford to Waterford, and north to Berlin." People coming to the Living Rock

Church on Sunday morning are not creating a relationship to the town any more than are people who come to the restaurant across the street from the church. Unlike the Congregational and Catholic churches, the Living Rock Church is not visible from the road. Hidden in the woods, it sends a message of retreat from the town's public space.

It may be merely chance, but I have never met anyone at a town event who told me that he or she was a member of the Living Rock Church. I have been to services and events at both the Congregational and the Catholic churches, but never at the Living Rock Church—not even a funeral. Neither has Catherine, whose work is to appear everywhere and with everyone. At times, Pastor Ryan will be asked to give the benediction at a town event—the local ministers take turns. He is noteworthy for the religious sectarianism he expresses on such occasions, as if he has no concern for the non-Christians in attendance. Or perhaps his concern is to use the occasion to bring to them the good news of Jesus Christ.

Unlike the Congregationalists and the evangelicals, the Catholics are a part of a global organization with its own hierarchy. The structure continually reproduces itself within the faith community: the local priest's authority derives entirely from the center.[45] Priests are assigned by the bishop for tenures that average around five years. Their power is quite independent of the community. It is the power to conduct the rituals of Mass and Communion, the other sacraments, and confession.[46] An individual priest may have charisma, he may be more or less engaged with his community, but his religious authority is independent of his personal qualities.

The town parish is a part of a diocese that covers the eastern half of the state, all under the direction of a bishop in Norwich. The local Catholic priest administers rites of transition—baptism, Communion, marriage, death—but in each instance renders them private matters standing under a structure of church authority. Compare the closed, private space of the confession to the openness of the Congregational meeting. To note this difference is not to suggest that the Catholic Church is uncharitable; it runs its own charities.[47] The local parish has a stewardship committee that regularly contributes to the town food bank, along with other regional charities. The Congregationalists also pursue charitable works.[48] But charity is not self-government. Contributing to a church charity drive is not preparation for participation in the give-and-take of a town meeting or the volunteer operations of town governance.

Of course, individual Catholics are no less active than others in town affairs. The point is rather that the authority structure of the Catholic Church does not offer support for the practices of self-government.[49] The church does not make up for the surfeit of Tocquevillian equality among residents. The priest has authority—more than that of the Congregational minister—but it does not align with the town. It is not too much to say that the parish is his town, while the Congregational Church is still understood by its members and by many other residents as the "town church."

The O'Sullivans, who are very engaged in both the Catholic parish and the town, emphasized how little influence the members of the parish have on assignment of priests. A parish, they commented, can make its views known to the bishop, but he is free to reject that advice. The Congregationalists, on the other hand, hire their minister. Reflecting on her nine years as minister, Martha Bays emphasized that she was an employee of the congregation. If she fell out of favor, she was entitled to three months' notice. "The church is owned by the people [and] they technically run it. They have the power." Despite this difference in formal authority, the Congregational minister can expect to have a position until retirement, while the priest is on a regular rotation. The former has traditionally been an integral part of the town; there is no such expectation with respect to the latter.

The Congregational Church of Killingworth originated with a grant from the General Court of the Connecticut Colony, but once it came into being, the parish was on its own.[50] It has had to navigate its own internal divisions, some of which have been deep, beginning with the Great Awakening of the late eighteenth century and continuing with the controversy over performing same-sex marriages. Unlike some of the neighboring Congregational churches, the Killingworth congregation rejected a proposal to be "open and affirming" of same-sex marriages. For some of its liberal members, this was unacceptable. They withdrew—not a small matter for a congregation already worried about its diminishing size. Decades before, another national controversy—abortion—disrupted the congregation. When the minister preached a sermon opposing abortion, some members strenuously objected and withdrew. Martha emphasized how careful she had to be when she preached a "political sermon": "And boy, if I ever wanted to preach a political sermon, I had to really think it through very carefully. I always felt if I met people where they were, I could move them a little

further into becoming . . . maybe just more open to looking at things in a different way." A community that depends on voluntary association must take care
not to so offend as to break the bonds within the congregation.

Until the arrival of substantial numbers of Catholics, the Congregational
Church meeting was a point of concentration—a general gathering of town residents. Its spirit was the same volunteerism that informs the town. As intertwined
sites of self-government, neither the church nor the town developed strong, formal structures of authority; both depended upon a community ethos of public
service. Residents once came to church as members of families embedded in
relationships of work, school, service, and friendship. Today, most of the town
is elsewhere on Sunday morning. Even within the congregation, they joke that
there are more cars in the parking lot weekday evenings than on Sunday morning. Those cars belong to members of the Lions, the karate club, and other community groups that use the church for a meeting space.[51]

When I asked Rob Rimmer, the church's trustee chair, whether the church
"put Killingworth first," he said that it did. He pointed to the large number of
groups using the building, as well as to the church's food programs and work with
seniors. Martha, too, spoke of "the amazing numbers" of community members
who "walk through the doors during the week." The church remains a gathering
place, even if Sunday morning attendance has declined. Many members like
to pause for coffee and conversation after the Sunday service. At the Catholic
church, parishioners tend not to linger after Mass.

Rob explained that many residents still think of the Congregational Church
as "the town's church." For Rob, this meant that he only came to feel fully a part
of the town when he and his wife joined the church, several years after moving
here. The idea of the "town church," however, has a broader meaning. Rob
spoke of people who see the church—the most prominent building in town—
and think of it as somehow theirs. They expect to have their funeral service
there. I was at one of those services a few years ago after a friend, Eric Auer Sr.,
died at a young age from brain cancer. Catherine and I went to the service. I
found it moving and assumed that Eric, who had lived in town for decades, had
been a member of the congregation. A couple of years later, I asked Eric Jr.
about his own participation in the Congregational Church. He told me he was
not a member and that his family had never been members. Still, I expect it was
his father's church.

The Congregationalists once put the weight of the sacred behind the institutions and mechanisms of self-government. Before disestablishment, this was formally proclaimed.[52] In 1891, when the congregation formally incorporated itself, its declaration stated, "We the members of the Congregational Church in Killingworth, Connecticut . . . do hereby constitute ourselves a body politic." There was nothing new in this. Neither of the "new" churches can step into the place of the Congregationalists, for both model forms of social organization that do not replicate the ethos of volunteerism.[53] Neither church comes from the New England tradition of orderly egalitarianism, combining responsibility and authority, and neither can transfer its form of authority—charismatic or bureaucratic—to support volunteerism in the town.

The O'Sullivans are extraordinary volunteers, within and outside of the Catholic Church, but they emphasized that volunteering in the church was primarily about religious education and church support. Martha, on the other hand, emphasized that the Congregationalists feel a sense of responsibility for the town and its history. She understood the "well-being of the community" to fall within her responsibilities.

One might think that the religions most likely to flourish today would be those that grate least against modern forms of knowledge. Ordinarily, people try to escape cognitive dissonance.[54] Why participate in a church whose doctrinal demands are difficult to reconcile with the premises of modern life, including modern science? For much of the twentieth century, it was widely assumed that forms of belief would gradually homogenize. The secular public schools would be the vehicle of this transition from religious faith to scientific proof.[55] Members of traditional religious faiths often fear the public schools for this reason. The growth of the home-schooling movement parallels the growth of religious fundamentalism.[56]

The shrinking of the Congregational Church suggests what was wrong with this assumption about the direction of religious belief. A church that makes few demands on the faithful may not offer enough to hold its parishioners' attention. A church that avoids cognitive dissonance is also one with little new or challenging to say.[57] It must compete with other demands on residents' time, as well as with alternative sources of advice and encouragement. If I am not going to hear anything different at church, the reasons for attending become less compelling. All the more so as the counseling function of the local minister is displaced by professional therapists and life coaches.

Many families find in the Catholic and the evangelical churches a counter to the authorityless individualism that they see around them. Church authority is attractive to families that feel adrift or overwhelmed by a civil society in which everything seems to be a matter of choice and personal opinion.[58] That authority structure, however, is a reverse image of the volunteerism upon which both the Congregationalists and the town rely.[59] To look to these religious authority figures is to look right past the borders of the town.

The figure the Congregational minister most closely resembles is the first selectman. Both must lead by doing; both exhort members to participate in collective projects for the good of the community. Both must match an aging institutional infrastructure to contemporary social practices. Both face the same difficulty of motivating a younger generation to take up an ethos of volunteerism. Both lack the power to shame, since any effort to do so would likely lead its target to withdraw from participation. Both can do little more than preach to whoever shows up. They are, for the most part, preaching to the faithful.

The town and the Congregational Church attract the same sort of person, a connection evident in the list of church leaders. Catherine's campaign manager is a member of the congregation, as is her husband, a past chair of the Democratic town committee. But so is the manager for Catherine's opponent in the 2019 election.[60] So is a recent member of the board of finance, and an ex-registrar of voters. Rob Rimmer told me that of the seventeen town committees and boards of which he was aware, Congregationalists sat on all but four.[61] He was in his fifth year serving on the board of finance and also chairs the charter revision commission.

Apart from the dwindling Congregationalists, religious practice today is more likely to take one out of, rather than into, the public life of the town. The churches compete with the town for the limited time Killingworth families have for anything beyond work and school. The disappearance of the ethos of the congregation from the public space of town meetings has contributed to three effects that together make it increasingly difficult for self-government to succeed.

First, most people no longer belong to an authoritative community—the congregation—that creates an ethical expectation of public service. Volunteering for the town becomes just another private choice. There is a general assumption that those who volunteer must enjoy the work; otherwise, they would not do it. Little appreciation is expressed publicly for those who volunteer or for the sacrifices they make.

Second, once volunteering has been drained of its ethical imperative, those who do it can be suspected of advancing private interests. Suspicion of others' motives can grow unchecked—especially when encouraged by media sources that constantly allege the self-interested motivation of those who govern. This puts a tremendous strain on those who serve on the town boards and commissions. When any controversy arises, volunteers are suspected of self-dealing. I saw roots of this problem in Cheryl Fine's enthusiasm for her church but skepticism toward the town. To me, she described the former as a community of volunteers with diverse views and backgrounds, united by working together on church missions. She described town governance, in contrast, as under the control of elites, pursuing their own self-interest. For her, this tension is expressed in attitudes toward less well-off seniors: the church takes care of them; the town, she believes, ignores them.

Third, absent an authoritative community, public institutions that rely on volunteers are vulnerable to the pathologies of harassment and capture. No one has the authority to discipline or shame the harassers; no one teaches factional interests that their responsibility is to pursue the public good.[62] Hearings and meetings can become sites for aggressive performance by those who want to impress their faction by challenging the legitimacy of those exercising public responsibility.

That the town no longer has a privileged place in the geography of religious faith carries no moral weight in itself. A concern for others can be as broad as the world. It suggests, however, that we may no longer have a civil society interested in local self-government. We are not going to reorder our religious practices in order to support local governance. But successful self-government continues to depend on habits of volunteerism that trace back to the Congregationalists. Those habits will not appear absent certain virtues of character, and those virtues must be taught. Where are they taught today?

Local Commerce: Entrepreneurs and Volunteers

The secular project of maintaining the town as a cooperative venture might once have been enough to create a thick community resting on an ethos of volunteerism. The cluster of postwar civic associations—the ambulance association, the library, the Lions, the Chamber of Commerce—and the enthusiasm with which older residents remember that period of activism support this view, as does the recent success of Parmalee Farm. On the other hand, the aging volunteers on town committees, the difficulty of staffing essential services, and the empty Town Meetings raise serious doubts. Religious life is not the only form of civic association that has changed in recent years.

Commerce and Leadership

Just as the town's religious life has transformed, so has its commercial character. This, too, bears on the viability of attitudes and practices on which the town continues to rely. Like religion, markets have moved outward, reducing the significance of the town for residents. As residents have become wealthier, the economic life of the town has become thinner, dramatically limiting the pool of potential town leaders. No longer able to rely on the willingness of competent residents to run for office or staff committees, some small towns are hiring professional town managers. Clinton—once the southern part of Killingworth—has hired its first town manager. Even the mention of this possibility in Killingworth has created controversy, with some residents objecting to both the cost and the implication that residents lack the skills to manage the town on their own. The issue, however, is not whether the skills exist in town but whether those who have them will volunteer for public service.

There has not been a consistent attitude, nationally or locally, toward the political role of business figures. Thomas Jefferson praised the virtues of independent farmers while viewing cities and commercial life with suspicion. Alexander Hamilton famously disagreed.[63] A generation later, as Americans took up the idea of a commercial republic, Hamilton's views were widely accepted.[64] During the nineteenth century, business came to be seen as a training ground for political leadership. By the twentieth century, the business of America was thought literally to be business. As former GM chairman Charlie Wilson came close to saying, in his 1953 confirmation hearing for secretary of defense, "What's good for General Motors is good for America."[65]

This view has always generated a vigorous reaction among populists, progressives, unionists, and liberals.[66] Still, something remains of the American appreciation for the managerial capacities of the successful businessman. We elected a businessman with no political experience as president in 2016; numerous candidates for lower offices campaign on their business success. The 2018 Connecticut gubernatorial campaign came down to a choice between two businessmen with scant political experience.[67]

The popular appeal of a business background rests on a few beliefs. Some citizens think government services are run inefficiently and waste tax dollars. They think successful businesspeople know how to control costs. Businesspeople are also thought to possess character traits supportive of a public role. The successful businessperson is a "pillar of the community." People's livelihoods depend upon the success of his or her enterprise. Economic success also functions as a proxy for class distinction: the wealthy serve as an American aristocracy to which are attached the obligations of class. Think of all the local libraries funded by Andrew Carnegie or the work of the Gates and Zuckerberg foundations today.

These factors also operate locally. Managerial and organizational skills are needed no less in local government. Successful planning requires a willingness to confront facts and anticipate future demands. Businesspeople are thought to have developed this skill in responding to market demands: either they get it right or they go under. In addition, some believe in a natural convergence of interests; a town where residents are not doing well is not good for local business. Local commercial interests, accordingly, have a direct stake in the town's success.

This last idea of a convergence of interests remains a factor in Killingworth politics. In 2019, the Republican candidate for first selectman was the owner of the largest and most expensive restaurant in town. One of his supporters made the connection between business and political leadership: "Having owned several successful restaurants (through a nasty recession I might add) [Francesco] understands holding the line on spending, how to make our money go further, how to make tough decisions, and how to look for inefficiencies in spending. Not everyone agrees that government is a business but, in my opinion, it is; it is a business with people at its heart and we should never lose sight of that, but it is still a business, and if not run correctly the town will suffer."[68] Convergence of town and business interests is also evident in some of the surrounding towns. The first selectman of nearby Essex owns and operates the town's largest manufacturing concern.[69] Other area towns have local lawyers as first selectmen. Wholly apart from public spiritedness, reputation counts in local commerce; leading the town and its civil society organizations is a way to build recognition.[70]

Despite the Republicans' recent turn to Francesco Lulaj, the model of businesspeople leading Killingworth has pretty much exhausted itself, for the age of small business has passed. When Catherine and I arrived, local lawyers, insurance agents, and developers were still attracted to town governance. Participation was a part of the responsibility of those who were commercially invested here. First selectmen, for several years, had been local lawyers. There are not many ways to achieve name recognition in town, and the position did not require a full-time commitment. David Denvir, for example, was first selectman from 2001 to 2005, having already been a selectman from 1993 to 2001. He also served on various regional and state boards or committees. Throughout this time, he practiced law, opening his own local office in 2001.

Today, local commerce is hardly visible in Killingworth. Those stores that remain—the hardware store, the liquor store—are often owned by nonresidents. For most of its history, the town was not only the place where one raised a family but also where one secured a livelihood. That started with farmers and extended to a range of supporting small businesses. In the early nineteenth century, the town used its abundant water to power mills of every sort: saw, grist, shingle, flour, paper, carding, felt, and fulling. It manufactured ax handles by the tens of thousands; it had tanneries, blacksmiths, and iron forges as well as stores, taverns, and doctors. This economy collapsed in the second half of the nineteenth century.

There are many more residents today but little of the robust commercial enterprise of the mid-nineteenth century. The mills and manufacturers are long gone. Retailers cannot compete with the large stores in neighboring towns or, increasingly, with Amazon. The same is true of the service professions. Medical practices are consolidating on the regional and state levels; lawyers in solo practice have become rare. Consolidated professional services locate where there are more people. Independent contractors in the construction trades remain, but they get their supplies elsewhere, and most of their job sites are elsewhere, too. Like their neighbors, they leave each morning and return in the evening. And their numbers have been greatly reduced since the recession of 2008.

In the twenty-five years Catherine and I have been here, the direction of local commerce has been mostly down.[71] Killingworth would like to encourage more small businesses, but there is substantial resistance to creating any sort of commercial strip.[72] The town lacks the transportation infrastructure for malls or manufacturing.[73] The last significant commercial employer—a pharmaceutical-related business—left a decade ago. The two large buildings it occupied, just off the traffic circle that marks the town center, are a sign of Killingworth's commercial decline. One has been converted to residential rental units; the other cannot find enough commercial tenants. In recent years, the hardware store moved to a larger building, Francesco Lulaj's restaurant opened—another closed—and a few small businesses related to construction, landscaping, and prepared food have opened. Some Killingworth residents run private businesses out of their homes, but these enterprises tend to be e-commerce, for whom the traditional attractions of building a local reputation no longer apply since the customers are elsewhere. Tim Gannon closed his photography business after more than thirty years of operating from a small studio on his property. When I asked him who was replacing him, he said that event photography has become a regional business and that, with the arrival of digital cameras, there is an endless supply of people claiming to be photographers. In short, there is not much possibility for a successful local photography business anymore. There is some new interest in town in micro-agribusinesses: a mushroom farm, a llama farm, a lavender farm, and some fresh produce stands. Still, the commercial geography of residents' daily life no longer aligns with the political geography of the town. The largest commercial enterprise operating in Killingworth today is likely Amazon.[74]

There is a chamber of commerce, but it has little visibility on issues of governance. Its primary purpose is to facilitate private networking and local advertising through its publication, the *Killingworth Krier*. The chamber does not pursue long-term commercial planning—perhaps because there is no realistic belief that much commerce will ever return to Killingworth. Recognizing the town's limited prospects, the local chamber recently merged with the county-level organization. The *Krier*, too, is feeling the loss of advertising revenue as local commerce declines. It is looking for alternative sources of revenue, including subsidies from some of the larger nonprofit groups in town. It may not survive.

The disappearance of local commerce is not just a matter of inconvenience for some residents. It has a dramatic effect on town governance.[75] Except for a few contractors, I rarely encounter a local business owner at a public meeting or event. The very idea of a local business leadership no longer makes sense. There is no frame of reference for such an idea. Francesco ran for office, but I have not heard of him attending town meetings or serving on any board or committee. Interestingly, the same is true of John, the leader of the Conservative Party, who has an HVAC business. He runs for the selectmen positions, but he serves in no volunteer positions in town of which I am aware.

Engagement with commerce today not only takes residents out of Killingworth but takes up most of their time. As the field of commerce expands, so does its demands. Success requires a willingness to meet those demands.[76] This inculcates habits of competition and private accumulation that reduce the interest in, and value of, volunteerism. Today, to turn to commerce is to turn away from the public life of the town, and people rarely turn back.

Commuting and Participation

Shortly after we moved to town, we met an elderly woman who remembered our house from her childhood, when it was owned by her grandparents. It was then a working farm with a small dairy operation, the remnants of which were still visible when we arrived. Its main cash crops were strawberries and raspberries. She remembered riding on wagons filled with berries as they were pulled into the barn. Another resident, who grew up at the same time just a mile away, described her childhood up until 1944: "We had no electricity, no running water and we got water for ourselves and the animals from the well. We had a wood stove for heat and cooking. Our cow provided milk and butter, we raised pigs for food, chickens provided eggs and we tended a vegetable garden for produce."[77] Those who can remember that Killingworth speak of "a mesh of connectedness among the old timers."[78] That mesh does not extend so far anymore.

In the postwar era, Killingworth changed from a more or less self-sustaining farm economy to a town of commuters. This was made possible by the arrival of paved roads, especially the turnpike, which opened in 1958. Those roads redefined the residents' economic reach. It became easy to get to the larger stores in the population centers along the coast, leaving Killingworth with a few small convenience stores. Convenience is a good way to describe most of the local businesses: the hardware store for when you do not want to drive to Home Depot; the local garage for when you do not want to go to the car dealership; the local hair salon and the lunch counter for the few who remain in town during the workday.

The residents' mobility limits the town's capacity for commercial growth. Killingworth competes with neighboring towns to persuade businesses already in the region to relocate, but that is not a general growth strategy. It may not even increase employment, since town residents may already work at those businesses. A few years ago, Killingworth attracted one such business. Immediately after it arrived, it started threatening to leave unless it received certain benefits. Within a few years, it was gone—perhaps trying to leverage similar demands in a neighboring town.

The likely sources of economic growth, online services and businesses, are invisible to the public life of the town.[79] They lead not to more engagement with the community but to less. They privatize commerce in the literal sense of keeping it within the home. At the same time, they focus the entrepreneur's attention elsewhere. Moreover, when the home becomes an online office, the result can be ever longer workdays, with even less time for volunteering. Those who stay in town to pursue their careers are literally staying at home.

Many residents commute to work in Hartford, New Haven, or New London. Each is thirty to forty minutes away. Each city is proliferating a range of commercial activities into its immediate suburbs. Killingworth has a fair number of knowledge professionals—teachers and scientists—who work at universities, colleges, and the laboratories that tend to grow up around such campuses. It has a fair number of health care professionals who work at the hospitals and medical centers associated with the universities and a fair number of managers who administer these operations or work in insurance and related businesses around Hartford. It has lawyers, financial consultants, engineers, and accountants. None of these careers entails contact with local governance or requires any volunteer investment in the town's operations or well-being. Local commerce, for these commuters, means some form of convenience store.

A town of commuters is ill-suited for self-government based on volunteerism. This phenomenon is well studied with respect to the suburbs, although researchers have reached no single conclusion. Postwar studies of the new suburbs saw them as sites of high levels of civic participation.[80] More recent studies have shown less engagement with civic society organizations.[81] There is a debate about whether levels of participation are a consequence of suburban living— for example, built into the architecture—or of the socioeconomic class of those who choose to live in the suburbs. This is not a debate that matters for Killingworth. Whichever view is right, declining participation threatens the town's self-governance.

Of course, there will always be civic-minded individuals who will engage with the town regardless of where they work and shop. But commerce no longer creates a civil society structure supporting volunteerism as a natural part of its operation and self-conception. Commuting itself tends to close off the possibility of seriously engaging with the town. It displaces the town from the center of one's personal geography. Residents who commute to New Haven or Hartford spend most of the daylight hours away. They may be more concerned with the economic health of the cities where they work than with that of Killingworth.

Commuters are likely to find themselves excluded from the politics of those cities, yet without time or interest for the politics of the town where they live. It can hardly be surprising that children growing up in a family of commuters do not linger in town. They do not imagine any link between adulthood and town.

Just as important as commuting's temporal and geographic displacements is its relationship to the media. The lone commuter in his or her car willingly occupies an ideological bubble and does so week in and week out. The radio normalizes and teaches forms of political discourse on both sides of our national divide. Does politics mean National Public Radio or right-wing talk radio? They not only have different views but speak different political languages.[82]

The commuter no longer listens to neighbors but to a national partisan voice. The only politics he or she regularly and intimately engages is likely to be through a voice that has little to do with the town. This voice creates expectations by supporting a political imaginary drawn to one side or the other in our polarized national politics. If there is a school of politics today, it is a correspondence course, with each of us studying on our own in a moving bubble.

Commuters are also pulled away from the town by their professions. Professional life today tends to be rich in commitments to a community: the firm, the college, the practice, the business, or the lab. Professions often involve high social functions of coordinating and managing. The community of the workplace, accordingly, competes with the town as a site of social identity. When people think of advancing to leadership, they think of the work community. When they think of reputation, they think of professional standing. In this world, volunteering to help run the town does not figure as a contribution.[83]

I spend long days dealing with colleagues as we collectively work to sustain and manage the law school community. Alongside classroom responsibilities, there is an institution to run, with its endless committees, meetings, programs, lectures, and workshops. There are budgets to manage and hiring decisions to be made. There is also a network of national and global scholars in conversation with whom one's substantive work goes forward. These are all communal exercises; they are no less social than activities at town hall. They are surely as exhausting.

Why would residents who find themselves in this situation think they have some special obligation to volunteer for the town? It is just not that important in their lives. They receive few public services. Their livelihoods come from a different community. Their faith may lead them to yet another community. Their friends and extended families are likely located elsewhere. The idea of filling a leadership office in town government is out of the question for most professionals—at least before retirement. Residence is a thin reed upon which to base a claim of collective self-governance.

Yet if public leadership is limited to those who have plenty of time, the town will lose out on the wide range of skills and expertise its residents possess. Governance will fall to the retired, the underemployed, and those who happen to enjoy participating in the volunteer services. This is the profile of the regular attendees at town meetings. Rarely are young adults there; even middle-aged adults are few. It is also the profile of those most active in the local political parties. This remains true despite ongoing efforts to recruit younger residents. They may come for a little while but soon find themselves too busy and town politics too frustrating.

Family and Town

Politics is an intergenerational enterprise. A group that organized itself only for a single event or to accomplish a single end would not properly be described as political. It might opportunistically seize hold of a political possibility, but it would not express any commitment to politics as an activity that has its own ends. Killingworth is a political community because some portion of its residents remain interested in its past—it recently celebrated a 350th anniversary—and committed to its future. If residents no longer cared about its past or future, the town would have become simply an administrative unit—something to be managed, not governed. What had been a political community would become just another form of corporate organization. Today, many residential communities—gated communities—are indeed private organizations.[84]

The political character of the town is evident when we compare it to the school district. In 1972, Killingworth joined the neighboring town of Haddam to form a regional school district. The state encouraged this consolidation; it was also efficient for both towns. Before this, Killingworth sent its teenagers to high schools in neighboring towns. When it built a kindergarten through eighth-grade school to replace its one-room schools in 1948, the school had only sixty-seven students. Twenty years later, it had more than four hundred—still not enough to sustain a high school.

Formally, the school district is a governmental unit separate from both Haddam and Killingworth. Residents of each town elect representatives to the school board. The board sets the budget, which is subject to a popular referendum in which the voters of the entire district act as a single unit. Despite these procedures, the school district has no independent political life. There is no sense of the district as a community with a unique history or a special future. The schools could be reorganized again without anyone complaining of a loss of a community identity, although residents might complain for other reasons.

Insofar as politics reaches the schools, it is the politics of each town.[85] Regularly, Killingworth residents approve the proposed budget while those of Haddam reject it.[86] We all know of this difference in town sentiments. We do not think of the pro and con forces as united across town lines; rather, we ask what each town will do. The question every year is whether the probudget voters in Killingworth will sufficiently outnumber the antibudget voters in Haddam. This difference partly defines each community's political identity. The formal structure of the school district has not created a single political community out of two towns.

The school board recently proposed closing one of the two elementary schools in Haddam. Because the school population is shrinking, the board argued, the cost of running two schools could no longer be justified. Many Haddam residents were deeply upset and mobilized to reverse the decision.[87] Despite Haddam's history of opposition to school spending, some residents were eager to continue this expense—estimated at about $1 million a year. They did not see it as a matter to be evaluated from the perspective of a larger political community constituted by the school district. It is entirely imaginable that the towns might return to two separate districts in the future. It is not imaginable that the towns would follow the school district and themselves merge into a single, larger town.

Young Families Buying in

The intergenerational character of politics means that the town depends upon the willingness of its younger families to take up the tasks of self-government. But does family life in Killingworth today make this a reasonable expectation? The town has young and middle-aged professionals who could contribute a great deal to governance, but few show up. No doubt part of the reason is that they are exhausted. Volunteering is not a realistic aspiration for those who spend ten hours a week commuting, the equivalent of one long day of work, and then confront the demands of childcare at home.[88]

Time is not the only issue. During Catherine's first political campaign, in

2007, she made a striking observation. She would ring the doorbell of a large home in one of the more expensive, new developments and find rooms largely empty of furniture. She was out campaigning with Marty, the first selectman running for reelection. He explained to her that there was no furniture because all of the family income went to paying the mortgage, the loans on the two cars necessary for the daily commutes, and other necessities. Outside the house, there was no landscaping beyond that done by the builder. In terms of both money and time, they could not afford to live where they had chosen.

That was before the real estate crash. Whatever these young couples thought about the financial wisdom of investing in a house they could barely afford, those beliefs most likely did not survive the Great Recession of 2008. Many families were left making payments on houses that were now worth less than their mortgages. No one likes to talk about it, but Killingworth had its share of foreclosures, auctions, and short sales. Development largely stopped.[89] Many contractors went out of business. Residents who opposed further development won the argument by default.

Before the Covid-19 pandemic, employment had generally recovered in the area, but income relative to expenses had not.[90] As in most places, the new jobs do not pay as well as the old. Those who work for government, including teachers, feel a particular threat. Even before the pandemic, financial insecurity was a dominant concern, voiced at town meetings whenever there was a proposal that would increase town expenses.

The election of 2016 brought a good deal of attention to the unemployed workers of the Midwest: people who were left without jobs when the mines closed and the manufacturers moved abroad. There is no unemployed working-class population in Killingworth, yet many residents are angry about their financial situation. People are not angry about the very rich; they are angry that they cannot achieve the lives that they were promised.[91] Alongside the gap between the 1 percent and the rest, there is an even more disruptive gap between expectations and the ability to achieve them.[92] Why did these young families buy houses they could barely afford? Why did their willingness to take on risk overcome their inclination toward financial security?

Family Economics: Privatization and Politics

Just as Killingworth has few residents near the bottom of the economic ladder, it has few near the top. The median household income in town was $113,068 for 2014–18.[93] There are wealthier areas close by, with real mansions, not Mc-Mansions. Killingworth poses the question of the political character of those who seem wealthy when measured against the economic distribution of the nation but are looking up at others far wealthier than themselves.

The wealth effect in Killingworth is not the one we are used to reading about—the claim that money has too much influence in American politics.[94] Generally, the wealthy influence elections by funding candidates directly, by contributing to political action committees that "independently" purchase ads for and against candidates, and by funding social media campaigns. That influence continues once candidates are in office, for there is always another election on the horizon. In addition, the wealthy—particularly wealthy corporations and interest groups—influence policy through lawyers and lobbyists.[95] They fund organizations that monitor legislative and regulatory activities in order to direct an agenda.

All of this is true at the national level; some of it is true at the state level and in large cities.[96] None of it is true in a small town. Wealthy residents in Killingworth do not try to control town politics. They would have difficulty even determining how to intervene effectively. More lawn signs? In the 2019 election cycle, there was a dramatic increase in local Republican campaign expenditure. Some of it was now going to online advertising and professional political consultants. It seemed to have little effect. The wealth effect that is so troubling is not intervention by the very rich but withdrawal of the middle class from public engagement. Families—especially well-off families—over the last generation have moved toward privatization.

By privatization, I mean purchasing for one's own family a range of goods and services that were once pursued through common efforts.[97] The McMansion not only strains the family budget but represents the taking into the household of what used to be common activities, ranging from education to entertainment. The families of Killingworth are wealthy enough to aspire to an ideal of privatization, but for the most part they are not wealthy enough to reach it.

While few individuals will achieve great wealth, we expect a modern society to offer everyone an opportunity for work that will support a life that they can find meaningful in the right sort of way.[98] The qualification "in the right sort of way" means only that we have no collective responsibility to support antisocial or self-destructive behavior. When there is no stable relationship between reasonable choice, hard work, and economic success, the society is in trouble. That is the felt meaning of a serious recession like that of 2008: from the individual worker's perspective, financial success and failure became arbitrary. The economy continued to feel that way for many people even after the recovery. Then the pandemic renewed that feeling.

Individuals pursue economic opportunities with an idea of what it would mean to succeed. They have some vision of a good life, meaning a life that is reasonable to expect and satisfying to live. A society that puts its idea of a good life beyond the reach of most individuals is in a deep economic crisis, regardless of its actual living standard. Happiness depends on expectations as much as on facts.[99] A society that holds out an image of success that is disproportionate to the means it provides to get there is failing by its own terms. It generates endless desire and corresponding anger. The former may be necessary to drive the economy, but the latter undermines normal politics.

A persistent mismatch between ideals and economic reality gives rise to a structural inability to perform politically. Even though we are a far wealthier society now than in the 1950s and 1960s, government at all levels operates with a sense of having few resources available. How can one of the wealthiest societies in all of history be unable to afford to invest in its schools, roads, parks, and public buildings, let alone the well-being of its citizens? The problem is not a lack of resources; it is a political problem. Our politics is disabled by a pervasive sense of not having enough. Our private wants exceed our grasp. Even normal politics today operates under structural conditions of unease, ready to burst into a crisis of anger and resentment.

No one thinks that Killingworth residents should be the recipients of wealth transfers or charitable giving. The needs of others are far more pressing. It is not mere whining, however, to point to the disjunction between wants and means. People are unhappy in their actual circumstances, not in the abstract. Consider an analogy to children in a well-off family. They grow up surrounded by a set of expectations that they gradually adopt for themselves. Parents, relatives, teachers, and community shape their imaginations. Just as children gain a view of how the natural world works, so they have an understanding of society and their place in it. No one is wholly constrained by this understanding, yet it is the point from which everyone begins to form individual aspirations. We are happy for children if they succeed and sympathetic if they fail despite their best efforts. If the life they were taught to seek is close to impossible to obtain under the material conditions they actually face, something is deeply wrong. We are becoming that society. I often hear Killingworth residents complain that their adult children cannot afford to live in Killingworth; they are downwardly mobile.[100]

The constant repetition of a limited set of images of success—in film, television, social media, and ubiquitous advertising, repeated in the classroom, the workplace, and the home—creates the background against which individual expectations are formed. Individuals can reject all of this; they are free agents. But most do not. Rather, they internalize these expectations.

That conventional image of success is the life to which most of Killingworth's families aspire: a married couple with two or three children, two careers, a large house, two cars, children succeeding at school and in after-school activities, easy access to the media, and sufficient resources for higher education and family vacations.[101] It includes long-term security, meaning that this life is insured against disabling shocks from illness, disaster, and old age. This is what families want and believe they need. Indeed, they believe they have a right to this if they have worked hard. Yet it is not what most are likely ever to be able to afford.

This mismatch is not just a consequence of the job insecurity that has followed the turbulent economics of the millennium's opening decades—although that worsened residents' financial insecurity. It is a deeper problem brought on by the overwhelming privatization of family life today. Every family is to acquire, on its own, private housing, private health care, private retirement accounts, private childcare, private transportation, private tutoring, private vacations, and, for some, private schools. Couple this privatization with the decline of the extended family and one has a recipe for endless anxiety. The middle class want a life that only the rich can afford.[102]

Families cannot imagine an alternative life that they would consider successful, yet they cannot earn enough to support the one that they are set on. This is not a problem of character, as if Killingworth's residents had uniquely inflated expectations. Families are choosing what has been held out to them as the goal for which they should aim. They do not think of themselves as extravagant; they think they spend cautiously. Yet they chronically want more than they can afford. Periodic bubbles may hide this fact for a while, but bubbles burst.

It is too easy to dismiss this mismatch as a consequence of exposure to relentless advertising. Advertisements do create desires for things we did not even imagine until very recently. How many smartphones does a family need? The structural issue, however, is not the advertisements themselves but that they succeed so easily in creating a need. That is made possible by the countless narratives of what success looks like, which have already shaped our collective moral imagination.[103]

The Impoverishment of the Well-Off

It is not hard to estimate the financial strain of the affordability gap that Killingworth residents confront. The median household income of about $113,000 is below what it costs to live in the style that most families imagine as reasonable and appropriate. The median price of a home is about $365,400, which means that many residents spend about $30,000 a year on housing, including mortgage, insurance, maintenance, and property taxes.[104] They pay federal income taxes of about $7,000 plus another few thousand in state taxes. They pay FICA taxes of upwards of $8,500. They are likely to have auto loan payments and auto insurance costs of over $10,000.[105] It is hard to imagine living in town and paying utility bills of less than about $5,000 a year, including heating costs, electricity, online services like Netflix and Amazon Prime, and the ever-increasing cost of cable and cell phones.[106] Even assuming that a family receives employer-provided health insurance, insurance costs are still likely to be over $6,000.[107] Already, we are approaching $70,000. Full-time daycare for a preschool child costs well over $10,000 at one of the centers in town. Then there are commuting costs, which can run to $4,000 for gas and parking for each adult. With two children, we may already be over $90,000, and we have yet to consider the costs of food, clothing, computers, dentists, orthodontists, optometrists, retirement or college-savings accounts, and supplemental lessons for the kids. To say nothing of entertainment or vacations. Forget about charitable giving. The median household income is below what it costs to lead what most families consider a modest middle-class life. Which of these expenses can a family give up? Furniture?

These are all rough estimates, but the point remains. Families with incomes in the second-highest quintile can barely afford to live here. As I watch the money flow out of our household, I often wonder how most Killingworth families manage at all. Many, I suspect, do not; they are in chronic debt. The economic data indicate that some families have a surprising amount of wealth in relation to their income.[108] In part, this reflects the value of their homes, but that does not help them pay their monthly bills. In part, it is money in retirement accounts, which also does not help with ordinary expenses. For some, it represents wealth that has accumulated in families over generations. These families are surviving by spending down their inheritance.

The unfurnished houses tell us that, whatever the statistics show, many families are not economically secure. They are living at the very limits of their income. They save little and feel they have very few options, for they have no discretionary income at the end of the month. An unexpected crisis could be financially disabling.[109] Nor does the situation improve dramatically for families who make it into the highest quintile. They face a decision that will dramatically and disproportionately increase their expenses: private schools. Aiming for elite colleges that cost over $70,000 per year, they must consider whether to send their children to private schools with tuitions that are not much less. With two or three children, the costs of private education are enormous for all but the very wealthiest. Even the well-off live in a highly competitive world in which they feel they have little control over their own lives or their families' futures. And these are the most successful among us.

Nothing I have described suggests any sort of irresponsible extravagance. Most families in Killingworth need either better-paying employment or less expensive housing, daycare, transportation, insurance, and higher education. Government-provided health insurance would surely help; so would free college tuition. But that is not the society in which they live. Their measure of success, and that by which others judge them, is a large house, two cars in the garage, and children at good colleges. Yet even if they settled for a smaller house and less expensive cars, they would still be living close to the financial edge. It is not a paranoid fantasy to wonder whether our economy seeks to keep them exactly on that edge: always needing to spend a bit more than they can afford.

All of this puts substantial pressure on residents' work lives. They cannot afford even short-term unemployment. They must advance if they are ever to escape indebtedness. For these reasons, no one complains when employers demand more and more hours. Others may find themselves working two jobs. The idea of a balance between work and family life disappears when individuals lose control of where and how that balance might be achieved.

Family Economics and Public Life

This financial strain has predictable consequences for residents' civic participation. It not only drains their interest in volunteerism but shifts their attitude toward town governance from something that residents do together to something that is done to them. Many see the town as just another demand on their limited resources. Government comes to mean taxes, when residents are already living beyond their means. They ask what they get in return and whether they can get it for less.

When people are living at the financial edge, it is no small matter when taxes go up even a little. Paying a higher property tax bill means spending less on something else. Even when the increase is quite small—as any single year's increase is likely to be—the anxiety caused by constant financial stress can bring disproportionate reactions. The sense is, "Enough already." Residents do not want to hear arguments; they want a lower bill. For some, this means being against everything the town proposes, for it all costs money. These are the CAVE people I described in chapter 3.

When interest rates are low, arguments that it is a good time to take on debt to finance capital improvement projects fall on deaf ears. It is never a good time for those who must pay the bills. It can be difficult to get approval to spend on routine maintenance, let alone long-term projects. In their perpetual financial stress, many residents want to put off expenses as long as possible. They vehemently reject the idea that the town budget should expand over time as the town takes on more common projects and responsibilities. For them, increasing privatization means that the town should do less, not more.

This does not mean that nothing happens. For the most part, opposition is unorganized and people are too busy to pay attention. That state of disengagement is, after all, the condition from which contemporary governance problems arise. Not a lot of residents actually read the town budget; few show up at town meetings. But opposition can flare up unpredictably with respect to any proposal, no matter what the need. Such arbitrary opposition can make planning difficult. It makes public officials anxious and defensive. They lower their ambitions, which means lowering the town's ambitions for itself.

Financial stress can make residents unneighborly. It undermines the trust and sympathy critical to the ethos of volunteerism. Constant financial anxiety makes residents suspicious about the uses to which their taxes are put and about the motives of public officials—hence the 2017 campaign signs proclaiming, "Drain the Killingworth Swamp." Arguments that good schools, senior services, and public amenities improve everyone's property values do not persuade at a time when property values are flat or falling. Worse, the argument endorses the general idea that taxes should be judged by the return on investment. As families privatize, it can be hard to find a sense of intergenerational responsibility: services should be paid for by those who use them.

Coupled with this suspicion is a fear of being taken advantage of by the undeserving. If one begins from the premise that each family is on its own, then any use of town resources to help others is aid to the "undeserving." It does not take much exposure to Killingworth political discourse to hear anger toward the poor—not so much those in town as those in nearby urban areas. Residents may have no sympathy for the difficulties of urban life for minority groups, because they have no contact with members of those groups. Some residents have memories of fleeing urban areas, and this continues to inform their idea of the city as a place that a responsible family would leave. To come to Killingworth, they believe, is to accept responsibility for supporting oneself and one's family.[110] No one remembers that the town's rapid postwar development was aided by white flight from the cities, which contributed to the economic plight of those left behind.

These beliefs, grounded in fear, ignorance, and personal financial stress, may explain why John Samperi, the Conservative Party candidate in 2017, could find some political success in Killingworth. Samperi repeatedly runs for office as a member of the Conservative Party, a splinter faction of the Republican Party. Although he does not win, he has substantial support. In the 2015 election, for example, he received 611 votes for a position as selectman. His total that year was more than that of Catherine's Republican opponent for first selectman, who received only 428 votes.

Before coming to town, Samperi had been an elected fire commissioner in nearby West Haven. He moved to Killingworth after undergoing an impeachment proceeding in West Haven prompted by an allegation that he had made racist remarks.[111] Samperi denied the allegation and sued the other commissioners who had carried out the impeachment.[112] By 2009, he was running in the Killingworth Republican primary for a selectman seat. That July, however, the town tax collector complained to the board of selectmen that Samperi had made sexist remarks about her at town hall. The selectmen unanimously issued a letter informing Samperi that his alleged remarks "create a hostile work environment for town officials and employees."[113]

A small town like Killingworth once stood to urban areas as a thick community stands to a society characterized by anomie. Towns were rich in personal relationships and strong in traditions. Urban society, meanwhile, was transient, anonymous, lacking in traditions, and frequently lonely. Today these character-istics are reversing. Killingworth families are no longer extended or mutually supportive. Each pulls into itself; many take on responsibilities that they are not capable of fulfilling. These self-centered households produce teenagers with little sense of place, for Killingworth will not remain their home. They do not know where they are going, only that they are not staying here. Today, if we are searching for the community values once associated with the small town, we are more likely to find them in the urban neighborhoods that are experiencing a renaissance as young families reject suburban privatization.[114]

Killingworth residents feel under assault by layers of public demands: first from the town, then from the state with its urban areas, and finally from the nation with its global commitments. Everyone wants from them, but no one gives them what they most want: the means to enjoy their spacious homes and watch their children move up in the world. These feelings of financial stress and social resentment can create a politics that shifts arbitrarily between carelessness and anger. A proposal that one expects to be controversial may go before a town meeting at which no one shows up. Another that responds to an obvious need may be derailed by a derisive ad hominem attack. There is no reason for either response. When the central complaint is "enough already," it can be voiced at any moment, against any proposal.

Most Killingworth residents live in an economic order that keeps them en-tirely dependent on others: the boss, the firm, the customer. One can imagine two different liberty-enhancing responses to the anxiety that arises from that dependence: a vigorous, participatory effort of self-government or a search for a private zone of independence, a turn to the town square or a retreat into the home. Over the past few decades, Killingworth residents have increasingly chosen privatization over participation. That is the same fateful choice made in middle-class communities across the nation.

When the aspiration for this sort of independence meets most residents' ac-tual financial limits, the response is often to seek a still more private world. The barren rooms become a secret. No one is invited in. Informal associations dis-appear. The house changes from dream to nightmare. People close their blinds rather than publicly reveal their difficulties. We know very little about what actually goes on in most homes. We can no longer assume that all is normal, for we see the effects not just in the arbitrary interventions in local politics but in the increased rates of substance abuse, domestic violence, anxiety, and depression. The Covid-19 pandemic has exacerbated all of these problems.

Residents return to town at the end of a workday exhausted and stressed. Public-spiritedness does not figure in their lives; it is not encouraged at work, in school, or in national political discourse. Private success is no longer related to the town's success. Many families remain in town with a feeling of being stuck. Today, homes lack not just furniture but children: the school-age population is shrinking.[115] Public policy today focuses on closing schools, not on building them. There is a raging disappointment that even this does not reduce the tax bill.

PART THREE

PUBLIC OPINION NATIONALIZES AND DIVIDES

By the early decades of the new millennium, Killingworth had lost the sense of success it had when my family and I moved to town twenty-five years ago. It stopped growing; its school-age population was in rapid decline. The new middle school will never reach capacity, and an elementary school in the district has been closed. The town has no idea how to make itself an attractive place for young families. There are few jobs for them, and the cost of living is high. The Killingworth town plan of 2018 offers a grim forecast: "Killingworth is predicted to lose significant population by 2040. Projections now indicate a steady loss of population with a reduction of 27.3% by 2040."[1] That is a lot of empty houses or, more likely, houses empty of children, occupied by retirees who cannot afford to sell.

These are the circumstances of uncertainty under which privatization goes forward. They are also the circumstances in which public opinion is formed. Public opinion in Killingworth, as in towns and cities everywhere, has been nationalized. We are all exposed to the same media, commentators, and information. Beyond a sort of neighborliness, it can be hard to identify a local public opinion in Killingworth—what I earlier called "common sense." Issues that gain public salience become occasions for a local replay of our national polarization. Our national debate looks for occasions to show itself locally: "Drain the Killingworth Swamp."

There is a deep connection between privatization and nationalization. As residents withdraw from a public to a private life, they turn to national sources of information and opinion. What flows on the internet flows everywhere; commuters listen to the same programming everywhere; Fox News is ubiquitous. The inward turn, then, is also paradoxically an outward turn, as residents follow information links leading them further and further from the town. Both privatization and nationalization speak to the loss of a middle ground once occupied by civic society institutions, on the one hand, and local public opinion, on the other. If we are each on our own, we are citizens of the nation, with opinions and views shaped by our polarized national debates.

When a crisis arrives, a community that listens to its pastor urging hope is not the same as one that listens to a radio voice urging hate. A community can turn toward each other, expressing concern and mutual support, or it can turn outward, seeing the town as a site for national movements. Those nightly reports of "Killingworth Copes" during the Covid lockdown were intended not only to inform but to support a local public opinion that affirmed community over isolation, volunteerism over retreat, and hope over despair. They were controversial not because those who complained had a different view of how the town should confront the crisis but because the critics were focused on national conflict.

Today, the priority of national political identity is self-evident in practice and in theory.[2] The Tocquevillian inversion is one consequence of nationalization. It raises a fundamental question: Can we have local self-government without a local public opinion? Will residents volunteer if they are focused on national controversies and receive information primarily from national sources? If they are not interested, they will not volunteer; they will not be interested if they have no information.

For most residents most of the time, there is no local politics. They have no local news sources: no newspapers, no television, and no radio. When they think about politics, they think of what they saw and heard on Fox News, CNN, MSNBC, and Facebook. There are some local social media sites. They do not cover local news as newspapers or television once did. Rather, they participate in it. The debates on social media are meant not to inform but to engage. When residents do engage on Facebook, they quickly bring to bear views and attitudes shaped by national public opinion.

5
Talking to Each Other

Thus in order that there be society, and all the more, that this society
prosper, it is necessary that all the minds of the citizens always be brought
and held together by some principal ideas; and that cannot happen unless
each of them sometimes comes to draw his opinions from one and the
same source and unless each consents to receive a certain number of
ready-made beliefs.
—Alexis de Tocqueville, Democracy in America

WE FIT NEW EXPERIENCES INTO A repertoire of narratives that we already use to explain ourselves, our communities, and our world. These are stories of progress or disruption, control or lack of control. They are centered on values and norms that we embrace or reject. We could not begin a conversation if we did not already share common ways of organizing our experience. These narratives circulate in fiction, histories, political speeches, and legal arguments. They fill the exchanges we have with each other, whether intimate friends or strangers. Taken together, these shared narratives constitute public opinion.

Public Opinion, Persuasion, and Freedom

Every genuine conversation follows a pattern of proposition, response, and reply. We say something, listen for a response, and then offer a reconsideration. In law and public debate, these three stages can be quite formal, marking a structure of debate. The pattern holds up an ideal of persuasion: we listen and respond.

Sometimes, we are persuaded to see things differently. If we refuse to change our views even slightly, we are not really listening.

This pattern of argument is more than a form of inquiry. It is our first and most immediate experience of freedom.[1] Only people argue with one another; only people are free. The first act of an authoritarian regime is to close down the possibilities for argument. In our present political environment, the claim of oppression is often put forward as a claim of silencing—that is, of exclusion from the public exchange of opinions.

Our sense of ourselves as free subjects is bound up with our capacity for discursive exchange, of which market exchange is a pale reflection. Alone on a desert island, it would make no sense to ask whether I was free. This link between speaking together and freedom is the origin of politics. Politics begins not with violence but with discourse. A free politics is one in which we can argue freely. This is why we value politics not just as an instrumental means for achieving private interests. Political exchange is an end in itself because in and through it, we realize ourselves as free subjects. Of course, we do not all argue in the chambers of Congress, but when we argue with each other about what we should do together, we are pursuing the retail exchange of opinions that is constitutive of political freedom. The Town Meeting was once the paradigmatic site of free exchange—the nineteenth-century "school for liberty." For many people, the attraction of local politics is that it provides a space for engagement and exchange—freedom—that is absent from national politics.

Political theorists sometimes try to imagine an original discursive exchange among those in a state of nature. All that these first people possess in common is a fear of death and a desire for safety.[2] The social contract is a built out of this very thin public opinion. Actual communities, on the other hand, have available a thick public opinion built on experiences, commitments, traditions, beliefs, and practices.

Polarization occurs when politically salient groups adhere to radically different public opinions. It is as if the world has split in two. Abolitionists, for example, no longer appealed to the same narratives as slaveholders. Where the latter spoke of protection of property, the former spoke of denial of humanity. These were not ordinary differences within a common world but markers of two different public opinions that intersected on a field of violence. Polarization of public opinion marks the point at which arguments on each side no longer make contact with the other. Absent a shared public opinion, a vote is as likely to divide a community as to unite it. Abraham Lincoln won the election in 1860; the nation divided. The national elections of 2016 and 2020 had just this character of exacerbating division.

These observations on language, politics, and freedom are as old as Aristotle, who began a tradition of describing man as both a "political animal" and a "speaking animal."[3] They are the grounds for thinking of democratic governance, in its ideal form, as a conversation between free and equal subjects.[4] When we focus on the vote rather than on the conversation, we misunderstand the nature of political freedom. Most immediately, we face the conundrum of democratic authoritarianism, when the voters become a mob—a group that refuses to listen to alternative views.

A majority vote is a fair decision rule in many circumstances, but standing alone it does not legitimate a political practice. It fails because it models freedom as individual choice rather than as reciprocal recognition and engagement. Individual choice may suffice as a model of freedom when deciding what to have for dinner, but even my dog makes choices when I set him loose in the backyard. That is not political freedom; it does not become so if I add more dogs.

Extending the right to vote is important not just to register more individual opinions but as an expression of respect for individual rights bearers. That, however, requires more than providing access to the voting booth. We respect others when we open ourselves to persuasion by them. We each have the right to vote because collectively we are concerned with each other as equal members of the same community. That concern is constitutive of political friendship. If Killingworth is to survive as a self-governing political community, it must sustain political friendship among its residents. Our national politics has become that of competing tribes.[5] These tribes are increasingly occupying the town, straining the bonds of friendship.

Persuasion and Polarization

In law school, we do not actually teach much law. There is too much of it to memorize, and it constantly changes. Instead, we teach our students how to reason within the law. They must learn how to take a set of facts and give a legal account of rights, injuries, and remedies. They must learn to tell a particular kind of story—a legal narrative—about the facts. They learn this by studying cases, focusing on the nature of these narratives in different areas of law.

Legal argument is not deduction; it is persuasion, not proof. Think of the recent controversy over the right of same-sex couples to marry. Both sides offered a narrative about the institution of marriage. On one side, the narrative involved recognition of a relationship between two loving persons. Advocates argued that the gay couple is analogous to the heterosexual couple in this critical respect. The other side constructed a marriage narrative centered on the social management of the production of children. They argued that intergenerational reproduction distinguishes the gay couple from the heterosexual. There were many positions in between, combining or challenging elements of each story. As these competing narratives circulate, they shape how members of the community think and talk about the issue. Participants in the debate may disagree, but each recognizes the arguments of the other. Where there is recognition, the possibility of persuasion remains.

Except for its formal, procedural quality, there is nothing special about legal argument. The marriage debate, for example, went forward not just in courts but also in diverse public and private forums. We all know how to speak of love and children; we all give accounts of family order, recognition, and social management. Many people were persuaded to change their opinions.[6] In politics, ideas count as they enter into reciprocal efforts to persuade. Persuasion breaches the distinction between thought and action. It is thought's political face, which is to say it is a free practice.

Public opinion constitutes less what we think than how we think. It refers to how we explain ourselves when asked to give an account of what we believe and why we are acting as we do. Just as one has to go to law school to learn what can be said in a courtroom, a stranger has to learn what can be said in a political community. I did not arrive in Killingworth knowing how neighbors persuade each other. When I proposed that the town use its power of eminent domain to obtain property for the new middle school, I was out of place. If I had continued to feel out of place, I would not have been able to see the town as my own, and its politics would not be, for me, a practice of freedom.

Public opinion does not govern in a democracy through the weight of a single belief or sentiment. That is not a democracy but a mob. Tocqueville saw evidence of this phenomenon of the mob in America: "I do not know any country where, in general, less independence of mind and genuine freedom of discussion reign than America. . . . In America the majority draws a formidable circle around thought."[7] Protecting the mechanisms by which public opinion is created is the object of the First Amendment, but law by itself will not create a vibrant public debate. For that, we need to speak to each other. We need to be political friends.

The danger that Tocqueville saw in mass opinion is not an idle worry in our age of cyber reproduction. Social media may have begun with an enthusiastic embrace of a democratic exchange of diverse views, but in practice, many of these sites empower the mob.[8] When people worry today about political correctness on college campuses, they are worrying about the same tendency toward uniformity.[9] This threat of drawing "a formidable circle around thoughts" can come from the right or the left. If we are each in our own circle, there is no exchange and no possibility of persuasion. Two closed minds do not constitute political pluralism. They constitute a competition between two authoritarians.

Public opinion governs in a democracy, then, not as the singular opinion of the mob and not as the manipulated opinion of organized propaganda, but as a practice of disagreement within a community of friends committed to persuasion. Unanimity endangers democracy because it endangers freedom. We can have nothing to say to each other because we do not care or because we already think the same thing. The first is a consequence of privatization, the second a consequence of nationalization. In either case, democracy cannot survive. A democracy is always stronger with two political parties than with one.

Ironically, voting can be a moment of unfreedom in a democratic polity, for it is the moment at which we stop trying to persuade each other and instead determine winners and losers. It is the moment that brings a temporary end to a contest of persuasion.[10] In a successful democracy, the decision is respected by all sides because the process by which it was reached respected all views. Even when my candidate loses, I can say, "We decided." The same is true at law: I can lose my case while affirming the decision. If we cannot move from "I" to "We" at the moment of decision, our institutions have failed in the face of polarization, and we are on our way to civil war.

In sum, democracy requires disagreement, but not too much. Disagreement must operate within a shared public opinion. Polarization undermines a democracy by dividing public opinion. No longer sharing a world, we can come to see each other as enemies. The absence of common narratives is evident, for example, in our disagreements over climate change. Neither side recognizes the other's assertions. They appear as false, incoherent, or fabulous. Those who deny climate change are not asserting a single fact but standing within an entire world that questions scientific expertise, education, centralization, and transnationalism. Arguments about climate change are not settled by referring to facts because they are not really about facts.[11]

In Killingworth, where self-government means volunteering more than it means voting, a shared public opinion is a condition of democratic success. Volunteering requires affirmation of a common world, reciprocal respect, and a willingness to learn from each other. Like dialogue, it is something we do together. When disagreement is severe, nothing gets done. Absent a local public opinion, volunteers will stay home, where they are entertained by national media sources. When they do go outside, they will bring our national civil war to Killingworth.

Accordingly, the threat that nationalization poses to local self-government is not just that members of the red and the blue will no longer speak to each other. It is that they will no longer work together. Neighbors who cannot speak to each other will quickly have no interest in each other at all. They will attack each other on Facebook and avoid each other in town. It will be as if they live in two different towns, for the meanings by which they navigate among themselves and their institutions will be completely different.

Killingworth long held out an ideal of public service without politics. The ideal described a natural process by which the "I" became a "We": individually, voters had preferences, but collectively, they were political friends. Joan Gay, who has lived in town for more than fifty years, expresses the idea directly. She was the first woman to serve as chair of the Democratic town committee and was, in the 1970s, elected to the board of finance. Reflecting on local politics of that era, she says, "Don't get me wrong, we wanted to win elections." But after the election, she stresses, everyone worked together in a nonpartisan spirit for the good of the town. Friendship did not depend on politics; elections came and went. Partisanship was limited because not much turned on who won which office. The work of the town was bounded by the common sense of the town.

Joan thinks this is less true today: "The political atmosphere has become more divided." When she was the Democratic chair, she used to get together with her Republican counterpart to organize debates among candidates. They would "establish rules to make sure everyone was heard." Today, this level of cross-party cooperation is hard to find. Instead, we have one party trying to keep another off the ballot or declining to participate in a debate. In 2019, when the chamber of commerce held a forum for the Republican and Democratic candidates for first selectman, the Democrats' video recorder malfunctioned. The Republicans declined to share their video of the event. Why this pettiness?

Cheryl Fine, at the opposite end of the political spectrum from Joan, observes a similar movement away from a single, common community. She offers a less political, and more class-based, explanation: "I just find that the town used to be regular people. . . . Everybody acted like a regular person and now we've morphed into this elitist attitude that if you can't afford to live here just move. We don't want you. We don't try to maintain that mix of incomes and ideas and personalities." Cheryl speaks of seniors who do not visit doctors because they cannot afford the copays. No doubt there are residents in such difficult circumstances, but the divisions in town do not really fall on lines of economic class. They are deeper and broader.

Political polarization can penetrate even traditionally nonpolitical spaces. The Congregational Church, for example, also presents itself as a public space without politics. Yet when I asked a member about controversies within the church, I was told of a division over whether to return to inside services in the midst of the pandemic. The speaker added, "You can imagine who fell on which side." The suggestion was that the church, too, had become a site of polarization. Another member told me much the same thing, only focused on the earlier conflict over recognition of same-sex marriage. She read the congregation's opposition as "political" and, most important, not her politics.

The Lions, too, try to maintain this ideal of separation of public service from politics. They prohibit discussion of politics at their meetings. The local chapter started in the early 1970s with thirty-eight members, most of whom were in their late twenties and early thirties, and already friends. It was, according to Charlie Smith—one of the founders—80 percent public service and 20 percent social. That sort of a group can easily imagine leaving politics to their other interactions. Today, the Lions are not keeping up with the growth of the town. They have grown by only a third, to fifty members, while the town population has more than tripled. Moreover, their pool of potential members dramatically increased with their decision to admit women in 2015. Today, the active members, of whom there are about thirty, are mostly new retirees.

Public service without politics is neither as imaginable nor as attractive as it was fifty years ago. It is not just that politics is more divisive; it is also more interesting—that is, it holds one's attention. The politics that interests residents, however, is national. Peg Scofield, the editor and publisher of the now-defunct

Killingworth Today, suggests that something deeper may be going on. She reported on local government for thirteen years, starting in 2003. She thought then that the Lions Club was "a huge political machine" that included most of the town "power brokers"—the people sitting on the important committees. She called it "a closed environment"—the "patronage" system to which Joan referred. By the time the Lions started admitting women—including Peg—those power brokers were "moving on." As political power in town has become more diffuse, a more hardcore national politics had displaced a local self-confidence. Interestingly, Peg thinks that the other site of power in town, some twenty years ago, was the Congregational Church. Joan also identified the church as a site of Republican power in her early years in town.

If it seems increasingly difficult to separate politics from governance, this may be less a reflection of difference from past practices than of our unease with the state of national polarization. The old separation may have been more appearance than fact. Entrenched power always looks apolitical until it is called out. The power brokers who ran the town were confident that they were apolitical. That is the attitude that produced exclusionary zoning, even as it produced the ambulance association. The need today is not to return to some neutral space that never existed but to turn away from our unbridgeable national divide and to focus on local differences. We need to embrace these differences and make them productive for the town. Killingworth cannot dispel our national civil war, but perhaps it can change the conversation a bit.

The Venuti Property

National polarization was so complete by the time of the 2020 election that the president and the speaker of the house had literally not spoken to each other in more than a year.[12] The carefully scripted confirmation hearings for Amy Coney Barrett, just before the election, were staged to avoid any actual exchange of ideas. She became the first Supreme Court nominee since 1869 to receive no votes from the opposition party. We share with that earlier era an atmosphere of civil war.

Nationally, we no longer share a common public opinion that grounds competing efforts to persuade. When national politics comes to Killingworth, we find much the same thing. The Trump and the Biden supporters did not argue with each other. Each side stood at the entrance to the dump, glaring at the opposition and wondering what they were plotting. Partisans competed to get to the dump earliest to stake out the best and largest territory. They took down the signs or blocked sight lines of the other side. Signs appeared in town saying, "Reelect Trump / Make Liberals Weep Again." The sign celebrated polariza- tion, as if the reason to vote for Trump was to offend Democrats—in alt-right phrasing, to "own the libs." There is neither respect nor engagement.

As Joan cautioned, however, the political life of the town cannot be reduced to election rhetoric.[13] Local public opinion has not been wholly displaced by national polarization. One sees an earnest commitment to the town as a neigh- borhood of mutual concern, for example, when newcomers introduce them- selves on social media. Neighbors extend a warm welcome. They urge partici- pation in the KWO and the PTO. They speak with pride of Parmalee Farm and their favorite hiking trails. They are committed to being committed to the town. They rarely speak about the political divide.

When public engagement avoids the national narratives of red and blue, res- idents remain capable of practicing self-government as reciprocal efforts to per- suade. For example, in describing the competition between the accounts of lib- erty as independence and as equal membership, I invoked some basic elements of local public opinion. The two accounts serve as narrative frames within which residents can organize their experience and aspirations. They also shape the accounts residents deploy to argue about particular issues. The accounts are public in the sense that everyone in town recognizes both narratives. That is why they can operate as tools of persuasion, holding us together even as we disagree. They are opinions because there is no truth of the matter that can settle the controversies.

The contrast between the political debate that unfolds in national media and the debate that can still occur in the world of folding chairs set up in the multi- function room of the elementary school was strikingly apparent at two town meetings held in June and September of 2018. At issue was whether the town should purchase a 350-acre parcel of undeveloped land—the Venuti property. This is the last large parcel of open space still available in town; it has been the subject of town discussion for some twenty years. In the late 1990s, the town voted to make the purchase, but the deal fell apart when problems with the title emerged. Purchase was again considered a few years later, when the town was looking for a site for the new middle school.

The land is owned by the Venuti family, which has been here since the 1950s.

Members of the family are active in town, including in the fire company. In 2018, they still ran a construction business on a small portion of the land. The significance and history of the question before the town, as well as the embeddedness of the family, brought the issue to the attention of many residents.

Some two hundred people showed up at each of two meetings to discuss the purchase, an extraordinary turnout these days. Because the purchase was already scheduled for a public referendum, the meetings were for information and debate. Nor were participants trying to persuade town officials to decide one way or another. Rather, residents were there to inform themselves and try to persuade each other. They listened to each other even when they disagreed. Moreover, because residents were familiar with the land—located just up the road from our home—and the family, there was little room for alternative facts or conspiracy theories. Residents were asked collectively to deliberate about what the town should do. Should we tax ourselves to make the investment, or should we allow private development of the land?

The land purchase was not an issue that fit within the red or blue narratives. Neither political party had a position on the purchase. The Venuti family is not particularly identified with one party or the other. The head of the land trust is a Republican, but many of the preservationists in town are Democrats. The selectmen themselves were divided across party lines. Long-range planning and short-term tactics were both at issue in deciding what to do. Personally, I was for the purchase, but not at the price that was being asked. I could have been persuaded to go forward if enough neighbors expressed enthusiasm to make the purchase now.

Each side framed its arguments in terms of the alternative narratives of autonomy and participation. Interestingly, both narratives were used by both sides. Those who believed strongly in liberty as autonomy did not just appeal to anti-tax sentiment to oppose the purchase, although some did. That narrative was also used to argue for the purchase, on the ground that it would contribute to a Killingworth of few people, empty woods, and minimal regulation. Those opposing purchase also used the equal membership narrative to argue that the town had already done enough to protect open space and was at the limit of what it could responsibly manage. To this argument, supporters of the purchase responded that ownership of the land would create a "land bank" that would preserve future residents' ability to govern themselves. We had to act as trustees for them.

The debate did not divide neatly between an antitax group and an antidevelopment group. It was far more sophisticated because the participants had access to multiple deeply embedded narratives that could give structure to their intuitions of what was best for the town. These narratives constitute important elements of the common sense—the public opinion—of the town. Everyone understood appeals made from both sides, even if they found one side more persuasive.

No one at these meetings made accusations of conspiracy or malicious intent or targeted particular members of the community. We took different positions, but we could do so while respecting those with whom we disagreed. There was only one tense moment, when one of the Venuti brothers suggested that a failure to purchase could lead to development of affordable housing, which in turn would lead to an increase in the number of special needs children in the schools. Some residents found these remarks disturbing; they prompted angry responses on Killingworth Stompin' Ground, which led to an apology from the speaker.

These town meetings exemplified local democracy. They were not a necessary condition of a decision. We could have gone straight to the referendum. But the meetings were a necessary condition of something else: democratic self-government as a practice of freedom. They were possible because residents were not strangers to each other. I do not mean that everyone in the room knew each other. Rather, they all shared in the common world of Killingworth, and that was enough to justify listening and responding. That is what it means to be "political friends."

Among friends, disagreement is possible because it does not threaten an underlying reciprocal commitment. That commitment, in a successful democracy, extends to the entire community. This is not just the enthusiasm and pride of the welcome wagon. It extends to care for all the community's children, even those who pose special costs. That commitment is carried by local public opinion. By bringing into the room different interpretations of our common interests, we were reenacting the very point of the Town Meeting as it was practiced when Tocqueville visited New England. There were no experts at the meetings, for no one was better qualified to decide than those of us sitting in the folding chairs.

The referendum occurred several weeks later; the purchase was rejected by a vote of 1,333 to 668. Because of the multiple arguments, however, the rejection did not send a single message. I did not come away thinking that the town would never buy the property. I thought the residents needed to do some more bargaining with the Venutis but felt even more strongly that the town should not let the land go into private development. Others thought the decision meant that we should support private development; still others came away disappointed that we did not make the purchase. The town will no doubt keep debating the issue as long as the parcel remains undeveloped.

National Displacement of the Local

Democracies are fragile because they require an openness to diverse points of view. This is hard enough to maintain in an academic department. In a polity, it requires bonds of care and commitment that can be hard to find today. It requires that citizens be friends. They need not be intimate or even close, but they must have a concern for each other. Given the decency and mutual respect on display at the town meetings on the Venuti property, I was surprised to hear that the disagreement had in some cases become personal. Friendships broke over the issue.

Only recently did I learn the source of the anger: social media. While I was observing the respectful efforts at person-to-person persuasion at the town meetings, an entirely different sort of engagement was occurring on Killingworth Stompin' Ground. Amanda Brackett, one of the site administrators, traces the collapse of civility on the group forum to this debate. At that point, she says, "the internet exploded."[14] Personal accusations flew back and forth. Amanda continues, "Stomping Ground was created to nurture conversation between people, not to create a forum where you can facelessly attack your neighbors . . . and that's what it absolutely became." She believes political discourse today has radically different appearances—in person and online—two faces that the same person can assume: "Social media has given somebody a voice [to say] what he might not have had the balls to say to your face at the gas station." People, she says, "got very dirty."

Many Killingworth residents today have little experience with politics as a practice of persuasion. To them, the expression of disagreement does not signal political success; rather, it raises fear of personal attacks. The relationship between the red and the blue tribes is hardly one of friendship. We listen to friends even when we disagree. Disagreement among friends can even be a source of strength. Among enemies, however, it is always a potential threat. Suspicion makes persuasion impossible. Instead, we will take steps to protect ourselves and our communities. Gun stores sold out of ammunition before the election of 2020. Before the inauguration of President Biden, the National Guard was brought into the District of Columbia to prevent violent attacks by those who suspect conspiracies behind political disagreement.

There was a time when the debate over purchase of the Venuti land would have been seen as important but ordinary. Town residents shared a public opinion that was the common sense of the town. Walt Adametz refers directly to the loss of this common sense: "Growing up in a small town and having the ability to work the land . . . tempers a person. . . . The biggest thing I take out of it is the common sense that you derive. . . . There doesn't seem to be the common sense today as there was." Politics then was not something apart from families and civil associations. That time of a local common sense, resting on a common experience, has mostly passed.[15]

The Venuti property debate is one of the few remnants of that time. It showed Killingworth political life at its best, but in total only a few hundred residents attended the meetings. One wonders how it could be otherwise. There is no such thing as Killingworth news. Neighbors may not know each other. Before suburbanization, many residents had extended families in town, but no longer. Nor are there the close networks of young families that Joan and Charlie found in the rapidly expanding town of the 1970 and 1980s.

Just as personal connections to the town are no longer deep, so local communications networks have grown weak. When I ask residents where they get their news about the town, all say essentially the same thing: "Nowhere." Most speak derisively of the available social media sites; all note the absence of traditional print or television news. Social media sites are filled with the clutter of lost dogs, advertisements, and requests for recommendations of local tradespeople. When politics does appear, it reflects the national polarization. Those who are not engaged, which are most users, want such news off the sites.

Just as there is little access to local news, there is also little to local history. The town is 350 years old, but most residents know nothing of its past. Few residents grew up here. Local stories have mostly been forgotten. We wonder why there is a street named Roast Meat Hill; no one remembers how that came to be. We see the beautiful lakeside lodge built by the Works Progress Administration during the Depression, but no one remembers that the WPA was in town. No one knows how so much land ended up in state park and forest. We see the well-preserved one-room schoolhouses, but few know whether they have been moved from their original locations to where they now serve as architectural ornaments. We have a town historian, but he is over eighty, and he may not have a successor.

Few local leaders grew up here. Lou Anino, the other Democrat on the board of selectmen, may be the last. He has served in town government for more than twenty years and occupies a position once held by his father. Family knowledge of the town will not pass on to the next generation, for they have no interest in it. The religious leaders in town all come from elsewhere. They may identify with their congregations, but they are not of the town. The small businesses in town are mostly owned by nonresidents. Catherine has led the town for twelve years. She did not arrive until middle age and brought with her values learned where she grew up—New York City.

Killingworth public opinion today is largely shaped by national sources.[16] If democratic politics depends on public opinion, and public opinion formation today is a national process, then a basic question arises: Is Killingworth still an appropriate subject of political inquiry? Does the idea of a local political community make any sense? Killingworth survives as a residential community, but can it survive as a political community distinct from various membership organizations and its few shops and restaurants?

Many residents have already exited in spirit. Others never arrived. Charlie Smith, who has been an active volunteer in numerous organizations for fifty years, notes a different attitude among the "newcomers"—particularly those in the expensive developments. He says he rarely meets them, for they have no interest in joining the Lions, the Killingworth Ambulance Association, the Congregational Church, or the chamber of commerce—to all of which he belongs. Tim Gannon says the same thing about the volunteers who do the work at Parmalee Farm. These newcomers have political identities shaped by national, not local, concerns. They vote in national elections; they do not come to town meetings. They have definite views about national politics, but they may know next to nothing about local politics. Residents have to comply with town ordinances and pay property tax, but do they see this as anything more than paying for services or complying with the rules? If I join a baseball team, I have to comply with its rules and pay dues. The town sets rules for the receipt of services and charges dues in the form of taxes, but what is political about it?

That this question arises at all tells us how far we have come since Tocqueville's visit in the 1830s. Then, the priority of the local as a political association was taken for granted. Before the arrival of electronic media, it could hardly be otherwise. Washington was far away and exercised a very limited mandate.[17] The writers of the Federalist Papers tried to assure those who worried about the creation of a powerful national government that state and local associations would always be first in citizen loyalty. This priority was, for them, as obvious as the precedence of family attachment over more distant relationships.[18] Today it is the other way around. National politics is pervasive, inescapable, and inter-generational. It grabs our attention wherever we look. The mandate of local government, on the other hand, is limited. Its presence in our lives is equally limited. It cannot compel our attention, but it does ask us to volunteer.

The disruption of the local governance by national politics was evident shortly before the 2020 election, when Tim Withington got into a shouting match on Facebook with the leader of the state Republican Party.[19] Tim, who has long worked in emergency response, had recently taken over as director of the town's emergency operations, after the abrupt resignation of the prior director. The Facebook altercation began after President Trump called for an "army of poll watchers" to take up his cause on Election Day. Tim responded intemperately, saying that if this army disrupted the Killingworth polls, he would "make their lives difficult." The Republican Party leader widely broadcast Tim's remarks, accusing him of threatening violence. Several town residents predictably ex-pressed outrage, first on Facebook, then communicating directly with Catherine. Saying that they did not feel safe at the polls with Tim on the loose, they de-manded police intervention. They wanted Tim locked up and fired immediately from his emergency response post. Tim quickly apologized for his intemperate remarks. Soon he resigned from his volunteer post. Killingworth lost its desper-ately needed, experienced emergency operations director.

The assault on Tim showed no care for him as a member of the community who had only recently stepped forward to solve a crisis in the town's emer-gency management operations. He was a volunteer upon whom even his critics relied in a real emergency. Nevertheless, once he was seen in terms of the na-tional political conflict, he became precisely no one to his attackers. He was only a figure around which to spin a partisan narrative of threat in a world already filled with threats. What, after all, was Trump's invocation of an "army," after his refusal to distance himself from violent right-wing groups? After the insur-rection of January 6, 2021, Tim's "threats" look very small compared to the real sources of violence in the nation.

Tim was sacrificed at the altar of national politics. Of course, he was drawn in by his own political passions. His political identity, no less than that of his critics, was formed in national presidential races. Accordingly, any effort to defend him would be read as a further partisan intervention. Killingworth thereby suffered twice: first, it lost Tim's expertise; second, it lost a sense of its own political identity. Tim and his critics were not arguing as neighbors but acting out roles in a national drama. The partisanship that counts today is all about national politics.

The displacement of local political identity by national politics grew stronger throughout the twentieth century, not only because Washington did more and became more accessible on radio and television. More important, national identity became a life-and-death matter. Over the century, we moved through national wars fought by mass conscription armies to threats of nuclear annihilation to fears of international terrorism. To live in the national security state is to live with a national political identity. Each of us knows that if we were ever to confront a terrorist, it would be our passport, not our driver's license, that matters.

At the beginning of the twentieth century, federalism was a doctrine of separate spheres for local and national political life.[20] The local was to be defended from "invasion" by the federal government's new regulatory agenda.[21] In that era, Killingworth was solidly Republican, even voting against Franklin Roosevelt.[22] This attitude lingered. When Joan moved here in 1968, the town was still heavily Republican. She remembers it as one of a small handful of towns to vote against Ella Grasso, the Democratic candidate for governor, in 1974.

By the end of the century, separation of the national and the local had been displaced by cooperation.[23] More and more local activities were funded and regulated by the national government. From education to the environment, from welfare to transportation and health care, one could no longer disentangle the national from the local.[24] The right question was no longer how diverse localities build a national order but how national political identity could be realized differently in and through local participation. This was the era during which partisan identity was quite fluid in Killingworth. Fred could move from the Democrats to the Republicans without jeopardizing his leadership positions in town.

By the third decade of the new century, this idea of difference within unity is fading. The difference that counts locally is the same as what counts nationally: red versus blue.[25] Party membership is no longer a fluid marker but a deeply entrenched identity. Catherine started serving on the board of selectmen in 2007. For twelve years, the board acted with striking unanimity; they reached a cross-party consensus. Since 2019, consensus is no longer an ordinary expectation or an ideal.

The twentieth-century transformation of the local was not just a matter of rural areas becoming suburban. The highways linking places like Killingworth to urban communities were supplemented by media connections—from radio and television to Facebook—that drew the entire nation to the same sources of public opinion. By the beginning of the new century, many could wonder what made Killingworth different. The answer for many residents was "nothing," which is what they wanted. They had been drawn to Killingworth by the promise that they could live the same life as anywhere else, for a bit less.

People often tell me that they moved to Killingworth because it was the closest place to New Haven, Hartford, or New London where they could afford the house they wanted. For those who wanted a new house, not a new life, the disappearance of a local difference was a measure of success, until our national politics took a pathological turn with the rise of populist authoritarianism. Then the question became whether Killingworth retains the resources to resist and, even more important, to aid in the recovery of a national community of political friends.

Nationalization—the penetration of the local by the national—brought us together through much of the twentieth century. Think of the Second World War. Today, it divides us. The pandemic is literally a national phenomenon penetrating the local, where it reproduces the national political divisions. I wonder what beliefs and norms I share with those who get their information from Fox News, just as they wonder what they share with those who get their news from the *New York Times*. Neither Fox News nor the *New York Times,* however, has anything to say about the Venuti property. Freed of the burden of the national, local common sense can anchor a conversation. Once we lose that anchor, national narratives take over.

I experience this gap between the national and the local when I speak with someone like Ed Ricciuti. On national politics, we completely disagree. He votes for Trump to defend his right to own guns; he thinks Washington is corrupt; he fears urban areas and thinks the BLM movement is a group of terrorists. But when we talk about Killingworth, we agree on most matters, including the importance of conservation, volunteerism, and good government. The challenge, accordingly, is twofold. First, can we preserve a Killingworth community from the corrosive effects of national division? Second, can we use the experience of self-governance in Killingworth to begin to overcome our national political pathology? The answer to both questions begins with an appreciation for a sense of place, of mutual responsibility for the life of a community that is simultaneously particular and national, unique and universal.

Within Living Memory

Even as residents work together on local projects, national political divisions are never far away. A couple of years ago, Killingworth faced a contentious referendum on the school budget. This was part of the extended controversy over the proposal to close one of the three elementary schools in the system. The teachers' union supported the budget and asked if they could use a conference room in town hall as a place from which members could make calls. State law does not allow the town to spend resources supporting either side in a referendum. The teachers, however, planned to use their own phones. There was disagreement among the board of selectmen as to whether mere use of a room constituted "town support." Catherine allowed them in on the ground that many different groups use the meeting space for their own purposes. She thought the union should be treated no differently. It was a close call.

The surprise was not the disagreement but the news that a Republican elected official reported Catherine's decision to the state elections enforcement commission, alleging a violation of the statute.[26] The official did not voice her concern to Catherine and try to work it out amicably within town hall. The commission subsequently took Catherine's side in the controversy. The incident is a sign of the suspicion already circulating in town and ready to attach to almost any issue.

Democrats and Republicans in town grow more and more divided even though it is hard to find any partisan division over the actual issues before the town. In the 2019 election cycle, the Killingworth Republicans ran on the slogan, "Killingworth Values," but when pressed they could not identify a single issue upon which they actually disagreed with Catherine and the Democrats. Why, then, was the Republican Party pouring more resources than ever into an election in which nothing seemed to be at stake? When I asked Catherine's opponents to explain why they were not supporting her—even though many had worked successfully with her on town projects—the most frequent answer was, "Time for a change." That is partisanship stripped of all supporting reasons. It explains as well why the state Republican Party suddenly seemed very concerned with the town: every party victory now signals support for a national, partisan identity.[27] Both parties want a presence everywhere because the nation is everywhere.

Instead of diversity among communities, we increasingly find everywhere the same political divide. Residents focus directly on the national political debate. When the Killingworth Conservative Party puts up signs saying, "Drain the Killingworth Swamp," it has no local reference. A government of volunteers offers little opportunity for corruption. There are no bureaucrats to fire; there can be no deep state in a town in which neighbors take turns volunteering. The sign functions as a signifier of national allegiance. Local politics becomes the local appearance of "Make America Great Again" versus "Build Back Better."

This is all quite new for us. Until well into the twentieth century, Killingworth, like other New England towns, was essentially on its own. Photos from the 1920s show oxen and horses used for plowing and transportation. No one went anywhere very quickly, and few came here. Recently I saw an excerpt attributed to a Middletown newspaper from 1915, which made fun of Killingworth's backward condition. After noting that the town has "neither railroad nor post office," it went on: "Killingworth is a wild region. Once in a while comes a story that a bear has chased a pretty school teacher over Roast Meat Hill way, or that some lanky nimrod has brought down a wild cat out on the Ninevah Falls road. It is a Godforsaken country, too, if all stories can be believed. More murders have been committed in Killingworth and Durham, which adjoins it, than in all the other townships in the county combined." Regular contact with the urban centers may have been not much more than the arrival of the kosher butchers, who shopped for livestock on local farms. Killingworth was where you came if you wanted to farm but had little money with which to purchase land. It was where a subsistence farmer traveling east from New York might end his search.

Today, connection has displaced isolation. Online, I can watch political events in all the major capitals of the world, but until very recently I could not find the Killingworth Town Meeting, let alone the biweekly meetings of the board of selectmen. The pandemic has forced an experiment in online meetings. This new accessibility, however, has not significantly changed attendance patterns. The meetings do not hold the public's attention. They are politics as the mundane business of government and usually interest only those who are directly involved. To sustain an interest, one needs a guide who can identify the issues, track their development, and articulate the divisions of opinion. For over ten years, Killingworth had such a guide in Peg Scofield, who published *Killing-*

worth Today. When she stopped publication in 2016, local government became a black hole for most residents.

Not so long ago, children grew up quickly in Killingworth. They had to contribute to family life and work. Growing up also meant participating in community self-government. Today, participation in politics can be infantilizing. The administrators of Killingworth Stompin' Ground recently admonished the trolls and aggrieved posters, "This kind of childish behavior is not welcome here. If you cannot keep civil, [your posts] will be removed." Online political discourse can quickly become entertainment unfit for serious people. Any number of residents have told me they want nothing to do with Stompin' Ground because the exchanges are so childish.

Walt Adametz, who was born in Killingworth in 1957, has observed this change in the character of political participation over his life. He was born into a large farm family that had lived in Killingworth for close to one hundred years. He had aunts, uncles, and cousins all living nearby. Family history merges with that of the town. His grandfather had supplemented his farmwork with real estate work, and when money was short, took land in place of a monetary commission, eventually acquiring over two hundred acres. That generation of the family was made up primarily of farmers: "No one had any money," and "everyone raised their own food." In the next generation, only Walt's father was "really geared to agriculture." His uncles started working for the state. Public employment was a way out of town. Only his parents stayed on the land, raising cattle and pigs. Walt learned farmwork as a child. That tradition is gone. His son, Jeremy, runs a local auto shop. One daughter went to work for a pharmaceutical company; another became an accountant.

The farms never produced enough income to sustain a family. Walt's grandfather produced charcoal, which he sold in New Haven, and gathered witch hazel, which he sold to a nearby processor. Walt's father ran a construction business alongside the farm. Walt himself continued to raise a few cows, but he worked in a private garage before joining the town road crew, of which he is now the foreman.

He speaks of his childhood with great nostalgia. Life was oriented entirely around family, farm, and town. There were no latch-key kids; mothers were home after school. Children were taught hard work and respect for adults. "Our parents were the boss. They let you know when you got out of hand." Family was a structure of authority with strong expectations. "Sunday dinner was required unless you were dead."

Town and family blended into each other. Walt's father started taking him to Town Meetings at age ten, the same age at which he started splitting wood to heat the home. These two images of childhood seem united in his mind. One expresses the narrative of participation; the other expresses that of autonomy. This was the traditional Killingworth: self-supporting families joining in self-government. The families were alone together. Walt traces each of these images of liberty in an account of decline. He stopped heating with wood when his grandfather died, in 1997. Shortly thereafter, most of the family land was sold to developers. Over the years, the Town Meeting has declined as fewer and fewer residents attend. Without using the term, Walt describes a local politics that is increasingly nationalized.

The town Walt remembers was a place with steady values, institutions, and families. When the teenagers went south to attend Clinton's high school, they were called "hicks." Walt says that with pride; it meant they were raised with local values. Killingworth, Walt pointed out, had no police force. The hicks, he says, knew how to behave, because they had no choice: family and town depended upon them.

The town offered authority without organization. There was the Congregational Church—an "integral" part of town, according to Walt. When I asked him about other organizations, he could recall only the 4H Club. Things were more "informal." "Basically," he says, "it was neighbor helping neighbor. . . . Everybody chipped in," and "everyone worked with everyone." At town meetings, discussions were "lively," but "at the end of the day, after the meeting, we were neighbors." They remained friends, visiting each other and sharing meals and tasks, whatever their political differences. Today there is "more animosity" and it does not end with the meetings.

Politics, Walt says, has become more "hardcore"—meaning polarized—over the past twenty years. He blames this on pressures from "employment and mortgages." The deeper story he tells, however, is of the absorption of Killingworth into the region, the state, and the nation. Newcomers did not want the life of a rural community. They did not want the "farm smell." They wanted the same goods and services that they had had in the urban areas from which they came. Killingworth did not change them; they changed Killingworth. Walt does not oppose this; it is after all, his family's story as well. Yet it is clear that the Killingworth he values most is the one he remembers from his youth.

Party identity, he thinks, has become far more important as the town has lost its neighborly familiarity. "Years ago, when people ran for office, party didn't matter as much." Residents were on the "same wavelength." They asked "whether this is the right person for the job." The focus was "more on the local, not the national scene." People switched parties as opportunities for service arose. Fred is the obvious example of a town leader switching parties, but so is Frank Cunningham, who was a Democratic selectman from 1985 through 1987. In 2003, he was elected to the board of finance as a Republican, and by 2006 he was chair of the Republican town committee. Frank explained that differences with the national Democratic Party were behind his switch. While party identity focuses on national politics, "at the local level . . . it's not really a Democrat, Republican, or unaffiliated that makes the difference, it's the person."[28]

Walt ran for selectman in 1989 with the short-lived Killingworth First Party, which formed when there was a split within the Republicans. He lost, but his party's candidate for first selectman, Jerry Lucas, won. Most people, Walt says, "did not vote a straight-line ticket." Intraparty division is not uncommon in Killingworth. In 2007, the Democrats split, with the incumbent Democratic first selectman, Marty Klein, forming a third party, to the advantage of the successful Republican candidate. More recently, the Republicans have split, with a group forming the Conservative Party.

By the time Walt's children were teenagers, the town had its own high school. By then no one could distinguish the kids of Killingworth from those of Clinton or anywhere else. They all hung out at the mall; all the malls looked the same. There were no farmers left. No one took their children to Town Meetings; everyone is busy and the children would be bored. Killingworth, Walt explains, has been penetrated by people with money, spreading up the coast from New York.

Walt expressed a sentiment of public responsibility that I have also heard from other old families: he tried to teach his children a "sense of giving back" to the town. He is proud of his children's pursuit of public service while they were in high school. His son worked with the fire company and one of his daughters with the ambulance association. They were following family tradition. Walt had been in the fire company in the 1970s, and his father had been a charter member of the Killingworth Ambulance Association. Today, the high school has a community service requirement, but students need only perform thirty hours of work that can be very casual. The parents to whom I speak do not take it seriously, except as a résumé builder for college admissions—a point that the high school emphasizes as well.

By the early 2000s, the developers had hold of most of the available land, including that which had been in Walt's family. That land was sold off by an uncle—an act that triggered an unsuccessful lawsuit. "When land prices went crazy, family farms got sold." Walt sold his last cow a dozen years ago. There is no point in raising cows anymore, he explains, because everyone buys prepared meals on their way home from work. Who is going to purchase hundreds of pounds of beef for the freezer? That freezer full of meat represented a commitment to the family dinner at the center of daily life—the Sunday dinner one dare not miss. Fewer and fewer families gather together over a meal at the end of the day. Parents come home "beat and stressed from the job," he says. They want to "chill." Instead of family dinner, they "throw twenty bucks to the kids" to go get a pizza. Family and town suffer from the same problem: "Everyone comes home from work and keeps to themselves." Residents no longer help each other: "Instead of coming to town meetings, people complain on social media," and "instead of finding a solution, people throw gasoline on problems."

No longer splitting wood or raising cows, Walt lives a life more suburban than rural. The town of which he feels so deeply a part is mostly a town of his memory. That town had more in common with the town of 1800 than with that of 2021. Once Walt's generation goes, there will be no memory of that Killingworth. Its habits of self-governance will also be gone.

An Unbridgeable Gap

In 2016, I was shocked by an exchange I had with Francesco Lulaj as I left his restaurant. He told me he was unhappy with his choices in the Republican presidential primary. When I responded that he might want to consider voting for Hillary Clinton, he looked at me as if I had asked him to consider cutting off his own right hand. When I pressed him on why this was an outrageous suggestion, he explained that he could not vote for Clinton because she is a "murderer." I thought this a bizarre statement. Now I understand that he had most likely received endless messages designed to normalize this belief. Hillary had become "Killary" because this was how right-wing social media, including Russian bots, referred to her. Francesco was probably the willing victim of an unlawful Russian effort to influence the American election through lies—"willing" because he, like many others, kept clicking long after the message left the domain of plausible belief.

The deeper point, however, is that plausible belief no longer looks the same on the right as on the left. This became a vivid political problem in the 2016 election. Right-wing media attacks included claims so outlandish that they struck *New York Times* readers as too absurd to entertain. Yet from the birther movement to the alleged pedophilia ring run out of a Washington pizzeria, they were taken seriously by large groups of voters.[29] In 2020, the right generated a torrent of stories, comments, and allegations that convinced most Republicans that the outcome of the presidential election was fraudulent. Neither the judges who rejected the claims as without evidence nor the election officials—including Republicans—who certified the results were able to persuade Trump's supporters that these claims were nonsense. They took it upon themselves to try to stop the electoral vote count in Congress by invading the Capitol.

When fictions become facts, compromise between parties becomes far more difficult. If, for example, climate change is not occurring, it makes no sense to address it in any way. This is quite different from debating alternative policies of remediation. If there is no structural racism, there is nothing to redress and certainly no discussion to be had about reparations. Similarly, if claims of voter fraud are fictions, there can be no agreement on forming committees to investigate.

The right's confusion of fictions with fact is not an innocent mistake.[30] It has been cultivated in a politics of entertainment for the purpose of assaulting an entire structure of authority that arose out of and supported a national public opinion. For a large share of the electorate, that attack has succeeded. Factual claims that they do not like are now labeled "fake news." This term once had a clear meaning: divisive propaganda made to look like factual journalism. Now it refers vaguely to any inconvenient information that emanates from the traditional sources of opinion formation.

Charges of fake news are not efforts to get to "the truth of the matter." Rather, they are efforts to discredit information sources. They divide the news media into friends and enemies, and from enemies there is nothing to learn. Democratic procedures are well suited to deal with controversies over how to respond to facts. They are not suited to settling questions of fact. We do not decide what is true by counting votes. When an electorate insists that it has the authority to decide issues of fact, its decisions will no longer be seen as legitimate by the opposition. In the 2020 campaign, this intersection of fact and opinion reached an extreme in the chants at Trump rallies to "Fire Fauci," the director of the National Institute of Allergy and Infectious Diseases. His effort to set out the epidemiological facts of the pandemic were labeled "fake news."

Public opinion in Killingworth today tracks the national division. How could it be otherwise, when polarization fills the media? With television, it is Fox News versus MSNBC, and then everybody else. Fox is winning this competition: its news programs are the most watched.[31] A similar division occurs with radio, which continues to have an outsized effect because so many people commute to work. The effects of those choices are amplified on social media. On Facebook, residents "friend" Catherine in order to send her stories about violent conspiracies that are well beyond anything I can imagine. They think she needs to know about pedophilia rings, communist conspiracies, and liberal threats of a violent coup. These residents are not just keeping their first selectman up to date, they are also arming themselves. Catherine signs a steady stream of concealed weapon permits.

These beliefs represent the penetration of the local by national media sources. As these sources grow, common sense declines. Politics based on fiction is wide open to conspiracy theories that range from claims that all laws passed after 1868 are invalid to unsupported claims of missing funds at town hall.[32] Released from facts, politics becomes at once comic and tragic. Or, more accurately, it is comedy until it becomes tragedy, when someone arrives with a gun or a mob bursts into the Capitol. Compare this to the solid grounding of local public opinion in the discussion of the Venuti property. The advantage of local politics used to be that we knew what we were talking about. Once the local becomes a site for national confrontation, we lose that advantage.

Our deeply divided national politics looks a good deal like a religious conflict. Sectarian divisions cannot be resolved through appeals to expertise. What could I have said to Francesco when he told me Clinton was a murderer? Had I directed him to other news sources, it is likely he would have dismissed them as "fake news." He was like Creationists who offer Genesis as proof to their secular neighbors. Telling them to read Darwin will not change their beliefs. The rabbi is not going to convert the Catholic parishioner. Little could I imagine in 2016 that Francesco would be the Republican candidate against Catherine just three years later. In 2016, I still thought of Fred as the face of the local Republican Party. He stood for self-government through local public opinion—that is, for common sense.

Public Character and Public Opinion

Killingworth depends on the public-mindedness of its residents, for they must take up the burden of volunteering. This requires mutual trust and respect; it requires that we all live in the same world of public opinion. Few Killingworth residents believe that town officials practice corruption in the form of kickbacks or misuse of public funds. Such cases happen, but they are very rare. Many residents, however, have a sense that "the system is corrupt," by which they mean that those running the town pursue projects to suit themselves and "their people." This suspicion is the same sentiment as that successfully directed at the national government by populist forces. It easily generalizes because it is based on beliefs about human nature—given power, individuals will use it to their own advantage. This belief is the ground of all conspiracy theories. Commentators on both the right and the left put it forward as if they were speaking truth to power.

We should not imagine that political debate was ever a neutral inquiry into facts. Debate is better thought of as a form of action than as a form of inquiry. It is persuasion, not proof. Politicians offer narratives of hope, anger, progress, and distress. These are matters of public opinion, not fact, but this does not make facts irrelevant. An informed and reasonable electorate will reject narratives that fail to correspond to what they know to be true. When the direction of transmission was from the local to the national, the common sense of a community could ground the entire enterprise. As opinion has come unmoored from lived experience, it has become a wide-open field for propaganda.

Politics is not science, but when the politician accuses climate scientists of perpetrating a hoax, politics has taken a pathological turn. The question for us as citizens is, "Why is this person attacking scientists?" The politician can argue that we should do nothing in response to a changing climate; he or she can argue that God will protect us or that some future discovery will cure the problem. These are matters that citizens can judge according to their own beliefs. But by attacking the scientist, a politician shows a lack of character. A population unable to see the difference between choosing to do nothing and attacking the scientist's good faith—especially when the finding comes not from one scientist but from thousands, employing many strands of evidence and expressing near unanimity—is failing at its own democratic responsibilities.

Citizens must decide to whom they are willing to entrust public responsibilities. Absent character, democracy does not produce results that deserve our respect. When the people elect a demagogue, they have become a mob. The right attitude to take toward figures like Recep Tayyip Erdoğan, Viktor Orbán, and Donald Trump is not respect for the fact of their election but protest at what they have done to democracy. In 2020, Joe Biden won the presidency after a campaign centered on his own character. He campaigned as a person who could be trusted. Trump immediately turned to conspiracy theories to challenge his loss. He demonstrated a lack of character, yet millions followed him.

I suspect that many of Trump's supporters are not misled by his endless misrepresentations. That they are victims of mistaken belief is what liberals hope. Mistakes about facts, they believe, can be corrected. This reaction, however, may tell us more about liberals than about populists. Trump's falsehoods work not because they are believed but because they are a test of faith. Trump's supporters make a deliberate choice to suspend disbelief. Forcing this choice is the very point of his misrepresentations. He asks, "Are you with me or with them?" To accept the lie is to join the movement. That truth can be a function of power is hardly a new discovery in the twenty-first century.[33]

Trump's style remains that of an entertainer offering an alternative reality. There was something of the carnival in his campaigns in 2016 and 2020: a mixture of entertainment, nihilism, revenge, and resentment leading to an inversion of ordinary values. His base celebrated a politics of the carnivalesque. Even in office, his favorite forum remained the campaign rally, where speech gave way to acclamation.[34] On January 6, when his supporters burst forth as a mob, there was a moment of surprise for them and for him. No one had any idea what they would actually do; no one had a plan. Instead, the revolution became a moment to take a selfie inside the capitol. This, too, was politics as entertainment— insurrection as reality TV.

In a carnivalesque politics, aligning oneself with falsehood is a test of commitment. An inverted world rejects a culture that privileges expertise. That is the culture of the modern university, the administrative agency, and the institutions of global governance. This culture of global elites rejects claims of privilege based on race, religion, ethnicity, and gender. Members of this elite question nationalism; they believe in meritocracy and due process. They believe politics is serious. To all of this, Trump responds with a loud, "What's in it for me?" By 2016, many Killingworth residents were ready to ask that question as well.

6

Killingworth Disrupted

Drain the Killingworth Swamp.
—Killingworth Conservative Party campaign sign, 2017

LONGTIME RESIDENTS OF KILLINGWORTH recount childhoods lived out of doors. Children traveled among homes by bicycle along unpaved roads. Everyone knew everyone. They were the town's kids.[1] All the adults watched over the children of the neighborhood. Today, there are no children on the streets and few adults at home. The vital connections today are on the internet, and for the most part, they are not local.

Turning inward now means turning to the larger world. Privatization leads to nationalization. Once a haven, the home is now a point of entry to the world. It is no surprise that parents often feel they have more to fear when their children are by themselves in their bedrooms than when they are playing outside. The very meaning of privacy has undergone a shift: no longer alone so much as secret. Private life online can be deeply social—for many, far more social than life in public. It may also be more dangerous, for while it is social, the online world is not a society. A society has rules, traditions, norms, and safeguards. It has ways to police and protect. Killingworth Stompin' Ground has been fighting a virtual civil war over norms of civility and forms of policing. It has become so intense that newly installed administrators insisted on anonymity because their predecessors had received personal threats. One member of the group exclaimed, "Stompin' Ground becomes swampin' ground." This is national polarization disrupting the local community.

When Killingworth residents look out from their homes today, they are likely to look right past their neighbors. There is little within the town's boundaries that stops their gaze. Facebook may connect the world, but it disconnects Killingworth. One hundred years ago, a resident's vision started to blur at the town's boundaries. Today, it is just the opposite: matters within the town appear in a blurred fashion, if at all. If Killingworth is to recover a sense of itself as a self-governing community, it will have to figure out how to shift residents' gaze back to the town. That is a matter of matching interests and information, for we pursue information about what interests us. The challenge is to create the conditions under which a virtuous circle of interest and information can arise.[2]

Participation in local governance, if it is to be something other than an iteration of national politics, requires local knowledge. Once that knowledge was carried in the common sense of the community. In Walt's lifetime, Killingworth has gone from a community of 300 households—many related to each other—to one of 2,700 households—mostly strangers to each other. Unless a resident is directly involved, she or he is unlikely to know what will be discussed at the next meeting of the board of selectmen, let alone that of the inland wetlands commission. She does not know what the land trust is doing or what problems the volunteer fire department confronts. The only way to follow the news is to attend the numerous evening meetings of boards and committees and then to volunteer in multiple service organizations. This would not be following the local news but making it. Tim Gannon, who was already a leader of the Lions Club and the chamber of commerce, says, "Until I got involved with the Parmalee Farm Committee I had really no idea of the workings of the town and where the money went." He had attended various town meetings but had not understood how the pieces of governance fit together or the various processes worked.

There are no media sources to bring these issues to residents' attention. Some information is posted on the town website, but it is not frequently visited and its concern is with the calendar, not the substance. Formal notices are also posted in the *Hartford Courant,* but they have the same problems as those on the town website. Apart from direct involvement, the only means of obtaining information about the issues confronting the town is through contact with friends and neighbors who are directly engaged. But these networks of local associations are weak for the same reasons that local information networks are weak.

The information that circulates on social media often looks like the tail end of a game of telephone. Participants lash out at plans for a crosswalk that do not exist or at a charter amendment to hire a town manager that no one has proposed. Rumors that the town is about to put down a dog in the pound will build up frenetically when there is no such plan. Few investigate to separate reality from fantasy.

Just as national events and issues are more accessible than local ones, so are personal contacts more easily formed and maintained outside the town. Professional associations and friendships with colleagues draw residents out of town. Not so long ago, families connected and formed friendships through their children's schools and sports activities. No doubt there is still some of this, but Catherine and I never saw much of it after our children's first few years of elementary school. It was strongest when they were in day care. I do not hear much about it today apart from very young families—of which there are fewer and fewer in town.

Children's activities today are managed by parents; they are no longer an occasion for casual community building. Serious sports activities, for example, are now more regional than local. Connections among parents can be limited to taking turns carpooling to practices. Parents are concerned about their children's classroom experience, but for the most part that fails to translate into a concern for the town that outlasts their children's time in the classroom. There are exceptions: the O'Sullivans moved from PTO and school board to a wide range of volunteer activities in town; Eileen Blewett, recently elected a selectman, was active in the PTO when her children were in school.

Jennifer Patton, who has two children in the schools, leads the managerial life of the modern parent. She volunteers in the classroom but does not find herself making many friends through the schools. Of sports she says, "Our kids do competition soccer out of Madison and one kid does hockey out of Hamden rink. A lot of our friends are that way." That way means a lot of driving to other towns, a lot of taking care of your own, and a lot of transitory associations. These are not community-building activities. Indeed, Tim Gannon thinks that these "travel teams" and the demands they put on young families are a big reason that parents cannot find the time to volunteer in town. Between travel, commuting, social media, and cell phones, he wonders how anyone can find the time to help out at Parmalee Farm.

The town's civil society organizations remain sites of information exchange. I learn a good deal about local problems when I go to the annual dinners of the firemen and of the ambulance association. I get a somewhat different slant at the Lions Club awards dinner or the Harvest Dinner at the Congregational Church. Of course, the members of these organizations meet regularly, not just at these dinners, but active membership is just not that big. Recall the dimensions of the recent demographic changes in Killingworth. Even the largest civil society groups—the Killingworth Women's Organization and the Lions—together have a participating membership of only about a hundred people.[3] Moreover, their information exchange function is limited by their insistence on avoiding political discussions. Important as they are, they cannot overcome the information gap that has accompanied town growth. They cannot change the pattern of self-contained homes, children not playing out of doors, and long commutes to work. Neighbors no longer have time for each other, in part because they do not think they need each other. Both Walt and Charlie have noticed the change. Both say that after work and family, residents are simply too tired and too busy for public service. Cheryl Fine emphasizes the same point, identifying it as the "big change" in the town: "[Residents] not getting home until six or seven o'clock every night. . . . That [leaves] no time to do anything in town and . . . no way to meet people in town." No doubt these observations also reflect the changing place of women in the workforce.

I was surprised to learn that most local civic organizations have a disdain for politics. The scholars and lawyers who are my colleagues enjoy talking politics and do it whenever we gather. Our graduates will move in and out of government offices, nongovernmental organizations, and private practice. In all these roles, they will have the same concerns and pursue many of the same conversations. In Killingworth, it is quite the opposite. At all of those civil society dinners I attend, it would be deeply inappropriate to bring up anything touching on politics, local or national. Catherine is there on behalf of the town to thank the members for their service. That message is not to be tainted by even bipartisan politics. Killingworth also teaches, however, that politics kept out of the local public square nationalizes and radicalizes.

A few years ago, the head of the library board objected when a new librarian offered to host some of the weekly "coffee with the First Selectman" events at the library. Politics, the board's chair thought, does not belong in a public library. Elected officials appear political, and politics is not public service. Similarly, neither the Lions nor the KWO will invite candidates for office to speak to members, let alone organize a political event. The PTO does not lobby or campaign even when issues directly involving the schools—including the budget—are up for a vote. It is a support group for the classroom. If members want to campaign in support of the school budget referendum, they form a separate political action committee.

In town, political opinion is treated like religious faith: not a subject for public discussion. Imagining politics as partisan contestation of elections, residents see it as antithetical to public-spiritedness. Partisanship suggests self-interest. As election contests become less and less civil, this view gains strength. Oddly, to act in the public interest, one must act without politics. Not discussed, local politics becomes invisible to most residents. It lingers on social media sites against the background noise of national politics, which never recedes.

The only exception to this general separation of the public from the political is the League of Women Voters. The league is nonpartisan, although its concern for participation and good government certainly has a partisan cast these days. I speak to the regional group on occasion. I do not hide my partisan views and have never confronted any opposition. Indeed, I am warmly received. The group, however, is just what one would expect. The meetings draw maybe twenty-five people, few of whom are actually from Killingworth and the great majority of whom are elderly. These are not people who would otherwise be online. They learned their politics in an earlier era, when a two-party system did not mean civil war.

This disdain for politics in the name of serving the public is self-defeating, for it undermines awareness of local self-government. If the Lions Club works on the community park, the food bank supports families in need, and the volunteer firefighters protect homes, residents wonder what the town does for them. If they understand the schools to be the responsibility of a regional district, then the town can seem like little more than the road crew and the dump guys. Everything else becomes invisible. Town hall becomes "the place where one pays one's taxes." Like the doctor's office, it may be necessary, but the less involvement with it the better. Again, like the doctor's office, it is likely to enter our awareness only when something goes wrong.

Ignorance and Alienation

The local information vacuum is strikingly clear during political campaigns. There is no media market in which residents are more than marginal. No one interviews candidates. Killingworth has issues with its schools, with economic development, with preserving open space, with drug use, with town facilities, with workforce management, and now with the response to the pandemic. None of this is discussed anywhere in the media—print or electronic, traditional or social.

Most immediately, this absence of local information means people tend to vote their party.[4] Even if formally unaffiliated, most voters align with one national party and stick to it. One resident explained to me that even though he has voted Democratic in every local election he can remember, he registers as an Independent as a sign of his willingness to listen to everyone. Many of the publicly engaged residents distinguish local from national elections, saying that they vote "the candidate, not the party." This may be true of those who actually know the candidates, but that is not many.

Party-line voting is quite evident in town. In every election in which Catherine has participated, one can determine a baseline of party support. The vote totals for the Democrats always cluster around that number. For example, in 2015, she received 1,088 votes. Lou, her running mate for selectman, received 1,096, and the Democratic candidates for treasurer and tax collector received 1,037 and 1,102, respectively. It takes a strong personal connection for people to make an exception to their practice of voting for a party.

Party identification may be all the voters know about local candidates. The meaning of that identification, however, is formed through polarized, national political campaigns that have little to do with local issues.[5] Because there is little to counter the influence of the national media, town politics easily becomes a site for the replay of national political drama. The single most important determinant of votes in a local, contested election may be attitudes toward the President, that is, attitudes toward that element of our politics most distant from the life of the town.[6] Catherine saw this work to her advantage in the election of 2019. The Republicans mounted their strongest effort ever to displace her. They had good reason to think they could succeed, since Fred had lost by fewer than two hundred votes in the previous cycle—a number less than that drawn off by the Killingworth Conservative Party. What the Republicans had not counted on, however, was that anger with President Trump would result in a 25 percent increase in voter participation.

From the perspective of a robust Tocquevillian ideal of local self-government, the problem is not just a lack of knowledge about local issues. There is a more general lack of knowledge of persons and offices. Informed Killingworth residents are able to identify their national representative and senators. They know the name of the governor. After that it is pretty much darkness. With respect to town officers, I would be thoroughly surprised if half the residents know the name of the first selectman.

Residents have no idea of who is responsible for what in the town or even what falls within the town's responsibilities and what they must do for themselves. Walt speaks of residents calling to complain of water and sewage service in a town where everyone is on their own well and septic system. Residents don't know who assesses their property or how that process works. They do not know that there is an independently elected board of finance with responsibility for the budget. When power lines go down in a storm, residents call town hall, not the power company. When the library terminates a longtime employee, residents want to hold Catherine accountable, as if the library were a department at town hall. Some residents live on state roads; they do not understand that it is the state's, not the town's, responsibility to maintain them. Developers know the office of the building inspector, but homeowners making improvements generally know nothing of the permitting process. Residents know there is a volunteer fire company, but they have no idea how or whether it is supported by the town. Most do not know how to join or what that would entail. I certainly don't know, and I tend to pay attention.

Residents generally have little idea of what anything costs, the size of the budget, or where their taxes go. They often think their taxes have gone up even when they have not. They confuse changes in the mill rate with changes in their taxes. The mill rate will increase if property assessments go down, just to keep the actual tax burden the same. Town budgets of a hundred years ago were immediately understandable: they listed amounts paid to townspeople for local services. The charges were for teachers, firewood, building materials, road repairs, and direct assistance to the poor. Today, budgets are complex, reflecting the multiple regulatory structures within which the town operates. In the 2019 budget, for example, there were seven different entries for insurance programs and five separate entries for information technology network support. The few people who show up at the Town Meeting to contest some budget items can appear less as concerned citizens than as outliers and cranks.

Residents know little of the town's plans for future development, the often-contentious relationship with the state, the problems the schools face as the number of children in town declines, or the negotiations with the municipal employees' unions. This information is not secret, but neither is it easily available. None of it is discussed by any media source to which there is regular and easy access. Little of it appears on social media sites. None of it finds its way into the political party positions or discussions within or across parties.

I cannot identify any local issue in recent years on which the parties took different positions. This is a strength and a weakness. It is a strength in the ordinary operation of our government institutions: members of different parties work together. Those who volunteer to staff the committees and offices frequently point to this as an attractive feature of public service. It is, nevertheless, a weakness in the broader political life of the town. Absent contestation over issues, there is little to promote interest and information among those residents who are not already engaged. In their ignorance about the town's problems, plans, office holders, and projects, residents' knowledge of town governance may come down to one thing: their tax bill. The absence of robust local debate, moreover, leaves an open field for the national debate—red versus blue—to shape town politics.

Ignorance of the actual workings of government exists at every level. Citizens notoriously overestimate how much of the federal budget goes to foreign aid or to social welfare programs.[7] How many citizens know how a law is enacted in Washington, understand the difference between state and federal courts, or can explain the role of administrative agencies? Law students require three years of intense study to begin to grasp these institutions and their roles. Ignorance about state and national government, however, occurs within a context of representative democracy. We elect representatives who develop the necessary expertise and staff to deal with issues and procedures we do not understand. We rely on political parties to set out the general contours of policy choices that voters can consider when deciding whom to support. We hold—or should hold—representatives and their parties accountable for the results; we do not try to govern ourselves.[8]

These mechanisms of accountability are absent from local government. In Killingworth, government is not representative, and the political parties have little role in shaping policy. Town residents are the legislators; regulation is self-regulation. Holding accountable means participating in local governance. There is no party that will do the voters' work for them. Can self-government remain a realistic possibility without knowledge of issues, offices, and procedures?

The stakes, moreover, are not limited to the quality of local governance. Representative government is unlikely to succeed anywhere if there is not actual self-government somewhere in our political system. If we are never more than voters, we take on a political role rather like that of stockholders delegating all decisions to company management. We focus only on the return on our investment—what we get for our tax dollars. When we lose contact with actual responsibility for governing at least some small part of our community, we become easy marks for the politics of entertainment.

Successful democracy requires common sense. Walt thinks one gains common sense by working the land. This is no longer a realistic possibility for most people, but the general point remains. One gains common sense only through some sort of anchoring practice that demands more than passing judgment on representatives. Speaking to this problem, Robert Putnam turns to John Dewey: "'Fraternity, liberty and equality isolated from communal life are hopeless abstractions. . . . Democracy must begin at home, and its home is the neighborly community.'" "'Only in local, face-to-face associations,'" adds Dewey's biographer Robert Westbrook, "'could members of a public participate in dialogues with their fellows, and such dialogues were crucial to the formation and organization of the public.'"[9]

For much of the twentieth century, the most visible anchor of democratic citizenship was conscription. The possibility of military service for self and family members focused the mind on the seriousness of politics. What forces us to be serious about politics today? Where do we act together as citizens, if not in governing ourselves locally?

Participation is not just a means to an end; it is education in citizenship. It is learning by doing. Participation teaches the value of politics in a full and meaningful life. It teaches the value of what Hannah Arendt called "public happiness," which is something we enjoy together or not at all.[10] The veterans I meet in town always speak of their years of service, whatever the personal burden, as among the most meaningful in their lives.[11] They achieved, then, a public happiness that many carry forward to a sense of public service for the town. For them, Catherine's most important achievement has been the creation of a veterans' memorial in front of town hall.

Without a commitment to participation, democracy means judging how well others are governing us. Instead of together providing for ourselves, we become consumers of government-provided goods. Regardless of whether the good is highways or hiking trails, we lose the experience of citizens mutually engaged in creating and maintaining a community. We become instead competitors for government benefits. We become suspicious of those who benefit when we do not. Absent participation, we may forget—or never learn—that politics requires openness to difference and a willingness to work with those with whom we disagree. Reduced to passing judgment on our representatives, citizens lose the experience of being held accountable to and by other citizens. Engaged and responsible locally, citizens confront the necessity of working together, of compromising and persuading. That is the pull of common sense. Absent that, we can fall victim to public nonsense.

With respect to national and state government, voting is the beginning and end of most citizens' political participation. A republic of voters, however, may not be much of a republic.[12] Voting becomes a mechanism for decision rather than an element within a larger process of participatory self-government. When the voters who supported a losing candidate do not see themselves represented by the winning candidate, the ideal of democratic self-government has died. Government no longer represents the people but only a faction, even as it has legal authority to decide on matters of public concern.

Local Politics as a Vocation

The absence of local media would not have been a problem when word of mouth was an effective form of communication in town. Residents grew up knowing who had authority and who took responsibility. To know the town was to know not just how it worked but also one's own role. This was the point of frequent elections and multiple offices. Over the course of a life, one could expect to rotate through many offices, as neighbors took turns.

The career of Rick Albrecht, who died in 2018, provides an example.[13] Rick had lived in Killingworth since childhood. Military service was the only extended period when he was away. He served on the board of selectmen for eight years, including two years as first selectman. Over a twenty-year period, he was repeatedly elected to the board of assessment appeals, often serving as chair. He was the town's representative to the regional water authority and the town's open burning official, supervising fires residents use to eliminate brush. He served repeatedly as assistant Democratic registrar. For decades, he was always elected moderator at Town Meetings. He was effectively the town parliamentarian and may have been the only person who understood the rules by which these meetings are run. He served for decades on the Democratic town committee, which he regularly chaired. He was a fifty-year member of the volunteer fire company and served more than forty years with the ambulance association. He was a deacon of the Congregational Church, commander of the Veterans of Foreign Wars, and the organizer and leader of the annual Memorial Day services. His official positions extended to state functions as well, serving as a deputy sheriff of the county and a state marshal. Even in his private life, he seemed bound to the town: he was self-employed, running a small business out of his home. He knew firsthand the past sixty years of town history, including who had done what to whom. He did not know all of the town's residents, but he knew everyone who participated in the life of the town. Along with everything else, he was a bit of a town gossip.

In this life of public service, Rick followed in the footsteps of his father, Walter. Civic responsibility in town often ran in families. Walter served on the board of selectmen, was elected town assessor for twenty-eight years, and served as zoning officer for ten years. He also served as the truant officer and as special constable for the Connecticut Water Company. He was a founder of the ambulance association. He served in virtually every position, including chief, in the volunteer fire company. He created something called the Killingworth Civil Defense Auxiliary Police, which remains today as the "auxiliary police" in the fire company—those who direct traffic around an incident. He was a member and sometimes chair of the Democratic town committee, as well as a life member of the VFW. Surprisingly, this committed Democrat received the GOP Citizen Award in 1975. It is unimaginable that his son could have followed in this, for that sort of bipartisanship no longer exists. Perhaps most telling of all is that when Walter died, at age ninety-one in 2010, all of his surviving children lived in town but none of his grandchildren did.[14] Public participation is no longer passed on within families.

Walter's and Rick's lives are evidence of the easy movement, over many decades, among positions in town government, political party, civil society, and church. Into the twenty-first century, they led lives typical of Killingworth before the postwar boom, suburbanization, and nationalization. Other leaders of Rick's generation had the same vocation. John McMahon, who died about the same time as Rick, lived here thirty-four years. I knew him as chair of the board of finance, on which he served for close to twenty years. He also served as president of the Lions, chair of the Killingworth Scholarship Association, and chair of the town Republicans. He was a member of board of youth and family services, the housing partnership committee, the Killingworth Foundation, and the scholarship association. Bruce Dodson, a forty-five-year resident, is another example. He has been chair of the zoning board of appeals—the place one goes for a variance—for twenty-five years. He has held all of the leadership positions of the Killingworth Land Conservation Trust, has been a member of the town's open space and Parmalee Farm steering committees, president of the Lions, and director of the historical society. Tom Lentz, who moved to Killingworth in the mid-1960s, has been chair of the planning and zoning commission for decades. He is also the Municipal Historian and author of several books and pamphlets about the history of the town. Bruce and Tom exemplify the way in which concern for the town's land is also concern for its history. Conservation and preservation go hand-in-hand as aspects of self-governance.

There was no sharp break in the ethos of volunteerism with the arrival of new residents in the 1960s and 1970s. This was the generation of Charlie, Joan, John, Bruce, and Tom. They embraced participation, not autonomy. The McMansions came later, along with a new lifestyle. That early generation is now withdrawing from public service. Most of those participating in self-government today do not have the town as their vocation. They may be no less dedicated, but they do not have the range of experience and knowledge that comes with decades of involvement.

Catherine had lived here less than fifteen years when she became first selectman in 2009. She had served one term as a selectman and part of a term on the board of finance. Not yet deeply of the town, she had to learn on the job. For most of the time she has served, the other two selectmen were Fred Dudek and Lou Anino. Both grew up here; both came from families dedicated to public service. Fred has since retired. Lou may be the last of the intergenerational volunteers. His father, Lou Sr., served as a selectman for twelve years, as well as on the board of finance, the board of assessment appeals, and many other committees and commissions.

The town's future is not with the next generation of Albrechts, Anninos, or Adametzes. It is rather with volunteers like Suzanne Sack, now in her fifth year as a member of the school board. She and her husband, Dave, bought a home in Killingworth about the same time we did. Originally it was their second home. That changed when her office moved from New York to Boston. Only after she retired in 2009 did she become seriously involved with the town. She brings to the school board twenty-five years of experience in financial services, including time as president of a regional bank. Eileen Blewett, a selectman, has also lived in town about twenty years. She, too, started her professional life in the finance industry but left it to raise four children in Killingworth. Active in the PTO, scouts, and school programs, she was elected to the school board in 2017. This is all to Killingworth's advantage. The town needs people like Suzanne and Eileen if it is to survive. But it cannot rely on the informal information networks that once produced a lifetime of service from families bound to the town.

Political Parties as Information Networks

Robust political parties might provide a local information anchor. Both Walter and Rick Albrecht played major roles in the Democratic Party; John McMahon served as chair of the Republican town committee. Again, however, the future is more likely represented by Suzanne, who is an Independent. Unaffiliated voters are now the largest group in town.[15] Unless the parties reconsider their roles, they will likely continue to shrink. If they do grow, it will be to bring national battles to Killingworth politics.

Party identification once served to transmit information to local voters. It signaled who, at the state and national levels, could be trusted to advance their interests.[16] At the local level, voters did not need such signals because they had direct experience. The parties linked that experience to the further reaches of government. They transmitted information from the top to the bottom but drew their energy from below. One version of this was Tammany Hall in New York or the Daley operation in Chicago. In both cities, ward captains practiced a politics attentive to local interests.[17] One reason the Tea Party was so effective in its early years was that it drew energy from the local and directed it to the national: recall all those pictures of members taking over town hall events.[18]

Party identification increasingly aligns on local, state, and national levels.[19] Citizens vote the party ticket as an act of national partisanship. That means that the parties have little need to consider local issues or differences among communities. When the parties appear locally, they campaign on national issues. For the most part, however, the state and national party organizations simply ignore Killingworth. When I asked the liaison of the state Democratic Party how he kept himself informed of local news, controversies, and persons, he had no idea how to respond. It had not occurred to him that this might be part of his responsibility. When I asked what resources he could contribute to local politics, he offered generalities about conveying information about the state party. Perhaps he could, but the state party's agenda has little to do with the problems of governance in Killingworth.

State parties can ignore local politics today because they have direct access to voters via the internet, social media, direct mail, and phone solicitations. In turn, the local parties have little interest or involvement in state issues. For most town residents, state politics—beyond the race for governor—is even less interesting and more opaque than local politics. Virtually no one follows the work of the state house.

The parties become most visible during a presidential election campaign, which is also the moment of maximum polarization. Voters know their party identity primarily through the presidential candidates. Everything else follows from that. Except for empty slogans like "Drain the Killingworth Swamp," no one tries to relate the candidates' national messages to local issues. The town and the parties become sites and players in the national campaigns.

Many voters are unaffiliated because they are put off by the intense polarization of the national parties. Decrying party affiliation, they think of themselves as open to a wide array of candidates, each of whom must be evaluated on the merits.[20] Their rejection of parties, however, is deeply problematic for the town's future. Acting as if they are shopping for candidates, they fail to realize that, as citizens, they are also responsible for running the store and even creating the merchandise. Candidates do not come from nowhere; they must be identified, persuaded to run, and trained to govern. This has been the work of the parties. A successful party takes responsibility for conveying the public life of the town to the next generation. Who else is going to do this?

Informing the Voters: Old and New Media

Campaigns for town offices begin with the problem of how to communicate to voters in the absence of local media. The community's rural character makes it difficult to walk door to door in most neighborhoods. Nor is there a shopping district where candidates might find a concentration of voters. The only site at which residents regularly gather is the town dump, where many Killingworth residents bring their trash on Saturday mornings. Candidates for office stand at the exit. As residents drive out, they see campaign signs; some stop to grab a leaflet, and a few stop to talk.

Other than that, communication usually consists of a mailed brochure and lawn signs. Only in the election of 2017 did the candidates begin to explore online advertising. In 2019, the Republican candidate for first selectman seriously invested in this form of communication. Despite the expenditure, he lost the race. If online ads are to have an impact on local elections, they will have to be tailored to target particular voters. This will require professional skills that, so far, are out of reach of local candidates.

Killingworth has always been too small to support its own dedicated media. But just three decades ago, there was still a vigorous regional press in the three cities that define the triangle within which Killingworth sits: Hartford, New Haven, and New London. The *Hartford Courant,* the oldest continuously published newspaper in the country, provided extensive reporting of politics in the state capitol.[21] New Haven has had the *New Haven Register* since 1812, and New London, the *Day* since 1881. All three covered state and local politics; all thrived right into the 1980s. Killingworth fell within the coverage areas of all three. Reading these dailies, a resident could feel that the community was enmeshed in state and regional issues. These newspapers mostly relied on the wire services or ownership networks for national and international news, but all had reporters with state and regional beats.

Today, all three papers are shadows of their former selves. The *Courant*'s news staff is a quarter of what it once was and may be shrinking further. The *Register* barely survived bankruptcy. For the most part, it now carries stories from the national wires and some local sports.[22] Unlike the others, the *Day* has an endowed trust to support its work.[23] Its circulation nevertheless dropped by a third from the mid-1980s to 2010. Financial support cannot create readers where there is little interest. None of these papers now offers serious coverage of small towns like Killingworth or even of state politics. When Catherine first took office in 2009, the *New Haven Register* still had a reporter whose beat included Killingworth. That did not survive her first term. I have never seen a reporter from any of these papers at a town meeting or event. Catherine gets calls from reporters only when there has been a major accident or fire in town.

In place of these three distinguished dailies, there is now a single weekly, the *Source*—a freesheet published out of nearby Madison. Its focus is boosterism for Madison businesses. Again, Killingworth appears only when tragedy strikes. The paper's one contribution to Killingworth politics is to carry a few letters to the editor before an election. Sometimes there is an exchange of views, but it will not publish anything "negative" in the two weeks before an election. There is no independent coverage of campaigns, let alone of ordinary public controversies.[24]

Killingworth went online at the turn of the millennium. It is possible to imagine a social media response to the withdrawal of local newspaper coverage. Facebook, after all, began as a way for college students on a single campus to communicate with each other, and the town is a bit like a campus.[25] From the perspective of the town as a residential community, some of this online communication has happened: there is a continuous flow of information about missing pets and recommended plumbers. From the perspective of the town as a site of self-government, however, it has not happened. Instead of helping to reconstruct local politics, social media have damaged it further, accelerating the movement toward privatization and contributing to nationalization.

Several online sites have tried to fill the local media vacuum. The first was by far the most successful: *Killingworth Today*. Maintained by Peg Scofield, a resident with professional website design experience, it lasted more than ten years, starting in 2003. Peg thought of herself as a journalist with a local beat and was a genuine source of local news. She provided access to the important town meetings and discussions. When she covered meetings, she did not hesitate to ask questions and demand clarifications. She says that she tried to get "into the nuts and bolts" of local issues. She covered local elections and candidates in the same way, asking questions of candidates and posting their responses. The site also allowed residents to exchange views, but it did not allow them merely "to throw out comments without accountability"—her complaint against Facebook. Because she actively managed the site, it did not fall victim to trolling.

Killingworth Today offered an example of what social media might contribute to local governance. It aimed for civility and objectivity. Nevertheless, it failed from lack of interest and support. Peg took up the project for a mix of professional and personal reasons. Philosophically, she is of the view that "everything is local." She sought passionately "to bring more people into this local world of politics." Her goal, she told me, was "to be inside [local government] and also to be able to let other people know what was going on. Like why were decisions being made the way they were. . . . There's an awful lot going on that you're not aware of but it's super interesting, and you can get involved." Her ability to take up this project, however, depended upon the contingencies of her own career path. *Killingworth Today* shut down when she went to work full-time out of town. As a news operation, it was a one-person production; no one volunteered to help.

Acting as a reporter—the lone reporter covering the town—Peg made a difference. "People," she says, "were more informed." I can attest to that, for I was a regular reader. But despite its success, there was no economic model by which the site could survive independently of her volunteer efforts. Peg thinks "people stopped appreciating any of it. They didn't realize how much effort it took." They were certainly not willing to support it. She would love to see something like *Killingworth Today* come back, but she is not hopeful, for "there is zero interest among younger people." Of Killingworth politics, she says that "the Old Guard is gone and there is no New Guard." Everyone, it seems, has moved on to a Facebook-driven world.

As she describes it, that is also a world of privatization. Today, she thinks that even the traditional power centers in town—like the chamber of commerce—are filling with people who have no interest in volunteering for public service. Peg personally experienced the synergy between volunteering and building a career. She thinks that message has been lost today. The current attitude is one of "I just want to do my job. I don't necessarily want to do anything outside." She also notes that ten years ago there were sixty residents actively volunteering at town hall, while today she puts it at forty.

The more recent Facebook site, Killingworth Stompin' Ground, has become as much an object of the news as a site for exchange of news. Brandy Richards, a Democrat, and Amanda, a registered Republican who describes herself as a libertarian, started the site in 2015. They wanted a site for friendly exchange on issues and events of interest to the community. They were both new to town and came up with the idea after a KWO meeting. They were not thinking of politics; they invited their friends from the KWO to join. Quickly, they had 250 members. Because Brandy and Amanda had not anticipated political controversy, the site literally had no rules for the first few years, beyond what Amanda describes as the "Don't be a dick" rule. Members could "flag" posts they thought inappropriate. The administrators would review them and take down those that they thought were not "helpful in any way" or used offensive language. Brandy says they asked, "Does it create conversation or community?"

There was no need for rules until the 2017 local elections. By then, the site had a thousand members. Some of them began to follow the model of the Trump campaign of 2016. According to Brandy, "Folks were being pretty outrageous with some of their comments." She continues, "I think some people felt empowered by the national election to have . . . their opinions out there on the stage. [It was] microactivism."

In 2017, while the site was being hit with the new Trumpian style of personal assault, Brandy was also managing Catherine's reelection campaign. She was quite aware of the possible conflict of interest. The site's response was to adopt a rule of no political endorsements for either party. Town issues could be discussed, but candidates could not be endorsed. Brandy, who was always more active in monitoring and removing than Amanda, says she tried to be even-handed in administering the site. Nevertheless, most of the offending posts were coming from the right: "It was pretty clear by just glancing at their own personal walls on Facebook . . . that they were more Trump leaning." Pretty soon, Brandy, who was known as a liberal Democrat, became the object of vicious personal attacks.

The battles of 2017 turned out to be just a warmup to those of 2019, when things became, according to both Amanda and Brandy, "dramatically uglier." In the years in between—the central years of the Trump administration—Brandy found that "people became more and more emboldened." Amanda describes that as a period in which users had become comfortable with their internet persona. She says that by 2019 the site they had created had "become a beast."

Brandy had, by the time of the 2019 election, moved from town. Theirs is a military family, and they were sent to a foreign posting. Under the military's rules, however, she could remain a voter in Killingworth. She wanted to stay involved with the site through the election, both to protect the site's integrity and to protect Catherine from malicious attack. Again, the site tried to enforce a "no endorsements" policy, but now monitoring was a "full time occupation." Brandy would turn off comments on a post when they became particularly vicious. In response, participants would, according to Amanda, "jump down her throat." Threats were made. Amanda says that "psychos" started showing up at Brandy's old house.

Amanda emphasizes that the personal attacks came from both sides. To me, it seems that Brandy was attacked by the right, while Amanda was attacked by the left. Brandy left after the 2019 election but remains an object of attack on the site. Some of the postings express a sense of victory for having driven her

away. By December 2020, Amanda was driven out. She cut all of her connections to the site because of baseless attacks accusing her of racism grounded in
her "white woman's privilege." Amanda, who is married to a person of Filipino
descent and was in the process of adopting a mixed-race child, had had enough.
She summed up her feelings about the site at the time of her departure: "They
can burn." The posters, she thought, were going after her family and soon would
be going after her business.

With the departure of the founders, new administrators were immediately
mired in their own controversy. Some moderators that Brandy and Amanda had
brought in tried to impose a liberal perspective on the site. Amanda criticizes
them for trying "to control the conversation." They did not last. The new administrators again tried to enforce civility under rules that included the following:
"There IS ZERO TOLERANCE FOR BIGOTRY OR DISCRIMINATION OF ANY KIND. This includes denials of systemic racism, use of the phrase "all lives matter," and ho-
mophobia, as well as personal attacks and threats." They prohibited "excessive
partisanship, hate speech, and bullying." Publication of these rules led to new
charges of partisan censorship. The charges were again relentless, and again threats
emerged. The new administrators, too, lasted only a few months. When they
resigned, one offered this explanation: "I am not bothered by messages I received
accusing me of being racist but what you don't see is the number of people
posting publicly about the admins being racists, being bigots, being xenophobes,
etc. You don't see the messages we receive saying people are going to go after
our jobs and contact our bosses or boycott admin owned businesses."

As of this writing, the site is on its third set of administrators who insist on
remaining anonymous because of the history of personal threats. The controversial rules have been withdrawn. The new rules seem to permit open political
combat respecting "local government, and issues that affect Killingworth." The
new standard is "good faith" under the admonition, "Do not make things political that do not need to be political." Under these rules, trolling has become
a regular phenomenon. Many users, weary of the continued vitriol, want all
politics—even all expressions of opinion—eliminated from the site.

Some members feel that the site moved from leaning left in the 2019 election
cycle to leaning right today. Those objecting to the former created a new Facebook site, Killingworth Connection, in November 2019; those objecting to the
latter created a new site, HK Progressives, in December 2020, also on Facebook. Killingworth Connection, I'm told, is fading as its members drift back to

Stompin' Ground, now that it is under new administrators. Members of HK Progressives are more and more alienated from Stompin' Ground. One of the founders wrote, "[I] am as disgusted as all of you with KSG. It has clearly become a vehicle for a right-wing agenda, and they aren't even trying to hide it anymore. That's why I created this group."[26] She went on to explain:

> Brandy created a wonderful resource for the town that has sadly been recently hijacked by a group with a political agenda. I wanted to create a safe space for those of us who want to connect and share with our community. I am usually one who avoids conflict and doesn't see a need to make things political when they don't need to be. However, at this point in time, we seem to all need to take a stand on our feelings regarding truth, oppression, conspiracy theories, equal rights, etc. Personally, I don't think these should be political issues, but rather moral issues.[27]

Sites and politics are beginning to align. Soon, no one will be talking to others across the line of political polarization. One participant told me that Killingworth Connection could not thrive because its members were all like-minded. They seek confrontation but can find it only in the more diverse membership of Stompin' Ground. Yet this person also worries that continued confrontation will ultimately undermine that site as more members lose patience with the incivility and leave. These seem to be our choices on social media: boring homogeneity or intolerable division.

Local Politics and the New Connectivity

The internet exploded into ordinary life just around the time we moved to Killingworth. It is hard now to remember how unexpected this shift was in the mid-1990s. I recall, for example, a colleague trying to persuade me to create an email account. I could not imagine why I would want such a thing. I told him that when I wanted instant communication with someone, I used the telephone. Wasn't it better to speak directly to someone than to write to them? I could not envision how email would fit into the social practices of my professional and personal life. One did not write letters to friends and colleagues; one wrote to professionals who were not friends. Was I supposed to start writing to my children instead of talking to them directly? Was I going to have written communications with my assistant? None of this was imaginable; none of it seemed necessary. All of it rapidly became true.

Our first project on moving to Killingworth was to build a study in an old barn. Looking ahead to changing technology, we put in an extra phone line connecting to the house. We thought that at some point we might want a phone line dedicated to electronic communication. That the study would be linked to the world through a wi-fi network and cell phone technology was not on our horizon.

These memories point to the communications revolution—social and technological—of the past two decades. We are now continuously linked to the entire world. That communication is continuous speaks to the intensity of the connection; that it extends to the entire world speaks to the displacement of the local. Both of these characteristics—intensity without a home—undermine the conditions that support the volunteerism upon which self-governance depends.

Continuous Connection

Continuous connection redefines the rhythms of daily life. It breaks down the separation of work from leisure, of office from home. There is no longer such a thing as "after work." It also breaks down the shape of a day, for we are now effectively present in multiple time zones. Communication is felt as a compulsion—a sort of overhanging presence. We are not exactly waiting for a call on the smartphone, as if it were simply a mobile telephone. Rather, we are always in the middle of any number of ongoing communications, only some of which involve dialogue.

Someone is always sending or posting something that is available to us, even if not directed at us. We feel the need to send out a continuous signal that says nothing more than, "I am here." Our phones do this automatically, but it is also the effective content of the endless postings on social networks. In this existential affirmation, pictures are displacing words. Ever more sophisticated technology is producing ever less sophisticated communication. Seeing and being seen: the affirmation of presence is what matters. The most sophisticated technology moves seamlessly toward the most primitive of uses, replicating the exchange of presence that is the sexual encounter.

Continuous connectivity creates a psychology of addiction.[28] We fear that were we to turn away, we might miss something. The worry is not that we will be disadvantaged but that we will not be present. The smartphone has us always looking into the near future; there is no moment of satisfaction in the present. The phone routinizes this shift of attention to what is about to happen by making what just happened banal. Nothing carries weight, nothing is worth lingering over, because it is all ephemeral. It is a moving wall, not a still life. The flicking finger on the screen is the momentum of time.

Online, individuals often relate to each other as reciprocal voyeurs; they look at each other's photo albums. These are not communicative exchanges in which the distinctive presence of the other requires recognition and response. No challenge is posed; no ethical demand is made.[29] This is hardly training for deliberative democracy, which requires discussion among those with different points of view. Cyber friends are usually not political friends in the sense in which I have used the term. Some are actual friends; many share an interest or point of view. But most are not bound to each other politically in a relationship of care across differences of opinion. Absent care, interventions online quickly turn uncivil and hostile. Absent care for the common, little is at stake in attacking others. Exit is always an option, when the exchange stops being entertaining. This is essentially the story of Killingworth Stompin' Ground. It begins as a site for real friends; it fails as a site for political friendship.

The political forums of exchange were once stable, even as participants expressed different opinions—rather like a court that structures controversy in order to reach a decision. Today's cyberforums seem fragile, threatened by the very exchanges they enable. Facebook's "news feed" is just the opposite of the news in a self-governing, political community. It is not a common resource; it is personal, not public. It is designed to entertain, not to inform. Worse, it is designed to addict, to keep the viewer online and clicking.[30] It is not an invitation for mutual engagement over common problems; it is more like a business scheme.

We learned in the 2016 election that an online vehicle designed to sell advertising through entertainment is easily converted into a tool for political manipulation.[31] That Trump governed through Twitter, while assaulting traditional news sources, revealed the ongoing collapse of politics into entertainment. That he still dominated social media in the 2020 election cycle explains why polarization continues as if the two sides lived in entirely different worlds. Effectively, they do.[32] This was even more evident in the postelection period when Trump supporters were continually reinforced in their belief that he had actually won.[33] Everywhere, social media exacerbates political conflict, for everywhere it offers a vehicle to extremists who had previously been marginalized by public opinion.

Facebook, which began as a vehicle for young people to present themselves to each other and "hook up," still bears this origin in its architecture. It trades on an idea of intimacy, of sharing experiences. Making the intimate public, however, does not create a forum of public interest. Instead, it circulates gossip: news as banal entertainment. Social media hardly invented this genre. Local news broadcasting had already moved in this direction. But gossip on social media is politically dangerous, not just because it is easily manipulated, but because it crowds out the news that is a necessary condition of self-government. We are too busy and too preoccupied for politics—or at least for a politics that demands the volunteerism of local self-government. But what are we busy doing when we flick the screen of a smartphone?

Global Connection

For most people today, the smartphone is their vital connection to the world. Without it, they feel lost. But if we are at home in cyberspace, what becomes of our actual hometown? The cyber community that now defines our nature as social beings is a place without borders. It always pushes toward a global reach; it aspires to be everywhere, with the result that it is nowhere. One symbol of this transformation is the changed nature of the area code. It no longer tells us anything about the place from or to which a connection is made. At most, it now figures in a personal history.

Distance no longer makes communication more difficult. There is no advantage in geographical closeness when everywhere is just one click away. Because of this design feature, there is no easy way for a local community to re-create itself on the web. Users can choose to link to other town residents, but what reasons do they have to define an online community geographically? Escape from local borders is exactly what social media and the worldwide web offer. Killingworth Stompin' Ground is for residents of Killingworth, but there is a continual suspicion that some of its postings are from "outsiders." Indeed, Amanda believes that the posters who attacked her personally were not residents.

The political nature of the town was a function of its borders, which were more than lines on a map separating one residential area from another. Politics begins with reciprocal commitments among a limited community. We may express concern for the well-being of all humanity, but a political community has a special regard for its own members. A universal community would be a church, not a polity.[34] Politics cannot begin without drawing a line; it cannot continue in the face of complete ease of exit. Ease of entrance and exit characterize commercial enterprises. When I am unhappy with a restaurant or store, I simply take my business elsewhere.[35] We understand such relationships as private and distinguish them from the public character of politics. I have no obligation of care toward the shopkeeper. In politics, I must care for community members whom I do not personally know.[36] Even more important, I must care for those I know but dislike. Borders define a geography of care for citizens.

Town boundaries were never hard limits; moving has always been an option. But this was never as easy as deciding to shop elsewhere. Family roots in a community made it difficult to leave, as did social, economic, and religious connections. Together, the web of connections grounded residents' sense of responsibility for the place. The more difficult it was to exit, the more one had to invest in cooperation with one's neighbors. To be a resident was literally to be of the town—part of a self-governing community. In Killingworth, we see the ease of exit growing across generations: from Walter Albrecht, whose children all stayed in town, to his grandchildren, who have all left.

The internet offers a costless exit option. Online, one no longer has to leave town to exit the community. Killingworth has lost control of itself as a point of discursive engagement. When the home becomes a portal, its effective address is its IP address, not its postal address. The former is nowhere in particular. It makes little sense even to talk about "exit" from a place that is nowhere. Individuals may at first find the ease of crossing borders—geographic, social, and cultural—to be liberating. Too much border crossing, however, may leave them feeling disempowered. Having nowhere in particular to go can be as disruptive as being unable to get out. A citizen of the world has no political presence whatsoever.[37]

Of course, new communities arise on the web—for example, chat groups or Facebook friends. They are mostly without borders, responsibilities, or authority. They may be communities of sentiment—sometimes strong sentiment—but they have no political responsibilities for which they are accountable. They have no power to tax, to compel, or to regulate those who do not consent. Ordinary politics is work, not entertainment. It requires attention, not distraction; commitment, not escape; and institutions, not mass gatherings.

No doubt some media networks can be meaningful to those who participate. The same, however, is true of some stores or restaurants; it is true of libraries and concert halls. The local bar can create a community; so can the New Haven Symphony Orchestra. But these are not political communities. They make no claim upon me once I withdraw my patronage. The owner of the bar has no commitment to me, only an interest in my business. The same is true of my relationship to the orchestra: making a contribution is not a political act. The wealthy may prefer making contributions to paying taxes, but often that is because they want to be free of political responsibility.

Politically motivated groups do use the web, and strong sentiments cultivated online can fuel political interventions—sometimes dramatically. This has been the story of Trumpism. One cannot disentangle the insurrection of January 6, 2021, from the online agitation about the results of the November election. But we see there as well that the mob could not exercise political authority; they could not even imagine it. This was vivid in the video recording of the mob breaking into the Senate chamber: once there, they seemed aimless.

Generally, cyber movements have a very hard time turning themselves into enduring political communities. This was the lesson of the Arab Spring that began in Tunisia in December 2010.[38] Politics requires institutions, which can develop only in communities with boundaries and citizens who care for each other. Trumpism will survive to the degree that it is able to colonize existing political institutions and organizations—particularly state legislatures, the federal courts, and the Republican Party.

When Killingworth was the site of livelihood and family, residents' connections to the town were as difficult to break as their bonds to the land. They had to defend this place, metaphorically and literally. They also had to take care of each other. I have been told that the very title of the town's elected leader, "Selectman," comes from the responsibility to select the family to which residents without families would be assigned for support and care.[39] In the first decades of the twentieth century, support for the poor—including payments for house repairs, wood, meat, and potatoes—was the town's third highest expense. Federal and state programs have taken over this welfare responsibility, vastly improving the lives of those in need. Still, the question arises of what exactly town residents care about if they no longer need to care for each other. They care about national politics, for that is what they see when they go online or turn to the media.

Into the twentieth century, state law assigned to the selectmen responsibility to walk the town borders to make sure they were well marked and visible along their entire length.[40] Killingworth is not yet as borderless as a cyber community, but its borders have less and less significance, apart from the tax rolls. No one walks them anymore. Most residents are not sure where they lie. Residents are out of town most of the workday (when there is not a pandemic), and when at home they spend far more time in cyberspace than out of doors.

The question is no longer whether most residents are willing to pursue a local politics of self-government. Most are not. They live thoroughly privatized lives in which the fundamental categories of family, work, and entertainment leave no space for the responsibilities of local self-government. They are citizens of the nation with political views shaped by the national debate. When they enter the polling booth, they bring with them the values of the web, whether red or blue. As national citizens, they will continue to vote, but will they volunteer? Killingworth needs citizens who are more than spectators in a politics of entertainment. So does the nation.

A Free Market in Ideas: Debate or Propaganda?

Here are some examples of what our polarized political rhetoric has meant in Killingworth. In a recent election, a large sign went up that said simply, "Where is the missing $500,000?" That sounds as if it were referring to a well-known controversy that had yet to be resolved. In fact, there was no such controversy; the sign referred to nothing. Its entire point was to raise suspicion by directing an accusation at public officials. Anyone reading it might think that they were personally uninformed. They might blame their ignorance on the lack of local media. Such an allegation creates a dilemma: How does one respond without lending credence to the story? For an official to defend his or her own integrity looks defensive; it can suggest that there is something to the accusation. Minimally, any response is likely to increase the circulation of the accusation.

Whoever put up the sign probably learned the technique from a website giving instruction in political dirty tricks. The same technique of inventing an issue is visible in a second example. In 2012, Jerry Lucas—previously a first selectman from the Republican and then the Killingworth First Party—along with Michael Board, a leader of an antitax group, submitted a complaint to the state's attorney, along with a notebook of "forensic evidence," charging Catherine with a conspiracy to defraud and mislead Killingworth taxpayers. The allegations arose out of a plan to lease an old farmhouse at Parmalee Farm to the historical society for one dollar a year—the same arrangement the town has with the library.

Lucas and Board charged that the plan was illegal. They further charged that Catherine and the board of selectmen had withheld information about the costs of renovations from the voters when the issue went to a Town Meeting. Lucas publicly stated, "They [the selectmen] did not want people to know the extent of the cost or future expenses." The complaint alleged a conflict of interest between the town and the historical society. Board announced, "I suspect this is only the beginning of what we're going to discover." The whole submission was a mishmash of accusations written in a way that sounded to me like someone trying to imitate what he or she imagined to be legal language. It was barely readable, but it made the local news, such as it is.[41] In making the charge, Lucas and Board were recycling a technique used fifteen years earlier against school superintendent Charles Sweetman. Allegations of financial improprieties involving insurance policies provided to the superintendent by the board of education led to lawsuits over Freedom of Information Act requests. The state ruled for the board of education on at least two occasions.[42] In 1996, when the superintendent left the district, in the middle of his contract term, "outspoken members of Haddam and Killingworth taxpayer groups, which [had] called for Sweetman's ouster, called his decision to leave a 'victory.'"[43]

Following his own professional rules, the state's attorney would say only that the complaint about the farmhouse had been turned over to the state police to determine whether the allegations merited investigation. Nothing came of that referral. Nothing more was heard from the state. Politically, however, official action may never have been the point. I realized this when I began to hear references to Catherine as someone under criminal investigation by the state's attorney. Again, there is no politically effective way to respond. Denying the allegation simply draws attention to it. Yet silence may suggest that one has no defense. This is accusation without accountability.

These perversions of local political discourse parallel those we saw nationally during Trump's rise to power. The allegation of missing funds looks a good deal like the allegation of a missing birth certificate. The allegation of criminality took national form in the anti-Clinton chant, "Lock her up." Both allegations created the same dilemma of how to respond without inviting a new round of accusations. Deceitful allegations like these undermine the idea that political speech can illuminate issues confronting the community.

Politics has always been a rough game. Yet it was not so rough in Killingworth, where neighbors worked together to maintain the town. The nature and effect of political speech has to be judged within the context in which it is set—including citizen expectations. Until recently, neighbors could speak to each other in a common language. Those who learned their political speech from Rush Limbaugh, Fox News, and Donald Trump are no longer trying to engage their neighbors in conversation. They are often trying to provoke, because that is what gains attention in a world where politics is entertainment.

Killingworth teaches yet another lesson about political speech as constructed outrage: purveyors pay no price. Whether or not they provoke a response, baseless allegations simply trail off without any determinate judgment or measure of accountability. There is no moment at which one must offer an explanation, let alone an apology. When the state's attorney decided to do nothing about the charges against Catherine, there was no moment of acknowledgment by Catherine's accusers. Moreover, the allegations linger in residents' memory as a vague sense of wrongdoing. Twenty-five years after insubstantial allegations of embezzlement were brought against the superintendent, I run into people in town who did not even live here then but "remember" that there was a superintendent engaged in "shady" dealings. They don't know anything but have a sense of "a problem." Those who brought the allegations, meanwhile, had moved on to new targets and new charges.

Often this destructive speech does not even identify an author. Traditionally, we protect anonymous speech with the thought that it allows critics to speak without fear of retaliation from powerful actors.[44] Today, anonymity supports misrepresentation. Rumors can be let loose without accountability. Classical rhetoric taught that speech becomes more effective as we trust the speaker, but that idea of speaker identity has little place on most social media.[45] What do we know about the character of someone who retweets rumors that were deliberately introduced to stoke anger and prejudice? We do not even know if we are viewing the actions of a person or a machine. Today, confidence comes from repetition, not character. Speech, we are learning, is both the beginning and end of democracy.

But is there anything new in this? There have always been two ways of approaching political speech. There was the First Amendment tradition of vigorous public debate as the foundation of enlightened public opinion. Free speech and a free press were to serve as the instruments of investigation and accountability. The thought was that in the exchange of ideas—the marketplace of ideas—truth and justice would win out as speakers were forced to defend their positions in public debate.[46] This view of free speech has always existed alongside a darker view of political speech as propaganda seeking to achieve political ends while bypassing deliberation.[47] As instrumentalized speech, propaganda plays to the passions: it creates an atmosphere of outrage and suspicion that is hostile to reasoned debate. Its end is to persuade without convincing, if by the latter we mean an argument that can withstand critical reflection.[48] Because it is only a means to an end, failed propaganda is replaced by more propaganda, never by a confession of error.

Democratic speech inevitably takes the form of both reasoned argument and propaganda. Thomas Jefferson wrote the Declaration of Independence and founded the University of Virginia; his library formed the initial core of the Library of Congress. He also secretly started the propaganda arm of what became the Democratic Party.[49] Apparently, he thought that the ends justified the means.

No one enters politics indifferent to outcomes; we all have positions that we seek to advance. Political debate is not an academic seminar. The temptation to treat citizens as means to our ends is always there. We all agree that buying votes undermines democracy, but is lying to obtain votes any different? A well-functioning democracy creates an ethos that tempers the urge to deploy propaganda, just as we resist the urge to buy votes. Propaganda untethered from reason builds a mob in place of a citizenry; it should be resisted precisely because we know it is effective.

A well-functioning democracy, therefore, tempers the inclination toward propaganda with a demand for critical, organized exchange. In part, this generates the platforms and policy papers that accompany modern campaigns.[50] A visible image of the continuing interest in organized debates between the candidates is the modern presidential campaign.[51] Of course, the debates are more than opportunities to display reasoned argument. Their impact may turn on a candidate's appearance, confidence, and self-presentation—wholly apart from the quality of the arguments. If the debates become only another site for the exchange of propaganda, they have lost their point.

There is no way to determine the "right" proportion of debate to propaganda in political life. Nevertheless, we should worry that modern communication, with its emphasis on entertainment, is pushing us too far in the direction of propaganda. The critical speech of political debate requires effort, not just from speakers, but from listeners. Extending respect in the form of listening requires us to place ourselves in uncomfortable situations and temporarily suspend judgment.

These are the practices of the classroom, not of social media. Even in the classroom, they are becoming difficult to maintain.

Earlier, I described the 2017 debate organized by the League of Women Voters in which Fred, the Republican candidate, declined to participate. In 2019, the chamber of commerce held a "candidate forum," which they insisted was not a "debate." Only about forty people attended, and virtually all were already committed to a candidate. The tension in the room led to outbursts from the audience. Our choices today seem to be nonparticipation or rampant partisanship. This is politics without friendship. Is it possible to have a local politics that asks less of "Which side are you on?" and more of "How shall we do this together?"

Is anyone listening to anyone else? The point of the communications model offered by Facebook, Instagram, Twitter, and other social media sites is that talk is easy. They all appeal to the quicker passions over reason. The ambition is to attract a crowd, and the way to attract a crowd is to entertain. Indeed, we don't know how much of contemporary politics has become only another merchandising vehicle. Is politics using entertainment to advance an ideology, or is marketing using ideology as entertainment to sell products?

The consequences of the turn toward propaganda and the use of wild allegations of criminality cannot be measured directly. They have certainly helped polarize our local politics. Where Walt remembers a fluid relationship between Republicans and Democrats, with cross-endorsements and candidates switching parties, those relationships are now frozen. In Catherine's first four elections, her vote totals were respectively: 977, 1,017, 1,074, and 1,088. The trend was up but not by much, despite her success in running the town. The Republicans kept losing because their vote was split with the Conservative Party and because they kept running candidates who attracted little interest beyond party stalwarts. In 2017, their strongest candidate, Fred, finally ran. This time, more Republicans came out, but again their vote was split with the Conservative Party. Catherine barely increased her vote total to 1,107, which was less than the total of 1,124 on the right. All of this changed in 2019, when nationalization of local politics did not just mean a stable polarization between Democrats and Republicans but an explosion of Democratic furor at Trump. The local election was now just a skirmish in the national battle. Catherine received 1,570 votes, while her opponents received a total of 1,263 votes. Her vote had increased more than 40 percent, the Republicans' only about 10 percent. Both sides were getting ready for 2020.

Politics, Pornography, and Accountability

Accountability is in short supply today in most forms of public discourse. The political pundit who promotes wildly implausible claims is not dismissed from the public space but may instead gain listeners. The more extreme the charges, the more enthusiastic the audience. When it all turns out to be wrong, the pundit simply moves on to the next wild speculation. Scientists who misrepresent their findings are banished from credible journals. Commentators who misrepresent get lucrative contracts.

When politics becomes entertainment, it is enough that the opinions are held—even if only briefly. Their significance is captured in political polls, which work like Nielsen ratings. No one asks whether the highest rated television shows are meeting some standard of excellence. The only "should" at stake is what advertising should cost in light of the ratings. Similarly, as politics becomes entertainment the idea of reexamination in the face of critique disappears. Fox News does not apologize for what it has said, even after it has paid large sums to settle civil cases.[52] Pointing out lies has little effect: no one expects entertainers to tell the truth. When we do not take arguments seriously, the only question is which side you are on, and the only measure that counts is the size of the audience. This is the attitude toward truth and ratings that Trump personified.

An example of punditry without accountability came to Killingworth shortly after the 2017 election. A few of the Republican town committees in the area, including Killingworth's, held a joint fundraising dinner. Their keynote speaker was Michelle Malkin, who reached national celebrity status by, among other things, arguing in support of the Japanese internment during World War II.[53] Even Congress has apologized for the internment, while the Supreme Court recently overruled the infamous decision upholding the practice.[54] When Catherine publicly criticized this choice of a speaker, the local Republicans predictably accused her of denying them their right to free speech. That such freedom comes with political responsibility for how it is exercised was a thought too far. There is no such thing as responsibility when politics becomes entertainment, but there is no legitimate democratic politics without responsibility.

The fantastical propaganda driving national politics has taken on the form and even the substance of pornography. This has not been limited to the famous *Access Hollywood* tape or Trump's alleged hush-money payments to an adult film star and a Playboy model.[55] The political actions of ordinary citizens are often modeled on behavior learned from online pornography, beginning with spectator anonymity. This anonymity has a dual aspect: it is both voyeuristic and moblike.

The internet is endlessly voyeuristic. One can observe without being observed. While the voyeur always fears exposure, the member of the mob has no such fears, for he is neither exceptional nor alone. He is free to act in ways he would not dare on his own. Cyber porn quickly moved from the relative passivity of voyeurism to aggressive violation that was euphemistically called "commenting." Commentators imagined themselves as part of a mob transgressing ordinary norms of civility.

The practice of commentary as violation has now spread throughout the net. This is what drove both Brandy and Amanda from the site that they created. Any number of ordinary websites, imagining they were creating a space for informed exchange of opinions, have had to take down their comments sections because they were infected by hate speech, sexual aggression, and threats of violence.[56]

The connection between sex, violence, and politics is ancient. Plato tells the story of the Ring of Gyges, which made its wearer invisible. The first thing Gyges did was to have sex with the king's wife; the next was to take his throne. All people, the story teaches, want sex and power. If they can violate the rules without being caught, they will. The internet offers everyone a Ring of Gyges.

The web is the great democratizer of power as a capacity for sexual transgression. It empowers the ordinary person, for voyeurism is not just a fictional image of sexual transgression but itself a transgressive activity. On the web, one need not be King David to have access to Bathsheba. But what does that access do to our political life? For David, taking Bathsheba was the turning point in his political career.[57] From that point forward, we see the dissolution of the moral and familial values that are a necessary condition of successful politics. His children turn on each other in acts of rape and murder; ultimately, they turn on him. If everyone has access to Bathsheba on the web, mob behavior can become the norm of political life.

From the Old Testament to Freud, the message has been that politics depends on controlling sexual desire. But then so does civilization itself.[58] The new forms of transgression run up directly against this ancient insight. What had been inappropriate public behavior becomes imaginable once it has been pursued online. This begins in the pornographic and extends through various forms of commenting and trolling. We need not think that the moral universe is falling apart because of the internet, but we do have to ask whether our online habits are undermining the forms of public life on which self-government relies. What, after all, is QAnon but an extended sexual fantasy projected on to national politics?

Habits of civility cannot be legislated online or anywhere else. They are there as common practices—Tocqueville's "mores"—or they are not there at all. Killingworth is in danger of losing its mores, in no small part because its residents spend so much time online. Absent those mores, shaming is no longer much of a norm-enforcing device.[59] New forms of transgressive politics are possible because local public opinion and civil society, the sources of effective shaming, are dramatically weaker than they once were. Amanda did not think that she could shame those who baselessly attacked her. Rather, she thought that any form of response would just provoke further personal attacks. She thinks it impossible to control this behavior, because people online abandon the mores that still control their behavior in the actual presence of others.

Another sign of the general weakening of public mores was the resurfacing of Jerry Lucas in 2012, beginning with his letter seeking Catherine's indictment over the Parmalee Farm building. Some fifteen years earlier, he lost reelection to the first selectman office after there had been a public report of police intervening in a domestic dispute in which he allegedly hit his wife. Lucas was charged with third-degree assault and breach of the peace.[60] He continued to live in town but without much public presence. He came back as a leader of the party of resentment. As far as I know, there had been no discourse of forgiveness among his followers.

One saw the politics of transgression at Trump rallies in 2016, where actual violence regularly occurred—at times with Trump's encouragement.[61] During his administration, there was a deliberate confusion of public and private violence. Trump could solicit the support of law enforcement while welcoming informal displays of biker and neo-Nazi violence. His speeches were full of innuendo suggesting more violence, particularly if he were denied an electoral victory. This came to national prominence in the first debate of 2020, when, on being challenged to renounce the far-right Proud Boys, he told them to "stand back and stand by."[62] The violence became a reality with the mob's invasion of the Capitol. This was an insurrection incited by a president who thought of politics as just another form of entertainment in which violence and sex drive up ratings.

In Killingworth, too, there was an air of violence in the 2016 election. One saw this most directly in the normalization of vandalism. Entering Killingworth during the campaign, one saw a sea of Trump signs on lawns, alongside the roads, and in public spaces. The effect was striking—it looked as if the entire town were supporting Trump. In fact, virtually no sign expressing support for Clinton could survive more than twenty-four hours. Every night, the signs that had gone up during the day would be stolen. This was not just ordinary adolescent misbehavior; it was orchestrated theft. When did vandalism become normal politics? This behavior went to the very heart of the idea of an election as a public airing of diverse views.

A town that had, for three centuries, modeled politics on debate among neighbors in the Town Meeting suddenly saw the appearance of widespread political aggression. No one knew where the limits now lay or even whether there were any limits. Had campaigning itself become a dangerous activity? Might one be attacked for supporting the Democrat? Might one's home be vandalized, one's children put at risk? By 2019, such threats were being made on Killingworth Stompin' Ground. Political life had become dangerous.

Shortly after the 2016 election, Fox News was dealing with a scandal involving employee allegations of sexual abuse directed at its most powerful figures: Roger Ailes and Bill O'Reilly.[63] From the charges, it appears that each thought his position entitled him to demand sex from employees and that his power provided immunity from any repercussions. Both, it seems, felt free to violate the law; both felt free to destroy the careers of those who might resist them. Over the next year, it became clear that they were not alone in this attitude and that such views are not limited to powerful actors on the right. Many powerful men, in both political parties, apparently thought they had hold of the Ring of Gyges.

Of course, sexual transgression as an abuse of power has always been a problem in institutions, including families, universities, businesses, and government. Its appearance at Fox News might be nothing more than a reminder of the pervasiveness of the problem. But to read it as no more than that is to let Fox off too easily. Fox has made its fortune by cultivating the transgressive politics that now permeates much of American life. In the world of politics as entertainment, O'Reilly is no less a political figure than Trump. His behavior was no different from Trump's. Both linked sex to power; both directed public opinion toward the normalization of transgression. As Killingworth politics nationalized, it, too, confronted patterns of transgression.

Politics as Bullshit

The right-wing media provides an endless stream of political speech not bound by ordinary norms of truthfulness and respect for others. Political speech becomes trolling. Those with whom one disagrees become the enemy, whose motives and intelligence are always questioned. This form of political discourse was modeled by President Trump, who called opponents enemies, the Democratic leader of the Senate a "clown," and the Speaker of the House, "lying Pelosi."

When the opposition is cast as the enemy, a politics of compromise looks like a violation of principle. Hillary Clinton was not the leader of a party with which a victorious Republican Party would have to work. Rather, she should be jailed. Similarly, anything the Obama administration had done was seen as an act of treachery or betrayal, for the enemy never acts to advance our well-being. Thus, we have not just a polarized politics but one in which each party must govern alone. President Biden took office promising to try to end this. The promise was no doubt sincere, but one could reasonably doubt the possibility of success.

More than a decade ago, Killingworth residents started imitating the political speech they heard on right-wing radio and television. They began believing that to speak politically was to speak in the mode of Rush Limbaugh. They were surrounded by Fox News at home, in the shop, and at bars and cafés. In the car, they listened to one right-wing radio host after another. The default mode of political speech became outrage.

While campaigning in 2017, Catherine approached John Samperi, her Conservative Party opponent, and asked why he was saying things about her that she believed he must know to be false. She recalls that he expressed surprise and explained that it was "politics." In 2019, I approached some campaigners standing by a large "Drain the Killingworth Swamp" sign. When I said, "This is insulting to my wife," they sheepishly acknowledged this, as if that was just an unfortunate consequence of political speech. Politics trades in personal insults, they all seemed to think, but is not to be taken personally.

Harry Frankfurt's extraordinarily successful little book *On Bullshit* helps to explain the character of political speech today.[64] Bullshit, he argues, is different from lying. Bullshit is speech without regard for truth. The point is not to represent a state of the world but to create an impression. To lie is to deliberately misrepresent in order to accomplish an end that turns on belief in the truth of the lie. Bullshitters will not bother to defend their claim, for nothing turns on the particular representation. When challenged, they will simply substitute another claim. The game they play is not that of finding the truth but of holding attention. We used to think this a sign of mental illness. Today, it is a sign of politics.

When we expect bullshit from politicians, we are caught up in entertainment. We suspend disbelief just as we do at the movies. Politics has always been a subject of entertainment. American literature, film, and television are full of political drama. Until recently, however, we could separate the entertainment value from the political value. Can we do that with Ann Coulter, Sean Hannity, or Alex Jones? If we cannot distinguish the entertaining from the serious, not only will we fail to distinguish democracy from mobocracy but we will neglect the ordinary, mundane cares of governance, in which little is entertaining.

America is not alone in the political turn to entertaining bullshit. Everywhere, new forms of populist politics follow new forms of communication. Social media operates everywhere and the smartphone is never turned off. One does not defeat bullshit by pointing out its errors but only by building an ethos that values truth and dignity. That is a serious project. Is there any longer a place for seriousness in our age of entertainment? This is the question that Killingworth confronts; so does the rest of the nation. Killingworth has some advantages—size, history, wealth—that may allow it to find a way forward.

7

What Can Be Done?

For all the folks . . . here in Killingworth who are frustrated with what is
happening nationally, the most important thing you can do is get involved
locally. Try to make your community a better place, [one] that reflects
your values. If you do that, it will spread . . . and eventually have an
impact at the national level.
—Senator Chris Murphy, at Killingworth Farmers' Market, July 19, 2019

I HAVE IDEALIZED KILLINGWORTH'S past practices, but then so did Tocqueville, for whom they were not even past. He has been accused of missing the messy facts of inequality, exclusion, and self-interest. In our defense, I would say that we need an ideal against which to measure our present situation. It is not a measure of the distance we have fallen, but of where we are in relation to where we believe we should be. Edenic myths function as regulative ideals, and self-government is ours. Our political Eden continues to look like the self-governing New England town.

Does that myth still serve a useful purpose? Most democratic government today is, and must be, representative. The importance of the Town Meeting no longer lies in legislating but in volunteering: it symbolizes an ideal of participatory self-government that models a practice of civic care and political friendship. The strongest argument for local self-government is that it inculcates the virtues necessary to the success of democracy at every level of government. We may learn politics from national media, but we learn citizenship locally. Are these lessons strong enough to offer some resistance to the pathologies of our national political life?

The Structure of Democratic Disappointment

We hope that democratic politics will make us better people; we fear it will make us worse. Trump got a lot of voters to the polls, proving that voter participation rates alone are a poor marker of the health of a democracy. We can identify two beliefs indicative of a troubled practice of self-government. Today, these beliefs are all too common.

Every Idea Is Only an Opinion

Democratic decision-making levels the forms of argument: moral claims stand alongside self-interested claims; informed views compete with uninformed. Neither those who argue that we have a moral obligation to save the planet nor those who would bring back the coal industry come to politics with any extra weight or privilege. Persuasion is the coin of the realm, but citizens are often persuaded by bad reasons.

Democratic politics treats assertions about truth and justice as opinions, but we misunderstand democracy if we take this as an expression of relativism. That beliefs count politically only to the degree that they persuade does not mean that all opinions have equal value. It does not mean that citizens can be indifferent to the sources of support for an opinion.

An opinion grounded in relevant scientific expertise should ordinarily be received as more persuasive than a position that ignores such expertise. There may be good reasons to reject the scientist's view, but preferring ignorance is not one of them. It remains a poor reason even if it aligns with one's self-interest. Similarly, an opinion should be more persuasive when it comes from a person of character than one put forward by an untrustworthy person. Citizens should be open to persuasion, but it does not follow that they should give up their common sense. Just the opposite: because they must be persuaded, they are accountable for their beliefs. A false claim or groundless opinion does not become better when it enters politics—even if it manages to persuade a majority of citizens.

Although both sides in a political controversy are entitled to try to persuade voters, it does not follow that they should be treated as equal. We see the perverse turn of the ethos of persuasion when the climate change deniers and the climate scientists are treated as equals.[1] The same perversion appears when xenophobic speech is given an equal hearing with compassionate speech in the debate over immigration, or when racists and civil rights defenders are both described as "fine people."[2] In Killingworth, we see this when those expressing hateful speech are quick to defend their right to speak when they are called to account for what they have actually said.[3] Democratic self-government that confuses the idea of openness with that of equal value is in danger of moving from a practice of debate to mob behavior. If we are to govern ourselves, we must do the work of deciding for the right reasons.

Democracy Is a Machine That Will Govern Itself

Belief in the equality of opinions is often linked to a belief in democracy as a "machine that would go of itself." A well-constructed polity is to work like a market, turning private vices into public benefits.[4] Politics, on this view, does not ask us to be better than we are. Rather, it transforms the pursuit of self-interest into a public good. The body politic will move toward the public good because members will eventually correct errors in judgment, provided they suffer the consequences of their own mistakes. This idea has considerable prominence in traditional arguments for judicial deference to legislative majorities.[5]

Before we buy an iPhone, we do not ask whether Steve Jobs was a person of character. We might care whether the produce we buy is organic, but beyond not wanting to be cheated, we do not care about the farmer's character. If the farmer is selfish or obstinate, most of us do not consider this a reason not to buy his or her brussels sprouts. Politics, however, does not permit the same separation of products from character. A person of character may gain our trust, in which case she or he may persuade us even when we are otherwise unsure of what is proposed. Conversely, we should be skeptical of arguments made by people we know to lack character, even when their proposals otherwise look attractive. The proposal to close an elementary school presented this issue. I was unsure about it, but I trusted the members of the school board because I knew how hard they worked and how publicly minded they were. Conversely, while I was sympathetic to the idea of keeping elementary schools very local, the proponents had not previously displayed, at least to my knowledge, any interest in the larger school system.

The view that political persuasion works among voters in the same way that competition works in markets is not just inaccurate but pernicious. It discourages publicly motivated action. Political altruism, it argues, will only advance someone else's self-interest. In other words, "Nice guys finish last." The protesting residents might keep their school, but the costs will be paid in cutbacks elsewhere in the school system, where the funds would have had a larger public benefit.

These two beliefs about opinions—leveling and self-regulating—create the vacuum that privatization and nationalization rush to fill. Nationally, the result has been a government broadly supportive of corporate deregulation, a populist politics of resentment directed at "underserving" others, and a foreign policy of unilateralism. Locally, these factors empty town meetings, reduce the willingness to volunteer, limit the town's ability to take on new projects, and make misrepresentation and ad hominem attacks accepted forms of political discourse.

These beliefs in leveling and self-correction rest upon a kind of moral laziness. They are opposed by the view that self-government is work and that the role of citizens can be performed well or poorly. Proper performance requires character and common sense. Many citizens who thought that Donald Trump posed a deep threat to our democracy focused less on particular policies and more on the absence of character. Some of his supporters in 2020 resorted to the argument that voters should ignore his character, which was merely a matter of personality, and focus on his policies. Character, however, does not come second in a democracy.

Politics today often has a coarseness designed to shock. Not long ago, we encouraged our children to read a newspaper as part of their education in democratic citizenship. Now we are not so sure. The news has become adult entertainment. Much of the political speech from the right has the same relationship to a free market of ideas that pornography has to a college seminar. Our political condition is as if the pornographers were threatening to take over the university. They might succeed if we made the professors defend their enterprise against the pornographers' attacks and then put the question up to a vote by the students. The pornographers would depict the professors as self-interested, corrupt, conspiratorial elitists. Their shrill attack would know no bounds; it would be titillating and entertaining. Once such speech is normalized, it is very difficult to stop. In 2016, Michelle Obama lectured the nation: "When they go low, we go high." Her party lost.

The downward spiral of political speech does not have a legal solution. We cannot ban speech because of its pernicious political effects. If we are to improve the character of our politics, we must first improve the character of citizens. No legal or regulatory shortcut will give us that result. The law cannot require people to be broad-minded, sympathetic, and just.

Putting Character First

The importance of local self-government no longer lies in asserting control over the forces that most affect our lives. Those forces have become far too complex to entrust to local government. Killingworth can barely manage its budget and its open spaces; it will never control the economic, health, environmental, and security policies that affect all of us today. If that was not already entirely clear when I began this work, it has become stunningly clear as I finish in the middle of a pandemic. Killingworth volunteers with sewing machines could temporarily fill the gap when more masks were needed, but they could not prevent the pandemic from sweeping through the town.

Nevertheless, local self-government remains important because character is necessary to the success of politics. The American Founders understood that institutional structure without individual character would not prevent the rise of democratic pathologies. They thought of institutional structure and individual character as equal foundations of self-government. Politics does not require citizens to be saints, but it does require—contra Kant—that they not be devils.[6]

George Washington gave direct expression to this concern for character in his Farewell Address. After warning of the possibility of political divisions arising between the distinct communities that the new nation brought together, he spoke of the importance of religion to politics:

> Of all the dispositions and habits which lead to political prosperity, religion and morality are indispensable supports. In vain would that man claim the tribute of patriotism, who should labor to subvert these great pillars of human happiness, these firmest props of the duties of men and citizens. The mere politician, equally with the pious man, ought to respect and to cherish them. . . .
>
> And let us with caution indulge the supposition that morality can be maintained without religion. Whatever may be conceded to the influence of refined education on minds of peculiar structure, reason and experience both forbid us to expect that national morality can prevail in exclusion of religious principle.
>
> It is substantially true that virtue or morality is a necessary spring of popular government. The rule, indeed, extends with more or less force to every species of

free government. Who that is a sincere friend to it can look with indifference upon attempts to shake the foundation of the fabric?[7]

Politics, Washington is saying, needs a moral supplement. The political role of religion is not doctrinal but moral. The state needs the church to form the character upon which a democratic political order depends. Washington is not arguing for a state religion but for a strong civil society. Religion, he believes, will serve as the school for character of democratic citizens. When the address was composed, the schools in Killingworth had only recently been transferred from the responsibility of the Ecclesiastical Society to that of the town.[8]

Skeptical as we may be of religion's role in civic education today, Washington's point remains true: a successful polity cannot reproduce itself through institutional design alone. Government is not a machine. The community must tend to the maintenance of what Washington termed an "enlightened" civil society. Self-government obligates the citizen to be the type of person who can responsibly participate in governance.[9] Most citizens no longer learn these lessons in church, but they must be learned somewhere.

In 1838, forty-two years after Washington's Farewell, Lincoln gave his first great speech, an address before the lyceum of Springfield, Illinois. In this speech, he, too, worries that a pathological form of democratic politics—a mob—will overwhelm the rule of law. No less than Washington, he is concerned with character as the foundation of democratic self-government. But he no longer believes that governance needs an external moral supplement. Faith in law can do the work that religious faith once did.

Lincoln begins his speech with the mob that takes law into its own hands; he ends with the Napoleonic figure who reorders the state to match his own ambitions. An antinomian character can express itself as less than law—the mob— or more than law—the dictator. As the Greeks had understood, these have a way of turning into each other. Mobs support dictators; dictators cultivate mobs. In response, Lincoln imagines the pedagogy of a civic community: "Let reverence for the laws, be breathed by every American mother, to the lisping babe, that prattles on her lap—let it be taught in schools, in seminaries, and in colleges; let it be written in Primers, spelling books, and in Almanacs;—let it be preached from the pulpit, proclaimed in legislative halls, and enforced in courts of justice. And, in short, let it become the *political religion* of the nation."[10] For Lincoln, the state becomes its own church, able to create for itself the citizen character that democratic success requires. This vision set the pattern for the next 150 years: constitutional democracy created citizens willing to sacrifice themselves to defend that state. The countless war memorials before town halls, including that of Killingworth, are reminders of Lincoln's political faith that linked law, sacrifice, and character. Today, conscription is gone, and practices of citizenship are uncertain.

Washington and Lincoln both believed that democracy is not a natural state. We are not, by nature, good citizens; individuals must be educated to citizenship. A virtuous political character embraces an empathetic imagination, a commitment to the public good, and a concern for equality under law. Absent that character, democracy can become mobocracy.

The town that Walt Adametz remembers from his childhood, where neighbors relied upon each other, put character first. As that farm community gave way to commuters, new residents like Charlie Smith and Joan Gay stepped forward. Their generation of arrivals created new civic society associations that took the place of the informal, reciprocal support among the old farm families. Charlie and Joan both commuted to urban areas, but they embraced Killingworth as their town. Charlie describes himself as "a joiner," but he was also a founder. He helped to create the Lions, the ambulance association, and the chamber of commerce. He helped to revitalize the Congregational Church. Joan was a trailblazer when she became the first woman to lead the town Democrats.

Looking back, Charlie repeats a dictum learned over the years, "Twenty percent of the people do 80 percent of the work." When I pressed him on whether that 20 percent can still be found in Killingworth, he confessed that he was worried. The newcomers are, for the most part, not interested; young families are too busy; the Living Rock Church has no presence; and those living in Beachwood's senior community, with a few exceptions, do not step forward. Joan remembers a time when there was no problem finding volunteers for town offices: "People were a bit more involved because everything was local." Today, it is "more of a commuter town."

In part, Charlie blames social media for absorbing residents' time and attention. More broadly, he acknowledges that residents are too occupied with family and work to take on the burden of volunteering for the town. Indeed, the change in family life predates the arrival of Facebook.

By the 1990s, the era of founding and joining was over. Our family arrived in mid-decade. So did that of Arjumund Abid. We moved into an old farmhouse; the Abids moved into one of the new, upscale developments. Both families had two daughters of about the same age. The Abid children went to private schools from the beginning; ours were in public school for several years. The families met when our younger daughter joined theirs at a nearby private school. Neither family joined a local religious group or made close friends through the schools. On arrival, the adults of both families commuted to the urban centers. We were all busy juggling careers, schools, and children's extracurricular activities, too busy to find a lot of time for civil society. Catherine stopped commuting after a couple of years; our younger daughter started college in 2007. That was also the first year Catherine ran for office. The house was empty, and Catherine was in town all day. A few years later, Arjumund, who was still commuting to work, participated in the founding of a branch of the Rotary Club. It quickly failed for lack of time and interest.

Civil society participation, today, often comes down to an occasional posting on Killingworth Stompin' Ground. Few commuters have time for much more. Online, Arjumund does not find a local community; he finds an argumentative hot house, in which a small group of participants take "cheap shots" at local leaders. After a couple of years, he says, he was "turned off" by the incivility of the discourse and mostly stopped posting.

"New retirees," Charlie says, are today's volunteers, but he notes that people are retiring later and later. These retirees are often the people with whom Catherine finds herself working. They are the people who make the Congregational Church skew older, as does every civil society organization in town. When I attend the annual volunteer firemen's dinner, there are always several people receiving their thirty—or even forty—year service pins. Is this a viable plan for the town's future as a self-governing community?

The Town as a School for Character

With public opinion deeply polarized, there are no grounds to believe that national politics can teach the lessons in citizenship on which democracy depends. Those lessons, if they are to occur at all, must begin in places like Killingworth—places where residents can take up a practice of volunteering. That may be government, but it also includes civil society associations—secular, political, and religious. What matters is the opportunity to take responsibility and to make judgments on matters that fall within the common sense of a community.

When we pursue these practices and make these judgments together, we are learning self-government. As Tocqueville put it, "By dint of working for the good of one's fellow citizens, one finally picks up the habit and taste of serving them."[11]

Suburban communities have long been criticized for disclaiming responsibility for the urban areas on which they rely economically and culturally.[12] Residents who direct their concerns locally may ignore their connections to those outside the town's borders. They may resist programs that would redistribute resources toward less well-off communities, even when they are next door. Many suburban residents fled the problems of the cities; they want to break, not embrace, the connection. Earlier, I discussed the appearance of this urban disregard in Killingworth.

The critique is no doubt correct, but the attitude it identifies is precisely that which makes it unlikely that jurisdictional borders will be redrawn—a frequent proposal from well-intentioned reformers. That, however, is not the only possible answer to the problem. The qualities of character that support local participation do not align automatically with a selfish localism. Charlie, among the most active of town volunteers, spends one day a week working at a soup kitchen in New Haven. Carolyn Anderson, who serves on the board of assessment appeals and recently managed Catherine's reelection campaign, runs an annual holiday gift drive for children in the Hartford schools. The KWO supports a women's shelter in Middletown. Catherine spends much of her time tending to regional management, which often means coordinating with other towns and cities. The problem of alienation from the broader community arises from the same forces of privatization and nationalization that work against participation in self-governance in town. Empathy and generosity—features of a virtuous political character—do not stop at the town borders.

The town must teach the beliefs necessary for its own flourishing. No one else will. Public education's first responsibility is political, just as politics' first responsibility is educational. Public education is not like a public water or sewage system: it is not just an efficient alternative to each family performing the function privately. Rather, public education has a duty to prepare students for their democratic responsibilities.[13] This duty is the local equivalent of the federal government's national security mandate, for the political community will not survive if it fails in this task. Of course, public schools must train students for the workforce, but that is because providing the means of individual success is itself a goal of democratic self-government.

Public education must be education in character formation because politics has an ethical complexity that resists any easy formulation of rules. That complexity arises from the continual need to bridge an aspiration for the universal—justice—and care for particular individuals. This is the same sort of ethical complexity that characterizes a family. My obligations to my children are, in the first instance, matters of care, not justice. I do not condition my care for them on justice. The relationship of care to justice is the other way around: caring for my children, I want them to be just. Similarly, caring for my community, I want it to be just. When it is unjust, I have a responsibility to work toward its reform, not to abandon it.

To navigate the ethical complexity of family—the relationship of justice to love—we need good judgment, which in turn requires character. Parenting demands character, not rules. Political education should train citizens in a similar form of ethical responsibility—that is, in an ability to navigate the relationship of justice and care. A proper political ethos sustains authority while creating responsibility. Citizens must learn that they have an obligation to pay attention to the issues and to the variety of voices in the community. Students should aspire to be citizens who can be trusted. Not so long ago, we trusted each other with our lives. Today, we still must trust each other with the well-being of ourselves and our children. That we have not trusted each other to maintain social distance and to wear masks to prevent the spread of the virus has been a political failure and a national embarrassment.

Self-government begins with taking responsibility for what we do together. About that, citizens often disagree. Disagreement makes many residents uncomfortable. Unable to speak in a single voice, they believe that politics, like religion, does not belong in the schools. To allow religion or politics into the classroom would invite conflict among students and proselytizing by teachers. Politics, on this view, is a matter of personal opinion rather than of public opinion formed through leadership, dialogue, and inquiry. To treat politics like religion, however, is not to respect politics but to undermine it. Religious differences are tolerated in a democratic polity; political differences are not tolerated but embraced as the very life of the community.

The schools should embrace diversity of belief as the soul of democratic self-government. They should teach students how to deal with disagreement.[14] Students must learn that self-government is about assessing different positions, deciding for oneself, and working alongside those with whom one disagrees. If schools avoid politics, where do we expect our children to learn to appreciate political differences? Political education is like sex education. If we do not teach sex education, children are likely to learn online by watching pornography; if we do not teach politics, children will learn from the incendiaries on broadcast and social media. Our children are already learning about sex from Howard Stern. Do we want them to learn politics from him as well?

Absent habits of civil discourse, political disagreement is vulnerable to trolls, conspiracy theorists, propagandists, and ideological extremists. We don't fight these patterns of political assault by banishing politics from the schools. *Killingworth Today* demonstrated that successful political debate requires a moderator willing to intervene to keep discussions on track, enforce rules of engagement, identify the real points of conflict, and ask questions of each side. Of course, there remains a place for independent speakers making their case on the metaphoric soap box in the park, but productive political debate has always required a moderator and rules of order. That is the lesson of the Town Meeting, and it should be the lesson in the schools.

Education in citizenship has ambitions across the entire curriculum. Not the civics class alone but history, literature, social studies, and even the sciences must teach citizenship. Witnessing today's attacks on scientific expertise, the science classroom may be where political education is most needed. Patterns of education easily reproduce a general assumption that there is a natural progression from the local to the global. The result is that local history is studied in elementary school, while high school is for politics and history of a broader reach. That sense of the local as elementary needs to be replaced with a sense that it is foundational and remains at the core of successful political life.

The educational role of local governance is to create and maintain the public character of citizens. This role is not limited to the schools. It includes practices of adult education. "Killingworth Copes" was such an effort, just as the endless meetings of boards and committees are as much about practicing citizenship as getting something done. At these meetings, citizens simultaneously take responsibility and exercise authority. Recently, for example, the planning and zoning commission has been considering alternatives to the town's demanding two-acre zoning model—a regulatory standard with exclusionary effects. The commission started out quite divided on the issue. Two members took the lead in exploring and explaining alternatives. Those who defended the old rule are beginning to imagine alternatives. The commission recently approved a substantial modification, allowing accessory apartments to be built. Members of the commission are enacting the meaning of character in politics: expansion of the imagination that comes with trying to see a situation from multiple perspectives.[15] Public practices, public character, and public opinion are all of a piece.

That character is a necessary part of politics is dramatically illustrated in Connecticut, where the state faced chronic budget problems even before the pandemic.[16] Officials claim they cannot raise taxes. The state, they say, has no more resources, and we must "live within our means." But Connecticut is one of the richest tax jurisdictions in the world. There is far more wealth now than there was in the mid-twentieth century, when the state built much of its public infrastructure. The problem is not economic; it is political. Wealth is concentrated in a small group of individuals. When wealth comes from finance rather than manufacture, raising taxes may lead to an exodus. Or so the wealthy threaten, and the politicians fear.[17]

The mobility of wealth, however, is not a fact of nature. It is a problem with many possible responses. The most effective of these come from the federal government, which has the power to tax regardless of residence and to structure the financial industry in ways that would lead to less concentration of wealth in the first place. Lacking similar regulatory powers, the state must persuade. It must persuade the wealthy that they have responsibilities for community well-being. They must be persuaded to see themselves as citizens.

This idea is hardly implausible, although it may strike many that way today. The wealthy create foundations, pledge to give away their fortunes, and take up public service in all sorts of ways, including military service.[18] The rich who want to flee from the tax jurisdiction are showing a failure of character just as much as the poor who see government as a source of benefits but not responsibilities. Not so long ago, all this was self-evident: when the country went to war in the 1940s, both rich and poor were expected to volunteer. Military service may be less important today, but responsibility for the well-being of the community through the project of self-governance remains. To turn away, to flee, to ignore, to shirk, and to free ride remain flaws of character.

Politics cannot take citizens as it finds them, for what we are becoming will not sustain our democratic institutions. In Killingworth, continuing as we are will mean that governance simply does not get done. At the state level, it means that one of the richest states in the country finds itself chronically short of funds. At the national level, it means illiberal democracy as voters elect autocratic populists.

We are reluctant to talk about the role of government in developing citizen character. We rightly worry that this could become an invitation to pursue cultural and social prejudices. There is a long history of equating Christian, northern European culture with civilization itself. Minority groups were thought to be incapable of governing themselves, let alone of sharing in the government of white men. Similar claims were made against women and the poor—none had the character required for self-government. This attitude justified colonialism abroad and social and economic subordination at home. This history is not so long past that we can dismiss it as irrelevant. For some, it is not past at all. Yet the response to this worry cannot be indifference to the role of character in politics.

As Killingworth Goes, So Goes the Nation

Politicians like to repeat a remark made by Winston Churchill: "Democracy is the worst form of government except for all those other forms that have been tried."[19] Democracy, however, has no single institutional form. Churchill's remark in no way reassures us that our particular political practices are better than other, equally democratic possibilities. The significant choice today is not between democracy and authoritarianism, for the most pressing challenges now come from democratic forms of authoritarianism.

Imagining alternative institutional arrangements is a useful exercise, however, only if taken up from a position within the existing political order. Absent the constraints of the actual, proposals for reform too easily become utopian fantasies. We need to consider instead what reconfigurations are possible—even if difficult—from the position we occupy. Imagining institutional reform under these constraints is itself a political act, for it self-consciously assumes the burden of persuasion.

Even if we need to imagine possible reforms from a particular position, why start from Killingworth? A small middle-class town, with a long history of volunteerism, situated in a deep blue state, cannot claim to be typical. Yet much about Killingworth today is typical of communities around the nation. Everywhere, participation in civil society organizations is declining; everywhere, politics is nationalizing. Families everywhere find themselves estranged from their neighbors and managing by themselves. Residents everywhere have little information about local practices and issues. All must deal with the political consequences of the changing media environment, including the rise of social media and the collapse of local reporting. Everywhere, mainline churches are shrinking while evangelical churches grow. Everywhere, families are financially over-extended while work is both more demanding and less secure. Wherever we live, we are assaulted by new leaders of public opinion who fail to distinguish news from propaganda, facts from fiction. Politics everywhere is tinged with violence as it becomes less and less civil. Nationalization brings polarization everywhere, even within deeply red or blue states. In short, Killingworth is buf-feted by the same changes that are storming across the entire American political and social landscape.

None of this is to deny that scale matters in politics. There is, as I said at the beginning, no direct path from Killingworth to Washington. Yet just as the town's small size allows us to analyze widespread democratic pathologies, so it allows us to think about concrete reforms. The exercise of imagining reform presses us to think about the relationship of broad political ends to particular institutional means. Killingworth's practices of volunteerism, for example, invite us to think about the nature of participatory democracy, just as the important role of local knowledge leads us to reflect on the willingness of some national political move-ments to disregard facts. We learn locally that politics neither begins nor ends at the ballot box. That, too, is a useful lesson everywhere.

Reform begins with a critical stance toward existing political institutions. The institutions of democratic governance must make sense to contemporary citizens. That they made sense two hundred years ago is not a good reason for keeping them, if they fail to meet our needs and values. First among those values is self-government. Institutions do not have a value independent of the politics they enable. This principle is as old as our Declaration of Independence: "When-ever any Form of Government becomes destructive of these ends [life, liberty, and the pursuit of happiness], it is the Right of the People to alter or to abolish it, and to institute new Government, laying its foundation on such principles and organizing its powers in such form, as to them shall seem most likely to effect their Safety and Happiness."

Direct Democracy Reconfigured

The New England Town Meeting figures in the myth of our nation's demo-cratic origins. It offers an image of direct democracy that serves as a measure of other democratic institutions—as if representative institutions are a second-best form, forced upon us by size. In Killingworth, however, the Town Meeting operates in a dramatically undemocratic fashion. Not only do few residents attend, but those who come are not representative. The meeting illustrates the rule I put forth in chapter 3: the closer a political institution is to the people, the less democratic it is.[20]

Killingworth also illustrates the problem with turning to referenda as an expanded form of direct democracy. A referendum enables wider direct participation than does a Town Meeting. Polls are open all day, and voting generally takes only a few minutes. No need to arrange for babysitters or give up a whole evening. Even so, referenda do not have a good record of voter participation. Rates are higher than at the Town Meeting, but nowhere near the turnout for a national election or even local elections.[21] The information voters rely on is often little more than what they can glean from lawn signs proclaiming, "Vote Yes," or (more often), "Vote No." Referenda do not create interest and attention where there is little.

Moreover, referenda do not advance volunteerism. They model politics as a one-off intervention. They convey no appreciation for the volunteers whose work is at stake in the referendum. Voters can reject these efforts without bothering to attend the public meetings where issues were considered or speaking with their neighbors who have put in the work. Those who spent many evenings doing their best for the town rightly ask of the voters, "Where were you when the work needed to be done?" When the town voted down the proposal to rebuild town hall, the committee members did not go back to the drawing board. They went home.

We may think that a referendum allows voters to focus on a single issue, but without a thorough and open debate on the issue, a referendum often becomes yet another site to replay our deeply divided politics. The deeper those divisions, the less sense it makes to decide issues by referenda, for the outcome will always be a loss for one side. Politics then becomes warfare by other means.

Democracy in the age of cyber reproduction is vulnerable to storms of populist propaganda driven by resentment, intolerance, and fear. These conditions can make moving toward more direct democracy the wrong response. Political practices of self-government demand collaboration and compromise; they rest on persuasion. The democratic response to division is dialogue, empathy, and compromise. Neither the Town Meeting nor the referendum, operating alone, matches participation to information. Working together, however, they suggest a possible path forward.

The process by which the town considered the Venuti property, which I described in chapter 5, offers a model. That process began with two well-attended meetings where information was shared and arguments presented. Those meetings succeeded, at least in part, because participants were not pressed to vote at the conclusion. They could take home what they had learned and continue to deliberate. The referendum occurred a few weeks later.

Tying a referendum to information sharing and debate in public meetings has additional benefits. Those meetings may have helped some residents resist the cyberwar that arose over the purchase. The discussion at the meetings also helped to broaden the grounds of decision beyond the issue of cost. Democracies must combat a fee-for-services view of government that is antithetical to public participation. Referenda will not do that on their own, especially if most of them deal with budget decisions. But linked to genuine deliberation, they can ask citizens to do more than look at their tax bill.

Either the public meetings or the referendum, without the other, would have been far less satisfactory: one because few would have participated, the other because any decision would have been uninformed. The need productively to link informing to deciding is a national problem. Bruce Ackerman and James Fishkin addressed the problem in their proposal for "deliberation day" before elections.[22] Killingworth shows us the possibility of using existing institutions in new combinations to accomplish the same ends.

The Town Meeting Reimagined

Although formally still the legislative body, the Town Meeting today is an anachronism that undermines democratic possibilities. Absent participation, the meeting signals citizen indifference. This problem is beyond cure: we cannot force the town into the room any more than we can force residents off social media. The Town Meeting's legislative authority should be abandoned, and the meeting should be reimagined as a part of the broad ethos of volunteerism already operating in the other boards and committees. It should be an occasion for residents to work together, simultaneously sharing and building the town's common sense.

Once stripped of its legislative function, town meetings could more directly address problems of information and deliberation. Without the authority to decide, the problem of capture disappears. Less formal meetings could be made more attractive as sites of exchange and debate. This is an instance in which less is more: less authority could lead to more participation.[23]

The effort should be to take the meeting to the people, to go where they are and make participation easy—a regular part of living in the town. Why hold meetings on weekday evenings, an impossibly busy time for many residents? Meetings could, for example, be scheduled alongside other events. Why not a town meeting after a soccer game on Saturday morning, right on the playing field? Why not at the weekly farmers' market or after a town picnic? Why not at the high school, with participation by students? Why not make a special effort to bring in senior citizens by meeting at the retirement community? Once we break free of the eighteenth- and nineteenth-century forms, the possibilities multiply.

The pandemic has already forced the town to innovate by moving meetings online. It might be possible to hold several online meetings over a week to talk about a particular issue in depth.[24] One could imagine presentations by experts, organized debates, question and answer sessions with officials, and sessions for open discussion of whatever citizens want to propose. Freed of the burden of legislating, the town could experiment with different ways of exchanging information and encouraging debate. The form of the meeting should be driven by the substantive goal, which is to make it easy for residents to come together to build local public opinion.

Representation and Political Parties

The town has far too many elected positions—some twenty offices were on the ballot in the last local election. This practice made sense when elections were held at the annual Town Meeting and neighbors took turns. This is still the practice in the Congregational Church. But today, what exactly are the grounds upon which voters decide whom to elect for the position of alternate to the board of zoning appeals?

No one knows why some officials and members of some boards are elected while others are appointed—accidents of history? The town clerk and the tax collector are elected, as are the two registrars of voters. The zoning officer, assessor, and public works director are appointed. Boards that exercise authority over zoning, assessments, and budget are elected. Boards that consider public health, public buildings, and local development are appointed. No one could draw a flow chart of authority. No one knows who gets the final say if a controversy arises. Who, for example, decides whether to defend a lawsuit or settle a claim? Does it matter whether the official sued is elected, appointed, or employed?

The selectmen are the most visible elected officials, but critical town functions are performed by elected officials who have no visibility—for example, members of the board of finance and of the planning and zoning commission. They effectively control town finances and development, but their public meetings attract only a handful of residents. Residents have little idea how the system works. When they vote for the selectmen, they think they are voting for their representatives, even though the board of selectmen lacks authority to pass a budget, enact ordinances, or raise taxes.

All of this should be reordered in a way that rationalizes responsibilities, encourages participation, and serves the teaching mission of town governance. Functions and offices should be consolidated; elections should be rationalized. Without focused responsibility and electoral accountability, participation will lag, interest will be diverted, and volunteerism will continue to suffer.

Senior executive and legislative positions in town should be elected. Managerial and professional positions should not be on the ballot. The town already concentrates its competitive political energies in the election for first selectman. Most voters treat the first selectman as a mayor, supervising the administration at town hall. The position should be reformed to match citizen expectations. That means some sort of mayor–town council system.

Killingworth is too small, however, to have council districts. Instead of electing councilpersons at large, why not have the elected heads of the three most important committees—finance, planning and zoning, and inland wetlands—serve on the town council? This would concentrate functions and expertise. If elections were limited to these top positions, voters could focus their attention and evaluate actual performance. The other volunteers who fill the numerous boards and committees could all be appointed.

Why not assign the appointment responsibility, in the first instance, to the local political parties? Let the parties take direct responsibility for putting forward members.[25] Giving the parties this responsibility might encourage them to imagine their role as service to the community rather than winning the electoral cycle for the national party. Minimally, it would encourage them to cultivate leadership across generations. Instead of the current minority representation requirement, there could be a requirement of some number of unaffiliated voters on each committee, who would be appointed by the town council. Unaffiliated voters are now the largest group in town; they, too, deserve a regular seat at the table.

The details of Killingworth's organizational reform are not particularly important. What matters is the directions in which they might point—encouraging flexibility, information, party responsibility, and clear lines of authority. Woodrow Wilson noted at the end of the nineteenth century that there was a tremendous gap between the way the national government worked and the way citizens imagined it worked.[26] Practices no longer corresponded to legal forms. That made effective citizen mobilization difficult if not impossible. Voters not only lacked information; they did not know even where they should be looking. This remains a problem in Washington; it is no less a problem locally. "Who governs?" is a question that continues to resonate. Citizens will not participate as long as they do not understand. An ethos of volunteerism depends upon transparency and functional rationality. This, too, begins locally.

Local Media and the Limits of a Political Community

Killingworth cannot create its own media market; it cannot even model reform for a national effort. One might have hoped that social media would provide an easy fix for the disappearance of local news. Such a fix is imaginable, but it will certainly not be easy. Several attempts have already failed, either financially or functionally. No one has a model that can sustain local reporting.

There is a saying about the internet: "Information wants to be free." From the local perspective, this means that information wants to be free of borders. On the internet, one thing literally leads to another, propelling us across endless borders. We gain access to the world, but at the cost of the local. This condition cannot be cured by creating firmer borders. The most we can hope to do is create conditions under which residents will want to get involved locally, informing each other of their mutual interests and concerns. Peg Scofield, who successfully ran *Killingworth Today* for more than ten years, does not think the Facebook model can serve this local function. Serious information requires serious reporting, but that requires serious funding. She has no idea where that might come from. *Killingworth Today* started as a way for her to learn and practice reporting and design skills. It was so successful that now, she says, it could not afford her services.

The disappearance of a local media supporting a local public opinion forces us to confront one last time the question of whether the town itself can or should survive as a political entity. Many of its functions have been stripped away as the state and the nation have taken on new responsibilities. Perhaps more should be. For example, Killingworth, with fewer than ten employees, negotiates union contracts for two bargaining units. This arrangement requires the town to hire lawyers, union negotiators, financial advisers, and actuaries. There is no reason to think that Killingworth's conditions of employment are different from those of neighboring towns. Why not a regional hiring authority, from which Killingworth could draw its employees as needed? This pattern repeats itself on many issues. The town, for example, maintains its own pension plan but has no particular financial expertise.

Despite regional efficiencies, the town remains a natural kind for many of its residents—particularly for those who are already volunteering. Connecticut never successfully developed county-level government.[27] Residents' sense of political jurisdictions moves from town to state to nation. This may not be the best organization, but in politics we are not free to make up new jurisdictions. When we try, they rarely gain citizen attachment.

Killingworth must remain the site of democratic pedagogy, for there is no plausible alternative for its residents. The political lessons that the town can teach come from tending to itself as a community of volunteers. That is more than enough. Volunteers cannot save the economy or stop climate change. They can, however, respond to emergencies, preserve our local forests, maintain our facilities, care for the elderly, and make the town a safe and engaging place in which to raise children. Doing these things together, we are promised something more than the sum of the parts—public happiness. If we can find this in our local communities, it gives us something to hold up to national politics. We can ask of national institutions why they are causing so much pain, instead of realizing their own forms of public happiness.

Taking responsibility in and for the town, residents participate in forms of volunteerism and cooperation that give meaning to a political life. The yearning for such meaning is why the myth of self-government through the Town Meeting remains so strong. The town can remind us of our political aspirations by asking us to live them, at least when the stakes are low. Because the stakes are low, however, residents are easily distracted. The fight for Killingworth's survival requires getting people out of their homes and into the streets, parks, and meeting rooms. Once there, they may not stop until they fill the Mall in Washington.

NOTES

Preface: Political Theory and Political Practice Today

1. Robert A. Dahl, *Who Governs? Democracy and Power in an American City* (New Haven, Conn.: Yale University Press, 1961).

2. See Leonard V. Kaplan and Rudy Koshar, eds., *The Weimar Moment: Liberalism, Political Theology, and Law* (Lanham, Md.: Lexington Books, 2012).

3. See, e.g., Andrew Nolan, Kate M. Manuel, and Brandon J. Murrill, "Judge Merrick Garland: His Jurisprudence and Potential Impact on the Supreme Court," *Congressional Research Service,* Apr. 27, 2016, https://fas.org/sgp/crs/misc/R44479.pdf (finding that then-Judge Garland's jurisprudence materially differed from Justice Scalia's in several key areas, including the role of the judiciary).

4. See Samuel Moyn, *Not Enough: Human Rights in an Unequal World* (Cambridge, Mass.: Belknap Press of Harvard University Press, 2018), 3–11; and Ganesh Sitaraman, "The Puzzling Absence of Economic Power in Constitutional Theory," *Cornell Law Review* 101 (2016): 1450–55.

5. See, e.g., Daniel Markovits, *The Meritocracy Trap: How America's Foundational Myth Feeds Inequality, Dismantles the Middle Class, and Devours the Elite* (New York: Penguin, 2019), 4–6; Thomas Piketty, *Capital in the Twenty-First Century,* trans. Arthur Goldhammer (Cambridge, Mass.: Belknap Press of Harvard University Press, 2014), 19–21; and David Singh Grewal and Jedediah Purdy, "Inequality Rediscovered," *Theoretical Issues in Law* 18 (2017): 78–82.

6. Judith N. Shklar, *Legalism* (Cambridge, Mass.: Harvard University Press, 1964), 28.

7. See, e.g., Arthur Vidich and Joseph Bensman, *Small Town in Mass Society: Class, Power and Religion in a Rural Community* (Princeton, N.J.: Princeton University Press, 1958), viii ("The community is viewed as a stage on which major issues and problems typical of the society are played out.").

8. *The Day,* a newspaper based in New London, Connecticut, recently proclaimed the "near extinction" of the New England Republican, "that collaborative problem solver who . . .

believed in providing good government through bipartisan consensus building and prudent fiscal restraint." Editorial Board, "Disappearance of the New England Republican," *Day,* Feb. 13, 2020, www.theday.com/article/20200213/OP01/200219717.

9. Stan Fisher, "Killingworth Primary Brings Little Change," *New Haven Register,* Sept. 10, 2013, www.nhregister.com/connecticut/article/Killingworth-primary-brings-little-change -11396249.php.

Chapter 1. A Constitutional Coup

Note to epigraph: Alexis de Tocqueville, *Democracy in America* [1835], ed. and trans. Harvey C. Mansfield and Delba Winthrop (Chicago: University of Chicago Press, 2000), 7.

1. In 2016, Hillary Clinton lost three key states: Wisconsin (by 23,000 votes), Michigan (by 11,000 votes), and Pennsylvania (by 44,000 votes).

2. See, e.g., Harry Enten, "How Much Did WikiLeaks Hurt Hillary Clinton?," *FiveThirty-Eight,* Dec. 23, 2016, https://fivethirtyeight.com/features/wikileaks-hillary-clinton; and Nate Silver, "The Comey Letter Probably Cost Clinton the Election," *FiveThirtyEight,* May 3, 2017, https://fivethirtyeight.com/features/the-comey-letter-probably-cost-clinton -the-election. In addition, a Senate report found conclusive evidence that Russia's interference with the 2016 election targeted African Americans. *Report of the Select Committee on Intelligence, United States Senate, on Russian Active Measures Campaigns and Interference in the 2016 U.S. Election,* vol. 2: *Russia's Use of Social Media with Additional Views,* S. Rep. No. 116-XX (2019), 38; see also Tim Mak, "Senate Report: Russians Used Social Media Mostly to Target Race in 2016," *NPR,* Oct. 8, 2019, www.npr .org/2019/10/08/768319934/senate-report-russians-used-used-social-media-mostly -to-target-race-in-2016.

3. See Jonathan Easley, "Trump Sex Tape Comments Frustrate GOP Supporters," *Hill,* Sept. 30, 2019, https://thehill.com/homenews/campaign/298753-trump-sex-tape-comments -frustrate-gop-supporters; Dara Lind, "Poll: Vast Majority of Republican Voters Don't Care Much About the Leaked Trump Tape," *Vox,* Oct. 9, 2016, www.vox.com/2016 /10/9/13217158/polls-donald-trump-assault-tape.

4. In the 2016 national election, turnout for the presidential election was 60.1 percent. "2016 November General Election Turnout Rates," *United States Election Project,* Sept. 5, 2019, www.electproject.org/2016g. In 2020, turnout increased to nearly 67 percent of eligible voters. "2020 November General Election Turnout Rates," *United States Election Project,* Dec. 7, 2020, www.electproject.org/2020g.

5. Since 2013, the Annenberg Public Policy Center at the University of Pennsylvania has conducted an annual civic knowledge survey. In 2019, the survey found that a mere 39 percent of American adults could name all three branches of government. "2020 Annenberg Civics Knowledge Constitution Day Survey Appendix," *Annenberg Public Policy Center,* 2019, https://cdn.annenbergpublicpolicycenter.org/wp-content/uploads/2019/09 /Annenberg_civics_2019_Appendix.pdf.

6. See Yochai Benkler, Robert Faris, and Hal Roberts, *Network Propaganda: Manipulation, Disinformation, and Radicalization in American Politics* (New York: Oxford Uni-

versity Press, 2018), 14 ("The behavior of the right-wing media ecosystem represents a radicalization of roughly a third of the American media system.").

7. For the last official week of his presidency, President Obama's approval rating was 59 percent. "Presidential Approval Ratings—Barack Obama," *Gallup*, https://news.gallup .com/poll/116479/barack-obama-presidential-job-approval.aspx.

8. By January 2017, unemployment was at 4.7 percent, a low the country had not seen since before the Great Recession. Danielle Kurtzleben, "What Kind of 'Jobs President' Has Obama Been—In 8 Charts," *NPR*, Jan. 7, 2017, www.npr.org/2017/01/07/508600239 /what-kind-of-jobs-president-has-obama-been-in-8-charts. Real median household income in 2016 had just bounced back to what it had been in 2007 before the recession— at $62,898 and $62,090, respectively. "Real Median Household Income in the United States," *Federal Reserve Economic Data*, https://fred.stlouisfed.org/series/MEHOIN USA672N.

9. See "Military and Civilian Personnel by Service/Agency by State/Country," *Defense Manpower Data Center*, https://dwp.dmdc.osd.mil/dwp/app/dod-data-reports/workforce -reports (using data sets from September 2008 and December 2016).

10. Trump's approval rating hovered around 40 percent during his entire presidency, from a high of 49 percent to a low of 34 percent. "Presidential Approval Ratings—Donald Trump," *Gallup*, https://news.gallup.com/poll/203198/presidential-approval-ratings-donald -trump.aspx.

11. Trump repeatedly touted tax reform ("biggest tax cut in history") and health care overhaul ("something much better" than Obamacare) as landmark policies of his administration. "Remarks by President Trump in Roundtable Discussion on the Economy and Tax Reform, Burnsville, MN," *Trump White House*, Apr. 15, 2019, https://trumpwhitehouse .archives.gov/briefings-statements/remarks-president-trump-roundtable-discussion -economy-tax-reform-burnsville-mn. Only 40 percent approved of the 2017 Tax Cuts and Jobs Act. Frank Newport, "U.S. Public Opinion and the 2017 Tax Law," *Gallup*, Apr. 29, 2019, https://news.gallup.com/opinion/polling-matters/249161/public-opinion-2017 -tax-law.aspx. And only 17 percent supported a recent GOP effort to replace Obamacare. Jacob Pramuk, "Rough Series of Polls Show Americans Broadly Disapprove of GOP Health-Care Plan," *CNBC*, June 28, 2017, www.cnbc.com/2017/06/28/senate-gop-health -care-bill-has-dismal-approval-rating-poll.

12. See John Bolton, *The Room Where It Happened: A White House Memoir* (New York: Simon and Schuster, 2020), 468–70.

13. See Jan-Werner Müller, *What Is Populism?* (Philadelphia: University of Pennsylvania Press, 2016), 32–40 (discussing how populist leaders claim to be exclusive channels for the voice of the "people," regardless of empirical evidence to the contrary).

14. Trump fired five inspectors general over the course of six weeks, in what became known as a "slow-motion" Friday night massacre. Aaron Blake, "Trump's Slow-Motion Friday Night Massacre of Inspectors General," *Washington Post*, May 18, 2020, www.washington post.com/politics/2020/05/16/trumps-slow-moving-friday-night-massacre-inspectors -general.

15. See Aaron Blake, "Trump's Government Full of Temps," *Washington Post*, Feb. 21,

2020, www.washingtonpost.com/politics/2020/02/21/trump-has-had-an-acting-official
-cabinet-level-job-1-out-every-9-days ("Trump has kept acting officials in charge of top
agencies and departments so much that they've accounted for 1 out of every 9 days in
those positions. Across 22 Cabinet-level jobs, acting officials have served a total of 2,736
days—more than seven years of combined time.").

16. Trump was very vocal about his dissatisfaction with NATO, threatening to punish countries not meeting the defense spending requirements by "get[ting] them on trade." "Remarks by President Trump in a Working Lunch with 2 Percenters," *Trump White House,*
Dec. 4, 2019, https://trumpwhitehouse.archives.gov/briefings-statements/remarks-president
-trump-working-lunch-2-percenters; see also Julian E. Barnes and Helene Cooper,
"Trump Discussed Pulling U.S. from NATO, Aides Say amid New Concerns over Russia," *New York Times,* Jan. 14, 2019, www.nytimes.com/2019/01/14/us/politics/nato
-president-trump.html. Trump also aligned himself publicly with President Vladimir
Putin, stating that a cooperative alliance between the United States and Russia is "what
is best for America." "Remarks by President Trump and President Putin of the Russian
Federation in Joint Press Conference," *Trump White House,* July 16, 2018, https://trump
whitehouse.archives.gov/briefings-statements/remarks-president-trump-president-putin
-russian-federation-joint-press-conference; see also Joshua Yaffa, "The Trump-Putin
Summit in Helsinki," *New Yorker,* July 16, 2018, www.newyorker.com/news/current
/trump-putin-helsinki. And contrary to the U.S. intelligence community's findings, Trump
repeatedly asserted that any accusations of Russian interference into the 2016 election
are "ridiculous" and "just another excuse." Reena Flores, "Donald Trump Weighs in on
Russia Hacking Election, CIA Intelligence," *CBS News,* Dec. 11, 2016, www.cbsnews
.com/news/donald-trump-weighs-in-on-russia-hacking-election-cia-intelligence.

17. A paradigmatic example of Trump's action by inaction was the administration's deliberate slowdown of asylum applications at the border. See Charles Davis, "Bureaucracy
as a Weapon: How the Trump Administration Is Slowing Asylum Cases," *Guardian,*
Dec. 23, 2019, www.theguardian.com/us-news/2019/dec/23/us-immigration-trump-asylum
-seekers.

18. Just a few days after officially taking office, Trump issued Executive Order 13,771, "Reducing Regulation and Controlling Regulatory Costs," requiring that any executive department or agency planning to publicly announce a new regulation must propose at least
two regulations to be repealed. Exec. Order No. 13,771, 82 Fed. Reg. 9339, 9339 (Jan.
30, 2017). The executive order had a significant deregulatory effect: after twenty-two
months in office, the Trump administration had taken just 229 "significant" regulatory
actions—65 percent fewer than the Obama administration and 51 percent fewer than the
George W. Bush administration at the same benchmark. Diane Katz, "Here's How Much
Red Tape Trump Has Cut," *Heritage Foundation,* Oct. 17, 2018, www.heritage.org
/government-regulation/commentary/heres-how-much-red-tape-trump-has-cut.

19. At the end of Trump's term, 228 of 757 executive branch positions requiring Senate
confirmation remained unfilled. "Tracking How Many Key Positions Trump Has Filled
So Far," *Washington Post,* Jan. 15, 2021, www.washingtonpost.com/graphics/politics
/trump-administration-appointee-tracker/database/?itid=lk_interstitial_manual_8.

20. Among Trump's "A team," the most influential advisers within the executive office, turn-

over was 35 percent in year one and 31 percent in year two. In contrast in the same years, Obama's "A team" experienced 9 percent and 15 percent turnover, respectively. Kathryn Dunn Tenpas, "Tracking Turnover in the Trump Administration," *Brookings,* January 2021, www.brookings.edu/research/tracking-turnover-in-the-trump-administration.

21. In 2019, the Regulatory Information Service Center outlined in a proposed rule a "fundamental shift of the Regulatory state" that "start[s] with confidence in private markets and individual choices" and reaffirms a commitment to deregulation. "Introduction to the Fall 2019 Regulatory Plan," 84 Fed. Reg. 71,086, 71,086 (Dec. 26, 2019).

22. Trump accused the WTO of "screwing [America] for years" and threatened to leave the organization "if it's not going to be fair." "Remarks by President Trump on American Energy and Manufacturing," *C-SPAN,* Aug. 13, 2019, www.c-span.org/video/?463437-1 /president-trump-delivers-remarks-us-energy-manufacturing. He similarly expressed that NATO "is not fair to the people and taxpayers of the United States." "Remarks by President Trump at NATO Unveiling of the Article 5 and Berlin Wall Memorials—Brussels, Belgium," *U.S. Embassy and Consulates in Russia,* May 25, 2017, https://ru.usembassy .gov/remarks-president-trump-nato. And at the Seventy-Fourth Session of the United Nations General Assembly, Trump delivered an explicit rebuke to the UN's philosophy of globalism, remarking that the "future belongs to patriots," not "globalists." Gabby Deutch, "Full Transcript: Donald Trump at the United Nations General Assembly," *Atlantic,* Sept. 25, 2019, www.theatlantic.com/international/archive/2018/09/trump-unga -transcript-2018/571264.

23. Joel Rose, "Despite Supreme Court's Ruling on DACA, Trump Administration Rejects New Applicants," *NPR,* July 15, 2020, www.npr.org/2020/07/15/891563635/trump -administration-rejects-1st-time-daca-applications-violates-scotus-order.

24. Trump did sign a criminal justice reform measure: the First Step Act in 2018. It was, however, hardly his initiative. A version of the bill had been first introduced in 2015 and was continuously championed by a bipartisan team of legislators. Notwithstanding President Trump's attempts to claim success for criminal justice reform, the Trump administration was accused of taking actions that "directly contradict[]the plain language of the First Step Act," refusing to grant inmates the sentence reductions they are entitled to under the act. Chandra Bozelko and Ryan Lo, Opinion, "One of Joe Biden's First Steps Should Be to Fix Donald Trump's Broken Criminal Justice Reform," *NBCNews THINK,* Jan. 21, 2021, www.nbcnews.com/think/opinion/one-joe-biden-s-first-steps-should-be-fix -donald-ncna1255038; see also Ram Subramanian et al., "Transition 2020–2021: A Federal Agenda for Criminal Justice Reform," *Brennan Center for Justice,* Dec. 9, 2020, 20, www.brennancenter.org/sites/default/files/2021-01/FederalAgendaCriminalJustice _Final.pdf (calling on the Biden Administration to "improve First Step Act implementation" in order "to fully realize the law's intended goals").

25. "Here Are Some of the People Trump Pardoned," *New York Times,* Jan. 20, 2021, www .nytimes.com/article/who-did-trump-pardon.html. At some point, Trump was rumored to be considering granting himself a pardon. Michael S. Schmidt and Maggie Haberman, "Trump Is Said To Have Discussed Pardoning Himself," *New York Times,* Jan. 7, 2021, www.nytimes.com/2021/01/07/us/politics/trump-self-pardon.html.

26. William Burke-White, "The Danger of Trump's New Sanctions on the International

Criminal Court and Human Rights Defenders," *Brookings,* June 11, 2020, www.brookings
.edu/blog/order-from-chaos/2020/06/11/the-danger-of-trumps-new-sanctions-on
-the-international-criminal-court-and-human-rights-defenders.

27. See, e.g., Donald J. Trump (@realDonaldTrump), *Twitter,* July 13, 2016, 12:54 a.m.
("Justice Ginsburg of the U.S. Supreme Court has embarrassed all by making very dumb
political statements about me. Her mind is shot—resign!"); Donald J. Trump (@real
DonaldTrump), *Twitter,* May 30, 2016, 5:45 p.m. ("I have a judge in the Trump University civil case, Gonzalo Curiel . . . who is very unfair. An Obama pick. Totally biased-hates
Trump."); see also "In His Own Words: The President's Attack on the Courts," *Brennan
Center for Justice,* Feb. 14, 2020, www.brennancenter.org/our-work/research-reports
/his-own-words-presidents-attacks-courts. Though Twitter permanently suspended Trump's
account following the attack on the Capitol, all of Trump's tweets have been archived at
www.thetrumparchive.com, and the tweets I cite throughout can be viewed there.

28. On November 19, 2018, Judge Jon S. Tigar of the Northern District of California granted
a temporary restraining order on Trump's bar of asylum for immigrants entering the
country outside a port of entry. East Bay Sanctuary Covenant v. Trump, 349 F. Supp. 3d
838 (N.D. Cal. 2018). In response, Trump suggested that the Ninth Circuit was populated
by "Obama judges," who were biased against him and threatened to break up the circuit
to create what he saw as less liberal-biased courts. See Donald J. Trump (@realDonald
Trump), *Twitter,* Nov. 21, 2018, 3:51 p.m. Earlier in his presidency, Trump suggested in
an interview that he would "absolutely" entertain proposals to break up the Ninth Circuit
for its "outrageous" rulings. Sarah Westwood, "Exclusive Interview: Trump 'Absolutely'
Looking at Breaking up 9th Circuit," *Washington Examiner,* Apr. 26, 2017, www.wash
ingtonexaminer.com/tag/donald-trump?source=%2Fexclusive-interview-trump
-absolutely-looking-at-breaking-up-9th-circuit; see also Russell Wheeler, "Trump Wants
to 'Break Up the Ninth Circuit': How Would That Help Him?," *Brookings,* May 16,
2017, www.brookings.edu/blog/fixgov/2017/05/16/trump-wants-to-break-up-the-ninth
-circuit-how-would-that-help-him (observing that in 2017, there were no fewer than five
bills proposed in Congress that proposed to break up the Ninth Circuit).

29. The Federalist Society played an outsized role in helping funnel judges with thoroughly
vetted conservative credentials into judicial appointments during the Trump administration. See David Montgomery, "Conquerors of the Courts," *Washington Post,* Jan. 2,
2019, www.washingtonpost.com/news/magazine/wp/2019/01/02/feature/conquerors-of
-the-courts.

30. Philip Rucker, "Trump Pressures Justice Department to Investigate 'Crooked Hillary,'"
Washington Post, Nov. 3, 2017, www.washingtonpost.com/news/post-politics/wp/2017
/11/03/trump-pressures-justice-department-to-investigate-crooked-hillary.

31. PEN America, a nonprofit organization representing free speech and press institutions,
filed a complaint against President Trump in 2019 for his "official acts . . . intended to
stifle exercise of the constitutional protections of free speech and a free press." The complaint details Trump's prolonged and sustained attacks on the integrity of the press, accusing Trump of "suspending the White House press credentials of reporters who the
President believes failed to show him sufficient 'respect'; . . . [and] directing the Department of Justice to challenge a vertical merger between Time Warner and AT&T because

of his antagonism to Time Warner subsidiary CNN and its news coverage of his Administration." Amended Complaint for Declaratory and Injunctive Relief at 1, Pen American Center v. Trump, 448 F. Supp. 3d 309 (S.D.N.Y. 2020) (No. 18-cv-9433-LGS).

32. The *Washington Post* reports that by the end of Trump's presidency, he had made 30,573 false or misleading claims. See *"*The Fact Checker," *Washington Post,* Jan. 20, 2021, www.washingtonpost.com/graphics/politics/trump-claims-database/?itid=lk_inline _manual_4.

33. Robert Woodward, *Rage* (New York: Simon and Schuster, 2020) (revealing that President Trump was deliberately lying when he said the virus would not be a problem).

34. On July 2, 2017, Trump tweeted a video of himself tackling and punching a man with the CNN logo photoshopped over his face. @realDonaldTrump, *Twitter,* July 2, 2017, 6:21 a.m. He has also praised Rep. Greg Gianforte for body-slamming a reporter, stating, "Any guy that can do a body slam, he is my type!" Meredith McGraw, "Trump, No Regrets for Praising Greg Gianforte for Body-Slamming Reporter," *ABC News,* Oct. 19, 2018, https://abcnews.go.com/Politics/montana-rally-president-trump-praises-greg -gianforte-body/story?id=58596529. See also Donald J. Trump (@realDonaldTrump), *Twitter,* Apr. 5, 2019, 1:41 p.m. ("The press is doing everything within their power to fight the magnificence of the phrase, MAKE AMERICA GREAT AGAIN! . . . They are truly the ENEMY OF THE PEOPLE!").

35. Trump also took aim at the integrity of higher education with Executive Order 13,864, which "enhance[s] the quality of postsecondary education" by "ensur[ing that] institution that receive Federal research or education grants promote free inquiry." Exec. Order No. 13,864, 84 Fed. Reg. 11,401 (Mar. 26, 2019). While facially neutral, most commentators agreed that this order was designed to protect far-right speakers. Patricia McGuire, "Whose Freedom of Speech?," *Insider Higher Ed,* Mar. 27, 2019, www.insidehighered .com/views/2019/03/27/trumps-free-speech-executive-order-protects-only-those-right -political-spectrum; Michael Stratford, "Trump Set to Sign Executive Order on Campus Free Speech," *Politico,* Mar. 20, 2019, www.politico.com/story/2019/03/20/trump-free -speech-devos-1230490.

36. My use of the term is to be distinguished from that of Jon Michaels, for whom it refers to the way in which government use of private contractors—"privatization"—threatens separation of powers. Jon D. Michaels, *Constitutional Coup: Privatization's Threat to the American Republic* (Cambridge, Mass.: Harvard University Press, 2017), 6.

37. See, e.g., characterizations of Russia's 2014 annexation of Crimea as "hybrid warfare." Some saw the sudden invasion as marking "a brave new world" where the difference between war and peace has become increasingly blurred and methods of conflict have grown to include "the broad use of political, economic, informational, humanitarian, and other non-military measures." Sam Jones, "Ukraine: Russia's New Art of War," *Financial Times,* Aug. 28, 2014, www.ft.com/content/ea5e82fa-2e0c-11e4-b760-00144feabdc0.

38. Giorgio Agamben writes of a "zone of indistinction" into which modern politics has entered—a "state of exception" that exits "between outside and inside, chaos and the normal situation." Giorgio Agamben, *Homo Sacer: Sovereign Power and Bare Life,* trans. Daniel Heller-Roazen (Stanford, Calif.: Stanford University Press, 1998), 19.

39. See Kim Lane Scheppele, "Autocratic Legalism," *University of Chicago Law Review* 85

(2018): 547–49; Müller, *What Is Populism?*, 44–46 (noting how populist authoritarian leaders colonize state bureaucracy, remaking it in their image).

40. See, e.g., Donald J. Trump (@realDonaldTrump), *Twitter,* July 27, 2020, 10:58 p.m. ("The Fake News Media is trying to portray the Portland and Seattle 'protesters' as wonderful, sweet and innocent people. . . . Actually, they are sick and deranged Anarchists & Agitators.").

41. See Maggie Haberman, Nick Corasaniti, and Annie Karni, "As Trump Pushes into Portland, His Campaign Ads Turn Darker," *New York Times,* Aug. 28, 2020 (reporting that federal agents arrived in unmarked vehicles to "swoop[] protesters off the street" without explanation). In early 2014, armed soldiers appeared on the streets of Crimea, carrying Russian weapons, speaking in Russian accents, and driving vehicles with Russian plates. Despite all evidence to the contrary, President Vladimir Putin insisted that there was no official Russian military presence in Crimea. Vitaly Shevchenko, "'Little Green Men' or 'Russian Invaders'?," *BBC News,* Mar. 11, 2014, www.bbc.com/news/world-europe -26532154.

42. See, e.g., Bruce Ackerman, *We the People,* vol. 2: *Transformations* (Cambridge, Mass.: Belknap Press of Harvard University Press, 1998), 261–71. But compare Keith E. Whittington, *Constitutional Interpretation: Textual Meaning, Original Intent, and Judicial Review* (Lawrence, Kan.: University of Kansas Press, 1999), 11.

43. The Supreme Court of the United States being one of the original resisters. The most famous examples of the Court's early antagonism to the New Deal are *Schechter Poultry* and *Carter Coal.* In both, the Court struck down economic recovery efforts as unconstitutional extensions of the federal government's powers to regulate interstate commerce. A. L. A. Schechter Poultry Corp. v. United States, 295 U.S. 495 (1935); Carter v. Carter Coal, 298 U.S. 238 (1936).

44. See Jon Butler, *Becoming America: The Revolution Before 1776* (Cambridge, Mass.: Harvard University Press, 2000), 50, 236–39; see also Bernard Bailyn, *The Ordeal of Thomas Hutchinson* (Cambridge, Mass.: Belknap Press of Harvard University Press, 1974), 196–220.

45. A formal constitutional amendment must first be proposed by either two-thirds of each house of Congress or two-thirds of the states. It must then be ratified by three-fourths of the states. U.S. Const. art. V.

46. Bruce Ackerman, *We the People,* vol. 1: *Foundations* (Cambridge, Mass.: Belknap Press of Harvard University Press, 1991), 266–94.

47. FDR won in 1932 by 7 million votes, with 472 electors; in 1936 by 11 million votes—an unprecedented margin—with 523 electors (to his opponent's 8); in 1940 by 5 million votes, with 449 electors (to his opponent's 82); and in 1944 by 3.6 million votes, with 432 electors (to his opponent's 99). See Jean Edward Smith, *FDR* (New York: Random House, 2007), 287, 373–74, 479, 628.

48. Greg Price, "Representative Democracy? Democrats Won Popular Vote for House, Senate and President but Control Only One," *Newsweek,* Nov. 11, 2018, www.newsweek .com/democrats-won-popular-vote-2018-midterms-1207230 ("Republicans had 41.5 percent of all votes cast in Senate races, and Democrats 56.9 percent. The GOP received more than 33.5 million votes to the Democrats more than 46 million.").

49. Thomas Piketty, *Capital in the Twenty-First Century*, trans. Arthur Goldhammer (Cambridge, Mass.: Belknap Press of Harvard University Press, 2017); see also George Packer, *The Unwinding: An Inner History of the New America* (New York: Farrar, Straus and Giroux, 2013) (telling the story of a variety of people across America who have been facing stagnating wages and widening economic inequality, the 2008 recession, and changes in the sociopolitical landscape); John S. Ahlquist, "Labor Unions, Political Representation, and Economic Inequality," *Annual Review of Political Science* 20 (2017): 409 (summarizing research showing that the decline of labor unions erode[s] workers' bargaining power" and exacerbates economic inequality); and Axel Dreher and Noel Gaston, "Has Globalization Increased Inequality?," *Review of International Economics* 16 (2008): 516 (demonstrating that globalization has increased inequality).

50. "Over the past 25 years, there's been a fundamental shift in the relationship between level of educational attainment and partisanship. The Democratic Party has made significant gains among voters with a college degree or more education—a group that leaned toward the GOP 25 years ago. . . . The Democratic Party's advantage with more highly educated voters has grown over the past decade and is wider than it was in both 2016 and 2012." "In Changing U.S. Electorate, Race and Education Remain Stark Dividing Lines," *Pew Research Center,* June 2, 2020, 6, www.pewresearch.org/politics/wp-content /uploads/sites/4/2020/06/PP_2020.06.02_Party-ID_FINAL.pdf. President Biden won 59 percent of all college-educated voters: 75 percent of college-educated voters of color and 54 percent of college-educated white voters. "What Happened in 2020: National Crosstabs," *Catalist,* 2021, www.dropbox.com/s/ka9n5gzxwotfu1a/wh2020_public_release _crosstabs.xlsx?dl=0.

51. Tocqueville well understood that facts alone don't carry meaning: "There is a society only when men consider a great number of objects under the same aspect; when on a great number of subjects they have the same opinions; when, finally, the same facts give rise in them to the same impressions and the same thoughts." Tocqueville, *Democracy*, 358.

52. The classic work on this is Thomas Frank, *What's the Matter with Kansas: How Conservatives Won the Heart of America* (New York: Metropolitan Books, 2004). Focusing on his home state of Kansas, Frank examines why working-class and low-income citizens vote for a Republican Party that pursues policies inimical to their economic interests. For a view closer to Catherine's and critical of Frank, see Katherine J. Cramer, *The Politics of Resentment: Rural Consciousness in Wisconsin and the Rise of Scott Walker* (Chicago: University of Chicago Press, 2016).

53. Tocqueville, *Democracy,* 502 ("The doctrine of self-interest well understood does not produce great devotion; but it suggests little sacrifices each day; by itself it cannot make a man virtuous; but it forms a multitude of citizens who are regulated, temperate, moderate, farsighted, masters of themselves; and if it does not lead directly to virtue through the will, it brings them near to it insensibly through habits.").

54. See, e.g., Cramer, *Politics of Resentment*, 208–14; and Michael J. Sandel, *The Tyranny of Merit: What's Become of the Common Good?* (New York: Farrar, Straus and Giroux, 2020), 18–31.

55. During the 2016 election, Secretary Hillary Clinton's comment that half of Trump's sup-

porters belonged in a "basket of deplorables" became both a rallying cry and a symbol of the way the elite demonized "hard working," "regular" Americans. See Hanna Trudo, "Trump Releases New Ad Hitting Clinton for 'Deplorables' Remark," *Politico,* Sept. 12, 2016, www.politico.com/story/2016/09/clinton-deplorables-trump-ad-228018.

56. J. D. Vance, *Hillbilly Elegy: A Memoir of a Family and Culture in Crisis* (New York: Harper, 2016); Arlie Russell Hochschild, *Strangers in Their Own Land: Anger and Mourning on the American Right* (New York: New Press, 2016).

57. See also Cramer, *Politics of Resentment*; and Cecilia L. Ridgeway, "Why Status Matters for Inequality," *American Sociological Review* 79 (2013): 10–12.

58. For example, in Cramer's discussions with mostly older, rural Wisconsin residents who express resentment toward government policies, there is virtually no mention of the benefits of Social Security and Medicare, which most of them must receive.

59. Black workers faced an entirely different welfare state. Social Security was designed originally to exclude them. Arguably, the reluctance to extend Medicaid benefits today still rests on racist attitudes. See Robert C. Lieberman, "Race, Institutions, and the Administration of Social Policy," *Social Science History* 19 (1995): 514–15 (explaining how the initial Social Security Act of 1935 deliberately excluded professions historically pursued by Black Americans, namely agricultural and domestic workers); see also Zinzi D. Bailey and J. Robin Moon, "Racism and the Political Economy of Covid-19: Will We Continue to Resurrect the Past?," *Journal of Health Politics, Policy and Law* 45 (2020): 939–41 (exploring the ongoing racist underpinnings of public support strategies).

60. See Paul Mohai, David Pellow, and J. Timmons Roberts, "Environmental Justice," *Annual Review of Environmental Resources* 34 (2009): 410–13 (reviewing the debate around the relation between class and environmental injustice).

61. Some programs do target the urban poor in particular, but it is partisan propaganda to claim that those programs constitute the center of the modern welfare state. Moreover, these programs are those that have been targeted since President Clinton declared "the end of welfare as we know it." Aid to Families with Dependent Children (AFDC), for example, was originally passed to support children of low-income, single mothers. Once it became clear that the majority of those benefiting from the program were minority—predominantly African American—families, political support for AFDC dropped, resulting in its ultimate repeal under Clinton's 1996 welfare reform efforts. See Alma Carten, "The Racist Roots of Welfare Reform," *New Republic,* Aug. 22, 2016, https://newrepublic .com/article/136200/racist-roots-welfare-reform; see also Sandra Wexler and Rafael Engel, "Historical Trends in State-Level ADC/AFDC Benefits: Living on Less and Less," *Journal of Sociology and Social Welfare* 26 (1999): 51–55. Temporary Assistance for Needy Families (TANF), meant to replace AFDC, has instead led to a definite increase in the number of children living in poverty. Kathryn Edin and H. Luke Shaefer, "20 Years since Welfare 'Reform,'" *Atlantic,* Aug. 22, 2016, www.theatlantic.com/business/archive/2016 /08/20-years-welfare-reform/496730.

62. Peter Steinfels, "Clinton Signs Law Protecting Religious Practices," *New York Times,* Nov. 17, 1993, www.nytimes.com/1993/11/17/us/clinton-signs-law-protecting-religious -practices.html.

63. See Burwell v. Hobby Lobby, 573 U.S. 682, 736 (2014).

64. Benedict Anderson observes that the "mass ceremony" of reading a daily newspaper, "incessantly repeated at daily or half-daily intervals" in "silent privacy" yet with the knowledge that the ceremony "is being replicated simultaneously by thousands (or millions) of others," is a "vivid figure for the secular, historically clocked, imagined community." Benedict Anderson, *Imagined Communities: Reflections on the Origin and Spread of Nationalism,* rev. ed. (London: Verso, 1991), 35.

65. Conservative media and the conservative movement identified this common public opinion as the "liberal bias" of the mainstream media, opposition to which was the organizing principle of the conservative movement right up until the election of Ronald Reagan. See Nicole Hemmer, *Messengers of the Right: Conservative Media and the Transformation of American Politics* (Philadelphia: University of Pennsylvania Press, 2016), xii–xvi. The mainstream media, for example, generally disdained Sen. Barry Goldwater's presidential ambitions, sharing the consensus held by "a number of educated, sophisticated professionals" that Goldwater was a "nice guy" representing the "paranoid fringe" of society. Rick Perlstein, *Before the Storm: Barry Goldwater and the Unmaking of the American Consensus* (New York: Nation Books, 2009), 439–40; see also Hemmer, *Messengers of the Right,* 172.

66. Roger Ailes was a point of direct connection: he produced Rush Limbaugh's television program before joining Fox News. See Hemmer, *Messengers of the Right,* 262–65.

67. Benkler, Faris, and Roberts, *Network Propaganda,* 97.

68. As of 2018, 20 percent of American adults reported that they often got their news from social media. Among eighteen- to twenty-nine-year-olds the number was even higher, at 36 percent. Elisa Shearer, "Social Media Outpaces Print Newspapers in the U.S. as a News Source," *Pew Research Center,* Dec. 10, 2018, www.pewresearch.org/fact-tank/2018/12/10/social-media-outpaces-print-newspapers-in-the-u-s-as-a-news-source.

69. Marshall McLuhan famously argued that "the medium is the message" and thus that "the personal and social consequences of any medium . . . result from the new scale that is introduced into our affairs by . . . any new technology." Marshall McLuhan, *Understanding Media: The Extensions of Man* (New York: McGraw-Hill, 1965), 7–8. Neil Postman pursues the same idea that the "forms of human conversation," or its medium, dictates "what ideas we can conveniently express" and "inevitably . . . the important content of a culture." Even before the advent of the small screen, Postman wrote, "public discourse increasingly takes the form of entertainment. Our politics, religion, news, athletics, education and commerce have been transformed into congenial adjuncts of show business." Neil Postman, *Amusing Ourselves to Death: Public Discourse in the Age of Show Business* (London: Heinemann, 1986), 3–4, 6.

70. See, e.g., the Massachusetts Act of June 14, 1642, which made it compulsory for parents to teach their children the principles of religion, under threat of fine from the town. Nathaniel B. Shurtleff, ed., *Records of the Governor and Company of the Massachusetts Bay in New England,* vol. 2: *1642–1649* (Boston: William White, 1853), 8–9; see also Marcus W. Jernegan, "Compulsory Education in the American Colonies: I. New England," *School Review* 26 (1918): 735–40.

71. Marbury v. Madison, 5 U.S. (1 Cranch) 173, 178 (1803).

72. In American history, Ben Franklin is the figure uniting the founding of newspapers and

the writing of constitutions. See Walter Isaacson, *Benjamin Franklin: An American Life* (New York: Simon and Schuster, 2003).

73. Contrast Jefferson, who rarely spoke in public. See John Adams, *Diary and Autobiography of John Adams,* vol. 3, ed. L. H. Butterfield (Cambridge, Mass.: Belknap Press of Harvard University Press, 1962), 335 ("Mr. Jefferson . . . had never spoken in public [while in the Continental Congress]: and during the whole Time I sat[] with him in Congress, I never heard him utter three Sentences together. . . . Mr. Jefferson had the Reputation of a masterly Pen . . . [but] could stand no competition with . . . any one . . . in Elocution and public debate.").

74. Lincoln was a master of both the long address and of biblical imagery. Each of the Lincoln-Douglas debates lasted about three hours. The biblical cadences of the Gettysburg Address and the Second Inaugural make them the most famous examples of American political rhetoric.

75. Johnny Dwyer, "Trump's Big Tent Revival," *Topic,* April 2019, www.topic.com/trump-s-big-tent-revival (quoting Jason Brennan, a political scientist at Georgetown, as describing Trump rallies as "quasi-religious . . . the kind of mechanisms that make mass religion work are all the things that make politics work"); Jeff Sharlet, "'He's the Chosen One to Run America': Inside the Cult of Trump, His Rallies Are Church and He Is the Gospel," *Vanity Fair,* June 18, 2020, www.vanityfair.com/news/2020/06/inside-the-cult-of-trump-his-rallies-are-church-and-he-is-the-gospel ("To attend a Trump rally is to engage directly in the ecstasy of knowing what the great man knows, divinity disguised as earthly provocation."). In some cases, Trump held campaign rallies in churches, quite literally taking the place of the preacher at the pulpit. See Michael Collins and Courtney Subramanian, "Trump Rails against 'Left-Wing Mob' in Arizona Megachurch Rally, Tours Border Wall," *USA Today,* June 23, 2020, www.usatoday.com/story/news/politics/elections/2020/06/23/trump-reelection-president-heads-battleground-states-after-tulsa/3235553001.

76. Unlike earlier radio programing, in which a show had a single sponsor—credited at the beginning and end—television started selling smaller and smaller slices of a program to advertisers.

77. The ratio of commercials to television content has increased in recent years: in 2009, broadcast networks played an average of 13 minutes, 25 seconds of advertisements per hour. In 2013, the number was up to 14 minutes, 15 seconds. That same year, the majority of television ads were for 30-second spots, meaning that the average American viewer could see twenty-eight different commercials over one hour. Joe Flint, "TV Networks Load Up on Commercials," *Los Angeles Times,* May 12, 2014, www.latimes.com/entertainment/envelope/cotown/la-et-ct-nielsen-advertising-study-20140510-story.html. Postman describes the commercial as "the single most voluminous form of public communication in our society" and argues that it acclimated American audiences to "instant therapy." Postman, *Amusing Ourselves to Death,* 131–32.

78. Trump was permanently banned from Twitter on January 8, 2021, after inciting an attack on the Capitol. Twitter, Inc., "Permanent Suspension of @realDonaldTrump," *Twitter Blog,* Jan. 8, 2021, https://blog.twitter.com/en_us/topics/company/2020/suspension.html.

79. The same is true of some expressions of religion: Is the televangelist an entertainer? See

Razelle Frankl, *Televangelism: The Marketing of Popular Religion* (Carbondale, Ill.: Southern Illinois University Press, 1987), 145.

80. The emerging split between Fox News commentators—for example, Tucker Carlson and Sean Hannity—and its more traditional news desk is a prominent example of the tension between network news and entertainment. See Daniel D'Addario, "Shep Smith Has the Hardest Job on Fox News," *Time,* Mar. 15, 2018, https://time.com/longform/shepard -smith-fox-news (describing the "increasingly uneasy" relationship between Fox's opinion hosts and its news reporters). News as entertainment has deep roots in American television history. See Daya Kishan Thussu, *News as Entertainment: The Rise of Global Infotainment* (Thousand Oaks, Calif.: SAGE, 2007), 3 ("As television news has been commercialized, the need to make it entertaining has become a crucial priority for broadcasters."); Tony Schwartz, "Why TV News Is Increasingly Being Packaged as Entertainment," *New York Times,* Oct. 17, 1982, www.nytimes.com/1982/10/17/arts/why-tv-news -is-increasingly-being-packaged-as-entertainment.html."

81. This is not just an American problem. The popular and successful Danish television series *Borgen* has this conflict at its center.

82. The FCC formally imposed the Fairness Doctrine in 1949; it abolished it in 1987. Thomas W. Hazlett and David W. Sosa, "Was the Fairness Doctrine a 'Chilling Effect'? Evidence from the Postderegulation Radio Market," *Journal of Legal Studies* 26 (1997): 281–85.

83. Ahead of the 2020 election, Twitter released its Civic Integrity Policy, under which they labeled certain tweets falsely claiming victory in an election as misleading and removed tweets meant to "incite interference with the election." Vijay Gadde and Kayvon Beykpour, "Additional Steps We're Taking Ahead of the 2020 US Election," *Twitter,* Oct. 9, 2020, https://blog.twitter.com/en_us/topics/company/2020/2020-election-changes.html. Similarly, Facebook announced that it would refuse to accept new electioneering ads the week before the presidential election, remove posts discouraging people from voting, and label misleading or false information about the election results. "New Steps to Protect the US Elections," *Facebook,* Sept. 3, 2020, https://about.fb.com/news/2020/09/additional -steps-to-protect-the-us-elections.

84. Our increased reliance on smartphones has given rise to the term *nomophobia*—the fear of being "detached from mobile phone connectivity." Sudip Bhattacharya et al., "NO-MOPHOBIA: NO MObile PHone PhoBIA," *Journal of Family Medicine and Primary Care* 8 (2019): 1297. Brain imaging has revealed that people literally love their phones—the parts of the brain that light up when you see or hear a ringing iPhone are those "associated with feelings of love and compassion." Martin Lindstrom, "You Love Your iPhone. Literally," *New York Times,* Sept. 30, 2011, www.nytimes.com/2011/10/01/opinion/you -love-your-iphone-literally.html.

85. Trump rallies had a history of turning violent, both before and after the election. See, e.g., Fabiola Cineas, "Donald Trump Is the Accelerant," *Vox,* Jan. 9, 2021, www.vox .com/21506029/trump-violence-tweets-racist-hate-speech (summarizing over five years of violence incited, encouraged, or inspired by Trump); Marissa J. Lang et al., "After Thousands of Trump Supporters Rally in D.C., Violence Erupts when Night Falls," *Washington Post,* Nov. 15, 2020, www.washingtonpost.com/dc-md-va/2020/11/14

/million-maga-march-dc-protests (covering the skirmishes between Trump supporters and law enforcement, and counterprotesters, the week of the election); "Today's Rampage at the Capitol, as It Happened," *New York Times,* Feb. 6, 2021, www.nytimes.com /live/2021/01/06/us/washington-dc-protests (providing a survey of live coverage of the Capitol Riot).

86. As historian Philip Dray notes, "Lynchings were an undeniable part of daily life, as distinctly American as baseball games and church suppers. Men brought their wives and children along to the events . . . as if they had been at a company picnic." Philip Dray, *At the Hands of Persons Unknown* (New York: Modern Library, 2003), 17–18.

87. Michael Cohen, Trump's one-time lawyer, testified that Trump ran for president to improve his own personal brand. Brett Samuels, "Cohen: Trump Described His Campaign as "the Greatest Infomercial in Political History,'" *Hill,* Feb. 27, 2019, https://thehill .com/homenews/house/431802-cohen-trump-described-his-campaign-as-the-greatest -infomercial-in-political.

88. The most frequently visited pornography site had 78 billion page views in 2014—more traffic than CNN, Buzzfeed, and Huffington Post. Shira Tarrant, *The Pornography Industry: What Everyone Needs to Know* (New York: Oxford University Press, 2016), 44.

89. See Brian Crecente, "Nearly 70% of Americans Play Video Games, Mostly on Smartphones (Study)," *Variety,* Sept. 11, 2018, https://variety.com/2018/gaming/news/how -many-people-play-games-in-the-u-s-1202936332; Harvard Mental Health Letter, "Violent Video Games and Young People," *Harvard Medical School,* October 2010, www .health.harvard.edu/newsletter_article/violent-video-games-and-young-people.

90. For all his lambasting of what he called "fake news," Trump and traditional media enjoyed a symbiotic relationship. In 2017, cable news entered a "golden age"—Fox News saw "the best quarter in the history of cable news"; MSNBC grew by more than 50 percent; and overall national cable news viewership grew by more than 40 percent. Derek Thompson, "The Donald Trump Show Is Eating Television," *Atlantic,* Apr. 9, 2017, www.theatlantic.com/business/archive/2017/04/the-trump-show/522372. In turn, news stations gave Trump nearly $2 billion in free media coverage in the early months of the 2016 election alone. Nicholas Confessore and Karen Yourish, "$2 Billion Worth of Free Media for Donald Trump," *New York Times,* Mar. 15, 2016, www.nytimes.com/2016 /03/16/upshot/measuring-donald-trumps-mammoth-advantage-in-free-media.html.

91. For example, Civis Analytics describes its data services in the following way: "At the end of the day, data is about people. It's about people pushing voters to the polls, improving the customer experience, enhancing city services, or turning supporters into volunteers and donors." "The Civis Approach," *Civis Analytics*, www.civisanalytics.com/the -civis-method. Alexander Nix, who was chief executive of Cambridge Analytica when it worked with the Trump campaign in 2016, went on to market the same psychographic services to the commercial advertising market. See Matthew Rosenberg, Nicholas Confessore, and Carole Cadwalladr, "How Trump Consultants Exploited the Facebook Data of Millions," *New York Times,* Mar. 17, 2018, www.nytimes.com/2018/03/17/us/politics /cambridge-analytica-trump-campaign.html.

92. The obvious exception is an endorsement by President Trump in the Republican primaries. See Natalie Andrews and Lindsay Wise, "Alabama, Texas Primary Results Show

Power of Trump Endorsements," *Wall Street Journal,* July 15, 2020, www.wsj.com /articles/alabama-texas-results-show-power-of-trump-endorsements-11594836019. But see also Nathaniel Rakich and Meredith Conroy, "Almost Everyone Trump Endorses Wins Their Primary . . . But Is He Padding His Record?," *FiveThirtyEight,* Aug. 26, 2020, https://fivethirtyeight.com/features/almost-everyone-trump-endorses-wins-their -primary-but-is-he-padding-his-record (noting that while Trump's 98 percent victory rate in GOP primaries "is nothing short of extraordinary," it reflects "a strategy of endorsing candidates who are already in a good position to win—perhaps with the explicit goal of inflating his top-line win rate, and therefore his reputation").

93. See Mark Memmott, "Romney's Wrong and Right About the '47 Percent,'" *NPR,* Sept. 18, 2012, www.npr.org/sections/thetwo-way/2012/09/18/161333783/romneys-wrong-and -right-about-the-47-percent.

94. See Benkler, Faris, and Roberts, *Network Propaganda,* 20 ("Trump represents the pres- ent state of a dynamic system that has been moving Republican politicians, voters, audi- ences, and media to the right at least since Rush Limbaugh launched this model of mass media propaganda on talk radio in 1988.").

95. Today, a majority of Republicans believe the social media messages from QAnon are mostly or partly true. See Tommy Beer, "Majority of Republicans Believe the QAnon Conspiracy Theory Is Partly or Mostly True, Survey Finds," *Forbes,* Sept. 2, 2020, www .forbes.com/sites/tommybeer/2020/09/02/majority-of-republicans-believe-the-qanon -conspiracy-theory-is-partly-or-mostly-true-survey-finds/?sh=1519dd005231; see also Matthew Rosenberg, "Republican Voters Take a Radical Conspiracy Theory Mainstream," *New York Times,* Oct. 19, 2020, www.nytimes.com/2020/10/19/us/politics/qanon-trump -republicans.html.

96. See Naomi Oreskes and Eric Conway, *Merchants of Doubt: How a Handful of Scientists Obscured the Truth on Issues from Tobacco Smoke to Climate Change* (New York: Bloomsbury, 2010), 169–215.

97. See Michael Kazin, *The Populist Persuasion: An American History,* rev. ed. (Ithaca, N.Y.: Cornell University Press, 2017), 3–5, 221–66 (describing the gradual decline of left-wing populism and the ascendancy of the conservative agenda); Laura Weinrib, *The Taming of Free Speech: America's Civil Liberties Compromise* (Cambridge, Mass.: Har- vard University Press, 2016) (detailing the gradual subsuming of "radical" theories of civil liberties pushed by labor movements and leftists in the early twentieth century into the more "respectable" theories of civil liberties acceptable to both the ACLU and the U.S. Chamber of Commerce).

98. See Frank, *What's the Matter with Kansas?*; Joshua Zeitz, "Does the White Working Class Really Vote Against Its Own Interests?," *Politico Magazine,* Dec. 31, 2017, www .politico.com/magazine/story/2017/12/31/trump-white-working-class-history-216200 (arguing that Trump supporters are willing to sacrifice economic well-being for preser- vation of the cachet of "whiteness"). Interest in why (white) working-class people sup- port conservative candidates has persisted for decades. See, e.g., W. E. B. Du Bois, *Black Reconstruction in America: An Essay toward a History of the Part Which Black Folk Played in the Attempt to Reconstruct Democracy in America, 1860–1880* (1935; reprint, Oxford: Oxford University Press, 2007), 573; and David R. Roediger, *The Wages of*

Whiteness: Race and the Making of the American Working Class, 3rd ed. (London: Verso, 2007), 176–81.

99. See Stephen Wertheim, "Instrumental Internationalism: The American Origins of the United Nations, 1940–3," *Journal of Contemporary History* 54 (2019): 265 (arguing that American leadership in the United Nations, particularly in the organization's infancy, was a direct result of an increasingly popular view within the State Department that international political organizations were an "indispensable tool for implementing postwar US world leadership" and "projecting . . . American power").

100. See, e.g., Sven Beckert, *Empire of Cotton: A Global History* (New York: Knopf, 2014), xv (contending that successes of early capitalism were due to "slavery, the expropriation of indigenous peoples, imperial expansion, armed trade, and the assertion of sovereignty over people and land by entrepreneurs"); Timur Kuran, *The Long Divergence: How Islamic Law Held Back the Middle East* (Princeton, N.J.: Princeton University Press, 2011), 5–11 (arguing that Islamic legal institutions, in preventing the development of private capital accumulation, large-scale production, widespread exchange, and corporations, hindered the economic development of the Middle East for centuries).

101. The best recent example may be the years-long crisis over Greek debt, to which the EU, the International Monetary Fund, and the European Central Bank all responded by affirming a global neoliberalism. See Rebecca M. Nelson, Paul Belkin, and Derek E. Mix, "Greece's Debt Crisis: Overview, Policy Responses, and Implications," *Congressional Research Service,* Aug. 18, 2011, 6–11. Numerous writers have expressed concern over the creation of a governing elite who dictate the substantive policy agenda of nations— with little input from the rest of the world. See, e.g., Irving L. Janis, *Victims of Groupthink: A Psychological Study of Foreign-Policy Decisions and Fiascoes* (Boston: Houghton Mifflin, 1972), 14–49, 101–35 (assessing how the concentration of elites in government contributed to pernicious groupthink, which played a role in international "fiascoes" such as the Bay of Pigs invasion and the Vietnam War); C. Wright Mills, *The Power Elite* (New York: Oxford University Press, 1956), 11 (arguing that military, civil, economic, and political leaders often have similar interests that inform the governing policies of much of society).

102. Consider, for instance, the abortion reform movement in the years before *Roe v. Wade*. In the late 1960s and early 1970s, several states, including New York and California, began to liberalize their abortion statutes through legislation. However, "with public support for reform growing, a well-organized minority mobilized in opposition." In the eyes of this "well-organized minority," abortion was tied to the other progressive issues of the day: for example, the antiwar movement, the sexual revolution, and the prodrug liberalization movement. By 1972, this one-time minority was recast as Nixon's Silent Majority, and the Democrats—who in 1964 won all but six states—were pilloried as the party of "Acid, Amnesty and Abortion." Linda Greenhouse and Reva B. Siegel, "Before (and After) *Roe v. Wade*: New Questions About Backlash," *Yale Law Journal* 120 (2011): 2056–59.

103. See Milliken v. Bradley, 418 U.S. 717 (1974) (relieving the suburbs of responsibility to desegregate neighboring cities).

104. Linda Greenhouse and Reva Siegel, *Before* Roe v. Wade*: Voices That Shaped the Abor-*

tion Debate Before the Supreme Court's Ruling, 2nd ed. (New Haven, Conn.: Yale Law School, 2012), 256–60 (showing that the transformation of abortion into a women's rights issue sparked a countermovement in defense of traditional family values led by the Catholic Church and later coopted by the Republican Party).

105. In the 2016 election, white, born-again and evangelical Christians—who constituted 26 percent of the electorate—voted for Donald Trump by an overwhelming margin (81 percent to Clinton's 16 percent). Jessica Martinez and Gregory A. Smith, "How the Faithful Voted: A Preliminary 2016 Analysis," *Pew Research Center,* Nov. 9, 2016, www.pewresearch.org/fact-tank/2016/11/09/how-the-faithful-voted-a-preliminary -2016-analysis. The *Washington Post* reported similar results in 2020: white evangelical Christians made up around 28 percent of voters and voted for Donald Trump by 76 percent to Biden's 24 percent. "Exit Poll Results and Analysis for the 2020 Presidential Election," *Washington Post,* Dec. 14, 2020, www.washingtonpost.com/elections/inter active/2020/exit-polls/presidential-election-exit-polls.

106. Roughly speaking, the first step was supported by Charles Koch's investment in numerous think tanks and "scholarly" programs such as the Cato Institute, the Heritage Foundation, Americans for Prosperity, and, of course, the various Koch family foundations. See Nancy MacLean, *Democracy in Chains: The Deep History of the Radical Right's Stealth Plan for America* (New York: Viking, 2017). The second step was supported by the media investments of the Mercer and Murdoch families. See Jane Meyer, *Dark Money: The Hidden History of the Billionaires Behind the Rise of the Radical Right* (New York: Doubleday, 2016); Amanda Carpenter, "The GOP Is a Propaganda Party: Media Parasites Have Taken Control of the Host," *Bulwark,* Nov. 30, 2020, www .thebulwark.com/the-gop-is-a-propaganda-party; and Carole Cadwalladr, "The Great British Brexit Robbery: How Our Democracy Was Hijacked," *Guardian,* May 7, 2017, www.theguardian.com/technology/2017/may/07/the-great-british-brexit-robbery -hijacked-democracy.

107. While the Creationism of William Jennings Bryan and the Scopes Monkey Trial had dissipated by the mid-twentieth century, "the new Bible" of the movement that would become known as creation science was published in 1961. Michael Ruse, "Creationism," *The Stanford Encyclopedia of Philosophy*, ed. Edward N. Zalta (Mar. 21, 2021), https://plato.stanford.edu/entries/creationism. As the authors of that text put it: "We are realistic concerning the reception this work may expect, by and large, from evolutionary scientists. We believe that most of the difficulties associated with the Biblical record of the Flood are basically religious, rather than scientific." John C. Whitcomb Jr. and Henry M. Morris, *The Genesis Flood: The Biblical Record and Its Scientific Implications* (Philadelphia: Presbyterian and Reformed Publishing, 1961), xxii.

108. See Neeela Banerjee, Lisa Song, and David Hasemyer, "Exxon's Own Research Confirmed Fossil Fuel's Role in Global Warming Decades Ago," *Inside Climate News,* Sept. 16, 2015, https://insideclimatenews.org/news/16092015/exxons-own-research -confirmed-fossil-fuels-role-in-global-warming.

109. See Oreskes and Conway, *Merchants of Doubt,* 59–65. More recently, consider the attacks on Dr. Anthony Fauci, who was the public face of the regulatory, public health response to Covid-19.

110. In 2019, Pew Research Center found that 59 percent of Republicans had a negative view of colleges' effects on society, while only 33 percent had a positive view of the same. Compare this figure to the 37 percent of Republicans who had a negative view of colleges in 2015. Kim Parker, "The Growing Partisan Divide in Views of Higher Education," *Pew Research Center,* Jan. 30, 2019, www.pewsocialtrends.org/essay/the -growing-partisan-divide-in-views-of-higher-education.

111. The exception here is former Fox commentator Bill O'Reilly, who has a graduate-school education. See "Bill O'Reilly," *Fox News* (last visited Jan. 28, 2021), https://web.archive .org/web/20101231213540/http://www.foxnews.com/bios/talent/oreilly.

112. For one example of the conservative critique of the undeserving other, see Nick Eberstadt, "The Rise of Entitlements in Modern America, 1960–2010," in *A Nation of Takers: America's Entitlement Epidemic* (West Conshohocken, Pa.: Templeton Press, 2012), 24–39; for a reply, see William Galston, "Have We Become a 'Nation of Takers'?," 93–113, in the same volume.

113. Both parties supported the same international institutions; neither was about to pull out of the Middle East or withdraw support from NATO and the EU; both supported free trade; both supported the projection of American military force through bases around the world; neither knew how to confront the rising power of China or bring peace to the Middle East.

114. Benkler, Faris, and Roberts, *Network Propaganda,* 7 ("The epochal change reflected by the 2016 election . . . was not that Republicans beat Democrats. . . . The critical change was that in 2016 the party of Ronald Reagan and the two presidents Bush was defeated by the party of Donald Trump, Breitbart, and billionaire Robert Mercer.").

115. See Kyle Cheney, "No, Clinton Didn't Start the Birther Thing. This Guy Did," *Politico,* Sept. 16, 2016, www.politico.com/story/2016/09/birther-movement-founder-trump -clinton-228304; Michael C. Bender, "Donald Trump Blames Hillary Clinton over the Tax Codes," *Wall Street Journal,* Oct. 4, 2016, www.wsj.com/articles/donald-trump -blames-hillary-clinton-over-the-tax-code-1475624308.

116. See Paul W. Kahn, "Sacrificial Nation," *Utopian,* Mar. 29, 2010, www.the-utopian.org /post/2340099709/sacrificial-nation.

117. In response to Gov. Andrew Cuomo's request for help to alleviate the medical supply shortage that threatened to overwhelm the New York City hospital system, Jared Kushner replied, "People are going to suffer and that's their problem." Katherine Eban, "'That's Their Problem': How Jared Kushner Let the Markets Decide America's Covid-19 Fate," *Vanity Fair,* Sept. 17, 2020, www.vanityfair.com/news/2020/09/jared-kushner -let-the-markets-decide-covid-19-fate.

Chapter 2. Killingworth Copes

Note to epigraph: Alexis de Tocqueville, *Democracy in America* [1835], ed. and trans. Harvey C. Mansfield and Delba Winthrop (Chicago: University of Chicago Press, 2000), 13.

1. Tocqueville, 6; see also at 7 ("To wish to stop democracy would then appear to be to struggle against God himself.").

2. Tocqueville, 53 ("Peoples can therefore draw two great political consequences from the

same social state: these consequences differ prodigiously between themselves, but they both issue from the same fact.").

3. Tocqueville, 491.

4. Dan Goldberg, "'It's Going to Disappear': Trump's Changing Tone on Coronavirus," *Politico,* Mar. 17, 2020, www.politico.com/news/2020/03/17/how-trump-shifted-his -tone-on-coronavirus-134246 (quoting Trump saying, "It's going to disappear. One day, it's like a miracle, it will disappear," on February 28).

5. In Killingworth today, many town meetings are formally "hearings." The formal Town Meeting is the body that exercises the legislative authority of the town. A Town Meeting is required to vote on the budget each spring. The board of selectmen will also call a Town Meeting whenever legislative authority must be exercised—for example, to pur-chase property or take on debt. To be clear, from this point on, I will use upper case (Town Meeting) to refer to formal meetings at which there is a vote of the town and lower case (town meetings) to refer to the many hearings that occur throughout the year.

6. Kyle Morris, "Black Lives Matter Co-Founder in 2015: 'We Are Trained Marxists,'" *Breitbart,* June 22, 2020, www.breitbart.com/politics/2020/06/22/black-lives-matter-co -founder-in-2015-we-are-trained-marxists; Joel Berry (@JoelWBerry), *Twitter,* Jan. 13, 2021, 3:05 p.m., https://twitter.com/JoelWBerry/status/1349447473593524226; see also Hollie Mckay, "Behind Susan Rosenberg and the Roots of Left-Wing Domestic Ex-tremism," *Fox News,* Nov. 17, 2020, www.foxnews.com/us/susan-rosenberg-left-wing -domestic-extremism-roots.

7. Caleb Parke, "Catholic Churches Burned, Vandalized over Weekend as Police Investi-gate: 'Where's the Outrage?,'" *Fox News,* July 13, 2020, www.foxnews.com/us/church -fire-florida-california-statue-burned-police-investigation.

8. As I write this, I read of the withdrawal of the public health officer in Ohio just hours after her appointment. She explained that she took the action after being "informed that the former director's family had faced harassment from the public." Brian Planalp, "Re-port: Ohio Health Director Candidate Withdrew Name Due to 'Harassment,'" *Fox 19 Now,* Sept. 11, 2020, www.fox19.com/2020/09/11/report-odh-director-candidate-withdrew -name-due-harassment. Accounts of such resignations of public health officials have been common over the time of the pandemic.

9. See "QuickFacts: Killingworth Town, Middlesex County, Connecticut," *United States Census Bureau* (last visited August 22, 2021), www.census.gov/quickfacts/fact/table /killingworthtownmiddlesexcountyconnecticut,US/PST045219.

10. The U.S. Census Bureau reports 2,300 households, but town hall maintains a mailing list of 2,700 home addresses.

11. But compare to J. Eric Oliver, who believes that social diversity—not homogeneity— contributes to good local government. He makes this argument, however, in the context of regional governance, charging that dividing *metropolitan* regions into smaller juris-dictions contributes to urban pathologies. J. Eric Oliver, *Democracy in Suburbia* (Prince-ton, N.J.: Princeton University Press, 2001).

12. The U.S. Census reports 4 percent in poverty in 2019 (compared to 10.5 percent across the United States). See QuickFacts: Killingworth, *U.S. Census Bureau.* City-Data.com reports a significantly lower number: just 1 percent below the poverty level in 2018. See

"Poverty Rates in Killingworth, CT," *City-Data* (last visited Jan. 29, 2021), www.city -data.com/poverty/poverty-Killingworth-Connecticut.html.

13. For a contrary view, see Paul E. Peterson, *City Limits* (Chicago: University of Chicago Press, 1981), 71 ("Because the interests of local and national governments diverge, the patterns of public policies promulgated by the two levels of government are different.").

14. See Catherine Iino, Opinion, "Small Town, Small Experience," *Washington Post,* Oct. 19, 2008, www.washingtonpost.com/wp-dyn/content/article/2008/10/17/AR2008101702530 .html.

15. Tocqueville, *Democracy,* 57–58.

16. See Chris Strohm, "Trump Presses Barr on Political Rivals as DOJ Shows Restraint," *Bloomberg,* Oct. 8, 2020, www.bloomberg.com/news/articles/2020-10-08/trump-presses -barr-to-target-political-enemies-as-doj-stays-mute.

17. "Why One Concerned Resident Is So 'Passionate' About KAA and Its Volunteers," *Killingworth Ambulance Association* (Nov. 11, 2019), www.killingworthambulance.org /2019/11/11/lally-why-im-so-passionate-about-kaa-and-its-volunteers.

18. See Daniel J. Hopkins, *The Increasingly United States: How and Why American Political Behavior Nationalized* (Chicago: University of Chicago Press, 2018).

19. See, e.g., Raj Chetty et al., "The Fading American Dream: Trends in Absolute Income Mobility since 1940," *Science* 356 (2017): 398 (finding that compared with 90 percent of children born in 1940, around 50 percent of children born in the 1980s are likely to have higher lifetime incomes than their parents); Penelope Muse Abernathy, "The Expanding News Desert," *UNC: Hussman School of Journalism and Media* (2018), www.usnews deserts.com/reports/expanding-news-desert (reporting that since 2004, more than 1,800 local newspapers have closed and many of the remaining newspapers are unable to provide meaningful coverage of local issues); Jeffrey M. Jones, "U.S. Church Membership Down Sharply in Past Two Decades," *Gallup,* Apr. 18, 2019, https://news.gallup.com /poll/248837/church-membership-down-sharply-past-two-decades.aspx (discussing statistics that demonstrate a decline in church membership from a high of 76 percent in 1947 to a low of 50 percent in 2018); and "The American Family Today," *Pew Research Center,* Dec. 17, 2015, www.pewsocialtrends.org/2015/12/17/1-the-american-family -today (noting that, in contrast to 1960, there is no longer any single dominant family form in America).

20. Compare Robert Ellickson, *Order Without Law: How Neighbors Settle Disputes* (Cambridge, Mass.: Harvard University Press, 1991), discussed below in chapter 3.

21. Tocqueville, *Democracy,* 7.

22. "In coming closer [the rich and the poor] seem to have found new reasons for hating each other, and casting glances full of terror and envy, they mutually repel each other from power." Tocqueville, 10.

23. Tocqueville, 10.

24. "By a strange concurrence of events, religion finds itself enlisted for the moment among the powers democracy is overturning, and it is often brought to reject the equality it loves and to curse freedom as an adversary." Tocqueville, 11.

25. Tocqueville, 29–30 (attributing this original condition to the equality of class among emigrants—"It is hardly the happy and the powerful who go into exile"—and the quality

of the soil, which could not produce enough "to enrich a master and a tenant famer at once").

26. Tocqueville, 31.

27. Tocqueville, 406, 12 ("[America] sees the results of the democratic revolution operating among us without having had the revolution itself."). Tocqueville is repeating a charge earlier made by Abbé Raynal. Thomas Paine replied that, quite to the contrary, "our style and manner of thinking have undergone a revolution, more extraordinary than the political revolution of the country. We see with other eyes; hear with other ears; and think with other thoughts." Thomas Paine, *Letter Addressed to the Abbé Raynal on the Affairs of North-America, in Which the Mistakes in the Abbé's Account of the Revolution of America Are Corrected and Cleared Up* (Philadelphia: Melchior Steiner, 1782), 49. John Adams also saw it differently—by his account: "The Revolution was effected before the war commenced. The Revolution was in the minds and hearts of the people, a change in their religious sentiments of their duties and obligations." John Adams to H. Niles, Feb. 13, 1816, in *The Political Writings of John Adams*, ed. George W. Carey (Washington, D.C.: Regnery, 2000), 708.

28. In Tocqueville's time, this accusation was directed against Andrew Jackson. Tocqueville was skeptical, writing that the time in America for such dictatorial undertakings had "not yet come." Nevertheless, he continued, "General Jackson is the slave of the majority: he follows it in its wishes, its desires, its half-uncovered instinct, or rather he divines it and runs to place himself at its head." Tocqueville, *Democracy,* 377.

29. Tocqueville thought America to represent the "natural limits" of the "great social revolution" of democracy, but he did not think that France should or would adopt the same governmental institutions: "I am very far from believing that [Americans] have found the only form of government that democracy can give itself." Tocqueville, 12.

30. Tocqueville, 227.

31. Before John Winthrop and his followers even set foot in New England, he declared that they "shall be as a city upon a hill," with "the eyes of all people . . . upon [them]." John Winthrop, "A Model of Christian Charity," in *The American Puritans,* ed. Perry Miller (New York: Columbia University Press, 1982), 83. President Reagan picked up on this theme at the end of the twentieth century, describing America as a model of freedom and liberty for the rest of the world. See, e.g., Ronald Reagan, "Shining City on a Hill: 1988 State of the Union Address," *C-SPAN,* Jan. 25, 1988, www.c-span.org/video/?c4746361 /shining-city-hill-ronald-reagan-1988-state-union-address.

32. I discuss the Founders' view in detail in Paul W. Kahn, *Legitimacy and History: Self-Government in American Constitutional Theory* (New Haven, Conn.: Yale University Press, 1992), 9–31.

33. Tocqueville, *Democracy,* 40.

34. See Tocqueville, *Democracy,* 57.

35. Henry David Thoreau, "Slavery in Massachusetts" [1854], in *Reform Papers,* ed. Thomas F. Glick (Princeton, N.J.: Princeton University Press, 1973), 99; Ralph Waldo Emerson, "Historical Discourse at Concord" [Sept. 12, 1835], in *Collected Works,* vol. 2, ed. Edward Waldo Emerson (Boston: Houghton Mifflin, 1903–4), 46–47. See also Lord Bryce, describing the Town Meeting as "the most perfect school of self-government in

any modern country." James Bryce, "National Characteristics as Moulding Public Opinion," in *The American Commonwealth* (Indianapolis, Ind.: Liberty Fund, 1995), 942.

36. Emerson, "Historical Discourse at Concord," 47.

37. See, e.g., Frank M. Bryan, *Real Democracy: The New England Town Meeting and How It Works* (Chicago: University of Chicago Press, 2004), 25–43 (tracing this history).

38. Town Ordinance of 1671, cited in correspondence from Town Historian Tom Lentz.

39. See "Population of Connecticut Towns, 1756–1820," *Connecticut Secretary of State*, https://portal.ct.gov/SOTS/Register-Manual/Section-VII/Population-1756-1820. That number included north and south Killingworth, which were divided into the separate towns of Killingworth and Clinton in 1838. The first separate census of the two towns occurred in 1840, at which point Killingworth had 1,130 residents. "Population of Connecticut Towns, 1830–1890," *Connecticut Secretary of State*, https://portal.ct.gov/SOTS/Register-Manual/Section-VII/Population-1830-1890.

40. See Michael Kammen, *A Machine That Would Go of Itself: The Constitution in American Culture* (New York: Knopf, 1986). Kammen's title was taken from an 1888 essay by James Russell Lowell to the Reform Club of New York, in which he warned that Americans have become "neglectful of our political duties."

41. See below, chapter 7.

42. Tocqueville, *Democracy,* 346.

43. See, e.g., J. H. H. Weiler, "COVID, Europe, and the Self-Asphyxiation of Democracy," in *Democracy in Times of Pandemic: Different Futures Imagined*, ed. Miguel Poiares Maduro and Paul W. Kahn (Cambridge: Cambridge University Press, 2020), 141.

44. Tocqueville, *Democracy,* 54. See also Theda Skocpol, "How Americans Became Civic," in *Civic Engagement in American Democracy*, ed. Theda Skocpol and Morris Fiorina (Harrisonburg, Va.: Brookings Institution, 1999), 27–80 (plotting the growth of civic associations and describing how they mediated among the local, state, and national, modeling the political relations among governmental units). Compare her other essay in the same volume, "Advocates Without Members: The Recent Transformation of American Civic Life," at 461 (describing a late twentieth-century shift in organizational structure, such that organizations are now created centrally—in D.C.—and recruit members directly from the national office. They no longer build up from the local to the national but rather move directly from the national to the individual member or contributor).

45. Robert Putnam, *Bowling Alone: The Collapse and Revival of American Community* (New York: Simon and Schuster, 2000).

46. Somewhat humorously, the sign actually said, "God love's Trump." The misplaced apostrophe remained on the sign in 2020.

47. Compare Bryan, *Real Democracy,* 20 ("Little towns allow us to gaze at the important inner space of politics.").

48. Arthur Vidich and Joseph Bensman, who wrote a well-known study of a small town in the postwar era, expressed well my ambition in this work: "[This] is not a study of a rural community. It is a study of how some of the major institutions of a society work themselves out in a particular community." Arthur Vidich and Joseph Bensman, *Small Town in Mass Society: Class, Power, and Religion in a Rural Community,* rev. ed. (Princeton, N.J.: Princeton University Press, 1968), xxix.

49. Compare Michael Sandel, *Democracy's Discontent: America in Search of a Public Philosophy* (Cambridge, Mass.: Belknap Press of Harvard University Press, 1996), 6 ("The republican conception of freedom, unlike the liberal conception, requires a formative politics, a politics that cultivates in citizens the qualities of character self-government requires.").

50. Tocqueville, *Democracy,* 291–92 ("In the United States, the sum of men's education is directed toward politics."); see also Amy Guttman, *Democratic Education* (Princeton, N.J.: Princeton University Press, 1987); and Norman Nie, Jane Junn, and Kenneth Stehlik-Barry, *Education and Democratic Citizenship in America* (Chicago: University of Chicago Press, 1996), 5–6.

51. Tocqueville, *Democracy,* 676.

Part II. Democratic Participation and Civil Society

1. See James Truslow Adams, *The Epic of America* (Boston: Little, Brown, 1931), 31 ("The American dream was beginning to take form in the hearts of men. The economic motive was unquestionably powerful, often dominant, in the minds of those who took part in the great migration, but mixed with this was also frequently present the hope of a better and a freer life, a life in which a man might think as he would and develop as he willed.").

2. See Frederick Jackson Turner, "The Significance of the Frontier in American History," in *Annual Report of the American Historical Association for the Year 1893* (Washington, D.C.: Government Printing Office, 1894), 197–227. Turner begins his essay by noting that the superintendent of the census declared the end of the frontier in 1880.

3. There is a substantial body of work theorizing a connection between suburban architecture and an autonomous lifestyle. See, e.g., Ray Suarez, *The Old Neighborhood: What We Lost in the Great Suburban Migration, 1966–1999* (New York: Free Press, 1999); and Phillip Langdon, *A Better Place to Live: Reshaping the American Suburb* (Amherst, Mass.: University of Massachusetts Press, 1994); see also William H. Whyte, *The Organization Man* (New York: Simon and Schuster, 1956), 330–49 (chapter 25, "The Web of Friendship"). But see J. Eric Oliver, *Democracy in Suburbia* (Princeton, N.J.: Princeton University Press, 2001), 154–74 (arguing that, aside from communities in the Sun Belt, the data do not support this architecture-based theory).

4. See David Foster et al., "Wildlands and Woodlands, Farmlands and Communities: Broadening the Vision for New England," *Harvard Forest, Harvard University* (2017), 6–7, http://mediad.publicbroadcasting.net/p/mpbn/files/201709/wildlands_and_woodlands _2017_report.pdf.

5. On privatization as a general phenomenon of suburban living, see Kenneth T. Jackson, *Crabgrass Frontier: The Suburbanization of the United States* (New York: Oxford University Press, 1985). Even within suburbs, there are degrees of privatization. Levittowns were quite the opposite of the modern developments, and the new McMansions push privatization to something of an extreme. See Herbert J. Gans, *The Levittowners: Ways of Life and Politics in a New Suburban* Community (New York: Vintage Books, 1967).

6. The trend had begun earlier with insurance companies. See Stacey Stowe, "Latest Merger Makes It Clearer Than Ever: Hartford Is No Longer the Insurance Capital," *New York*

Times, Nov. 21, 2003, www.nytimes.com/2003/11/21/nyregion/latest-merger-makes-it
-clearer-than-ever-hartford-no-longer-insurance-capital.html ("After the Connecticut
Mutual Life Insurance Company merged with MassMutual in 1996, the company's headquarters moved to Springfield, Mass. When the Connecticut General Life Insurance
Company merged with the INA Corporation to become Cigna in 1983, the home office
became Philadelphia.").

7. The classic work tracing this movement away from community associations and toward
   individualism is Robert D. Putnam's *Bowling Alone: The Collapse and Revival of American Society* (New York: Simon and Schuster, 2000).

8. Alexis de Tocqueville, *Democracy in America* [1835], ed. and trans. Harvey C. Mansfield and Delba Winthrop (Chicago: University of Chicago Press, 2000), 481.

Chapter 3. Self-Government as Volunteering

1. The political scientist's equation of democracy and voting traces in large part to Joseph
   A. Schumpeter's *Capitalism, Socialism, and Democracy* (New York: Harper and Brothers,
   1942). Robert D. Putnam, for example, sees this connection: *Bowling Alone: The Collapse and Revival of American Society* (New York: Simon and Schuster, 2000), 494, n. 2.

2. See J. Eric Oliver, Shang E. Ha, and Zachary Callen, *Local Elections and the Politics of
   Small-Scale Democracy* (Princeton, N.J.: Princeton University Press, 2012), 55–56, 64–
   86. Compare Jane J. Mansbridge, *Beyond Adversary Democracy* (Chicago: University of
   Chicago Press, 1983), 132 ("In Bedford . . . turnout soared to 74 percent in 1834 and to
   75 percent in 1843, averaging 63 percent in the twelve contested meetings between 1833
   and 1846. But in towns where there were no bitter controversies, like Lincoln, Acton, Car-
   lyle, and Lexington, turnout averaged 30 percent to 43 percent in the period 1821–40.").

3. One influential view in the social science literature, for example, argues that the threat that
   residents will move to other jurisdictions that align better with their interests is sufficient,
   by itself, to ensure that government leaders are responsive to residents' self-interest. On
   this view, low participation rates can be a sign of governmental success. See Charles M.
   Tiebout, "A Pure Theory of Local Expenditures," *Journal of Political Economy* 64
   (1956): 419–20.

4. Bryan makes this mistake. He contrasts representative democracies with the "real democracy" of the Town Meeting: "Real democracy (for good or ill) occurs only when all
   eligible citizens of a general-purpose government are legislators; that is called to meet
   in a deliberative, face-to-face assembly and to bind themselves under laws they fashion
   themselves." Frank M. Bryan, *Real Democracy: The New England Town Meeting and
   How It Works* (Chicago: University of Chicago Press, 2004), 3–4.

5. See Oliver et al., *Local Elections,* 28.

6. Oliver, *Democracy in Suburbia,* 6 ("To meet their social needs and facilitate the process
   of self-rule, American localities traditionally have relied on the voluntary activities of
   their residents."). For social scientists who model choice as a calculation of costs and
   benefits, government as volunteerism is a difficult concept, for the cost is always more
   than the benefit to the individual. Paul Peterson expresses this form of reasoning: "A
   convenient way of roughly calculating whether or not a policy is in the interest of a city

is to consider whether its benefits/tax ratio is more or less than 1.0, that is, whether the marginal benefits exceed the marginal cost to the average taxpayer." Paul E. Peterson, *City Limits* (Chicago: University of Chicago Press, 1981), 42. Efforts to reconcile the fact of volunteering with the method of calculation turn to the subjective satisfactions that volunteers find in their activities. That, however, reduces governance to a hobby, which is fundamentally an antipolitical stance.

7. See Putnam, *Bowling Alone*, 275 ("Much of the decline of civic engagement in America during the last third of the twentieth century is attributable to the replacement of an unusually civic generation by several generations [their children and grandchildren] that are less embedded in community life.").

8. New Haven has famously been the site of studies of these conflicts. See Robert A. Dahl, *Who Governs? Democracy and Power in an American City* (New Haven, Conn.: Yale University Press, 1961), 3. But compare G. William Domhoff, "Who Really Ruled in Dahl's New Haven?," *Who Rules America?* (blog), Sept. 2005, https://whorulesamerica .ucsc.edu/local/new_haven.html.

9. See Oliver et al., *Local Elections,* 10 ("The political terrain of most American localities is defined by the concerns of local stakeholders with the quality of their living environments, the maintaining of property values, and the balance between low taxes and basic service provision. The small size, limited scope, and low bias of most places greatly attenuate most of the political cleavages that fracture large, urban places."); see also Robert A. Dahl and Edward R. Tufte, *Size and Democracy* (Stanford, Calif.: Stanford University Press, 1973), 14 ("Smaller democracies make it easier for a citizen to perceive a relation between his own self-interest or understanding of the good and a public or general interest, the interests of others, or general conceptions of the good.").

10. Tocqueville, *Democracy,* 489. ("Americans of all ages, all conditions, all minds constantly unite. Not only do they have commercial and industrial associations . . . but they also have a thousand other kinds: religious, moral, grave, futile, very general and very particular, immense and very small.").

11. This point was brought to my attention on several occasions by Lt. Gov. Nancy Wyman—most recently at the swearing-in ceremony in Killingworth in 2017.

12. See Oliver et al., *Local Elections*, 18, n. 8 (analogizing Town Meetings to faculty meetings).

13. Mansbridge observed these same patterns in Town Meetings some fifty years ago: "In [the] town meeting, as in many face-to-face discussions, the fears of making a fool of oneself, of losing control, of criticism, and of making enemies all contribute to the tension that arises in the settlement of disputes." Mansbridge, *Beyond Adversary Democracy,* 70.

14. Jenn McCulloch, "Longtime Selectman Fred Dudek (R) Says 'Time to Step Up,'" *Zip06,* Oct. 24, 2017, www.shorepublishing.com/news/20171024/longtime-selectman-fred-dudek -r-says-x2018time-to-step-upx2019.

15. Robert Frost, "Mending Wall," in *North of Boston,* 2nd ed. (New York: Henry Holt, 1915), 11, 13.

16. Ed Ricciuti, "Killingworth Stompin' Ground," *Facebook,* Dec. 4, 2020.

17. Killingworth Town Code art. VI, § 500-43(A)(7).

18. Teachers in the public schools do not work for the town but are instead employees of Regional School District 17, formed in 1973.

19. Joe Murphy, Corky Siemaszko, and Phil Helsel, "Georgia Gov. Brian Kemp Sues Atlanta Mayor over City's Face Mask Mandate," *NBC News,* July 16, 2020, www.nbcnews.com /news/us-news/georgia-gov-brian-kemp-bans-local-governments-mandating-masks -n1234046 (noting that even as Kemp forbade local governments from imposing a mask mandate, Georgia's attorney general announced that "the State of Georgia continues to urge citizens to wear masks."); "Florida Governor Ron DeSantis Says Masks Should Be Voluntary," *CBS Miami,* June 19, 2020, https://miami.cbslocal.com/2020/06/19/florida -governor-ron-desantis-says-masks-should-be-voluntary ("While DeSantis won't man-date the use of masks, he has encouraged them—as has state Surgeon General Scott Rivkees."). Even President Trump came to speak in this way. Daniel Victor, Lew Serviss, and Azi Paybarah, "In His Own Words, Trump on the Coronavirus and Masks," *New York Times,* Oct. 2, 2020, www.nytimes.com/2020/10/02/us/politics/donald-trump-masks .html.

20. This sentiment is hardly unique to Killingworth. Activists in California attempted—and ultimately failed—to include a proposition on the 2018 ballot to exempt adults without dependent children from paying any taxes funding public education. "Should People Without Kids Not Have to Pay School Taxes?," *CBS Sacramento,* Nov. 10, 2017, https:// sacramento.cbslocal.com/2017/11/10/public-education-taxes-initiative.

21. "Mary Robbenhaar-Fretz," Killingworth Ambulance Association, May 19, 2019, www .killingworthambulance.org/2019/05/15/mary-robbenhaar-fretz.

22. "Lara Hajek," Killingworth Ambulance Association, Apr. 6, 2019, www.killingworth ambulance.org/2019/04/06/lara-hajek/.

23. The ambulance association, unlike the fire department, has a source of third-party fund-ing from health insurance policies that cover the cost of a trip to the hospital. The differ-ence is reflected in the town budget. The fire department is listed in the town's budget, but the ambulance association takes care of its own budget. See Cathy Iino, "We Need to Start Now," *Zip06,* July 11, 2019, www.zip06.com/news/20190711/iino-we-need-to -start-now ("The Killingworth Ambulance Association [KAA] has some income from insurance reimbursements; the town provides the land for KAA's headquarters, but the association has been able to cover its own budget and, in fact, has donated equipment and programs to the town.").

24. There is also the Haddam-Killingworth Recreation Department and the Haddam-Killing-worth Youth and Family Services. They are both privately incorporated but funded by the towns—the same structure as the library and the fire department. A mix of volunteers and professionals staffs both.

25. Margery C. Hennan, "Our First Ten Years," *Killingworth Library,* Nov. 15, 1973, https:// killingworthlibrary.org/about-us/our-first-ten-years.

26. "QuickFacts: Killingworth Town, Middlesex County, Connecticut," *U.S. Census Bureau* (2019), www.census.gov/quickfacts/killingworthtownmiddlesexcountyconnecticut.

27. Approximately 6 percent (12 of 204) of the students at the elementary school were eli-gible for free lunch and an additional 2 percent (5 of 204) for reduced lunch for the 2019–20 school year. "Killingworth Elementary School," *National Center for Education*

Statistics, https://nces.ed.gov/ccd/schoolsearch/school_detail.asp?Search=1&DistrictID =0903539&ID=090353900760.

28. Compare Katherine J. Cramer, *The Politics of Resentment: Rural Consciousness in Wisconsin and the Rise of Scott Walker* (Chicago: University of Chicago Press, 2016). She finds that rural residents deeply resent urban power centers and particularly state employees. The communities she studies are close to the Killingworth of the early twentieth century—impoverished and declining. Resentment is surely present in today's Killingworth, but it does not rest on community decline. It arises from privatization and nationalization; it has a broad, national focus.

29. Oliver argues that homogeneity tends to suppress resident participation in local politics because, absent differences of interest, politics will simply be less interesting. With little at stake, why get involved? Oliver, *Democracy in Suburbia,* 75. No doubt, Killingworth town meetings might draw more residents were the issues of greater weight. People volunteer, however, not to advance particular interests but to do their part in and for the community.

30. A variation on its name, "Kenilworth," was first used in 1667 by the General Court of the Colony of Connecticut. The General Court would later become the General Assembly. The spelling of "Killingworth" remained unstable through the beginning of the eighteenth century. Thomas L. Lentz, "The History of Killingworth, Connecticut," *Killingworth Historical Society,* 2016, www.killingworthhistorical.org/town-history.html.

31. "An Act for Securing the Rights of Conscience in Matters of Religion, to Christians of Every Denomination in this State," in *Acts and Laws of the State of Connecticut, in America* (New London: Timothy Green, 1784), 21–22.

32. Conn. Gen. Stat. §§ 7-7, 7-8.

33. The town does not generally keep attendance records beyond approximately ten years. A check of those records showed an attendance of sixteen at a Special Town Meeting in February 2010, called to approve a $475,000 transfer of funds to complete athletic fields; the annual Town Meeting to approve the budget in 2010 had just twenty-nine residents present; in 2012, there were sixty-three; in 2013, there were forty-five; and in 2019, just twenty-four.

34. Zimmerman reports that in 1996 the average length of a Connecticut Town Meeting was forty-five minutes. He also comments on the packing of Town Meetings by interest groups, such as environmentalists, families, and teachers. Joseph F. Zimmerman, *The New England Town Meeting: Democracy in Action* (Westport, Conn.: Praeger, 1999), 121, 124.

35. Conn. Gen. Stat. § 9-167a.

36. See Mansbridge, *Beyond Adversary Democracy,* 252–69. She observes the drive toward consensus in a small town but does not connect it to an ethos of volunteering.

37. I can find no record of an assessment challenge going to court in the twenty-five years we have lived here. During that same period, I have found six recorded cases involving zoning decisions.

38. "Plan of Conservation and Development, 2018–2028," *Town of Killingworth,* Aug. 9, 2018, 88, www.townofkillingworth.com/documents/2018/POCD%20Aug%209%202018 %20final.pdf.

39. Robert C. Ellickson, *Order Without Law: How Neighbors Settle Disputes* (Cambridge, Mass.: Harvard University Press, 1991).

40. Ellickson, 48–53, 70–71.
41. Ellickson, 167.
42. Thomas L. Lentz, *Timeline of the History of Killingworth, Connecticut, 1600–2016* (Killingworth, Conn.: Killingworth Historical Society, 2016), 8.
43. The twentieth-century interest in studying town meetings was driven in substantial part by an interest in testing the thesis that local government was controlled by business interests. See Bryan, *Real Democracy,* 40–45 (reviewing literature from Lynds to Wildavsky); see also Thorstein Veblen, *Absentee Ownership and Business Enterprise in Recent Times: The Case of America* (Boston: Beacon Press, 1967), 408–11 (discussing the relationship between business and civil government); Arthur J. Vidich and Joseph Bensman, *Small Town in Mass Society: Class, Power, and Religion in a Rural Community,* rev. ed. (Urbana, Ill.: University of Illinois Press, 2000), 109–70 (describing control of government by business and farm interests); and Aaron Wildavsky, *Leadership in a Small Town* (Totowa, N.J.: Bedminster Press, 1964), 253–81 ("The boundary line between what is private and what is public is often thin and tenuous. What the government does affects private persons and what they do may have a profound impact in the government. This is particularly true in cases involving . . . the relationship of the business community to other segments of the population.").
44. Killingworth has an owner-occupied rate of 93.8 percent. See "QuickFacts: Killingworth."
45. Turnout for the 2020 election was approximately 88 percent. "2020 Presidential Election, Voter Turnout by Town," *Connecticut Secretary of the State Election Center*, https://ctemspublic.pcctg.net/#/voterTurnout. Turnout for the 2016 election was just over 87 percent. "2016 Presidential Election, Voter Turnout by Town," *Connecticut Secretary of the State Election Center*, https://ctemspublic.pcctg.net/#/voterTurnout.
46. Voter turnout for the 2019 election was 60 percent. "November 2019 Municipal Election, Voter Turnout by Town," *Connecticut Secretary of the State Election Center*, https://ctemspublic.pcctg.net/#/voterTurnout. Voter turnout for the 2017 election was 48.6 percent. "November 2017 Municipal Election, Voter Turnout by Town," *Connecticut Secretary of the State Election Center*, https://ctemspublic.pcctg.net/#/voterTurnout.
47. In 2021, the participation rate on the school budget referendum was 13.9 percent.
48. Putnam puts the points well: "When most people skip the meeting, those who are left tend to be more extreme, because they care most about the outcome." Putnam, *Bowling Alone,* 342.
49. There is a 15 percent rule on charter revisions. Conn. Gen. Stat. § 7–191(f).
50. Compare Zimmerman, *New England Town Meeting,* 54. He sees these boards as a check on the potential democratic pathologies of the Town Meeting.
51. The board has since adopted new regulations that permit some exceptions to the two-acre rule, including accessory apartments.
52. In 2014, the Affordable Care Act included an option for states to expand their Medicaid programs with substantial federal funding. See "State and Federal Spending under the ACA," *MACPAC* (2020), www.macpac.gov/subtopic/state-and-federal-spending-under-the-aca.
53. This is similar to the resentment that Michael Sandel places at the core of the populist

anger fueling American politics today. Sandel thinks of that resentment as a reaction to meritocratic elitism. That analysis, however, makes little contact with the volunteerism of Killingworth. Michael Sandel, *The Tyranny of Merit: What's Become of the Common Good?* (New York: Farrar, Straus and Giroux, 2020), 24–31.

54. On the failure of institutional design in the absence of a strong civil society traditions, see Robert D. Putnam, *Making Democracy Work: Civic Traditions in Modern Italy* (Princeton, N.J.: Princeton University Press, 1993), 83–120.

55. Compare Dahl, *Who Governs?,* 11–86 (detailing the gradual transition in New Haven's political system "from oligarchy to pluralism"). Killingworth governance is not exactly the pluralism that Dahl saw; it is more eclectic, disorganized, and opportunistic.

56. See Verified Complaint, Samperi v. Mooney, No. 3:17CV01643 (D. Conn. Sept. 29, 2017). Following Samperi's withdrawal of action, the judge dismissed the case.

57. See Oliver, *Democracy in Suburbia,* 194 (discussing reasons for rejecting Charles Tiebout's rational choice model of residential choice).

Chapter 4. Civil Society

1. Eric Oliver expresses concern about an analogous form of mismatch: creating independent towns, with their own governments, within large metropolitan areas. Government is, thereby, detached from the civil society arrangements of jobs, commerce, culture, entertainment, and services. This becomes particularly problematic when it creates racially homogenous governmental units. See J. Eric Oliver, *Democracy in Suburbia* (Princeton, N.J.: Princeton University Press, 2001), 5–15, 99–133.

2. See Jane J. Mansbridge, *Beyond Adversary Democracy* (Chicago: University of Chicago Press, 1983), 97–114 (on inequalities of power within a unitary democracy).

3. Alexis de Tocqueville, *Democracy in America* [1835], ed. and trans. Harvey C. Mansfield and Delba Winthrop (Chicago: University of Chicago Press, 2000), 274 ("I consider mores to be one of the great general causes to which the maintenance of a democratic republic in the United States can be attributed.").

4. Tocqueville, 183.

5. Hannah Arendt, "What Is Authority?," in *Between Past and Future* (New York: Penguin, 2006).

6. See Hannah Arendt, *On Revolution* (New York: Viking, 1963), 200–211.

7. On the Constitution's "excellence," consider its original treatment of enslaved persons. U.S. Const. art. I, § 2, cl. 3 (counting slaves as three-fifths of persons for the purpose of allocating representatives); art. I, § 9, cl. 1 (prohibiting Congress from ending the importation of slaves before 1808); and art. IV, § 2, cl. 3 (requiring that runaway slaves be returned to their owners); see also Mark A. Graber, *Dred Scott and the Problem of Constitutional Evil* (Cambridge: Cambridge University Press, 2006).

8. Arendt, *On Revolution,* 201; Alexander Bickel, *The Least Dangerous Branch: The Supreme Court at the Bar of Politics* (New Haven, Conn.: Yale University Press, 1986), 16.

9. See Jed Rubenfeld, "Of Constitutional Self-Government," *Fordham Law Review* 71 (2003): 1755.

10. See also Paul W. Kahn, *The Reign of Law:* Marbury v. Madison *and the Construction of*

America (New Haven, Conn.: Yale University Press, 1997), 173 ("New legislation must be part of a single, continuous system of law. It may not, therefore, contradict prior law. The Court inverts the traditional legislative rule that the later displaces the earlier. New law is now either the same as antecedent law—meaning a part of a single whole—or it is negated as not-law. New law under the Constitution is never really new; it falls within the paradigm of reform, not revolution" [footnotes omitted].).

11. See Paul W. Kahn, *Making the Case* (New Haven, Conn.: Yale University Press, 2016), 53–56.

12. See Robert N. Bellah et al., *Habits of the Heart: Individualism and Commitment in American Life* (New York: Harper and Row, 1985), 333 ("[A community] almost always has a history and so is . . . defined in part by its past and its memory of its past.").

13. On the general trend of decline in civil society associations, see Robert D. Putnam, *Bowling Alone: The Collapse and Revival of American Community* (New York: Simon and Schuster, 2000); and Theda Skocpol, *Diminished Democracy: From Membership to Management in American Civic Life* (Norman, Okla.: University of Oklahoma Press, 2003).

14. The business of self-help is a multimillion-dollar-per-year industry, with thousands of new titles released annually; one study suggests that up to 85 percent of psychologists recommended that their patients read self-help books in addition to pursuing traditional forms of treatment. Richard E. Redding et al., "Popular Self-Help Books for Anxiety, Depression, and Trauma: How Scientifically Grounded and Useful Are They?," *Professional Psychology: Research and Practice* 39 (2008): 537–38; see also Sandra K. Dolby, *Self-Help Books: Why Americans Keep Reading Them* (Urbana, Ill.: University of Illinois Press, 2005); and Tom Tiede, *Self-Help Nation: The Long Overdue, Entirely Justified, Delightfully Hostile Guide to the Snake-Oil Peddlers Who Are Sapping Our Nation's Soul* (New York: Atlantic Monthly Press, 2001).

15. While I know a number of religious figures, I know only one life coach. Here is how he introduces himself on his website: "My name is Peter Rubin, and I'm a transformational coach for men. I help men realize their dreams and unlock their full potential, and I'm so glad you're here." "Welcome," *Peter Rubin, Transformational Coach for Men*, www .peterkrubin.com.

16. John Rawls, *A Theory of Justice* (Cambridge, Mass.: Harvard University Press, 1971), 12, 136–42.

17. Thomas Hobbes is often seen as the father of modern political theory because he derives political authority—in the form of the social contract—from this individualism of self-regard. Thomas Hobbes, *Leviathan* [1651], ed. Edwin Curley (Indianapolis, Ind.: Hackett, 1994).

18. This phenomenon is not limited to the New England town meeting or even the United States. For an exploration of the effects of this self-regard in the closing days of the Soviet Union, see Svetlana Alexievich, *Secondhand Time: The Last of the Soviets*, trans. Bela Shayevich (New York: Random House, 2016).

19. See Michael E. Mann and Tom Toles, *The Madhouse Effect: How Climate Change Denial Is Threatening Our Planet, Destroying Our Politics, and Driving Us Crazy* (New York: Columbia University Press, 2016), 72.

20. See, e.g., Brett Samuels, "Trump Retweets Game Show Host Who Said CDC Is Lying

About Coronavirus to Hurt Him Politically," *Hill,* July 13, 2020, https://thehill.com /homenews/administration/507011-trump-retweets-game-show-host-who-said-cdc-is -lying-about-coronavirus.

21. See, e.g., Nancy L. Rosenblum and Russell Muirhead, *A Lot of People Are Saying: The New Conspiracism and the Assault on Democracy* (Princeton, N.J.: Princeton University Press, 2019), 59–78; Jenna Johnson, "'A Lot of People Are Saying . . . ': How Trump Spreads Conspiracies and Innuendoes," *Washington Post,* June 13, 2016, www.wash ingtonpost.com/politics/a-lot-of-people-are-saying-how-trump-spreads-conspiracies -and-innuendo/2016/06/13/b21e59de-317e-11e6-8ff7-7b6c1998b7a0_story.html.

22. Tocqueville, *Democracy,* 495.

23. The effect of an absence of traditional authority in egalitarian groups was noted well before the arrival of social media. For example, speaking of the absence of authority in the postwar suburban communities, Whyte writes, "Sometimes [meetings] appear to be chiefly a medium by which anxious, uncertain people can vent aggressions. . . . Without the disciplining effect of a dominant older group and of custom, they are enticed into precocity [that] stimulates many to a form of free expression in which name-calling and rancor seems to be an end in itself." William H. Whyte, *The Organization Man* (1956; reprint, Philadelphia: University of Pennsylvania Press, 2002), 288.

24. On traditional role of professionals, see Theda Skocpol, "Advocates Without Members," in *Civic Engagement in American Democracy*, ed. Theda Skocpol and Morris P. Fiorina (Washington, D.C.: Brookings Institution Press, 1999), 461, 495 ("When U.S. professionals were a tiny geographically dispersed stratum, they understood themselves as 'trustees of the community.' . . . Working closely with and for non-professional fellow citizens in thousands of towns and cities, lawyers, doctors, ministers, and teachers once found it quite natural to join—and eventually to help lead—locally rooted cross-class voluntary associations.").

25. Thomas L. Lentz, *History of the Congregational Church in Killingworth, Connecticut* (Baltimore, Md.: Gateway, 2007), 63 ("At the end of the eighteenth century and into the first half of the nineteenth century, the church had the practice of calling into account offenders who violated any of the Ten Commandments or the scriptures.").

26. Lentz, 164.

27. Lentz, 64 ("All persons were required to attend public worship as far as possible."); and Brooks B. Hull and Gerald F. Moran, "The Churching of Colonial Connecticut: A Case Study," *Review of Religious Research* 41 (1999): 168 ("All town inhabitants [of colonial Connecticut], regardless of membership status [in the Congregational Church], had to attend Sabbath services; anyone failing to do so was fined.").

28. Thomas L. Lentz, *A Photographic History of Killingworth* (Killingworth, Conn.: Killingworth Historical Society, 2004), 2.

29. This emphasis on the central place of the congregation is evinced in the Fundamental Orders of Connecticut, which were adopted in 1639 when the Connecticut Colony was formally established. While coming together to form "an orderly and decent Government . . . according to God," the settlers' primary goal in "enter[ing] into Combination and Confederation" was "to maintain and preserve the liberty and purity of the Gospel . . . [and] the discipline of the Churches, which according to the truth of the said Gospel is now

practiced amongst us." "Fundamental Orders of 1639," *Avalon Project*, https://avalon .law.yale.edu/17th_century/order.asp.

30. Lentz, *Photographic History*, 6–7.

31. See Diana Ross McCain, "'Andover to Woodstock: How Connecticut Ended Up with 169 Towns," *ConnecticutHistory.org,* June 15, 2016, https://connecticuthistory.org/andover -to-woodstock-how-connecticut-ended-up-with-169-towns (explaining how ecclesiasti- cal societies were often "harbingers of new towns").

32. See William Miller, *Historical Discourse of the Congregational Church in Killingworth, Connecticut* (New Haven: Hoggson and Robinson, 1870), 39 ("During the one hundred and thirty-two years since the organization of the church, there have been seven pastors, making an average for each of about nineteen years. . . . The first six pastorates averages [sic] twenty-one years and eight months.").

33. Lentz, *History of the Congregational Church*, 13–18.

34. Lentz, 93–94 (describing the "enormous" tax voted in 1818 to build the new meeting- house). Lentz explained to me that only members of the Episcopal Society were exempt from having to pay the Ecclesiastical Society tax for the new building.

35. Lentz, 77 ("In 1896, the Corporation applied to the Connecticut Home Missionary Soci- ety for a grant of $100. These requests for aid increased in subsequent years reaching a peak of $800 in 1954.").

36. The Congregational Church is currently running a capital campaign to save the building from decay. The fundraising appeal begins: "The Killingworth Congregational Church is not only a place of faith, worship, and fellowship. It has been a beloved treasure of our quintessential New England town since 1820. Its reach goes far beyond the current con- gregation. Important rites of passage have occurred here throughout the years—bap- tisms, confirmations, marriages, and funerals. Our steeple has guided pilots home. Our bell and our carillon have brought joy and inspiration to those around us." "Preservation 2020," *Killingworth Congregational Church*, www.killingworthchurch.org/preservation -2020/.

37. Scott D. Gerber, "Law and Religion in Colonial Connecticut," *American Journal of Legal History* 55 (2015): 155 ("In October of 1644 the general court enacted two laws to provide financial support for the ministry. The first specified that the proposition made by the commissioners of the United Colonies of New England 'shall stand as an Order for this Jurisdiction.'").

38. J. Hammond Trumbull, ed., *The Public Records of The Colony of Connecticut: Prior to the Union with New Haven Colony, May 1665* (Hartford, Conn.: Brown and Parsons, 1850), 111–12, 112 n.*, available at www.cga.ct.gov/hco/books/The_Public_Records_of _the_Colony_of_Connecticut_1665.pdf.

39. Association of Statisticians of American Religious Bodies, "Middlesex County (Con- necticut): Religious Traditions, 2010," *Association of Religion Data Archives*, www.the arda.com/rcms2010/rcms2010.asp?U=09007&T=county&Y=2010&S=Name.

40. "Our Story," *Living Rock Church of Killingworth*, https://living-rock.org/our-history.

41. After the American Revolution, "the Church of England was all but destroyed, for as a religious body it was discredited as being Tory at heart." Richard J. Purcell, *Connecticut in Transition, 1775–1818* (Washington, D.C.: American Historical Association, 1918), 8.

In the years following, however, "strong [Protestant Episcopal] parishes were formed at Killingworth, Kent, and Norwich," notwithstanding temporary setbacks during the War of 1812. Purcell, 58. In 1815, there were thirty-six Episcopalian families in Killingworth. Thomas L. Lentz, "Churches in Killingworth," in *Celebrating 350 Years: Town of Killingworth since 1667*, ed. Karen Milano (2017), 35.

42. George B. Gilbert, *Forty Years a Country Preacher* (New York: Harper, 1940).

43. See Loren A. Broc, "Evangelicalism," in *Oxford Encyclopedia of American Cultural and Intellectual History*, ed. Joan Shelley Rubin and Scott E. Casper (Oxford: Oxford University Press, 2013).

44. The church website describes its history as follows: "Living Rock Church was founded in 1984, by Senior Pastor, Rev. Ryan Young. It was in Pastor Ryan's first meeting with the group of believers that would become the church congregation, that God prophetically declared he would become the Pastor of this newly established church. After a year of planning the church was established as Rock Church. 8 years later Rock Church bought land in Killingworth and began constructing the building we have today." "Our Story," *Living Rock Church of Killingworth*, https://living-rock.org/our-history.

45. See *Code of Canon Law* (1983), Can. 519 ("The pastor [*parochus*] is the proper pastor [*pastor*] of the parish entrusted to him, exercising the pastoral care of the community committed to him under the authority of the diocesan bishop in whose ministry of Christ he has been called to share, so that for that same community he carries out the functions of teaching, sanctifying, and governing, also with the cooperation of other presbyters or deacons and with the assistance of lay members of the Christian faithful, according to the norm of law."); and Can. 377, §1 ("The Supreme Pontiff freely appoints bishops or confirms those legitimately elected.").

46. "Roman Catholicism," in *The Oxford Dictionary of the Christian Church*, ed. F. L. Cross and E. A. Livingstone, 3rd rev. ed. (Oxford: Oxford University Press, 2005), 1418 ("[Catholicism] presents itself as an organized hierarchy of bishops and priests with the Pope at its head. This structure has been built up during a long history and rests its claims on the powers entrusted by Christ to His Apostles in general [Jn. 20: 23] and to St. Peter in particular [Mt. 16: 18 f.; Lk. 22: 32; Jn. 21: 15–17], as whose successors the Popes are traditionally regarded.").

47. See "Who We Are," *Catholic Charities, Diocese of Norwich*, www.ccfsn.org/About/Who-We-Are ("Last year, Catholic Charities served more than 60,000 residents throughout Eastern Connecticut, regardless of race, religion or national origin, through our four community-based offices.").

48. See "Missions and Outreach," *Congregational Church in Killingworth*, www.killingworthchurch.org/learn-and-serve/#missions.

49. Compare Tocqueville, *Democracy,* 276–77 ("Catholic priests in America have divided the intellectual world into two parts: in one, they have left revealed dogmas, and they submit to them without discussing them; in the other, they have placed political truth, and they think that God has abandoned it to the free inquiries of men.").

50. See *The Constitution of the United Church of Christ*, art. V, ¶ 18 (2018), www.uccfiles.com/pdf/UCC_Constitution.pdf ("The autonomy of the Local Church is inherent and modifiable only by its own action. Nothing in this Constitution and the Bylaws of the

United Church of Christ shall destroy or limit the right of each Local Church to continue to operate in the way customary to it; nor shall be construed as giving to the General Synod, or to any Conference or Association now, or at any future time, the power to abridge or impair the autonomy of any Local Church in the management of its own affairs.").

51. In Connecticut, the proportion of adults who attend weekly religious services is only 28 percent, compared to 35 percent who "seldom or never" attend religious services. Pew Research Center, "Attendance at Religious Services Among Adults in Connecticut," *Religious Landscape Study* (2014), www.pewforum.org/religious-landscape-study/state /connecticut; see also Jeffrey M. Jones, "U.S. Church Membership Down Sharply in Past Two Decades," *Gallup,* Apr. 18, 2019, https://news.gallup.com/poll/248837/church -membership-down-sharply-past-two-decades.aspx.

52. See Paula G. Shakelton, Comment, "Remembering What Cannot Be Forgotten: Using History as a Source of Law in Interpreting the Religion Clauses of the Connecticut Constitution," *Emory Law Journal* 52 (2003): 1008–9. ("Connecticut's Standing Order . . . believed that the church and the state were tightly linked. This Puritan view took institutional shape in the form of church establishments. The church and the state each had its own unique function, but only through mutual support could each bring stability, harmony, and prosperity to the community. In short, Puritans believed that the state must provide aid to the church, and the church must provide aid to the state. . . . They supported an established church because they considered a common church the best way to ensure unity among members of a community."); and Hull and Moran, *Case Study,* 167 ("From the beginning, Connecticut congregationalism enjoyed established status in two respects—state prohibition of religious competition and taxpayer support of the local minister.").

53. On the differences among religious congregations in their relationship to secular civil society organizations, see Robert Wuthnow, "Mobilizing Civic Engagement: The Changing Impact of Religious Involvement," in Skocpol and Fiorina, *Civic Engagement in American Democracy,* 331, 341–46 (observing that attendance in mainline Protestant churches is connected to about 50 percent more civic engagement with other organizations than attendance in evangelical churches, with Catholics falling in between).

54. See, e.g., Leon Festinger, *A Theory of Cognitive Dissonance* (Stanford, Calif.: Stanford University Press, 1962); Joel Cooper, *Cognitive Dissonance: Fifty Years of a Classic Theory* (Los Angeles: Sage, 2007); Eddie Harmon-Jones, ed., *Cognitive Dissonance: Reexamining a Pivotal Theory in Psychology* (Washington, D.C.: American Psychological Association, 2019).

55. See, e.g., John Dewey, *Democracy and Education: An Introduction to the Philosophy of Education* (1916; reprint, New York: Macmillan, 1961), 230 ("Science represents the fruition of the cognitive factors in experience. Instead of contenting itself with a mere statement of what commends itself to personal or customary experience, it aims at a statement which will reveal the sources, grounds, and consequences of a belief. . . . The function which science has to perform in the curriculum is that which it has performed for the race: emancipation from local and temporary incidents of experience, and the opening of intellectual vistas unobscured by the accidents of personal habit and predilection.").

56. In 2016, the National Household Education Surveys Program asked parents homeschooling their children to report the "important reasons" behind their decision to homeschool.
Fifty-one percent of respondents pointed to a "desire to provide religious instruction"; 67
percent to a "desire to provide moral instruction"; and 80 percent to "concerns about the
environment of other schools." The proportion of respondents who listed these reasons
were even higher in rural areas. Jiashan Cui and Rachel Hanson, "Homeschooling in the
United States: Results from the 2012 and 2016 Parent and Family Involvement Survey,"
table 2, *National Center for Education Statistics* (2019), https://nces.ed.gov/pubs2020
/2020001.pdf.

57. See Stanley Hauerwas and William H. Willimon, *Resident Aliens: Life in the Christian
Colony* (Nashville, Tenn.: Abingdon, 1992), 19–24 (criticizing "apologist" Christian
theologians for their "attempts to fit the Bible into the [modern] scientific world view,"
as "the theologian's job is not to make the gospel credible to the modern world, but *to
make the world credible to the gospel*").

58. Writing under the attraction of the secularization thesis in 1967, Peter Berger predicted
that most people will come to "prefer religious products that can be made consonant with
secularized consciousness." Nevertheless, he also saw a "countervailing movement" in
which people "refuse to accommodate themselves . . . and continue to profess the old
objectivities as much as possible as if nothing had happened." Berger thought that in this
tension between accommodation and intransigence, the former is winning. Peter Berger,
The Sacred Canopy: Elements of a Sociological Theory of Religion (New York: Doubleday, 1967), 145–53. Much has changed in Killingworth since the 1960s to undermine
Berger's conclusion, beginning with the arrival of Saint Lawrence's (1966) and Living
Rock (1992).

59. The nation's Jewish communities have similarly turned toward more authority-based
forms of practice. Throughout the latter half of the twentieth century, Reform and Conservative congregations dominated American Jewish life. Today, Orthodox congregations are growing while the others are shrinking. The Orthodox are not only stricter in
practice and belief; they also support claims of authority and insist on deference from
members. See "A Portrait of American Orthodox Jews: A Further Analysis of the 2013
Study of U.S. Jews," *Pew Research Center: Religion and Public Life,* Aug. 26, 2015,
www.pewforum.org/2015/08/26/a-portrait-of-american-orthodox-jews ("A variety of
demographic measures in the survey suggest that Orthodox Jews probably are growing,
both in absolute number and as a percentage of the U.S. Jewish community.").

60. Checking the Saint Lawrence Parish website revealed only one member of the leadership
who also held a leadership position in town—on the board of finance. More interesting
is the fact that Francesco, who ran for first selectman in 2019, prominently expressed his
membership in the Catholic Church.

61. See Putnam, *Bowling Alone,* 77 ("Historically, mainline Protestant church people provided a disproportionate share of leadership to the wider civic community, whereas both
evangelical and Catholic churches put more emphasis on church-centered activities.").

62. Compare Arthur J. Vidich and Joseph Bensman, *Small Town in Mass Society: Class,
Power and Religion in a Rural Community,* rev. ed. (Princeton, N.J.: Princeton University Press, 1958), 38–39 (describing how a small town was able "to absorb, protect and

care" for the "cranks, psychotics and 'odd' personalities," just "so long as non-conformity does not interfere with the normal functioning of the town").

63. Compare Thomas Jefferson, *Notes on the State of Virginia* [1785], ed. William Peden (Chapel Hill, N.C.: University of North Carolina Press, 1982), 165 ("While we have land to labour then, let us never wish to see our citizens occupied at a work-bench, or twirling a distaff. Carpenters, masons, smiths, are wanting in husbandry: but, for the general operations of manufacture, let our work-shops remain in Europe. . . . The mobs of great cities add just so much to the support of pure government, as sores do to the strength of the human body."), with Alexander Hamilton, "Final Version of the Report on the Subject of Manufactures," Dec. 5, 1791, in *The Papers of Alexander Hamilton*, vol. 10, ed. Harold C. Syrett (New York: Columbia University Press, 1966), 230, 236 (advocating for federal support of manufacturing and challenging the assertions of those, who like Jefferson, argued that agriculture is "the only productive species of industry").

64. See John A. Krout, "Alexander Hamilton's Place in the Founding of the Nation," *Proceedings of the American Philosophical Society* 102 (1958): 127 (outlining the influence of the "Hamiltonian System" on succeeding generations of American statesmen, including John C. Calhoun, Henry Clay, John Marshall, and Abraham Lincoln).

65. *Hearing on Nominee-Designate Charles E. Wilson to Be Secretary of Defense Before the Senate Committee on Armed Services*, 83rd Cong. 26 (1953) (statement of Charles E. Wilson, president, General Motors) ("For years I thought what was good for our country was good for General Motors, and vice versa.").

66. See Benjamin C. Waterhouse, *Lobbying America: The Politics of Business from Nixon to NAFTA* (Princeton, N.J.: Princeton University Press, 2014), 2 ("At times, particularly amid economic unrest, American voters have felt drawn to the notion that a captain of industry might hold the secrets to renewed prosperity. Yet just as often, such appeals have faltered in the face of longstanding concerns over unchecked corporate power and the unseemly pursuit of profit. The mix of admiration and skepticism with which the American public views corporations and their leaders has deeply shaped the nation's political values and traditions.").

67. Tyler Pager, "Ned Lamont, a Democrat, Wins Connecticut Governor's Race, Defeating Bob Stefanowski," *New York Times,* Nov. 7, 2018, www.nytimes.com/2018/11/07/nyregion /ned-lamont-defeats-stefanowski-connecticut.html ("Ned Lamont, a Democrat and wealthy business owner . . . defeated Bob Stefanowski, the Republican candidate and a former business executive."). Lamont had served as a Greenwich selectman for one term starting in 1987. He had also served on the Greenwich finance board.

68. Laura Lefko, "The First Selectman's Election in Killingworth: In Support of Francesco Lulaj," *Haddam-Killingworth, CT Patch,* Oct. 28, 2019, https://patch.com/connecticut /thehaddams-killingworth/first-selectmans-election-killingworth.

69. "About Senator Needleman," *State Senator Norm Needleman,* www.senatedems.ct.gov /needleman-about ("State Senator Norm Needleman . . . also serves as First Selectman of Essex. . . . Norm launched his own business, Tower Laboratories. He built the company to pre-eminence in its field, employing more than 150 people at three locations in Connecticut.").

70. See Herbert Gans, *The Levittowners: Ways of Life and Politics in a New Suburban Com-*

munity (New York: Vintage Books, 1967), 139 ("The lawyers, salesmen, realtors, and local retailers who needed to advertise their presence in the community, and had to do so at once, provided the community with leadership talent.").

71. Tellingly, the two largest employers in Killingworth as of 2015 were the local middle and elementary schools. Killingworth Planning and Zoning Commission, "Plan of Conservation and Development, 2018–2028," *Town of Killingworth,* Sept. 1, 2018, 36, table 2-9, www.townofkillingworth.com/documents/2018/POCD%20Aug%209%202018%20 final.pdf (hereafter cited as *Development Plan*).

72. *Development Plan,* 80 ("Commercial cluster developments or village-type developments should be encouraged instead of development occurring along uniform front lots which parallel roadways. . . . The intent of the Plan is to avoid commercial development being lined up along the entire highway that is zoned for commercial development and to minimize the number of driveways and commercial traffic congestion.").

73. *Development Plan,* 82 ("Reports concluded that it is unlikely Killingworth could attract suitable industry or compete with neighboring towns. Reasons for this include lack of suitable sites for industrial uses, lack of access to convenient transportation and suitable highway access, absence of necessary services and infrastructure such as road network, sewer and water utilities, communications, natural gas, and waste disposal options, and the necessity for protecting the Town's water resources. It would not be an efficient use of town resources to direct efforts toward attracting new business and industry that is highly unlikely to locate in Killingworth.").

74. All of this is to say that economically, Killingworth has become a suburb. On the economy of the suburbs, see Kenneth T. Jackson, *Crabgrass Frontier: The Suburbanization of the United States* (New York: Oxford University Press, 1985), 284–96; and J. John Palen, *The Suburbs* (New York: McGraw-Hill, 1995), 101–15, 184–87.

75. See Mansbridge, *Beyond Adversary Democracy,* 43 ("This lack of economic self-sufficiency has implications for [local] politics. . . . The automobile takes [residents] away each day to work; the city lures its young away for life; and the coordination of schools, roads, welfare, and the environment with those outside has gradually eroded its governmental autonomy.").

76. See Daniel Markovits, T*he Meritocracy Trap: How America's Foundational Myth Feeds Inequality, Dismantles the Middle Class, and Devours the Elite* (New York: Penguin, 2019).

77. Betty Gutt, "School Days as Told by a Lifelong Resident," in Milano, *Celebrating 350 Years,* 26.

78. Kathleen Amoia "Remembering Christmas Past," in Milano, *Celebrating 350 Years,* 46, 48 (quoting Carolann Annino).

79. *Development Plan,* 82 ("While the traditional telecommuting model typically fits well within residential districts, the Town should support growth of these activities beyond the residential setting. Larger facilities in the commercial district could support many types of mobile work including telecommuting and customary home occupations.").

80. See, e.g., Gans, *Levittowners* (finding that social and organizational activities multiply in the suburbs); and Whyte, *Organization Man,* 267 (noting that it is the "organization people" who come to dominate the "new suburbia [in which] they are concentrated," as

they are the ones who "organize[] the committees, run[] the schools, select[] the ministers, fight[] the developers, make[] the speeches, and set[] the styles").

81. Oliver, *Democracy in Suburbia*, 95 ("In contrast to the conclusions of previous researchers as well as the conventional wisdom, I do not find a positive relationship between affluence and participation. Instead, civic participation is significantly lower in cities with higher median household income and in cities that are more economically homogeneous.").

82. See, e.g, David Barker and Kathleen Knight, "Political Talk Radio and Public Opinion," *Public Opinion Quarterly* 64 (2000): 167–68 ("When Limbaugh levels criticism toward particular ideas, groups, or individuals on at least half of his broadcasts, regular listeners show a marked tendency to buy the Limbaugh message—displaying hostility toward those items beyond what can be accounted for by ideology, party identification, exposure to other conservative messages, affect for Limbaugh, or a host of other factors. Moreover, regular listening not only correlates with attitudes that reflect Limbaugh's message; listening also relates to opinion change toward greater conservatism and antipathy toward Limbaugh's favorite targets."); GangHeong Lee and Joseph N. Cappella, "The Effects of Political Talk Radio on Political Attitude Formation: Exposure versus Knowledge," *Political Communication* 18 (2001): 378 ("Listeners who are exposed to more conservative [political talk radio] evaluate Democrats more negatively and Republicans more positively, while those exposed to more liberal and moderate talk show the opposite relationship.").

83. Putnam considers and rejects the idea that the workplace community is replacing the traditional community as the site for building social capital. He sees a decline in social capital in both forms of community. Some features of modern work-life may build social capital—for example, an emphasis on team work and creative interaction—but they tend to be overwhelmed by increased insecurity around employment. See Putnam, *Bowling Alone,* 85–92.

84. See Larry J. Smith et al., "Gated Communities: Private Solution or Public Dilemma?," *Urban Lawyer* 29 (1997): 413; see also Edward J. Blakely and Mary Gail Snyder, *Fortress America: Gated Communities in the United States* (Washington, D.C.: Brookings Institution Press, 1997), 22–27 (describing the rise of "microgovernance" in the context of homeowners' associations in gated communities); and Robert E. Lang and Karen A. Danielsen, "Gated Communities in America: Walling Out the World?," *Housing Policy Debate* 8 (1997): 875 (noting that civic engagement within gated communities tends to be higher but that such internal engagement comes at the detriment of participation in civic affairs beyond the gated community).

85. The division between Haddam and Killingworth with regard to educational policy dates to the formation of District 17: Killingworth voters overwhelmingly supported the merger (by a vote of 370–81), while Haddam voters were more ambivalent (586–568). "2 Towns Vote to Form Regional School District," *Hartford Courant,* Apr. 18, 1972, 21. Haddam, at the time, was drawing substantial tax income from a nuclear power plant that has since closed. In the early years of the district, Haddam tended to vote to approve budgets while Killingworth disapproved. The positions reversed after Haddam not only lost its revenue stream from the plant but was ordered by a court to pay some of it back.

86. See, e.g., Stan Fisher, "Voters Pass Region 17 School Budget; Killingworth Tally Carries

Day as Haddam Narrowly Rejects Plan," *New Haven Register,* May 4, 2011, www.nhregister
.com/news/article/Voters-pass-Region-17-school-budget-Killingworth-11568990.php
("Reverting to historic trends, Killingworth voters carried the day for the budget, approv-
ing it by a vote of 338 to 261, while Haddam residents—for the 38th time in district
history—voted it down, 504 in opposition to 481 in favor. . . . Unusual for district voting
history, Haddam had approved the budget in the last two referendums, voting 487–448 in
favor in last year's referendum, a 39-vote margin of approval that compares to the 23[-]
vote margin of defeat registered this year.").

87. Cassandra Day, "Haddam Parents Pushing for Elementary School to Remain Open," *Middletown Press,* Dec. 7, 2018, www.middletownpress.com/news/article/Haddam-parents
-pushing-for-elementary-school-to-13448312.php.

88. See Phillip Langdon, *A Better Place to Live: Reshaping the American Suburb* (Amherst,
Mass.: University of Massachusetts Press, 1994), 4–6 (noting that "punishing" commutes
make it difficult for suburbanites to find the time "to involve themselves in social and
community affairs"); and Putnam, *Bowling Alone,* 213 ("In round numbers the evidence
suggests that each additional ten minutes in daily commuting time cuts involvement in
community affairs by 10 percent.").

89. Between 1990 and 2006, an average of forty-two housing permits were issued per year
in Killingworth. Between 2007 and 2017, an average of seven housing permits were
issued per year. "Annual Housing Permit Data by County," *Connecticut Department of
Economic and Community Development,* https://portal.ct.gov/DECD/Content/About
_DECD/Research-and-Publications/01_Access-Research/Exports-and-Housing-and
-Income-Data.

90. In 2006, the Killingworth unemployment rate was 3 percent. After the financial crisis,
Killingworth unemployment rates peaked in 2011, reaching 6.4 percent. In 2019, before
the Covid-19 crisis, the unemployment rate in Killingworth was 2.4 percent. After
Covid-19 arrived, unemployment rates returned to historic highs, reaching 7.8 percent in
May 2020. "Historical Labor Force Monthly Data w/ Annual Averages by Town," *Con-
necticut Department of Labor,* www1.ctdol.state.ct.us/lmi/laus/laustown.asp; see also
Drew DeSilver, "For Most U.S. Workers, Real Wages Have Barely Budged in Decades,"
Pew Research Center: Fact Tank, Aug. 7, 2018, www.pewresearch.org/fact-tank/2018
/08/07/for-most-us-workers-real-wages-have-barely-budged-for-decades.

91. See Annie Lowrey, "Millennials Don't Stand a Chance," *Atlantic,* Apr. 13, 2020, www
.theatlantic.com/ideas/archive/2020/04/millennials-are-new-lost-generation/609832.

92. See Markovits, *Meritocracy Trap*; and Michael J. Sandel, *The Tyranny of Merit: What's
Become of the Common Good?* (New York: Farrar, Straus and Giroux, 2020).

93. "Median Household Income by Town: Killingworth, 2015–2019," *Connecticut Data
Collaborative,* http://data.ctdata.org/visualization/median-household-income-by-town.
Nearly two-thirds of Killingworth households (66.6 percent) fall at or above the third
quintile for state incomes. In Killingworth, 37.2 percent of households make at least
$150,000 per year, and 17.2 percent make more than $200,000 per year. American Community Survey, "Income in the Past 12 Months (in 2018 Inflation-Adjusted Dollars),
ZCTA5 06419," *U.S. Census Bureau* (2018), https://data.census.gov/cedsci/table?q=income
&g=8600000US06419&tid=ACSST5Y2018.S1901&hidePreview=true.

94. See, e.g., Robert C. Post, *Citizens Divided: Campaign Finance Reform and the Constitution* (Cambridge, Mass.: Harvard University Press, 2016); and Lawrence Lessig, *Republic, Lost: How Money Corrupts Congress—and a Plan To Stop It* (New York: Twelve, 2011).

95. See Daniel Markovits, "Hope and Fear for Democracy in America," *Boston University Law Review Online* 98 (2018): 1.

96. There are numerous examples of corporate enterprises overtly influencing contemporary urban politics. See, e.g., Elizabeth Weise, "Why Amazon, Apple, Microsoft and Uber Are Spending Billions on Local Politics," *USA Today,* Nov. 6, 2019, www.usa today.com/story/news/2019/11/06/amazon-apple-dive-into-local-politics-with-big -money-influence/4168382002; Jim Brunner and Benjamin Romano, "Amazon's Growing Spending on Seattle Politics Includes a Spate of Donations from Jeff Bezos' 'S Team,'" *Seattle Times,* Oct. 20, 2019, www.seattletimes.com/seattle-news/politics /amazons-growing-spending-on-seattle-politics-includes-a-spate-of-donations-from -jeff-bezos-s-team; Nellie Bowles, "Cupertino's Mayor Urges Apple to Pay More Tax: 'Where's the Fairness?,'" *Guardian,* May 5, 2015, www.theguardian.com/technology /2016/may/05/apple-taxes-cupertino-mayor-infrastructure-plan; and Sean Hollister, "Welcome to Googletown: Here's How a City Becomes Company Property," *Verge,* Feb. 26, 2014, www.theverge.com/2014/2/26/5444030/company-town-how-google-is-taking -over-mountain-view.

97. See Putnam, *Bowling Alone,* 210 ("More than sixty years ago urbanist Lewis Mumford observed that 'suburbia is a collective effort to lead a private life.' Now, however, the privatization of suburban life has become formalized and impersonal.").

98. See Sandra L. Hanson and John Kenneth White, "Introduction: The Making and Persistence of the American Dream," in *The American Dream in the 21st Century,* ed. Sandra L. Hanson and John Kenneth White (Philadelphia: Temple University Press, 2011), 1, 8 ("The linking of the American Dream to equality of opportunity is particularly important to understanding the Dream's endurance. Equality of opportunity is a powerful concept, because, unlike other individual rights that can be easily taken away by authoritarian governments [e.g., freedoms of speech and religious worship], it is a state of mind that is virtually impossible to eliminate.").

99. See Herbert W. Marsh and John W. Parker, "Determinants of Student Self-Concept: Is It Better to Be a Relatively Large Fish in a Small Pond Even If You Don't Learn to Swim as Well?," *Journal of Personality and Social Psychology* 47 (1984): 213.

100. *Development Plan,* 5 ("It is recognized that housing in Killingworth is expensive and often beyond the reach of children of residents or the elderly who may wish to scale down from a large house to a more manageable residence.").

101. See Economics and Statistics Administration, "Middle Class in America," *U.S. Department of Commerce* (January 2010), 4–5, www.commerce.gov/sites/default/files/migrated /reports/middleclassreport.pdf (concluding that aspirations defining the middle class include "home ownership," "a car for every adult," "a college education for children," "health security," "retirement security," and "family vacations").

102. See Hanson and White, *American Dream,* 6 (recognizing that changing economic circumstances since the 1990s have made it increasingly difficult for Americans to achieve

the American Dream as they "hit a glass ceiling" in terms of income and upward mobility).

103. See Teresa A. Sullivan, Elizabeth Warren & Jay Lawrence Westbrook, *The Fragile Middle Class: Americans in Debt* (New Haven, Conn.: Yale University Press, 2000), 136–40 (describing the role played by advertising campaigns in the proliferation of credit cards among people who had never before needed or had access to such easy—and ultimately destructive—lines of credit).

104. These calculations are based on projected expenses for a particular property listed for sale in September 2020 with an asking price of $370,000. Assuming that a purchaser with good credit (720–739) makes a 20 percent down payment, the mortgage payment would come to around $1,500/month or $18,000/year. Other costs include around $2,500/year on insurance (www.insurance.com/average-home-insurance-rates), $3,600/year on maintenance, (www.thebalance.com/home-maintenance-budget-453820), and $5,400/year in property taxes.

105. The ordinary monthly loan payment on a $26,000 car would be about $370, or $4,400/year. "Auto Loan Calculator," *Bank of America*, www.bankofamerica.com/auto-loans/auto-loan-calculator. Connecticut car owners paid, on average, around $1,500/year on car insurance. Liz Knueven, "The Average Cost of Car Insurance in the US," *Business Insider,* Aug. 28, 2020, www.businessinsider.com/personal-finance/average-cost-of-car-insurance. Killingworth also assesses a property tax on vehicles; for a car with an assessed value of about $18,000, this would amount to around $480/year. This total annual cost of about $6,380 is for one car. A household with two working adults (and two cars) would likely spend upward of $12,000/year on automotive expenses.

106. The average Connecticut household in 2019 spent about $1,800/year on electricity. "2018 Average Monthly Bill—Residential," *U.S. Energy Information Administration* (2019), www.eia.gov/electricity/sales_revenue_price/pdf/table5_a.pdf. A household using propane for heat could expect to spend $720/year on gas. "Get a Quote," *Amerigas*, www.amerigas.com/go.

   Internet providers in Killingworth charge from a low of $400/year (*Frontier Communications*, https://internet.frontier.com/order-online/plan-package, quote for a Killingworth address) to a high of $720/year (*Xfinity*, www.xfinity.com/learn/internet-service/deals, quote for internet service at the same address with higher speeds).

   A household with two cell phones could expect to pay $1,440/year for cell service. See *AT&T*, www.att.com/plans/wireless; *T-Mobile*, www.t-mobile.com/cell-phone-plans?lines=2; *Verizon*, www.verizon.com/plans/unlimited (plans for two lines and unlimited talk, text, and data usage).

   A household could pay about $225/year for streaming services. "The Amazon Prime Membership Fee," *Amazon*, www.amazon.com/gp/help/customer/display.html; "Choose the Plan That's Right for You," *Netflix*, www.netflix.com/signup/planform.

107. "Employer Health Benefits: 2019 Summary of Findings," *Kaiser Family Foundation,* Sept. 25, 2019, 1 fig. A, http://files.kff.org/attachment/Summary-of-Findings-Employer-Health-Benefits-2019.

108. In 2017, the average household net worth in Killingworth was around $1.5 million. www.arcgis.com/home/item.html?id=93d6c84a70bd46139bbd38c379bf2693.

This net worth can be compared with that of New Haven—$242,000—on the one hand, and that of Old Greenwich—over $3 million—on the other. Another indication of Killingworth residents' wealth: only 40 percent of property tax payments are made by banks holding escrow accounts on mortgages.

109. See, e.g., Sullivan et al., *Fragile Middle Class,* 141–71 (chapter 5, "Sickness and Injury"); and David U. Himmelstein et al., "Medical Bankruptcy: Still Common Despite the Affordable Care Act," *American Journal of Public Health* 109 (2019): 432.

110. Consider in this regard the (in)famous image of the "welfare queen," the Black single mother who abuses the welfare system to sustain a life of drugs, alcohol, and luxury cars. See, e.g., Bryce Covert, "The Myth of the Welfare Queen," *New Republic,* July 2, 2019, https://newrepublic.com/article/154404/myth-welfare-queen; Martin Gilens, *Why Americans Hate Welfare: Race, Media, and the Politics of Antipoverty Policy* (Chicago: University of Chicago Press, 1999), 67; and Carly Hayden Foster, "The Welfare Queen: Race, Gender, Class, and Public Opinion," *Race, Gender and Class* 15 (2008): 164. In 1980, Clarence Thomas, addressing a meeting of Black conservative policymakers, described his own sister in similar terms. Juan Williams, "Black Conservatives, Center Stage," *Washington Post*, Dec. 16, 1980, A21 (quoting Thomas, who declared that "[my sister] gets mad when the mailman is late with her welfare check. That is how dependent she is.").

111. Associated Press, "Metro Briefing, Connecticut: West Haven, Fire Commissioner Ousted," *New York Times,* July 5, 2001, www.nytimes.com/2001/07/05/nyregion/metro-briefing-connecticut-west-haven-fire-commissioner-ousted.html.

112. See Samperi v. Deloatch, No. CV010074924S, 2001 WL 984713 (Conn. Super. July 24, 2001) (allowing Samperi's lawsuit against the commissioners who impeached him to go forward).

113. Stan Fisher, "Selectmen Respond to Worker's Complaint," *New Haven Register,* Aug. 27, 2009, www.nhregister.com/news/article/Selectmen-respond-to-worker-s-complaint-11633737.php.

114. See Yongsung Lee, Bumsoo Lee, and Md Tanvir Hossain Shubho, "Urban Revival by Millennials? Intraurban Net Migration Patterns of Young Adults, 1980–2010," *Journal of Regional Science* 59 (2019): 538.

115. The number of students enrolled in Regional School District 17, which serves Haddam and Killingworth, has fallen by over 20 percent since 2007, from 2,552 pupils in the 2007–8 school year to 2,026 for 2018–19. "Strategic School Profile 2007–08: Regional School District 17," *Connecticut State Department of Education,* https://edsight.ct.gov/ssp/2007-2008/217-00.pdf.

Part III. Public Opinion Nationalizes and Divides

1. "Plan of Conservation and Development, 2018–2028," *Town of Killingworth,* Aug. 9, 2018, 33 www.townofkillingworth.com/documents/2018/POCD%20Aug%209%202018%20final.pdf.

2. Nationalization has been the subject of considerable recent social science research. See, e.g., Alexander Hertel-Fernandez, *State Capture: How Conservative Activists, Big*

Businesses, and Wealthy Donors Reshaped the American States and the Nation (New York: Oxford University Press, 2019), 5–6 (noting that "cross-state conservative networks" have successfully coordinated and pushed right-wing policy agendas in state legislatures across the country); Daniel J. Hopkins, *The Increasingly United States: How and Why American Political Behavior Nationalized* (Chicago: University of Chicago Press, 2018), 13 ("Americans today are primarily engaged with national and above all presidential politics. The evidence is extensive: contemporary Americans' disproportionate engagements with federal politics is evident in their knowledge, descriptions of politicians, web searches, campaign contributions, and turnout decisions."); and Chris Tausanovitch and Christopher Warshaw, "Representation in Municipal Government," *American Political Science Review* 108 (2014): 620–21 ("Policy outcomes in city and town governments can be predicted by the policy conservatism of their citizens. . . . Not only is city government political, but . . . it may have more in common with state and national politics than previous scholars have recognized.").

Chapter 5. Talking to Each Other

Note to epigraph: Alexis de Tocqueville, *Democracy in America* [1835], ed. and trans. Harvey C. Mansfield and Delba Winthrop (Chicago: University of Chicago Press, 2000), 407.

1. See Paul W. Kahn, *Political Theology: Four New Chapters on the Concept of Sovereignty* (New York: Columbia University Press, 2011), 102–3.

2. Thomas Hobbes, *Leviathan* [1668], ed. Edwin Curley (Indianapolis, Ind.: Hackett, 1994), 76.

3. See Hannah Arendt, *The Human Condition* (Chicago: University of Chicago Press, 1958), 27; see generally Charles Taylor, *The Language Animal: The Full Shape of the Human Linguistic Capacity* (Cambridge, Mass.: Belknap Press of Harvard University Press, 2016).

4. See, e.g., Jürgen Habermas, *Between Facts and Norms: Contributions to a Discourse Theory of Law and Democracy*, trans. William Rehg (Cambridge, Mass.: MIT Press, 1996); Bruce Ackerman, *Social Justice in the Liberal State* (New Haven, Conn.: Yale University Press, 1980); and Robert Post, "Meiklejohn's Mistake: Individual Autonomy and the Reform of Public Discourse," *University of Colorado Law Review* 64 (1993): 1109.

5. "Political sectarianism" may be the best label for this intense competition: "Political sectarianism consists of three core ingredients: othering—the tendency to view opposing partisans as essentially different or alien to oneself; aversion—the tendency to dislike and distrust opposing partisans; and moralization—the tendency to view opposing partisans as iniquitous. . . . When all three converge, political losses can feel like existential threats that must be averted—whatever the cost." Eli J. Finkel et al., "Political Sectarianism in America," *Science Magazine* 370 (2020): 533.

6. Public support for same-sex marriage has been steadily increasing in the past decade: in 2009, 37 percent of Americans were in favor of same-sex marriage; by 2019, that figure jumped to 61 percent in favor. "Attitudes on Same-Sex Marriage," *Pew Research Center,* May 14, 2019, www.pewforum.org/fact-sheet/changing-attitudes-on-gay-marriage.

7. Alexis de Tocqueville, *Democracy in America* [1835], ed. and trans. Harvey C. Mansfield and Delba Winthrop (Chicago: University of Chicago Press, 2000), 244.

8. On the self-reinforcing, closed character of right-wing cyber sites, see Yochai Benkler, Robert Faris, and Hal Roberts, *Network Propaganda: Manipulation, Disinformation, and Radicalization in American Politics* (New York: Oxford University Press, 2018), 76–100.

9. See Keith E. Whittington, *Speak Freely: Why Universities Must Defend Free Speech* (Princeton, N.J.: Princeton University Press, 2018); and Anthony T. Kronman, *The Assault on American Excellence* (New York: Free Press, 2019).

10. See Robert A. Burt, *The Constitution in Conflict* (Cambridge, Mass.: Belknap Press of Harvard University Press, 1992), 27–28.

11. Compare Dan Kahan's characterization of the debate over gun control: "The gun debate is about *values* . . . about *who* you are and who you aren't. . . . What makes the gun control debate so intense is not a disagreement about the facts—does private ownership of guns promote or deter violent crime?—but a disagreement about alternative views of what America is and ought to be." Dan M. Kahan, "The Gun Control Debate: A Culture-Theory Manifesto," *Washington and Lee Law Review* 60 (2003): 6 (quotation marks and citations omitted).

12. The Speaker walked out of an October 2019 meeting at the White House when the president called her a "third rate" (or "third grade") politician and proclaimed he "hate[d] ISIS more than her." For almost a year afterward, Pelosi spoke only to intermediaries for the White House, refusing to meet directly with Trump. Trump, for his part, insisted that his refusal to speak with either Pelosi or Schumer was "taking the high road." Cristina Marcos, "Pelosi Defends Not Speaking to Trump for Almost a Year," *Hill,* Sept. 14, 2020, https://thehill.com/homenews/house/516320-pelosi-defends-not-speaking-to-trump -for-almost-a-year.

13. See Robert D. Putnam, *Bowling Alone: The Collapse and Revival of American Community* (New York: Simon and Schuster, 2000), 35 ("Voting is . . . the most common form of political activity, and it embodies the most fundamental democratic principle of equality. . . . On the other hand, in some important respects voting is not a typical mode of political participation. . . . 'It is incomplete and misleading to understand citizen participation solely through the vote'" [quoting Sidney Verba, Kay Lehman Schlozman, and Henry E. Brady, *Voice and Equality: Civic Voluntarism in American Politics* (Cambridge: Harvard University Press, 1995), 23–24].).

14. Brandy Richards, the co-administrator of the site, dates the disintegration a bit earlier— to the election of November 2017.

15. Peter Berger speaks of a similar passing of the world-constituting function of common sense among traditional religions: "The world as defined by the religious institution . . . was *the* world, maintained not just by the mundane powers of the society . . . but much more fundamentally maintained by the 'common sense' of the members of that society." Peter L. Berger, *The Sacred Canopy: Elements of a Sociological Theory of Religion* (Garden City, N.Y.: Doubleday, 1967), 134.

16. See Devin Caughey, James Dunham, and Christopher Warshaw, "The Ideological Nationalization of Partisan Subconstituencies in the American States," *Public Choice* 176

(2018): 141–44 (finding that partisan identity, rather than regional identity, has come to explain nearly all of the variance in people's positions on economic, social, and racial issues); Daniel J. Moskowitz, "Local News, Information, and the Nationalization of U.S. Elections," *American Political Science Review* 115 (2021): 126–27 (confirming the hypothesis that the decline of local news sources has increasingly nationalized public opinion on down-ballot races and issues).

17. Tocqueville observed that because the central government did not entail centralized *administration*, local governments could still act as a counterbalance to an overzealous national majority. He also observed how Americans have much greater affection and attachment to their townships over the national government, because a township is freely formed and closer to everyday existence. Tocqueville, *Democracy,* 250, 63–65.

18. See "The Federalist No. 46" (James Madison), in *The Federalist Papers*, ed. Clinton Rossiter (New York: Mentor Books, 1962), 294, 294 ("Many considerations . . . seem to place it beyond doubt that the first and most natural attachment of the people will be to governments of their respective States.").

19. See Zach Murdock, "Connecticut Republican Chairman Calls on Democrats to Condemn Election Day Threat Made by Killingworth Town Volunteer After GOP Asks for Volunteers for 'Army for Trump,'" *Hartford Courant,* Oct. 14, 2020, www.courant.com /politics/hc-pol-jr-romano-condemn-threat-20201015-isfp6dor6rchjahu2x4thzdlam -story.html.

20. See, e.g., Carter v. Carter Coal Co., 298 U.S. 238, 294 (1936) ("While the states are not sovereign in the true sense of that term, but only *quasi*-sovereign, yet in respect of all powers reserved to them they are supreme—'as independent of the general government as that government, within its sphere, is independent of the States'" [citation omitted].).

21. See Hammer v. Dagenhart, 247 U.S. 251, 276 (1918).

22. Killingworth voted against FDR in all four of his presidential elections, by fairly large margins (relative to the small voting population of the town). In 1932, Killingworth went to Herbert Hoover with 104 votes to Roosevelt's 74; in 1936, it went to Alf Landon with 152 votes to Roosevelt's 141; in 1940 to Wendell Willkie with 179 votes to Roosevelt's 145; and in 1944 to Thomas E. Dewey with 203 votes to Roosevelt's 126. See Statements of Vote for 1932, 1936, 1940, and 1944, on "General Election Statements of Vote, 1922—Current," *Office of the Secretary of the State of Connecticut*, https://portal.ct.gov /SOTS/Election-Services/Statement-Of-Vote-PDFs/General-Elections-Statement-of -Vote-1922.

23. See Heather K. Gerken, "Federalism and Nationalism: Time for a Détente?," *St. Louis University Law Review* 59 (2015): 997–98 (describing the rise of "the nationalistic school of federalism," which argues in part that devolution of centralized power can in fact further "traditional nationalist . . . aims"); and Abbe R. Gluck, "Our [National] Federalism," *Yale Law Journal* 123 (2014): 1996 ("National Federalism [is] nationalism and federalism, simultaneous and in tension—and generated entirely by federal statutes. . . . It incorporates experimentation, variety, and state historical expertise . . . into national law.").

24. Regularly, the courts would try to do so in order to protect some imagined aspect of state sovereignty. They searched for the "truly local," but it was a chimera. For example, the

Supreme Court found that the 1974 amendments to the Fair Labor Standards Act would "significantly alter or displace the States' abilities to structure employer-employee relationships in such areas as fire prevention, police protection, sanitation, public health, and parks and recreation," all activities "typical of those performed by state and local governments." It held that the amendments were unconstitutional insofar as they "interfere[d] with the integral governmental functions" of states and their political subdivisions. National League of Cities v. Usery, 426 U.S. 833, 851 (1976). Just nine years later, the Court overruled this holding, rejecting "as unsound in principle and unworkable in practice, a rule of state immunity from federal regulation that turns on a judicial appraisal of whether a particular governmental function is 'integral' or 'traditional.'" Garcia v. San Antonio Metropolitan Transit Authority, 469 U.S. 528, 546–47 (1985).

25. Katherine Cramer argues for the importance of considering place in constructing political identity, arguing in particular for the importance of the rural versus urban divide. Her research into rural political identity was completed around 2012, and it is striking that she makes no mention of social media, very little of the internet, and only one footnote on the power of Fox News. Katherine J. Cramer, *The Politics of Resentment: Rural Consciousness in Wisconsin and the Rise of Scott Walker* (Chicago: University of Chicago Press, 2016).

26. See In re Complaint by Lauren Blaha, Killingworth, File No. 2019-094 (Conn. Elections Enforcement Comm'n Nov. 20, 2019).

27. To the surprise of local residents, on election night 2019, Sue Hatfield, the vice-chair of the state Republican Party, appeared in the school multipurpose room to await the results with the rest of us. With elections going on throughout the state, why was she in this very small town? She was quite visibly disappointed when the results came in. I suspect that the state party was expecting an easy victory here.

28. Charles Stannard, "Former Democratic Selectman Picked to Lead Town Republicans," *Hartford Courant,* Apr. 4, 2006, www.courant.com/news/connecticut/hc-xpm-2006-04 -04-0604040202-story.html.

29. The *New York Times* published an in-depth dissection of the origins and arc of the "wild" #PizzaGate "conspiracy theory." Gregor Aisch, Jon Huang, and Cecilia Kang, "Dissecting the #PizzaGate Conspiracy Theories," *New York Times,* Dec. 10, 2016, www.nytimes .com/interactive/2016/12/10/business/media/pizzagate.html. While readers of this article would have clearly viewed the theory as obviously fake news, at least one man took the conspiracy seriously enough to visit the alleged site of the pedophilia ring armed with an AR-15 rifle. Cecilia Kang and Adam Goldman, "In Washington Pizzeria Attack, Fake News Brought Real Guns," *New York Times,* Dec. 5, 2016, www.nytimes.com/2016/12/05 /business/media/comet-ping-pong-pizza-shooting-fake-news-consequences.html.

30. For earlier, deliberate iterations of this effort to subvert a factual consensus, see Naomi Oreskes and Erik M. Conway, *Merchants of Doubt: How a Handful of Scientists Obscured the Truth on Issues from Tobacco Smoke to Climate Change* (New York: Bloomsbury, 2010).

31. In the first quarter of 2020, Fox News averaged 3.4 million primetime viewers. In comparison, MSNBC and CNN had only 1.9 million and 1.4 million, respectively. Brian Flood, "Fox News Channel Ratings for First Quarter of 2020 Are the Highest in Network

History," *Fox News,* March 31, 2020, www.foxnews.com/media/fox-news-ratings-2020
-best-history.

32. On charges of missing funds, see discussion in chapter 6, below.

33. Stalin's Moscow Trials are a prime example of how an authoritarian regime creates truth through political showmanship—as Max Radin observed at the time, the "trial" of high-ranking members of the "Old Bolshevik" faction was more public demonstration of guilt than actual fact-finding mission. Max Radin, "The Moscow Trials: A Legal View," *Foreign Affairs* 16 (1937): 66.

34. Compare Carl Schmitt on the role of acclamation in constituting a people. Carl Schmitt, *Constitutional Theory*, ed. and trans. Jeffrey Seitzer (Durham, N.C.: Duke University Press, 2008), 275 ("Public opinion is the modern type of acclamation.").

Chapter 6. Killingworth Disrupted

1. See Robert D. Putnam, *Our Kids: The American Dream in Crisis* (New York: Simon and Schuster, 2015).

2. See Daniel J. Hopkins, *The Increasingly United States: How and Why American Political Behavior Nationalized* (Chicago: University of Chicago Press, 2018), 62 ("Political engagement—that is, interest in politics, a sense of political efficacy, and basic political knowledge—is an important attitudinal prerequisite to political participation" [citations omitted].).

3. The KWO has 42 members; the Lions have 54 members. See *Killingworth Women's Organization,* August 2021, www.kwoct.org/contact-us; and "Lions in Action," *Killingworth Lions Club* (August 2021), www.e-clubhouse.org/sites/killingworth.

4. See Hopkins, *Increasingly United States*, 55–58; see also Brian F. Schaffner and Matthew J. Streb, "The Partisan Heuristic in Low-Information Elections," *Public Opinion Quarterly* 66 (2002): 573 (finding that "citizens, particularly less educated citizens, are less likely to state a vote preference when partisan information is unavailable").

5. See Alan I. Abramowitz and Kyle L. Saunders, "Is Polarization a Myth?," *Journal of Politics* 70 (2008): 554 ("Polarization in America is not just an elite phenomenon. The American people, especially those who care about politics, have also become much more polarized in recent years."); and William L. Benoit, LeAnn Brazeal, and David Airne, "Functional Federalism and Issue Emphasis in Political Television Spots," *Human Communication* 14 (2011): 383 (analyzing 526 federal congressional ads and 687 presidential campaign ads and finding that 56 percent of congressional ads and 66 percent of presidential ads "emphasized national issues more than local issues").

6. See, e.g., Steven Rogers, "National Forces in State Legislative Elections," 667 *Annals of the American Academy of Political and Social Science* 667 (2016): 209 (arguing that "instead of being local affairs, state legislative elections are dominated by national politics" and finding that "compared with individuals' assessments of the state legislature, changes in presidential approval have at least three times the impact on voters' decision-making in state legislative elections").

7. See, e.g., "2013 Survey of Americans on the U.S. Role in Global Health," *Kaiser Family Foundation,* November 2013, 1 www.kff.org/wp-content/uploads/2013/11/8508-f-2013

-survey-of-americans-on-the-u-s-role-in-global-health.pdf ("On average, Americans think 28 percent of the federal budget is spent on foreign aid, when it is about 1 percent.").

8. See Frances McCall Rosenbluth and Ian Shapiro, *Responsible Parties: Saving Democracy from Itself* (New Haven, Conn.: Yale University Press, 2018), 236–37 ("We have argued that competition between two strong parties is the best basis for public-regarding policies for five overlapping and related reasons. . . . The upshot of these five features is the government's ability to offer, and be held accountable for, public policies that give most voters what they want most of the time.").

9. Robert D. Putnam, *Bowling Alone: The Collapse and Revival of American Community* (New York: Simon and Schuster, 2000), 337 (quoting John Dewey, *The Public and Its Problems* [New York: H. Holt, 1927], in Robert B. Westbrook, *John Dewey and American Democracy* [Ithaca, N.Y.: Cornell University Press, 1991], 314).

10. Hannah Arendt, *On Revolution* (New York: Viking, 1963), 115, 126.

11. Vietnam was the last war fought by conscripts. It was also the last war marked by widespread protest. For many of that generation, including myself, the protests represented an alternative form of "public service." Like some veterans, we, too, look back to that experience as a ground for public happiness.

12. Compare Sidney Verba and Norman H. Nie, *Participation in America: Political Democracy and Social Equality* (Chicago: University of Chicago Press, 1972), 46–47 ("We suggest that there are four broad modes of political participation that are used, in ordinary circumstances, by citizens: voting, campaign activity, citizen-initiated contacts, and cooperative participation. . . . These four modes of participation represent a significant set of activities because they encompass a number of alternative ways in which the citizen can attempt to influence the government.").

13. Brian McCready, "Obituary: Richard (Rick) Walter Albrecht, 69, of Killingworth," *Haddams-Killingworth, CT Patch,* July 13, 2018, https://patch.com/connecticut/the haddams-killingworth/obituary-richard-rick-walter-albrecht-69-killingworth.

14. "Walter George Albrecht," *New Haven Register,* Nov. 9–10, 2010, www.legacy.com /obituaries/nhregister/obituary.aspx?n=walter-george-albrecht&pid=146535408&fhid =11561.

15. In October 2020, there were 1,539 Republicans, 1,463 Democrats, and 2,285 unaffiliated voters registered in Killingworth. "Registration and Party Enrollment Statistics," *Connecticut Secretary of the State,* Oct. 27, 2020, 3, https://portal.ct.gov/-/media/SOTS /ElectionServices/Registration_and_Enrollment_Stats/2020-Voter-Registration-Statistics .pdf.

16. See Rosenbluth and Shapiro, *Responsible Parties,* 95–127 (discussing the weakening of U.S. political parties, in general, and their inability to set forth a coherent policy agenda, in particular).

17. "Tammany Hall," *New York City Landmarks Preservation Commission,* Oct. 2019, 4, https://s-media.nyc.gov/agencies/lpc/lp/2490.pdf ("Precinct captains were responsible for keeping tabs on what was happening in the city's neighborhoods, helping families in time of need, and making sure that they voted for Tammany candidates.").

18. Martha Shanahan, "5 Memorable Moments When Town Hall Meetings Turned to Rage,"

NPR, Aug. 7, 2013, www.npr.org/sections/itsallpolitics/2013/08/07/209919206/5-memo rable-moments-when-town-hall-meetings-turned-to-rage.

19. Hopkins, *Increasingly United States*, 36–58.

20. This is the attitude that one finds on the League of Women Voters website in the section on "how to choose a candidate." It mentions party exactly once as an issue to consider, with no elaboration of why party matters. Of course, they are a nonpartisan group modeling independence as a virtue. See "How Do I Choose a Candidate in Connecticut?," *League of Women Voters of Connecticut*, https://my.lwv.org/sites/default/files/how_to _choose_a_candidate_in_ct_-_final.pdf.

21. The *Hartford Courant* began in 1764. In December 2020, it announced that it was closing its newsroom. Katie Robertson, "The *Harford Courant's* Newsroom Is Closing Down," *New York Times,* Dec. 4, 2020, www.nytimes.com/2020/12/04/business/media /the-hartford-courants-newsroom-is-closing-down.html.

22. *NHR Insider* began in 2019 and includes independent reporting on Bridgeport, Norwalk, Stamford, Greenwich, and Danbury, as well as regional investigative reports. See Paul Bass, "*Register* Goes 'Inside(r)' to Make News Pay," *New Haven Independent,* Oct. 17, 2019, www.newhavenindependent.org/index.php/archives/entry/nhinsider.

23. See "Our History," *Day,* Aug. 4, 2021, www.theday.com/article/99999999/STATIC01 /140739950.

24. Recently a similar freesheet that had focused on Haddam expanded to include Killingworth: *Haddam Killingworth News.* It, too, prints letters to the editor in which local issues, particularly before an election, can be raised.

25. Mark Hall, "Facebook," *Britannica,* July 8, 2021, www.britannica.com/topic/Facebook ("Harvard students who signed up for the service could post photographs of themselves and personal information about their lives, such as their class schedules and clubs they belonged to.").

26. Lisa Connelly, Comment on Post of Jan. 23, 2020, "HK Progressives," *Facebook.*

27. Connelly, Comment.

28. There are now numerous studies of "internet addictive disorder," showing that it can lead to severe psychological and social problems. See, e.g., Kimberly S. Young, "Internet Addiction: The Emergence of a New Clinical Disorder," *CyberPsychology and Behavior* 1 (1998): 237 (investigating the parallels between compulsive internet usage and other forms of addiction); and R. A. Davis, "A Cognitive-Behavioral Model of Pathological Internet Use," *Computers in Human Behavior* 17 (2001): 187 (distinguishing between general pathological internet use and pathological internet use related to specific purposes, such as online gambling).

29. The paradigmatic encounter is not face to face as Levinas imagines; it is pornographic. The former is embedded in the possibility of language; the latter drives out language. See Emmanuel Levinas, *Totality and Infinity: An Essay on Exteriority,* trans. Alphonso Lingis (Pittsburgh, Pa.: Duquesne University Press, 1969), 71, 78–81; see also Roger Scruton, *Beauty: A Very Short Introduction* (Oxford: Oxford University Press, 2011), 133 ("Pornography, like slavery, is a denial of the human subject, a way of negating the moral demand that free beings must treat each other as ends in themselves.").

30. Tim Kendall, Facebook's former director of monetization, has testified about the website's addictive qualities: "We took a page from Big Tobacco's playbook, working to make our offering addictive at the outset." See "Testimony of Tim Kendall," *House Committee on Energy and Commerce,* Sept. 24, 2020, 1, https://energycommerce.house .gov/sites/democrats.energycommerce.house.gov/files/documents/09.24.20%2CPC%20 Witness%20Testimony_Kendall-UPDATED.pdf.

31. See Kathleen Hall Jamieson and Doron Taussig, "Disruption, Demonization, Deliverance, and Norm Destruction: The Rhetorical Signature of Donald J. Trump," *Political Science Quarterly* 132 (2017–18): 619 (analyzing the rhetoric of President Trump's tweets as they relate to political institutions).

32. See Yochai Benkler, Robert Faris, and Hal Roberts, *Network Propaganda: Manipulation, Disinformation, and Radicalization in American Politics* (New York: Oxford University Press, 2018), 295–310.

33. See Anton Abilov et al., "VoterFraud2020: A Multi-Modal Dataset of Election Fraud Claims on Twitter," Jan. 21, 2021, https://arxiv.org/abs/2101.08210 (analyzing "a multi-modal dataset with 7.6M tweets and 25.6M retweets from 2.6M users related to voter fraud claims").

34. See Paul W. Kahn, *Sacred Violence: Torture, Terror, and Sovereignty* (Ann Arbor, Mich.: University of Michigan Press, 2008), 140–43.

35. See Albert Hirschman, *Exit, Voice, and Loyalty: Responses to Decline in Firms, Organizations, and States* (Cambridge, Mass.: Harvard University Press, 1970), 21 ("The availability to consumers of the exit option, and their frequent resort to it, are characteristic of 'normal' (nonperfect) competition.").

36. See Benedict Anderson, *Imagined Communities: Reflections on the Origin and Spread of Nationalism,* rev. and extended ed. (London: Verso, 1991), 6.

37. See Hannah Arendt, *The Human Condition* (Chicago: University of Chicago Press, 1958), 257 ("For men cannot become citizens of the world as they are citizens of their countries.").

38. See, e.g., Marc Lynch, "After the Arab Spring: How the Media Trashed the Transitions," *Journal of Democracy* 26 (2015): 90 ("The political uprisings affected the media landscape directly, enabling the rapid launching of dozens of new independent television stations, newspapers, and websites. Within a few years, however, most of the attempted democratic transitions had failed—and the media had surely had something to do with it.").

39. I have found no actual support for this claim, but the story was told by someone whose family roots extend back to the earliest European settlers. She may have been speaking with knowledge of the practices of her ancestors.

40. *Acts and Laws of His Majesties Colony of Connecticut in New-England: Printed in 1702 and Now Reissued* (Hartford, Conn.: Case, Lockwood & Brainard, 1901), 8 ("Two or more Persons shall by the Selectmen in each Town, be appointed to renew the bounds between their Towns, at least once in every year."); see also Allegra di Bonaventura, "Beating the Bounds: Property and Perambulation in Early New England," *Yale Journal of Law & the Humanities* 19 (2007): 123–24 (describing the practice of perambulation in the Connecticut Colony). In 1979, the legislature abolished the perambulation requirement.

41. The Killingworth "Watchdog," "State Attorney to Send Killingworth 'Watchdog' Com-

plaint on Parmelee Farm to State Police for Investigation," *Durham-Middlefield, CT Patch*, Mar. 12, 2012, https://patch.com/connecticut/durham/bp--state-attorney-to-send -killingworth-watchdog-comp68bf6c80fa; Lauren Sievert, "Killingworth Residents File Complaint with State's Attorney over Parmelee Farm," *New Haven Register,* Feb. 12, 2012, www.nhregister.com/news/article/Killingworth-residents-file-complaint-with -11531612.php; and Eileen McNamara, "Killingworth Residents File Complaint Against Town," *Durham-Middlefield, CT Patch,* Feb. 10, 2012, https://patch.com/connecticut /durham/local-residents-file-complaint-against-town.

42. See In re Complaint by Mike Board & Killingworth Taxpayers Association, Docket #FIC 93-125 (Conn. Freedom of Information Comm'n Apr. 27, 1994). The commission declined to review that decision in a subsequent case, In re Complaint by Elizabeth Allen, Docket #FIC 94-45 (Conn. Freedom of Information Comm'n Feb. 2, 1995).

43. Peter Marteka, "Sweetman Will Leave District 17 in Early '97," *Hartford Courant,* Dec. 14, 1996, www.courant.com/news/connecticut/hc-xpm-1996-12-14-9612140359-story .html.

44. See, e.g., McIntyre v. Ohio Elections Commission, 514 U.S. 334, 357 (1995) ("Under our Constitution, anonymous pamphleteering is not a pernicious, fraudulent practice, but an honorable tradition of advocacy and of dissent. Anonymity is a shield from the tyranny of the majority. It thus exemplifies the purpose behind the Bill of Rights, and of the First Amendment in particular: to protect unpopular individuals from retaliation—and their ideas from suppression—at the hand of an intolerant society." [citation omitted]).

45. See Eugene Garver, *Aristotle's Rhetoric: An Art of Character* (Chicago: University of Chicago Press, 1995).

46. Classically expressed by Justice Holmes: "The best test of truth is the power of the thought to get itself accepted in the competition of the market." Abrams v. United States, 250 U.S. 616, 630 (1919) (Holmes, J., dissenting).

47. Jason Stanley, *How Propaganda Works* (Princeton, N.J.: Princeton University Press, 2015), 125–222; see also George Orwell, *1984* (1949; reprint, New York: Plume, 1983).

48. See Bryan Garsten, *Saving Persuasion: A Defense of Rhetoric and Judgment* (Cambridge, Mass.: Harvard University Press, 2009), chapter 2, "Persuading Without Convincing: Rousseau."

49. Thomas Jefferson was one of the founders of the *National Gazette*, published from 1791 to 1793, in response to Alexander Hamilton's *Gazette of the United States*. Jefferson was responsible for hiring Philip Freneau, who simultaneously served as a translator in Jefferson's State Department, to edit the *National Gazette*. Jefferson directed Freneau to engage in partisan attacks on many of the policies of the administration, leading Hamilton to allege that Jefferson and Freneau were actively working "to vilify those to whom the voice of the people has committed the administration of our public affairs." See Julian P. Boyd, ed., *The Papers of Thomas Jefferson*, vol. 20 (Princeton, N.J.: Princeton University Press, 1982), 718–53.

50. Remarkably, in 2020, the Republican Party declined to put forward a new platform, preferring to campaign on Trump's personality alone. See "Resolution Regarding the Republican Party Platform," *Republican National Committee* (2016), https://prod-cdn-static .gop.com/docs/Resolution_Platform_2020.pdf.

51. There is substantial controversy over the impact of presidential debates on the outcome of an election. Compare Rachel Nuwer, "Presidential Debates Have Shockingly Little Effect on Election Outcomes," *Scientific American,* Oct. 20, 2020, www.scientificamerican .com/article/presidential-debates-have-shockingly-little-effect-on-election-outcomes (discussing recent research finding "that debates neither helped undecided voters to make up their mind nor caused those who had already made a decision to switch candidates"), with Alan I. Abramowitz, "The Impact of a Presidential Debate on Voter Rationality," *American Journal of Political Science* 22 (1978): 686 (analyzing the 1976 Carter-Ford debate and finding that "there was a clear tendency for Ford and Carter supporters to adopt their candidate's position" as expressed at the debate); John G. Geer, "The Effects of Presidential Debates on the Electorate's Preferences for Candidates," *American Politics Quarterly* 16 (1988): 487 (challenging other political scientists who argue that debates have little impact, instead submitting "that debates influence a large number of people in important ways, and that in tightly contested races these verbal exchanges between the nominees can be decisive events in the November election"); and Thomas M. Holbrook, "Political Learning from Presidential Debates," *Political Behavior* 21 (1999): 84 (suggesting that, "on balance, the evidence points to [presidential] debates as an important source of candidate information during presidential campaigns").

52. See Ben Smith, "Fox Settled Lawsuit over Its Lies. But It Insisted on One Unusual Condition," *New York Times,* Jan. 17, 2021, www.nytimes.com/2021/01/17/business/media /fox-news-seth-rich-settlement.html.

53. Michelle Malkin, *In Defense of Internment: The Case for "Racial Profiling" in World War II and the War on Terror* (Washington, D.C.: Regnery, 2004).

54. Civil Liberties Act of 1988, Pub. L. No. 100-383, § 2, 102 Stat. 903, 903–4; Trump v. Hawaii, 138 S. Ct. 2392, 2423 (2018).

55. Jonathan Allen and Jonathan Stempel, "FBI Documents Point to Trump Role in Hush Money for Porn Star Daniels," *Reuters,* July 18, 2019, www.reuters.com/article/us-usa -trump-cohen/fbi-documents-point-to-trump-role-in-hush-money-for-porn-star-daniels -idUSKCN1UD18D.

56. See, e.g., Klint Finley, "A Brief History of the End of the Comments," *Wired,* Oct. 8, 2015, www.wired.com/2015/10/brief-history-of-the-demise-of-the-comments-timeline; Scott Montgomery, "Beyond Comments: Finding Better Ways to Connect with You," *NPR,* Aug. 17, 2016, www.npr.org/sections/thisisnpr/2016/08/16/490208179/beyond -comments-finding-better-ways-to-connect-with-you; and "A Farewell to Comments," *Above the Law,* Apr. 12, 2016, https://abovethelaw.com/2016/04/a-farewell-to-comments.

57. See Moshe Halbertal and Stephen Holmes, *The Beginning of Politics: Power in the Biblical Book of Samuel* (Princeton, N.J.: Princeton University Press, 2017), 83–88.

58. Sigmund Freud, *Civilization and Its Discontents* [1930], ed. and trans. James Strachey (New York: W. W. Norton, 1962), 46–54.

59. Compare Robert C. Ellickson, *Order Without Law: How Neighbors Settle Disputes* (Cambridge, Mass.: Harvard University Press, 1991), 56–59 (residents of Shasta County are often successful in using "truthful negative gossip" to shame so-called deviants into abiding by "norms of neighborliness").

60. Tracey Thomas, "Killingworth First Selectman Accused of Hitting His Wife," *Hartford Courant,* Jan. 31, 1995.

61. See, e.g., Fabiola Cineas, "Donald Trump Is the Accelerant: A Comprehensive Timeline of Trump Encouraging Hate Groups and Political Violence," *Vox,* Jan. 9, 2021, www .vox.com/21506029/trump-violence-tweets-racist-hate-speech.

62. James Rainey and Melissa Gomez, "Asked to Condemn White Supremacists, Trump Tells Proud Boys Hate Group to 'Stand By,'" *Los Angeles Times,* Sept. 29, 2020, www .latimes.com/world-nation/story/2020-09-29/asked-to-condemn-white-supremacists -trump-tells-proud-boys-hate-group-to-stand-by.

63. See Emily Crockett, "Roger Ailes, Bill O'Reilly, and Fox News: The Ongoing Sexual Harassment Scandal, Explained," *Vox,* Jan. 10, 2017, www.vox.com/2016/7/19/12215974 /roger-ailes-fox-megyn-kelly-gretchen-carlson-sexual-harassment-explained.

64. Harry Frankfurt, *On Bullshit* (Princeton, N.J.: Princeton University Press, 2005). I am hardly the first to make this connection. See Jennifer R. Mercieca, *Demagogue for President: The Rhetorical Genius of Donald Trump* (College Station, Tex.: Texas A&M University Press, 2020), 10 ("Part of Trump's rhetorical strategy was in crafting an image of himself as either an authentic 'truth teller' or, if not that, then as someone who used 'truthful hyperbole' for strategic advantage. One way to make this distinction is that Trump was either telling the truth or he was using 'bullshit.'").

Chapter 7. What Can Be Done?

1. See Naomi Oreskes and Erik M. Conway, *Merchants of Doubt* (New York: Bloomsbury, 2010), 214–15; Maxwell T. Boykoff and Jules M. Boykoff, "Balance as Bias: Global Warming and the U.S. Prestige Press," *Global Environmental Change* 14 (2004): 126–27.

2. "Full Transcript and Video: Trump's News Conference in New York," *New York Times,* Aug. 15, 2017, www.nytimes.com/2017/08/15/us/politics/trump-press-conference-transcript .html.

3. See the discussion on Michelle Makin in chapter 6, above.

4. Bernard Mandeville, "The Moral," in *The Fable of the Bees* [1714], ed. Phillip Harth (Harmondsworth, Eng.: Penguin, 1970), 76 ("So Vice is beneficial found, / When it's by Justice lopt, and bound; / . . . Bare Vertue can't make Nations live / In splendour; they, that would revive / A Golden Age, must be as free, / For Acorns, as for Honesty.").

5. See, e.g., James B. Thayer, "The Origin and Scope of American Constitutional Law," *Harvard Law Review* 7 (1893): 149. A similar argument appeared among early advocates of originalism. See Lino A. Graglia, "'Interpreting' the Constitution: Posner on Bork," *Stanford Law Review* 44 (1992): 1044 ("To effectively limit judicial policymaking and protect representative self-government, originalism should be understood as requiring a strong presumption of constitutionality. Judicial invalidation of the elected representatives' policy choices should be permitted only when (as would very rarely be the case) the choice is clearly disallowed by the Constitution" [citation omitted].); and Michael J. Perry, "The Question of Minimalism," *Northwestern University Law Review* 88 (1993): 95 ("Many people who find originalism an attractive approach to constitutional interpre-

tation do so, like Bork, at least partly because and some of them principally, because they believe that originalism entails a minimalist judicial role. They believe that the original-ist approach, if properly understood and followed, entails—that it necessarily eventuates in—a relatively small or passive judicial role in constitutional adjudication; they believe that originalism entails a process of constitutional adjudication that is more 'legal' than 'political.'").

6. Immanuel Kant, "Toward Perpetual Peace: A Philosophical Sketch" [1795], in *Toward Perpetual Peace and Other Writings on Politics, Peace, and History*, ed. Pauline Klein-geld and trans. David L. Colclasure (New Haven, Conn.: Yale University Press, 2006), 67, 90 ("Establishing a state, as difficult as it may sound, is a problem that can be solved even for a nation of devils [if only they possess understanding].").

7. "Washington's Farewell Address 1796," *Avalon Project*, https://avalon.law.yale.edu/18th _century/washing.asp; see also Philip Gorski, *American Covenant: A History of Civil Religion from the Puritans to the Present* (Princeton, N.J.: Princeton University Press, 2017), 66–72 (on the Christian Republicanism of Founders).

8. See Thomas L. Lentz, "Schools in Killingworth," in *Celebrating 350 Years*, ed. Karen Milano (2017), 39, 39 ("North Killingworth formed a school society in 1795 that over-saw the schools until 1856.").

9. See Paul W. Kahn, "Democracy and the Obligations of Care: A Demos Worthy of Sacri-fice," in *Democracy in Times of Pandemic: Different Futures Imagined*, ed. Miguel Poi-ares Maduro and Paul W. Kahn (Cambridge: Cambridge University Press, 2020), 196. Woodrow Wilson expressed this same idea: "Every man in a free country is . . . put upon his honor to be the kind of man such a polity supposes its citizens to be." Woodrow Wil-son, *Constitutional Government in the United States* (New York: Columbia University Press, 1908), 23.

10. "The Perpetuation of Our Political Institutions: Address Before the Young Men's Ly-ceum of Springfield, Illinois, January 27, 1838," in *Abraham Lincoln: His Speeches and Writings*, ed. Roy P. Basler (Cleveland, Ohio: World, 1946), 76, 81.

11. Alexis de Tocqueville, *Democracy in America* [1835], ed. and trans. Harvey C. Mans-field and Delba Winthrop (Chicago: University of Chicago Press, 2000), 488.

12. See, e.g., J. Eric Oliver, *Democracy in Suburbia* (Princeton, N.J.: Princeton University Press, 2001), 207–13; Richard Briffault, "The Local Government Boundary Problem in Metropolitan Areas," *Stanford Law Review* 48 (1996): 1142 ("Local boundary lines have often been drawn in order to take advantage of the opportunity local government law provides incorporated communities to control local land use and to escape from the fiscal burdens of the surrounding metropolitan region.").

13. See the discussion in chapter 2, above.

14. For a radical pedagogical proposal moving in this direction, see Robert Litan, *Resolved: Debate Can Revolutionize Education and Save Our Democracy* (Washington, D.C.: Brookings Institution Press, 2020).

15. Hannah Arendt, *Between Past and Future: Eight Exercises in Political Thought,* rev. ed. (New York: Viking, 1968), 220–21.

16. The state has promised some $88 billion in pension and retirement benefits, but it has proven unable to fund more than half of that obligation. "Financial State of the States,

2020," *Truth in Accounting,* Sept. 22, 2020, 120–21, www.truthinaccounting.org/library
/doclib/FSOS-Booklet-2020.pdf. The state comptroller notes that the unfunded pension
obligations represent "a crushing debt that increasingly crowd out other state budget
priorities." "Pension Funding Agreement," *Office of the State Comptroller* (2017), www
.osc.ct.gov/pension/index.html. And Governor Lamont has struggled in his efforts to correct the state's finances. See, e.g., Keith M. Phaneuf, "Connecticut's Legacy of Debt
Weighed Heavy on Lamont's First Budget," *CT Mirror,* Dec. 11, 2019, https://ctmirror
.org/2019/12/11/connecticuts-legacy-of-debt-weighed-heavy-on-lamonts-first-budget.

17. See, e.g., Kenneth Scheve and David Stasavage, "Wealth Inequality and Democracy,"
Annual Review of Political Science 20 (2017): 464–65 (surveying recent studies examining the extent to which the wealthy have "captured" democracy to serve their own ends
and suggesting the need for more robust empirical analyses before the existence of such
capture is proven).

18. Billionaires Warren Buffett and Bill Gates established the Giving Pledge in 2010; those
who sign the pledge commit to dedicate at least 50 percent of their fortune to philan-
thropic activities. By 2020, more than two hundred people had signed the Giving Pledge.
Chuck Collins, Helen Flannery, Omar Ocampo, and Kalena Thomhave, "The Giving
Pledge at 10: A Case Study in Top Heavy Philanthropy," *Institute for Policy Studies,*
Aug. 3, 2020, https://inequality.org/wp-content/uploads/2020/08/GivingPledge-Brief-Aug3
.pdf. In December 2020, MacKenzie Scott—a pledger herself—announced that she had
given away nearly $4.2 billion since July 2020, with a focus on supporting organizations
dedicated to meeting basic needs and fighting systemic injustice. MacKenzie Scott, "384
Ways to Help," *Medium,* Dec. 15, 2020, https://mackenzie-scott.medium.com/384-ways
-to-help-45d0b9ac6ad8.

19. 444 Parl. Deb. HC (5th ser.) (1947) col. 207 (UK) (speech by Winston Churchill, Leader
of the Opposition).

20. Rosenbluth and Shapiro reach a similar conclusion: "The seeming truism—that increasing
voters' direct control of decisions and politicians enhances democratic accountability—
has, in fact, the opposite effect. . . . Rebuilding well-functioning democracies means reversing this trend." Frances McCall Rosenbluth and Ian Shapiro, *Responsible Parties:
Saving Democracy from Itself* (New Haven, Conn.: Yale University Press, 2018), 3.

21. For example, the referendum on the 2019–20 Haddam-Killingworth School Budget drew
1,100 voters from Killingworth, whereas the 2020 presidential election drew 4,386 and
the 2019 municipal election 2,833.

22. Bruce Ackerman and James Fishkin, *Deliberation Day* (New Haven, Conn.: Yale University Press, 2004).

23. Stripped of a legislative role, meetings would no longer be subject to the state requirement of five days' formal notice of the agenda, which effectively eliminates spontaneity.
Conn. Gen. Stat. § 7-3.

24. See Morris P. Fiorina, "Extreme Voices: A Dark Side of Civic Engagement," in *Civic
Engagement in American Democracy*, ed. Theda Skocpol and Morris P. Fiorina (Washington, D.C.: Brookings Institution Press, 1999), 395, 414–17 ("We should give a fair
hearing to proposals for newer, lower-cost forms of political participation. In particular,
we need to reconsider the notion that people must be physically present, or must invest

large blocks of their time. Ross Perot's talk of electronic town halls was met with deri-
sion among academics, but the possibilities offered by modern communications deserve
investigation, if only because they may be the only practical remedies.").

25. They already do so when they put forward just one candidate for a reserved, minority
representation seat. *Conn. Gen. Stat.* § 9-167(a).

26. Woodrow Wilson, *Congressional Government: A Study in American Politics* (1895; reprint, Boston: Houghton Mifflin, 1901), 6 ("We are really living under a constitution
essentially different from that which we have been so long worshiping as our own pecu-
liar and incomparable possession. . . . The noble charter of fundamental law given to us
by the Convention of 1787 is still our Constitution; but it is now our *form of government*
rather in name than in reality.").

27. In 1960, Connecticut dissolved its counties, which had existed since 1666. The Office of
Legislative Research notes that there were a variety of reasons behind the abolition, including the fact that the counties had not been reorganized since 1785, despite significant
changes in the labor market, transportation, and communication, as well as the general
"ineffectiveness" of the county governments. Judy A. Watson, "County Government
Abolishment," *OLR Research Report,* Jan. 30, 1998, www.cga.ct.gov/PS98/rpt%5Colr
%5Chtm/98-R-0086.htm.2

INDEX

Abid, Arjumund, 80, 209–10
abolitionism, 140
abortion, 13, 17, 25, 27, 29, 113
Access Hollywood (television program),
    4, 21, 198
accountability, 62, 174, 197
Ackerman, Bruce, 11, 218
"acting" appointees, 7
Adametz, Jeremy, 79
Adametz, Walt, 79, 88, 151, 170, 173,
    209; local roots of, 158–59, 161; town
    politics viewed by, 52, 159–60, 196
advertising, 130–31
affirmative action, 17
Afghanistan, 6
Ailes, Roger, 200
Albrecht, Rick, 176–77, 179
Albrecht, Walter, 177, 179, 190
American Revolution, 11
Americans with Disabilities Act (ADA),
    65
Anderson, Carolyn, 80, 211
Anderson, Steve, 80
Anino, Lou, 152, 172, 178
Anino, Lou, Sr., 178
antiwar movement, 25
Arab Spring (2010), 191
Arendt, Hannah, 102, 106, 175

Aristotle, ix, 141
Auer, Eric, Jr., 92, 114
Auer, Eric, Sr., 92, 114
authority, 100–117

Barr, William, 81
Barrett, Amy Coney, 146
Bays, Martha, 109, 113–14, 115
Biden, Joe, xiii, 2, 150, 165, 201
birther movement, 20, 23, 26, 28, 162,
    193
Black Lives Matter (BLM), 6, 10, 36–37,
    43, 45, 82
Blewett, Eileen, 63, 169, 179
Board, Michael, 192–93
border wall, 5, 6
Bowling Alone (Putnam), 52
Brackett, Amanda, 150, 183–85, 189,
    198, 199
Breitbart News, 21
Brinkley, David, 17
Bristol-Myers Squibb, 56

Cabral, Richard, 59
Capital in the Twenty-First Century
    (Piketty), 12
capture, 51, 92–93, 97, 101, 117
Carlson, Tucker, 20

Carnegie, Andrew, 119
Catholicism, 110–11, 112–13, 115–16
Centers for Disease Control (CDC), 4, 29
China, 24
Christian right, 25
Churchill, Winston, 215
civil rights, 8, 25
Clark, Rob, 44, 74
Clarkson, Walter, 66
climate change, 10, 23, 26, 27, 143–44,
    162, 204–5
Clinton, Bill, 16
Clinton, Hillary, 4, 5, 18, 22, 27–28, 161,
    201
Comey, James, 4
commuting, 122–24, 126
Congregational Church in Killingworth,
    18, 87, 89, 110, 116, 146, 159; de-
    clining influence of, 50, 109; early
    history of, 100, 107–9, 113, 115;
    modern governance rooted in, 106–8;
    older members of, 34, 210; political
    conflict and, 145; as "town church,"
    113, 114
Congregationalism, 50, 77, 112
conscription, 102–3, 175
conspiracy theories, 5, 18, 22, 23, 35,
    36, 47, 95, 163; attitudinal roots of,
    164; Trump's embrace of, 165
constitutional amendment, 11
consumer protection, 15
Cook, Annette, 33, 34
Coulter, Ann, 202
county government, 222
Covid pandemic, 3–4, 13; essential
    workers during, 89; in Killingworth,
    32–36, 38, 40, 129, 136, 138; masking
    requirements during, 72; Trump's
    mismanagement of, x, 9, 11, 29, 35,
    104
creationism, 26, 163
Cronkite, Walter, 17
culture wars, 13
Cunningham, Frank, 160

Dahl, Robert, ix
Daley, Richard J., 179
Day (New London newspaper), 181
Declaration of Independence, 102, 195,
    216
Deferred Action for Childhood Arrivals
    (DACA), 8
democratic pathology, 100–101, 105
Denvir, David, xiii, 120
Dewey, John, 175
direct democracy, 32, 50–51, 59–60, 101,
    216–17
domestic violence, 40, 136
Dotson, Bruce, 71, 73, 178
drug abuse, 40
Dudek, Fred, 154, 160, 164, 178; as
    candidate, xiii, 63–64, 79, 97, 172,
    196
Dudek, Linda, 79

Eliot, Jared, 108
Ellickson, Robert, 87, 89
Ely, Henry, 107
environmental protection, 6, 7, 15, 23;
    development vs., 40
Episcopalians, 110
Epstein, Jeffrey, 18
Erdoğan, Recep Tayyip, 165
European Union, 7, 24
evangelicalism, 13, 15, 19, 110–12,
    115–16, 216
Exxon Corporation, 26

Facebook, 20, 138, 182–83, 188–89
fairness doctrine, 19–20
Fauci, Anthony, 163
Federalist Papers, 16, 152–53
feminism, 25
financial regulation, 15
Fine, Cheryl, 36–37, 89, 96, 109, 117,
    145, 170
First Amendment, 143
Fishkin, James, 218
Food and Drug Administration (FDA), 4

Forty Years a Country Preacher (Gilbert), 110

Fox News, 17, 19, 21, 37, 46, 138, 155; popularity of, 163; sexual misconduct at, 200–201; Trump's links to, 20, 23; unrepentance of, 197

Frankfurt, Harry, 201–2

Franklin, Benjamin, 51, 108

free riding, 24, 72, 87, 89

free speech, 8, 194–95

fundamentalism, 23, 24, 25, 44, 115

Gannon, Tim, 71–72, 89, 94, 121, 152, 168, 169

Gates Foundation, 119

Gay, Joan, 78–79, 144, 147, 151, 154, 178, 209

gender identity, 13

Gettysburg Address, 102

globalization, 12, 23–24, 44

Grasso, Ella, 154

Great Awakenings, 19, 113

Great Recession, xi, 127, 129

gun laws, 13, 27, 29, 45–46, 155

Haddam, Conn., 69, 85, 125–26

Haggerty, Tom, 39

Hamilton, Alexander, 118

Hannity, Sean, 23, 27, 202

harassment, 93–94, 96, 98, 101, 117

Hartford Courant, 181

health care, 6, 13

Helping Hands (food bank), 34, 42, 45, 46, 90

Hillbilly Elegy (Vance), 14

Hochschild, Arlie, 14, 15

Hogarty, Lucinda, 70, 75–76

Hogarty, Tom, 70, 83

home-schooling, 115

Hungary, 7, 10

Hutchins, Joseph, 79–80

identity politics, 23

Iino, Catherine, 13, 40–41, 61, 69, 71,
109, 112, 152, 154, 181, 197; attacks on, 42, 43, 81, 94–95, 156, 192–93, 194; as candidate, 59, 63, 126–27, 134, 163–64, 172, 184, 196–97, 201, 210; during Covid pandemic, 34; as first selectman, xiii, 2, 33, 47, 65, 68

immigration, 7, 17, 205

incivility, 37–38, 41–42

inequality, x–xi, 12

informal amendment, 10, 11, 12

inspectors general, 7

International Criminal Court, 8

internet, 20–21, 180, 190, 198

Iran nuclear agreement (2015), 7

Iraq, 6

Jefferson, Thomas, 118, 195

Jobs, Steve, 205

Jones, Alex, 23, 202

Kant, Immanuel, 207

Kennedy, Ted, 16

Killingworth, Conn., xii–xiv, 1–2, 16, 29–30; ambulance service and emergency management in, 33, 44, 60, 61, 65, 70, 72–73, 74, 104, 146, 153; anti-tax sentiment in, 16, 39–40, 56, 72, 73, 90, 93, 95–96, 104, 133–34, 136, 148, 173, 192–93; Black Lives Matter and, 36–37; business and economy in, 118–22, 127–34; childrearing in, 160, 167, 169; churches in, 34, 45, 50, 76, 77–78, 89, 90, 106–18, 145; common good and common sense in, 63–67, 151; commuting from, 122–24, 126; Covid pandemic in, 32–36, 38, 40, 129, 136, 138; demography of, 38, 50, 55, 170; early history of, 77, 107–8; fire protection in, 44, 51, 60, 70, 73, 74, 109; governance in, 50–51, 59–60, 62–64, 219–20; homogeneity of, 38, 76; information vacuum in, 171–74; law enforcement in, 40, 69, 86, 87–89; library in, 34, 60, 70, 74–76, 89, 104,

Killingworth, Conn. (*continued*)
   109; local finance in, 16, 35, 36,
   39–40, 62, 92, 173; parent-teacher
   organization (PTO) in, 60, 89, 170–71;
   political campaigning in, 180–81;
   politics as vocation in, 176–79;
   population loss in, 137; privatization
   in, 128, 130, 133, 135, 138, 167;
   profusion of elective offices in, 50,
   219–20; public and private land in,
   68–70, 71, 147–50; public employees
   in, 69; public meetings in, 83–84;
   referenda in, 82, 90, 91, 92, 217; road
   maintenance in, 43, 65; schools in,
   61–62, 64, 69, 72, 76, 79, 82–86,
   91–96, 125–26, 137, 156, 205; suburbanization in, 56, 76, 78; topography
   of, 38–39; Trump support in, 16, 32,
   44, 52–53, 80, 95, 147, 200; urban
   areas contrasted with, 134–35; vandalism in, 200; volunteerism in, xiv,
   2, 16, 30, 33–34, 37–40, 44, 46, 47,
   57, 60–61, 67–76, 82–91, 101, 106,
   109–10, 116–17, 123, 138, 144, 210,
   215, 222; zoning in, 65, 84–85, 146,
   213–14
Killingworth Stompin' Ground (Facebook group), 46, 149, 150, 158, 167,
   183–89, 200, 210
Killingworth Today, 83, 146, 157–58,
   182–83, 213, 221
Killingworth Women's Organization
   (KWO), 43, 60, 64, 70, 89, 170, 211
Klein, Marty, 65, 127, 160

Lally, Jim, 44, 70
League of Women Voters, 171
Lentz, Tom, 93, 106, 107–8, 178
LeVasseur, David, xiii
Limbaugh, Rush, 17, 19, 22–23, 27, 194,
   201
Lincoln, Abraham, 28, 102, 141, 208–9
Lions Club, 33, 34, 60, 64, 71, 78, 92;

declining membership of, 89, 146,
   170; politics abjured by, 145
Living Rock Church, 110–12, 209
Lucas, Jerry, 160, 192–93, 199
Lulaj, Francesco, 34, 39, 119, 120, 121;
   as candidate, xiii; conspiratorial beliefs
   of, 161–62, 163; development backed
   by, 80
Luther, Martin, 18
lynching, 20

Madison, James, 16
Malkin, Michelle, 197
market research, 22
marriage, 142, 145
McCain, John, 25
McMahon, John, 177–78, 179
Medicare, 15, 25
Milano, Mike, 70
military service, 102–3, 154, 175, 214
Murphy, Chris, 203

narratives, 139, 141–42, 149
nationalization, of local issues, 52, 57,
   137–38, 143, 150–56, 167, 206
NATO (North Atlantic Treaty Organi-
   zation), 7
neoliberalism, 24, 52
Network Propaganda (Benkler, Faris,
   and Roberts), 18
New Deal, 10, 11
New England, 32, 39, 48, 49
New Haven Register, 181
Newsmax, 21
New York Times, 155

Obama, Barack, 6, 23, 44, 45, 201
Obama, Michelle, 206
Obamacare, 6, 13, 15, 16
Occupy movement, 6
On Bullshit (Frankfurt), 201
Orbán, Viktor, 165
Order without Law (Ellickson), 87

O'Reilly, Bill, 200–201
originalism, 102
O'Sullivan, Dan, 90, 113, 115, 169
O'Sullivan, Jan, 90, 113, 115, 169

Palin, Sarah, 25, 40
pardons, 8
Paris climate accord (2015), 7, 23
Parmalee Farm, 70, 73, 88, 89, 117, 168, 169, 192, 199; volunteerism at, 71, 152
Patton, Jennifer, 67, 80, 169
Pfizer Inc., 56
Pierson, Abraham, 108
Piketty, Thomas, 12
Plato, 198
Podesta, John, 4
Poland, 7, 10
polarization, 12, 14, 17, 29, 38, 47, 57, 140, 159, 180; social media linked to, 19–20, 44, 138, 143, 150, 196
polling, 22
populism, x, 105
pornography, 21, 198–99, 213
printing, 18
privatization: of family life, 128, 130, 133–34, 192; nationalized politics linked to, 57, 137–38, 143, 167, 182, 206, 211; social media linked to, 182, 183; suburbanization linked to, 135; of workplace, 123
Proud Boys, 199–200
public education, 15, 211–12
public opinion, 2, 8, 11, 16–18, 57, 65, 137–44
public speaking, 18
Putnam, Robert, 52, 175

QAnon, 199

radio, 17, 19, 20, 124, 163
Rawls, John, ix
referenda, 82, 90, 91, 92, 217–18

religion, 13, 15–16
Religious Freedom Restoration Act (1993), 16
revival meetings, 19
Ricciuti, Ed, 44–46, 66, 77, 78–79, 80, 155
Ricciuti, Mercedes, 42–46
Richards, Brandy, 183–86, 198
Rimmer, Rob, 114, 116
Roe v. Wade (1973), 27
Roman Republic, 102
Romney, Mitt, 22, 27
Roosevelt, Franklin D., 10–11, 154
Russia, 10; disinformation by, 4, 161–62; Trump's admiration for, 7

Sack, Dave, 178
Sack, Suzanne, 178–79
same-sex marriage, 142, 145
Samperi, John, 64, 73, 90, 97–98, 121, 134, 201
sermons, 18
Sessions, Jeff, 8
Seward, William, 107
Schumer, Chuck, 16
Scofield, Peg, 71, 83, 145–46, 157–58, 182–83, 221
shaming, 106, 199
Shklar, Judith, xii
slavery, 47–48, 140
smartphones, 18, 187–88, 189
Smith, Charlie, 89, 145, 151, 152, 170, 178, 209–11
smoking, 26, 27
social contract, 140
social media, 180, 209; polarization linked to, 19–20, 44, 138, 143, 150, 196; privatization linked to, 182, 183; Russian manipulation of, 4
Social Security, 15, 25
Source (weekly newspaper), 181–82
Soviet Union, ix
Stern, Howard, 20, 213

Strangers in Their Own Land (Hochs-child), 14
substance abuse, 14
suburbia, 56, 76, 78, 135, 211
supermajorities, 11–12
Supreme Court, 8, 29
Sweetman, Charles, 193

Tammany Hall, 179
tax cuts, 6
Tea Party, 179
television, 17, 19, 20
Thoreau, Henry David, 49
tobacco industry, 26
Tocqueville, Alexis de, 3, 97, 139, 203;
    civil society stressed by, 49, 105, 211;
    Civil War presaged by, 51; egalitarian
    dilemma viewed by, 31–32, 47–48, 53;
    local governance praised by, 41, 52,
    53, 62, 149, 152; mob rule viewed by,
    142, 143; mores stressed by, 101, 199;
    participation and democracy linked
    by, xiv, 50, 52, 56–57; Town Meet-
    ings viewed by, 32, 49–50, 52; well-
    informed citizenry viewed by, 13
town manager system, 41, 118
Town Meetings, 30, 59–60, 140, 149;
    budgets approved by, 35; lessons of,
    203, 213; myth vs. reality of, 49–50,
    97, 216–17; proposed reforms of,
    218–19; self-organization of, 82–83;
    sparse attendance at, 50–51, 91–92,
    97, 104, 107, 133, 135, 159; Tocque-
    ville's view of, 32, 49–50, 52
Transportation Security Administration
    (TSA), 4
Trump, Donald, xiii; as authoritarian
    populist, 2, 3, 5, 7, 10, 22, 165;
    character lacking from, 206; Covid
    response bungled by, x, 9, 11, 29, 35,
    104; cronies pardoned by, 8; election
    results rejected by, 8, 28, 162, 165,
    188, 191; evangelicalism linked to,
    19; gun owners' support for, 45, 155;
    higher education maligned by, 9; im-
    peachments of, 7; institutions dis-
    mantled by, 3–4, 6–7; Killingworth
    support for, 16, 32, 44, 52–53, 80, 95,
    147, 200; mendacity of, 9; Obamacare
    opposition exploited by, 15; opposition
    energized by, 98, 172; as pitchman,
    20, 165–66; "poll watchers" recruited
    by, 153; press muzzled by, 8–9; prose-
    cutions threatened by, 42; Republican
    Party reshaped by, 27; sex and vio-
    lence exploited by, 21, 199–200; social
    media banishment of, 20; stable sup-
    port for, 4, 5–6; truth disdained by,
    197; vituperative tone set by, 184,
    194, 201
Turkey, 10
TV Guide, 19
Twitter, 19–20

unions, 12, 23
United Nations, 7
U.S. Court of Appeals, 8

Vance, J. D., 14, 15
Venuti, Peter, 71
Venuti property, 80, 146–51, 155, 163,
    218
video games, 21
violence, 21
volunteering: capture as threat to, 92–93,
    117; commerce as threat to, 121–22;
    during Covid pandemic, 33–34, 38,
    40, 46–47, 61, 207; declining interest
    in, 16, 30, 44, 57, 88–91, 101, 116–18,
    124, 132, 183, 206, 209; in election
    campaigns, 60, 64; for military
    service, 102–3, 214; as obligation,
    109–10; partisanship and harassment
    as threats to, 42–43, 76, 93–98, 117;
    for private gain, 116–17; public and
    private merged in, 76–76; religious
    roots of, 106; by retirees, 210; root-
    lessness as threat to, 122–23, 126;

self-government linked to, xiv, 2, 57,
   59–99, 106, 112, 114, 144, 174, 187,
   189, 203; Tocqueville's view of, 52,
   62; virtue linked to, 46–47

Washington, George, 51, 207–8
Westbrook, Robert, 175
white nationalism, ix, x
WikiLeaks, 4, 22
Wilson, Charlie, 118
Wilson, Woodrow, 221

Withington, Tim, 153–54
Works Progress Administration (WPA),
   151
World Health Organization (WHO), 7
World Trade Organization (WTO), 7, 24

Yale Law School, 1
Young, Mike, 71, 95–96
Young, Ryan, 111, 112

Zuckerberg, Mark, 18, 119